Public Choice

AN INTRODUCTION TO THE
NEW POLITICAL ECONOMY

PUBLIC CHOICE

AN INTRODUCTION TO THE
NEW POLITICAL ECONOMY

DAVID B. JOHNSON
LOUISIANA STATE UNIVERSITY

Bristlecone Books

Mayfield Publishing Company
Mountain View, California
London • Toronto

To my son, Tedford, with the hope that his private
and public choices will improve his life and the lives of his family,
friends, and community.

Library of Congress Cataloging-in-Publication Data

Johnson, David B.
    Public choice : an introduction to the new political economy /
David B. Johnson.
        p.   cm.
    "Bristlecone books."
    Includes index.
    ISBN 1-55934-022-3
    1. Economics—Political aspects. 2. Social choice. 3. Public goods.
    4. Political science—Decision making.   I. Title.
    HB73.J64 1991
    338.9—dc20   90-46311
                                                                      CIP

Manufactured in the United States of America
10 9 8 7 6 5 4 3 2 1

Bristlecone Books
Mayfield Publishing Company
1240 Villa Street
Mountain View, California

Copy editor, Andrea McCarrick; text and cover designer, Jeanne M. Schreiber;
illustrator, Willa Bower. The text was set in 10/13 Palatino and printed on 50#
Finch Opaque by Edwards Brothers, Inc.

PREFACE

During the past 30 years economists have extended to politics and government the analytical tools they have traditionally applied to the private market. They have analyzed the demand and supply of public goods, political parties, voting rules, pressure groups, bureaucracies, and migration among political units. This relatively new field is called public choice: the subject matter is that of political science, but the methodology employed is from economics. Although numerous Nobel laureates have been recognized for their contributions to this field and much research is now being conducted by political scientists and sociologists as well as economists, most of the work has been relegated to journal articles and a few technical books. The purpose of this book is to present public choice analysis in a relatively nontechnical format that can be understood by those who have not had intensive training in economics. Since it contains most of the topics in the expanding field of public choice, it could be used as a textbook in public choice, political economy, or public finance classes and by those who want to familiarize themselves with this new field. No previous training in economics or political science is assumed.

One hallmark of this book is the application of the same economic methodology to both private and political markets. The first part of the book presents some fundamental postulates of economic methodology, a brief analysis of private market structures, and causes of private market failures. It incorporates many applications of private market theory to policy issues to show the reader how economic analysis can be utilized in the real world. One reason for reviewing private market theory and its applications is that students unfamiliar with private market economics have more difficulty understanding political market economics and placing it in its proper perspective. Another reason for including material traditionally covered in a principles of microeconomics course is to present the fundamental theories of the private and the political markets in one book. This book leads the reader through the workings of the private market and its many failures and then through the workings of the political market, or public sector, and its many failures. The subject matter of public choice can be better understood if the student constantly keeps in mind that one market is an alternative to the other and that both of them are subject to failures and imperfections. Thus, chapters 2 and 3 and the first part of chapter 11 review private market topics. The author has found that most students who have taken numerous courses in economics could benefit from this review. Those students who have not had a thorough course in economic principles should definitely read and comprehend these three chapters.

The purpose of the book is to analyze and discuss a wide range of public choice topics in relatively simple language, including applications and institutional material, which is often lacking in public choice literature. Some supplemental material providing institutional richness not traditionally presented in public choice texts—such as a history of American political parties, the experience of several countries with proportional voting, and the alternative methods of determining proportional representation—are covered in three appendices. Since examples often are worth more than a thousand words in understanding complicated material, some chapters (especially chapters 2, 3, 6, and 11) have rather detailed examples. The examples are not difficult, although they do require a few minutes of concentration to work through them.

A list of questions and answers is provided at the end of each chapter. Some of the questions and answers are lengthy and some are very short. Some questions do not have definitive answers but are provided to encourage the student to think about concepts, problems, alternatives, or ways of analyzing issues. Many of the questions explore political or economic issues in some depth and are minicourses for the relevant applications of concepts discussed in the chapter. Students are strongly encouraged to work through the question-and-answer sections. Those who do will be rewarded with a much better understanding of the material and the applications of the various concepts.

In order to appeal to the widest range of readers, I took considerable care to present the material in clear and easily understood terms. Mathematical models were avoided, and only a few simple graphs are used to illustrate the concepts.

I'm grateful to James Buchanan, George Mason University; Dwight Lee, University of Georgia; and Gordon Tullock, University of Arizona, for their valuable suggestions and comments. I also thank Andrea McCarrick for her sharp-eyed editorial assistance and Gary Burke, publisher, for his enthusiasm and patience.

CONTENTS

PUBLIC CHOICE

AN INTRODUCTION TO THE
NEW POLITICAL ECONOMY

CHAPTER ONE

INTRODUCTION

But there are no colonies of which the progress has been more rapid than that of the English in North America. Plenty of good land, and liberty to manage their own affairs their own way, seem to be the two great causes of the prosperity of the new colonies.
—ADAM SMITH, THE WEALTH OF NATIONS, 1776

We hold these truths to be self-evident, that all men are created equal, that they are endowed by their Creator with certain inalienable rights, that among these are life, liberty and the pursuit of happiness—that to secure these rights, governments are instituted among men, deriving their just powers from the consent of the governed.
—THE DECLARATION OF INDEPENDENCE, 1776

THE FOUNDING FATHERS

The year 1776 was a very good year. It was the year the Founding Fathers, possessing an endowment of wisdom, knowledge, and insights that should astonish current generations of Americans, wrote and signed the Declaration of Independence, which proclaimed their revolutionary message of self-evident truths to the world. While the Founding Fathers were contemplating the implications of their Declaration of Independence, 3,500 miles away in the country from which the Founding Fathers were severing all allegiances, a 53-year-old academic scribbler was putting the finishing touches on a book that would have nearly as much impact on the future of the rebellious colonies. Adam Smith, a mild-mannered Scot who had taught ethics, theology, jurisprudence, and moral philosophy at the University of Glasgow, was completing a book entitled *An Inquiry into the Nature and Causes of the Wealth of Nations*, which had a remarkable parallelism to the Declaration of Independence. A few notable paragraphs from Smith's book follow:

(1) Man has almost constant occasion for the help of his brethren, and it is in vain for him to expect it from their benevolence only. He will be more likely to prevail if he can interest their self-love in his favor, and show them that it is for their own advantage to do for him what he requires of them. Whoever offers to another a bargain of any kind, proposes to do this. Give me that

1

which I want, and you shall have this which you want, is the meaning of every such offer; and it is in this manner that we obtain from one another the far greater part of those good offices which we stand in need of. It is not from the benevolence of the butcher, the brewer or the baker, that we expect our dinner, but from their regard to their own interest. We address ourselves, not to their humanity but to their self-love, and never talk to them of our own necessities but of their advantages.[1]

(2) The difference of natural talents in different men is, in reality, much less than we are aware of; and the very different genius which appears to distinguish men of different professions, when grown up to maturity, is not upon many occasions so much the cause, as the effect of the division of labor. The difference between the most dissimilar characters, between a philosopher and a common street porter, for example, seems to arise not so much from nature, as from habit, custom and education.[2]

(3) It is the highest impertinence and presumption, therefore, in kings and ministers, to pretend to watch over the economy of private people, and to restrain their expense, either by sumptuary laws, or by prohibiting the importation of foreign luxuries. They are themselves always, and without any exception, the greatest spendthrifts in the society. Let them look well after their own expense, and they may safely trust private people with theirs. If their own extravagance does not ruin the state, that of their subjects never will.[3]

(4) When the judicial is united to the executive power, it is scarce possible that justice should not frequently be sacrificed to, what is vulgarly called, politics. The persons entrusted with the great interests of the state may, even without any corrupt views, sometimes imagine it necessary to sacrifice to those interests the rights of a private man. . . . In order to make every individual feel himself perfectly secure in the possession of every right which belongs to him, it is not only necessary that the judicial should be separated from the executive power, but that it should be rendered as much as possible independent of that power.[4]

The Declaration of Independence and *The Wealth of Nations* laid the foundations for a limited constitutional government and a free market economy in the new United States. Paragraph (1) above sets forth the basic message of *The Wealth of Nations*, which was expounded first by Smith and then expanded by subsequent generations of economists: The pursuit of private interest and the facilitation of private trade leads to an increase in the welfare of citizens. In his 900-page book Adam Smith described how

---

[1] Adam Smith, *An Inquiry into the Nature and Causes of the Wealth of Nations* (1776; reprint New York: Random House, Inc., The Modern Library, 1937), 14.

[2] Ibid, 15.

[3] Ibid, 329.

[4] Ibid, 681.

individuals allowed to pursue their natural "propensity to truck, barter and exchange" could become more prosperous than those who lived in a restricted, mercantilistic society, which predominated at the time. Paragraphs (2), (3), and (4) are samples of Smith' s concern with many of the same ideas that occupied the attention of the Founding Fathers. Adam Smith, the founding father of economics, believed in the basic equality of men and thought that only their occupations made them dissimilar, that governments were likely to squander money and should not be allowed to tell individuals how to spend theirs, and that one of the necessary "checks and balances" was an independent judiciary. Adam Smith possessed many of the same values and objectives as the Founding Fathers, but he wrote more extensively about integrating elements of individual self-interests and the advantages of limiting government's role in the economy. Smith, who viewed himself as a political economist, said that the study of the nature and causes of the wealth of nations was more properly called political economy, and he devoted a large portion of his book to a discussion of the reasons for government.

The authors of the Declaration of Independence and the Constitution devoted their attention to forming a federal republic with limited powers assigned to a federal government. They did their work well. Although the United States is one of the youngest major nations, more than two centuries later it is the oldest surviving republic. Adam Smith's "Invisible Hand" came under severe intellectual attack in the twentieth century, but it, too, survived more than two centuries; during the eighties and into the nineties it was resuscitated and reinvigorated from Des Moines to London to Taipei, and the fingers of the Invisible Hand are wiggling in Prague, Warsaw, Moscow, and Beijing. The democratic freedoms espoused by the Founding Fathers and the economic freedoms championed by Smith supported and reinforced each other, and it is doubtful that either would have survived more than two centuries without the other. Unfortunately, Smith's broad interest in political economy was not continued by subsequent generations of economists who narrowed, modelized, graphed, mathematized, disembodied, and explored the rarified theoretical nuances of the private market mechanism. Nineteenth-century economists largely ignored the public sector, except for arguing for a limited government that should provide only national defense, police forces, and courts.[5]

---

[5] An exception was Karl Marx, who developed a provocative but confusing economic theory of the state at a time when most other economists had not even begun to consider the topic. Marx stated that the state is the instrument through which the ruling class dominates the oppressed classes. According to Marx, the government is the "executive committee of the bourgeoisie"; it protects the property of the capitalist classes and makes policies to serve their interests. Marx's theory of the state was based upon his theory of rational and self-interested motivated social classes that were defined by property ownership.

THE EVOLUTION OF POLITICAL ECONOMY

At the beginning of the twentieth century only one branch of economics dealing with government had been developed by economists. It was *public finance,* which dealt mainly with the principles of taxation but not with the efficiency of government expenditures made possible by the tax revenue. Another branch of economics was in the initial throes of development, but it would not occupy the center stage in economics until the thirties. Although it is not widely known, classical economists had built some fairly strong sections of what would later be called macroeconomics. After John M. Keynes published his famous book, *The General Theory of Employment Interest and Money,* in 1936, macroeconomics became the separate focus of many economists, and it remained a major center of economic inquiry until the latter 1960s. Even today, many people think that an economist is one who deals exclusively with interest rates, inflation, unemployment, and monetary and fiscal policies. The overwhelming majority of classical economists continued their development of private market analyses.

By the beginning of the twentieth century the discipline of economics, with its rigorous models of competitive behavior and rational, self-interest-motivated buyers, sellers, and investors, had a set of sophisticated models that laid out the workings of the economic market and the precise conditions necessary to maximize economic welfare. Political science, which emerged as a separate discipline in the latter nineteenth century, never developed a comparable methodology for the political market, or public sector, which is the major alternative to the private market. The term "political market" is not meant to have any normative connotations, nor does it refer to the buying and selling of votes. Individuals attempt to reveal and satisfy their preferences for private goods through the price mechanism of the private market. Individuals also attempt to reveal and satisfy their preferences for public goods through the collective decision-making mechanism of the political market. Analytical slippages can be most easily avoided if the word "market" is used to designate these two sets of institutions, which are alternatives and supplements to each other. The political market is the public sector in which individuals allocate resources, provide goods and services, and satisfy wants through collective decision making. The major differences between the private and political markets are the choice mechanisms and institutions each employs to determine and to satisfy individual preferences and the type of goods each can provide most efficiently.

While nineteenth-century economists were focusing their analysis on the private market, the emerging profession of political science did not view the political market as a clear alternative to the private market, and most political scientists devoted their efforts to political and philosophical history, political institutions, political power, data collection and surveys, and to a seemingly endless search for morally or socially correct government policies that would achieve the "common good." They did not develop a systematic theory describing or explaining the actions of individuals participating in the political market. They had no model specifying the conditions necessary for maximizing the welfare of individuals making decisions in the political market. This is not intended to be a criticism of the development of political science. It pursued a separate and distinct development track, which produced much institutional richness absent in economics. It was the separate development tracks of economics and political science, not the superiority or inferiority of either economic or political science, that produced serious and long-lasting problems in policy analyses. There is considerable room for a division of labor among social scientists. We can learn much from the traditional approaches of political scientists as well as from the new approach of political economists.

This separate and unbalanced development of economics and political science had an impact in the real world that, perhaps, is best characterized by the ancient legend of the Roman emperor who, being asked to judge a contest between two singers, heard only the first singer and gave the prize to the second, assuming he could do no worse. This legend describes the asymmetrical intellectual approach to the private and political markets that existed during the latter part of the nineteenth century and through more than half of the twentieth century. The asymmetry was so severe that one might conclude that *The Wealth of Nations* produced more *harm* to the private market than any other book. The reason for this seemingly blatant anomaly is that Adam Smith and those economists who followed him during the nineteenth century developed a tightly reasoned framework of the conditions necessary for the efficient operation of the private market. They drew a clear blueprint of sophisticated interaction among individuals in the private market and the required conditions necessary for an efficient private market—competition, easy entry into industries, rational and knowledgeable individuals, lack of spillover effects in production and consumption, and U-shaped cost curves.[6] This blueprint made it simple for critics of the private market to systematically analyze its failures and to recommend solutions that involved government intervention. Any shortfall in competitive vigor or a lack of an encyclopedic knowledge by consumers, workers, and producers could be rectified by government

---

[6] The meanings and significance of these terms will be fully explained in chapters 2 and 3.

action. Undesirable spillover effects, or externalities as they were later called, could be remedied by government taxation. Goods with "social priorities" provided in insufficient quantities by the private market could be stimulated by government subsidies. "Social evils" such as low wages or high rents could be corrected by minimum wages and rent controls. The asymmetrical treatment of the private and political markets was abetted by economists emphasizing the pristine theory of competitive markets and debating with each other about the number of competitive firms that could fit on the head of a pin while ignoring the increasing divergences between their beloved models and the real world. However, the major cause of the asymmetrical treatment of the private and political markets was a lack of an Adam Smith and a *Wealth of Nations* in political science. The failures of the private market were obvious because economists knew how the economy should operate in the absence of the failures. No one, however, had developed a systematic model of the political market in pure theory *or* in the real world.

Scholars and practical people had romantic notions about the political market. The government, it was easily assumed, acted for the common good and could correct deficiencies in the private market without imposing any costs on citizens. Terms such as democracy, the will of the people, the common good, corrective taxes, and equity were tossed around indiscriminately and without any clear idea of what these terms really meant. The set of conditions necessary for democracy to work efficiently or even equitably were unknown. Individuals who demanded and supplied goods in the private market were assumed to do so out of materialistic self-interest, but when these same individuals reflected their preferences for public goods in the voting booth, they were assumed to be rational and knowledgeable angels who based their decisions on the common good of all citizens.

While welfare statism, socialism, and communism were bursting on the democratic, capitalistic nations during the first half of this century, social scientists had no analytical tools that could make comparisons between the two markets. One wonders if communism would have been so attractive and capitalism so repulsive to many European and some American intellectuals or if the world would have been divided into ideological camps throughout most of this century if a *Wealth of Nations* had been published for the political market during the nineteenth century. The lack of an integrated theory of the political market did not eliminate criticisms of the political market. Bureaucrats were either lazy and incompetent or empire builders. Politicians bought votes and accepted bribes. The defense budget was too large or too small. Some argued that the rich had too much political influence; others argued that the poor had too much political influence. Friends and supporters of politicians were appointed to administrative and judicial positions. Wars were instigated by greedy corporations that controlled politicians. The list of complaints about the political market was seemingly endless. But these ad hoc criticisms made by both scholars and average citizens were not systematized and integrated into a model of the political market that enabled one to make positive comments, predictions, or modifications of the basic model. Such criticisms were largely ineffective, misunderstood, inapplicable, or wrong. For one hundred years most social science scholars and policy makers participated in the "grass is always greener on the other side of the fence" fallacy. Aided by the clear framework of economic methodology, they were able to identify the obvious failures of the private market and to recommend corrective government intervention. The grass was wilted and contaminated on the economic side of the fence, and this unhealthy state of affairs, it was thought, could be remedied only by crossing the fence to the luxurious green grass on the political side. Scholars and social critics did not consider that a smoothly functioning political market required a list of conditions much longer, more restrictive, and less likely to prevail in the real world than the purely competitive private market. Critics laid one private market failure upon another—monopolies, false and misleading advertisements, unequal wealth, externalities, barriers to entry, incomplete knowledge of alternatives, and discrimination—and they called for solutions by government without considering the simple fact that very similar failures also existed in the political market. It did not occur to them that if they analyzed the relative roles that each market should play in a democracy, methodological consistency as well as simple logic should lead them to compare the pure theory of the private market with the pure theory of the political market; if they modified the theory of the private market by including its failures and inefficiencies, then they must also use the modified theory of the political market including its failures and inefficiencies. Comparing apples with apples and oranges with oranges is an American saying as old as the Declaration of Independence, but it was neglected by virtually all social science scholars throughout the nineteenth and most of the twentieth century.

There were scholars who were exceptions and who attempted to focus attention on public sector analysis, but they truly wrote far "before their time," and most of their research was ignored or not developed. One of the best known early pioneers of applying the deductive reasoning used in economics to the public sector was Thomas Hobbes (1558–1679), whose *Leviathan* was published in 1651. Hobbes was much impressed by the deductive reasoning employed in geometry, and he wanted to establish a deductive science of human behavior based on elementary axioms.

Rational man, argued Hobbes, would see that life in the state of nature would be "solitary, poor, nasty, brutish and short" and that the only escape was to set up Leviathan, a ruler with absolute authority. One of Hobbes's arguments was that one cannot prove the Pythagorean theorem by repeatedly measuring the sides of the right triangles and the hypotenuse. The theorem is proven by starting from abstract and simplified definitions and gradually adding variables to the analysis. Hence, it is not surprising that some of the earliest deductive and analytical research in the public sector was the systematic examination of alternative voting procedures made by French mathematicians around the time of the French Revolution.[7]

The first person to develop a mathematical theory of voting was Jean-Charles de Borda (1733–1799), a member of the French Academy of Sciences who made many contributions to mathematical physics. Borda's paper[8] on voting shows that a simple plurality voting, the most widely used voting system, could easily return a candidate who, on the average, was the least preferred by the voters. Borda recommended a substitute voting system in which each voter ranked his preferences, and weights were assigned to each ranking (see chapter 6). One of the most prolific French writers on voting, as well as mathematics, was Marie Jean Antoine Nicholas Carital, Marquis de Condorcet (1743–1794), commonly known as Condorcet.[9] He was a member of the French Academy of Sciences and the Legislative Assembly and an early supporter of the French Revolution, but like so many other early supporters, he was imprisoned after the revolution and died while still a prisoner. Condorcet also recognized that the single vote plurality system was flawed and he suggested that the candidate who received a simple majority over *each* of the alternatives ought to be elected. He also discovered the "contradictory set" of aggregate preferences, which 150 years later professor Kenneth Arrow would call a "cyclical majority" (see chapter 6). Pierre-Simon, Marquis de Laplace (1749–1827),[10] used different reasoning than Borda but arrived at the same

---

[7] The following paragraphs provide only a cursory overview of the early writers on voting. See chapter 5 for a more detailed examination of their arguments.

[8] "Memoire sur les Elections au Scrutin," *Histoire de l'Academie Royale des Sciences*, 1781.

[9] Condorcet's writings had considerable influence on French revolutionaries and philosophers, including Rousseau. He was a member of the Academy of Sciences and the Legislative Assembly. In 1785 he published his *Essai sur l'application de l'analyse a' la probabilite des decisions rendues a' la pluralite des voix*, which provided valuable contributions to probability theory and voting theory, but its heavily mathematical nature obscured its signficance until resurrected by Duncan Black in the 1950s. Due to exhaustion or poison he died in prison in 1794. His wife, who divorced him while he was in hiding, subsequently translated Adam Smith's *Theory of Moral Sentiments* into French.

[10] *Theorie Analytique des Probabilites* (1814).

conclusion that the best voting system was one in which the voter ranked his preferences and weights were assigned to each rank. The high-quality work done by Borda, Condorcet, and Laplace was ignored by academicians except for a few mathematicians and one remarkable individual who became famous not for his contributions to voting theory but for his literary work. Most Americans know the Reverend Charles Dodgson (1832–1898) as Lewis Carroll, who wrote *Alice's Adventures in Wonderland* (1865), *Through the Looking-Glass* (1872), and *The Hunting of the Snark* (1876), but he also wrote on mathematics, logic, and on many topics concerning Christ Church, Oxford, where he spent virtually his entire life. His strong commitment to Christ Church, his dislike of H. G. Liddell, dean of the College, and his infatuation with the dean's daughter, Alice, propelled Dodgson to write a series of pamphlets on the theory of elections directed at obtaining more efficient voting procedures in the governing committees of Christ Church.[11] His work on voting was written during the 1870s in apparent ignorance of contributions made by French authors nearly a century earlier. Dodgson wrote about glaring deficiencies in all voting methods, and he was well aware of cyclical majorities, successive elimination, weighted rankings, and exhaustive majorities, which were to occupy the attention of scholars nearly 100 years later. Dodgson's works, too, were ignored by political theorists and practitioners, and voting was not systematically examined until the post–World-War-II era.

Knut Wicksell, a Swedish economist in the latter nineteenth century, sought to extend economic analysis to government decision making. He argued strongly that taxes and expenditures debated in Parliament should be considered as one fiscal bill and that such bills should "pass" only if they secured unanimous approval (see Chapter 6). Wicksell reasoned that majorities could pass expenditure bills that benefited them while levying taxes on the minority. If unanimous consent was required, then the majority would have to bargain with the minority, and only fiscal bills that benefited everyone could pass. Wicksell's view of government as a quid pro quo process of exchange among citizens underlies much of the public choice literature in the sixties and seventies. Wicksell had a tremendous influence on Nobel laureate James Buchanan who began serious scholarship on public choice in the fifties. Eric Lindahl's important work[12] in 1919 laid

---

[11] *A Discussion of the Various Methods of Procedures in Conducting Elections* (1873); *Suggestions As to the Best Method of Taking Votes, Where More Than Two Issues Are to Be Voted On* (1874); *A Method of Taking Votes on More Than Two Issues* (1876); *The Principles of Parliamentary Representation* (1884). Yes, Alice Liddel was the inspiration for the "Alice" in Wonderland.

[12] Wicksells' best known paper, *A New Principle of Just Taxation* (1896) and Eric Lindahl's *Just Taxation—A Positive Solution* are repinted in R. T. Musgrave and A. T. Peacock, *Classics in the Theory of Public Finance* (New York: St. Martin's Press, 1967).

the foundation for the subsequent development of public goods theory based on the essential concept that the value that individuals place on marginal units of the public goods should equal the price they pay for such units through their taxes.

The modern scholarly interest in applying economic methodology to government emerged out of the economic subdiscipline of public finance, which prior to the mid-twentieth century was limited to traditional tax analysis. During the fifties public finance began branching into new dimensions, as public finance scholars started examining not only government taxes but government expenditures and then voting as well. Although not well known in the academic community in his native Britain, nor among many political scientists in the United States, economist Duncan Black was the modern pioneer of voting theory.[13] He researched the history of voting analysis, and he carefully analyzed the efficiency of alternative voting mechanisms. An American economist, Anthony Downs wrote the *Economic Theory of Democracy* in 1957, which has yet to be surpassed for its original, cogent, and insightful analysis of political parties (see chapter 6).

The increasing interest in, and respectability of, economic analysis of the political market is reflected in the fact that three economists who have written in this area have received the Nobel Prize.[14] Kenneth Arrow's *Social Choice and Individual Values*, published first in 1951, became more widely read after it was revised in 1963. This highly technical and abstract work stimulated discussion of voting and social welfare analysis by showing that no social welfare function meeting certain minimum acceptable properties could be constructed from individual preferences.[15] Arrow is often credited with introducing the concept of cyclical majority, even though the French writers had written about it 150 years earlier and Duncan Black had rediscovered and expanded on it in 1949. Paul Samuelson made important contributions in two seminal articles in the mid-fifties that

---

[13] Duncan Black, "On the Rationale of Group Decision Making," *Journal of Political Economy* 56 (1948): 23–34; "The Decisions of a Committee Using a Special Majority," *Econometrica* 16 (1948): 245–61; "The Theory of Elections in Single-Member Constituencies," *Canadian Journal of Economics and Political Science* 15 (1949): 158–75; "Some Theoretical Schemes of Proportional Representation," *Canadian Journal of Economics and Political Science* 15 (1949): 334–43; and *The Theory of Committee and Elections* (Cambridge: Cambridge University Press, 1958).

[14] The Nobel Prize for Economics was first awarded in 1969. Paul Samuelson received the award in 1970, Kenneth Arrow in 1972, and James Buchanan in 1986.

[15] The desirable characteristics were (1) collective rationality, (2) Pareto optimality, (3) nondictatorship, and (4) the independence of irrelevant alternatives. Arrow proved in his famous Impossibility Theorem that these desirable characteristics are "contradictory" because it is always possible to find individual preferences that would violate one of the characteristics. However, Arrow did not analyze individual and voter behavior, and he implicitly endorsed public officials making value judgments without guidance by citizens. *Social Choice and Individual Values*, Cowles Commission Monographs, no. 12 (New York, 1951, 2d ed., 1963).

expanded on and formalized Lindahl's work on public goods theory and provided a technical definition of a public good.[16]

THE EMERGENCE OF PUBLIC CHOICE

By the latter fifties and early sixties economists began to realize that their analytical tools describing and explaining consumer and firm behavior could be applied to the behavior of voters, government, and political representatives. The economist who recognized this most clearly was James Buchanan, the third person who received the Nobel Prize for his contributions to modern political economy. He began analyzing government decision-making institutions and mechanisms around 1950. Subsequently joined at the University of Virginia by his creative collaborator, Gordon Tullock, these prolific men wrote a series of books and articles during the sixties and seventies that formed the foundation of a new subdiscipline in economics and political science called "public choice." They were the first to argue convincingly that an analysis of the political market, like the analysis in the private market, must be grounded on rational individuals pursuing their own self-interests. They argued forcefully that the state is not an organic body apart from the collection of individuals comprising it and that the central role of the economist is to analyze how efficiently government institutions enable individuals to express and to realize their preferences about public goods and policies.

Prodded and stimulated by Buchanan and Tullock, articles on government, voting, bureaucracy, collective choice, and constitutional rules began to flood the academic journals during the seventies and eighties. The traditional public administration and political science theory of bureaucracy was challenged first by Gordon Tullock, Roland McKean, Anthony Downs, and William Niskanen,[17] who refused to accept the view that bureaucrats simply sought the common good of the country or took orders from Congress or from their superiors in the bureaucracy. Like all individuals, bureaucrats had their own preferences and goals, such as higher salaries, influence, and prestige, which they could achieve by enlarging the size

---

[16] Paul Samuelson, "The Pure Theory of Public Expenditure," *Review of Economics and Statistics* (November 1954): 387–89; "Diagrammatic Exposition of a Theory of Public Expenditures, *Review of Economics and Statistics* (November 1955): 350–56.

[17] Roland N. McKean, "Divergences between Individual and Total Costs within Government," *American Economic Review* (May 1964): 243–49; Gordon Tullock, *The Politics of Bureaucracy* (Washington: Public Affairs Press, 1965); Anthony Downs, *Inside Bureaucracy* (Boston: Little, Brown, 1967); and William Niskanen, *Bureaucracy and Representative Government* (Chicago, Aldine, 1971).

of their budgets and agencies. Closely related to the economic analyses of bureaucratic behavior is the concept of rent seeking, and its accompanying resource wastage, which was introduced by Gordon Tullock, Richard Posner, and Anne Krueger, who invented the term.[18]

As a result of these individuals' pioneering work, economists now clearly recognize that there are at least two major institutional mechanisms in which individuals can express and realize their preferences: the private market and the political market. The private market consists of the production and allocation of private goods in a decentralized market process in which individuals can express and realize their relative preferences. The political market, on the other hand, involves the collective expression of individual preferences through an aggregate decision-making process such as voting. A more popular but less appropriate distinction is that dollar "votes" signal the provision and allocation of goods in the private market and that political votes determine the provision and allocation of resources in the political market.

Public choice is the study of the political market. Essentially, it is economic methodology applied to political science. The subject matter of political science and public choice is pretty much the same: theory of the state, voting, apathy, party politics, bureaucracy, and policy analysis. However, the methodology in traditional political science differs from the methodology employed in public choice. Public choice applies two important economic postulates from private market analysis to political market analysis: (1) Individuals are the basic decision-making units, and governments, parties, and legislatures are merely convenient terminological shortcuts. (2) Individuals strive to achieve their personal goals in the political market as well as in the private market. When applying the postulate of rational self-interest to the political market, one must recall the central message in Adam Smith's *Wealth of Nations:* The motivation for individuals' actions is not a good indicator of the results of such actions. Individuals motivated by self-interest and guided by private market restraints tend to promote the general welfare even though they do not intend to do so and are often unaware that their actions are promoting the public interest. Had Adam Smith defined the role of self-interest in the political market he might have written: It is not from the benevolence of the voter, bureaucrat, or politician that we get our highways or welfare systems, but out of their regard for their own interests. There is no analytical reason or empirical evidence that suggests that individuals who

---

[18] Gordon Tullock, "The Welfare Costs of Tariffs, Monopolies, and Theft," *Western Economic Journal* (June 1967).

are "greedy materialists" while pursuing their objectives in the private market become sacrificing angels when they enter the voting booth. If the individual is motivated by personal benefits and costs when making decisions as a consumer, worker, or investor, that individual is going to be motivated by personal benefits and costs when making decisions in the voting booth, in the halls of Congress, and in the conference rooms of the bureaucracy. Previously, social scientists and political commentators assumed a curious dichotomy in human motivations where self-interest ruled supreme in all transactions within the private market but self-sacrifice predominated in the individual's relationship to the state.

Public choice is now well established as a subdiscipline, and many political scientists and scholars from other fields have joined economists in it. There is an active Public Choice Society, and the journal *Public Choice* now has more than 2,000 subscribers. There are active public choice societies in Europe and Japan. Public choice articles have appeared in major economic and political science scholarly journals, and substantial portions of public finance textbooks are now devoted to public choice theories. As a result of public choice research, economists are more aware that market failures exist in the political market as well as in the private market, and they are more cautious in recommending government remedial action for all private market failures. The greatest failure of public choice scholars is their inability or unwillingness to communicate their research to scholars in other areas and to the public at large. Virtually all the work of public choice scholars is directed at other public choice theorists. Many social scientists, social critics, and editorial writers and commentators continue to make statements that reflect their ignorance of developments in political economy and public choice. Such statements will continue as long as public choice theorists talk only among themselves. There are few books that bring together the various pieces and threads of past and present progress in political economy[19] and none that explains past progress in terms understandable by someone not majoring in political economy. While this is a common characteristic of technical material, the academic work done in public choice will have value only if other scholars, officials, representatives, and ordinary citizens become familiar with it. Hopefully, this book will remedy some of these deficiencies. Since public choice utilizes the terminology and methodology of economics, we will begin with a simple explanation of economic analysis in Chapter 2.

---

[19] One excellent book for someone trained in economics is Dennis Mueller's *Public Choice II* (Cambridge: Cambridge University Press, 1989).

QUESTIONS AND ANSWERS

No analyses, tools, or methodologies were discussed in this chapter, so specific questions and answers will not be presented. However, the student should read and contemplate the following:

1. Many economists and political scientists believe that a free market is absolutely essential for the existence of political freedoms.

a. Do you think that "freedom of the press" would have much significance if the government had a monopoly on newsprint?

b. Do you believe that local television stations, which must periodically apply for government operating licenses, or local newspapers are more likely to reflect current government opinion? Why?

c. Would the Fifth Amendment have much force if the government were the only employer? Why?

d. Do you believe that the democratization of Eastern Europe is possible without the establishment of a free market? Why?

e. From the following list, make a ranking of those whom you believe would benefit most from a significant growth in the political market and a decrease in the private market. Save your list and return to it after you have finished this book.

Street sweeper	Doctor
Professor	Psychologist
Economist	Political scientist
Politician	Government manager
Lawyer	Blacks
TV news commentator	Hispanics
Artist	Assembly line worker
Small firm manger	Large firm manager
Social worker	Farmer
Accountant	Editorial writer

2. Many economists believe that a political democracy that "softens the harshness" of the private market is absolutely essential for the continued existence of the private market.

a. Do you believe that a private market is more likely to exist in a dictatorship or in a democracy? Why?

b. What laws do you believe would encourage the development of the private market, and what laws would discourage it? Why?

c. Franklin Roosevelt's New Deal legislation is often credited with saving capitalism during the Depression of the 1930s. Do you agree? Why?

d. Why did workers lead the Polish Solidarity revolt against communism and in favor of democracy and the free market?

e. "Government is necessary to resolve interpersonal conflicts." Can you think of other ways interpersonal conflicts might be resolved?

3. Do you think that the word "free" means the same thing when it is used in the phrase "free market" as when it is used in "free press," "free speech," "free associations," "free governments," and "mankind yearns to be free"? Why?

4. Certainly, you have heard about "fair prices," "fair interest rates," "fair wages," "fair shares."

a. How would judge whether each of these is "fair"?

b. When you were young, did you and your mother agree on what constituted your "fair share" of the cake? If you went to a grocery store to buy a cake today, do you think that you and the grocery store owner would always agree on what was a fair price?

c. When you are about to deposit money in a bank, is a "fair interest rate" a high rate or a low rate of interest? When you are about to borrow money from a bank, is a "fair rate of interest" a high rate or low rate of interest?

d. When your boss tells you that your wage rate is going to be decreased and you say "that is unfair," what do you mean? When the university increases its tuition and you say "that is unfair," what do you mean?

e. Why do you think people use the word "fair"?

f. Can you think of other words in the English language whose meanings are as clear and precise as the word "fair"?

CHAPTER TWO

ECONOMICS: THE STUDY OF CHOICE BEHAVIOR

Man is a reasoning animal.
—LUCIUS SENECA, A.D. 50

The difficulty in life is the choice.
—GEORGE MOORE, *THE BENDING OF THE BOUGH*

The ideas of economists and political philosophers, both when they are right and when they are wrong, are more powerful than is commonly understood. Indeed the world is ruled by little else. Practical men, who believe themselves to be quite exempt from any intellectual influences, are usually slaves of some defunct economist.
—OBLIGATORY QUOTE IN ECONOMIC TEXTS, JOHN MAYNARD KEYNES, 1936

THAT DISMAL SCIENCE

Individuals have unlimited wants, but nature provides limited resources to satisfy them. Due to the insatiability of wants and to the stinginess of nature, humans are forced to choose the resources that should be employed, the combination in which they should be utilized, and the order in which these wants should be satisfied. Nature has made the capacity of rational choice a distinguishing characteristic of the human species. One need not dwell on its philosophical implications or derivations to observe that individuals do choose. They select their friends, spouses, careers, cars, soaps, and their politicians. Few, if any, of these choices are based on a complete knowledge of alternatives, nor do all individuals have identical alternatives available to them. College applicants, for example, are unacquainted with the strengths and weaknesses of all the world's colleges, and no husband or wife ever surveyed the delicate qualities of all potential mates in the world before marrying one. Choices are subject to constraints of time and space, of endowments and capabilities, of culture and experience, and by the choices of other persons.

Economics is that discipline which systematically studies individual choice behavior and the institutions within which such decisions are made.

16

Contrary to the layman's belief that economics is confined to a study of the stock market, inflation, or the production and consumption of material goods to satisfy material wants, economics is much more general. There is an economics of love, an economics of time, an economics of crime and punishment, as well as an economics of material goods; most importantly, these are not separable "economics." Each of these "economics" is based upon a foundation of a common set of analytical tools. Economics is not defined by the subject area it studies, since its domain has become the limitless field of human choice. Any attempt to delimit as dynamic a discipline as economics would not be an easy task, but a good first approximation would be a delineation by methodology. More than other social sciences, economics is a way of thinking, a method for approaching a subject, a framework of mental organization. Persons who learn and utilize this methodology will change. Perhaps they will lose the sweetness of naiveté and become cynics; perhaps they will become wise and recognize their ignorance. Whatever they become, there is no turning back; once baptized, the mark remains, and they become different persons and, hopefully, but not necessarily, better ones.

Economics is not an inherently dull or boring discipline, although it can become so with considerable ease. Pursued with a receptive, imaginative, and disciplined mind, economics in general—and political economics in particular—is quite exciting. It opens new vistas to explore, and it provides the tools for accomplishing the exploration. It is academic and practical; it is general and specific; it is rewarding and demanding. But anyone wishing to understand political economy and public choice must thoroughly understand the fundamental analytical tools of economists and their relevance to the private and political markets.

METHODOLOGICAL FRAMEWORK

ECONOMICS AS A SCIENCE

A discipline is termed a science if it employs the scientific method, which is nothing more nor less than the process of an orderly abstraction from reality—the development of a theoretical framework—in order to gain an understanding of the interrelationships among basic variables, followed by the systematic criticism and modification of these basic theories. All scientific theories are unrealistic in that they are abstractions from the confusing interplay of thousands of variables simultaneously affecting the object being studied: physics, for example, has its pure theory, or law, of frictionless falling bodies, and thermodynamics has its theory of pure gas.[1]

---

[1] Economics, too, has been known to have theories of pure gas.

These sciences have advanced not because their pure theories presented a realistic picture of the real world, but because they provided a theoretical foundation upon which the framework of further work and empirical verification could be constructed. The human mind has a limited capacity to process billions of bits of information and millions of interrelated variables. A sure way to become confused about reality is to consider too much information. Hence, the value of a theory depends not only on the realism of its assumptions but also on the extent to which the model enables one to understand events in the real world and to make reliable predictions.

Some critics of a particular theory believe they can destroy its validity by arguing that "it is only a generalization." Such arguments, of course, are meaningless. All scientific theories are generalizations; indeed, progress in any discipline would be impossible without them. It is only through generalizations that the nature of things can be observed, understood, and modified. This is as true for the social sciences as it is for the so-called hard sciences. Without a generalized analytical framework, it is as difficult to evaluate an economic system, a legislative act, or a social movement as it is to construct a skyscraper without a blueprint. Ideas, values, and facts are the lumber, cement, and nails; theories are the blueprints.

Theoretical models in economics are as esoteric as any in the physical sciences, but physical scientists are more fortunate in that they can isolate more easily, but not completely, the extraneous variables when testing their theories. When economists attempt to test their favorite theories they often are unable to isolate the relevant variables from the multifariousness of the real world. Another problem confronting the social, but not the physical, scientist is the unpredictable variability in individual values and motivations. It is difficult for the physical scientist, for example, to determine the earth's precise gravitational force at a certain place and under particular conditions. Once it is determined, however, it generally can be assumed that the law of gravity will not reverse itself. On the other hand, even if social scientists can determine the values and motivations of individuals, they may discover that, due to entirely unpredictable and initially unexplainable reasons, the values and motivations have been suddenly altered.

Apart from differences resulting from studying subjects with varying resistances to empirical verifications, the social and physical sciences differ in more subtle aspects. The social scientist, unlike the physical scientist, must analyze a group or set of which he or she is a member. As a result, personal prejudices easily become intermingled with analysis. If electrons, for example, wrote physics textbooks, it is likely that we would be reading that protons revolve around electrons. Similarly, a political scientist or economist receiving research funds from the federal government might conclude the analysis by claiming that the country can survive only if more research funds are channeled through Washington.

There are advantages, however, to being a member of the set one is analyzing. The social scientist can extrapolate his or her own introspections to other members of the set and, thus, can gain knowledge that would otherwise be denied. A physics textbook written by an electron, while probably not being entirely objective, might at least provide insights into the intricacies of the atom that are not yet available. Although economists tend to agree about economic analysis—as opposed to economic policy—much more than laymen realize, we should not expect to see the achievement of the definitive results in economic analysis that are obtained in the physical sciences. As long as individuals can choose freely from among alternative ends and means, economics might better be called the study, not the science, of human choice.

Political economists recognize the existence of personal motivations other than those selfish interests associated with *homo economicus*, but even altruistic behavior can be understood with economic analysis. More importantly, as anyone who has visited an orphanage or a nursing home knows, love is indeed a scarce resource. Economists emphasize those human institutions in which self-interest can produce tolerably acceptable results; they emphasize voluntary but self-interested exchanges among free individuals. In the process, and often without the intention of doing so, they highlight and clarify the moral issues that require the ministrations of the preacher and the philosopher.

Political economists search for institutional mechanisms that harness and direct the self-interests of individuals to achieve the public interest. They stress the manipulation of private incentives rather than changes in individual values; they focus attention on the mechanisms of decision making rather than the outcomes of such decision making. Most economists are reluctant to conclude that certain values or outcomes are preferable, and this reluctance has led them to ignore the ethical trade-offs of decision making. It is becoming increasingly clear, however, that ethical choices made by individuals and policy officials have significant impacts on both the political and economic systems, and some economists are now beginning to examine the effects of alternative ethical systems. One important advantage of economic analysis is that it reveals the opportunity costs of alternative ethical decisions, thereby facilitating ethical decision making. Furthermore, the self-interest postulate does not mean that individuals are greedy materialists who care only about themselves. It merely suggests that the decisions of both the humanitarian and the egocentric respond to changes in personal costs and benefits. A humanitarian, for example, would be more inclined to do good if his or her own personal costs of doing so were low rather than high.

One who reads most of the technical journals in economics might easily conclude that economics is irrelevant for most social issues. One reason for this is the presentation of economic arguments in mathematical terms, seemingly devoid of real-world implications; the other reason is that economics is the oldest of the social sciences, and the fundamental analyses have been written and rewritten many times. The new and the different analyses necessarily become more arcane and esoteric as a discipline matures. Economists, perhaps, have not been suitably sensitive to the fact that diminishing returns are as applicable to their own profession as they are to fertilizer—an example, intone the critics, that is *most* relevant to economics. Nevertheless, the fundamental economic theories are tremendously rich and effective in aiding our understanding of the social, political, and economic environment, and they are surprisingly relevant to a wide range of social policy issues. Many critics charge that the assumptions utilized by economists lack realism, and they cite the episode where a graduate student interrupted his economics professor by saying, "Sir, in the real world. . . . " The professor snapped back, "The real world is a special case, and, therefore, we don't have to consider it." Milton Friedman has answered these critics by persuasively arguing that the usefulness of a theory should not be judged by the realism of its assumption but by its ability to make good predictions.

Even the most practical and avid theory hater among us uses theories every day. When we look for the sunrise in the east or predict cold weather in Minneapolis in January, we are implicitly employing some of the most complicated theories known to man. We "couch potatoes" implicitly put some faith in the "calorie theory," which states that the weight of an individual is a positive function of caloric intake per some time period (a day or a week). One simple conclusion of this theory is that if we want to lose weight, we should reduce our caloric intake. A practical man or woman of the world could easily criticize the realism of this theory. No one has seen a calorie, and most of us don't really understand how calories are converted to weight. More importantly, shout the critics, the theory ignores age, sex, weight, height, heredity, exercise, and body metabolism. It appears to be an unrealistic theory, but we notice that when we eat more cakes, pies, and meat, we gain weight. We accept the theory because it makes reasonably good predictions. Further, medical experts are able to offer an explanation of the logical connection between caloric intake and weight gain. A good theory does not have to be "realistic" in the sense that it includes all possible variables; it might include only one or two of the relevant factors. It might not accurately describe or predict every occurrence, but if it explains and predicts most occurrences, it is a good theory.

A good theory does more than make predictions, however. It should enable us to think clearly and logically. It should enable us to separate issues that are not necessarily related to each other. It should be an efficient pedagogical tool in which rather severe initial abstractions are made in order to understand relationships among the most salient variables. After these relationships are understood, the severe assumptions can be systematically relaxed or altered. A good theory should stimulate a way of thinking and analyzing problems, and it should enable us to systematically modify variables appropriate to the real-world problem being examined.

EQUILIBRIUM IN ECONOMIC ANALYSIS

Equilibrium analysis is an important methodological tool widely used in the physical and biological sciences, but among the social sciences it has traditionally been confined to economics. Equilibrium means that a state of balance exists between opposing forces or that there is a state of rest, the achievement of which means that there are no incentives for further changes. For example, two units of hydrogen and one unit of oxygen may each be in separate equilibrium (assuming constant temperature, pressure, etc.), but when they are mixed together, they are in temporary disequilibrium until H_2O is formed, at which time they are once again in equilibrium. Economists use equilibrium analysis to examine alternative arrangements or conditions in the market. One of the first lessons a new student in economics learns is that given a particular set of costs and demand conditions, a market equilibrium price for the good will be reached. The price will remain unchanged until some variables change the demand or supply conditions for that good. For example, let's consider the invention of an inexpensive substitute for a good, say margarine for butter. The demand curve for butter would shift down, and a lower equilibrium price and quantity for butter would result. Economists compare the original equilibrium price with the new equilibrium price and conclude that the development of an inexpensive substitute for butter resulted in a lower equilibrium price for butter. Equilibrium analysis is used to analyze variable changes in both the private and political markets.

FUNDAMENTAL POSTULATES, PRINCIPLES, AND DEFINITIONS

All scientific theories are based on selected postulates or assumptions about how the world operates. Political economy is no exception. Its postulates, of course, differ from those in the natural sciences in that most of them pertain to human behavior, and economists might argue about which postulates are the most important. However, most economists would agree that the following are among the most significant postulates.

Postulate 1: The basic decision-making unit and, hence, the unit of analysis is the individual.

This is the most important postulate in economics and one that is most frequently ignored by political commentators, scholars, editorial writers, and average citizens. Individuals—not the U.S. government, General Motors, AFL-CIO, or the Democratic party—make decisions. Although it is convenient to refer to these aggregates in casual conversation, much chaos in the analytical process can result if such artificial entities are treated as though they actually make decisions or are capable of performing morally good or bad acts. This postulate is particularly significant when analyzing the political market, because many scholars use the individual as a unit of analysis in examining private market decision making but incorrectly revert to the group, Congress, government, or party as the unit of analysis in the political market. Consistency, if nothing else, demands that the individual be the basic analytical unit in both markets. When it becomes convenient to analyze the behavior of a group of individuals, such as a firm or a political party, it should at least be noted that the entity is composed of individuals and that the presumed behavior of the entity might not characterize all, most, or many of the choices of the individuals comprising it.

Individuals have differing preferences for both private and public goods, and economists do not examine whether these preferences are "good" or "bad," "true" or "false." Economists take preferences as given and then analyze the institutional efficiency in which these preferences are reflected and realized. Most economic principles books address this distinction as the difference between positive and normative analysis. *Normative analysis* is concerned with desirable actions or policies. A statement such as "We need more guns (or butter)" is a normative statement. *Positive analysis* is concerned with "if X, then Y" statements, which can be tested both by the internal logic of the relationship and empirical evidence. An example of positive analysis is the statement that if the price of good X is increased and other variables such as income and the prices of other goods are held constant, then the quantity demanded of X will decrease. Although the logical relationship of this relationship is more complicated than it might seem, this is a simple positive statement that can be subjected to empirical verification. There is no implication that changes in the quantity demanded of X are desirable or undesirable.

When economic analysis is applied to specific policies it might become more difficult for many analysts to separate the positive from normative analysis. For example, if an economist is analyzing a policy of enacting or increasing a minimum wage, the differences between positive and normative analysis can become clouded. The economist might take a simple theoretical model that assumes certain demand and supply curves for labor. When the minimum wage is injected into this model, the results may show that the real wages of those workers who remain employed will increase but some workers will become unemployed. This is positive analysis because it is identifying the consequences of the policy, which, hopefully, can be tested empirically. It does not state that the minimum wage is desirable or undesirable or good or bad policy. That would require a normative conclusion based on value judgments about the desirability of increasing the wages of some workers while other workers were losing their jobs.

So far the differences between positive and normative are fairly distinct. Now assume that the economist also builds a theoretical model that shows that if real wages increase because of minimum wage legislation, firms will lay off the least productive workers and that, among workers of approximately equal productivity, employers will refuse to hire workers from certain racial, religious, or ethnic groups. Hence, the economist might state that if minimum wage legislation is passed, unemployment will increase among the least-educated workers, the handicapped, the aged, and racial and ethnic minorities. Is this a positive or normative statement? Narrowly construed, it is a positive statement because it is put in the classic "If X, then Y" format, and there is no explicit statement about the desirability of the minimum wage law. However, the analyst selected only one consequence of the minimum wage legislation, that is, the impact on the unemployed. Not mentioned were the other effects of a minimum wage law, including the increase in the real wage rate of those workers still employed. Were the analyst's own value judgments slipped into the analysis that reported only the conclusion about the effects on the unemployed?

The positive-normative debate can get more complicated. Assume there are two economists, Able and Baker. Able's values tend to favor the minimum wage; Baker's values are opposed to the minimum wage. Now assume that each economist makes the following statements:

Able: If Congress wants to increase the real wage rate of a large number of poorly paid workers and increase their standard of living, then it should pass the minimum wage.

Baker: If Congress does not want to increase the unemployment rate among the most uneducated, the handicapped, and certain racial and ethnic minority groups, then it should reject the proposed minimum wage.

Are these positive or normative statements? If a single economist had made both statements, would they be normative or positive? Does the very selection of some questions and not others slip the analyst into normative economics? Economists' answers to these questions are not uniform. Some hang their answer on the "if . . . then" statement and conclude that they are positive, while others emphasize the word "should" and conclude that they are normative. Any scientist can inject normative implications into positive analysis by the proper selection of the questions he or she seeks to answer. This does not necessarily make the analysis less useful, but it should be considered by the reader or policy official who is interested in an expanded list of questions.

It is extremely important for the reader to understand that when economists use the individual as a unit of analysis, they do not sanction a political philosophy sometimes termed "rugged individualism" or extreme conservatism. Economists distinguish between methodological individualism and philosophical individualism. *Methodological individualism* is a system of analysis in which the individual is assumed to be the ultimate decision maker and both a consumer and producer of goods and services. In this methodology, the analyst must consider the possibility that some individuals might want to obtain additional collective goods by sacrificing private goods. *Philosophical individualism*, on the other hand, is the term applied to a set of values that implies that collectivism is undesirable and that individuals should be free to pursue their goals with minimal interference from the collectivity or government.

Although philosophical individualism is said to be normative because it directly involves the making of value judgments and methodological individualism is said to be positive because it is value free, the latter does imply some subtle, although generally widely accepted, values. For example, the most important value upon which methodological individualism is based is that individuals should be and are free to express and to work towards the realization of their preferences. If, on the other hand, we were to assume that a desirable societal objective is that some individuals should sacrifice themselves to the fire gods, no matter what their individual preferences might be, economists would be forced to work in a different ethical environment, and the conclusions about efficiency and how the system works would be much different from the individualistic assumption employed in economics.[2]

---

[2] A positive methodology could be developed, however, that would examine the most efficient way to coerce people to sacrifice themselves to the fire gods. Efficiency in this content would have a different meaning than efficiency in economic analysis. The point is that efficiency has no meaning other than that given by the normative objective of the analysis.

To summarize, methodological individualism is positive in the sense that it analyzes and evaluates the interrelationship of variables according to the criterion that individual decision makers do pursue their own goals. It shows what would happen to certain dependent variables if there were a change in one or more independent variables. However, it is normative in its implied assumption that individuals should be able to express and to realize their preferences and in its analysis of efficiency based on the premise that individuals should get what they want. This is especially true in political economy and public choice, where economists often analyze the efficiency of alternative institutional arrangements based on individuals being able to express their preferences. They sometimes even posit certain preferences, such as "If individuals want to limit the power of government, these are some institutional arrangements they can establish to reach that goal."

Economists generally assume that *individuals act rationally.* This does not mean that individuals are cold computers utilizing perfect information and making calculations with unerring precision. Individuals, however, do make some calculations in their attempts to achieve their goals. The information they possess or the goals they pursue might be different from ours, but these differences should not be interpreted as constituting irrationality. As we shall see later in the book, it is often rational for people to remain ignorant, because the expected benefits from obtaining additional information are less than the personal costs of procuring that information. Furthermore, economic rationality appears to exist even among individuals we initially might think do not act rationally. A series of studies of patients in mental hospitals showed that patients reacted very rationally when confronted with varying prices and wage rates.[3] They were offered tokens that could be traded in for candy, cigarettes, and other items in the hospital store. Higher token wage rates generated an increased number of workers for menial jobs that, otherwise, were avoided. When the token prices of some goods were raised, the patients purchased less of those goods and more of others. When they were not paid for the work, the patients chose not to work. Their reactions to the wages and prices were those economists would have predicted from their analytical tool of

---

[3] R. C. Battalio, "A Test of Consumer Demand Theory Using Observation of Individual Consumer Purchases," *Western Economic Journal* 11 (December 1973): 411–28; T. Allyon and N. H. Azrin, "The Measurement and Reinforcement of Behavior of Psychotics," *Journal of Experimental Analysis of Behavior* 8 (November 1965); R. C. Winkler, "An Experimental Analysis of Economic Balance: Savings and Wages in a Token Economy," *Behavior Therapy* 4 (January 1973): 22–40; David G. Tarr, "Experiments in Token Economies: A Review of the Evidence Relating to Assumptions and Implications of Economic Theory," *Southern Economic Journal* 43 (October 1976): 1136–43.

a rational individual. Even rats were observed to have negatively sloping demand curves. When the price of a tasty liquid went up in the form of the number of times they had to push a bar to obtain a liquid, they consumed less of that good and more of the lower-priced (fewer pushes) goods.

Postulate 2: Individuals have insatiable wants.

Most economists talk about individual wants rather than individual needs because the word needs has emotional connotations, and the needs of virtually every American citizen, if interpreted as that amount of goods necessary for continued existence, have been met.[4] Individuals have wants for goods, services, love, respect, power, prestige, and so on from which they obtain pleasure, satisfaction, happiness, or, as economists call it, welfare or utility. A good has *utility* if a person obtains some benefits from it or if it satisfies some want. Many people have the mistaken belief that economic theory assumes that all individuals are crude economic men or women who wish only to maximize their consumption of "materialistic" goods and services. This "outside" view of the economist's preoccupation with *homo economicus* is understandable in light of the existence of numerous economic texts that vehemently reject any reliance on the economic-man hypothesis in the introductory chapters and then vigorously employ the concept in the chapters that follow. But economic analysis is not chained to *homo economicus,* and it can incorporate the individual's choices among the entire set of goods that are believed to be "good" for that person. This might include food, cars, television, leisure, prestige, power, social approval, knowledge, and the welfare of other individuals, to list just a few.

Postulate 3: Resources and goods are scarce.

Goods are often classified into two broad categories: economic goods and free goods. An *economic good* is one that is scarce, relative to people's wants, while an *economic bad* is one that is more plentiful than individuals wish it to be. Scarcity, in a strictly physical sense, does not define an economic good. For example, goat milk in the United States is very scarce, but it is not considered to be a highly valued economic good because individuals do not demand it. Hence, an economic good is one that is scarce relative to people's wants and, thus, commands a positive price on the market. Even in the affluent United States there is a scarcity of goods. We are unable to obtain all of the computers, books, education, stereos,

---

[4] Americans, who have an average annual income per capita of approximately $14,000, sometimes forget that it is possible to live on much lower incomes. The average citizen of Bangladesh, for example, lives on an annual income of $110.

thick carpets, VCRs, European trips, medical care, strawberries, and housing that we would like. People must make choices among the goods they would like to have. They are willing to pay money, or to sacrifice other goods, in order to obtain more units of a particular economic good. Goods may yield negative as well as positive utility. Such negative-utility-yielding economic goods are sometimes called economic bads, and they exist when the quantity is greater than people wish it to be. Polluted water is an example of an economic bad. Economic bads command a negative price, or cost, because individuals are willing to pay some price to dispose of them.

If individuals are unwilling to pay some price to obtain or to dispose of marginal quantities of some good, that good is a *free good* and will command no positive or negative price. The ubiquitous example of a free good is air, because individuals would not pay a price, positive or negative, to obtain or dispose of additional units. This statement must be qualified, however, for clean air is an economic good not only to astronauts and aquanauts but also to contemporary urban-nauts. Fresh air in the western plains of the United States in the nineteenth century would be considered a free good, whereas fresh air to residents of smog-bound Los Angeles would not be. Note that goods also encompass services provided in the market. Hereafter, when the term *goods* is used, reference is being made to economic goods including services.

Postulate 4: Consumers are willing to substitute goods in consumption, and the value of any good depends upon the relative quantity of current consumption of that good.

There are no superior goods, because there is always *some* quantity of other goods an individual would be willing to sacrifice to obtain one more unit of a particular good. Even individuals in primitive societies sacrificed some food and clothing for a little bit of art and music. These sacrifices of additional food and clothing for art represent one of the most useful concepts in economics known as *marginalism*, which emphasizes that all choices are made about incremental or additional quantities of goods rather than about absolute amounts. For example, an economist would *not* ask whether shirts or shoes are more valuable, because if the consumer had, say, 500 pairs of shoes and two shirts, an additional, or marginal, shirt would be more valuable than an additional, or marginal, pair of shoes. If the same consumer had 500 shirts and two shoes, then an additional pair of shoes would be valued more highly. Thus, the value an individual places on a marginal unit of any good depends upon the relative quantity of that good the individual has consumed during some period of time. The concept of marginalism is also applied to costs. The cost of producing a marginal unit of a good is known as the marginal cost. The marginal cost could be greater than or less than the average cost. Assume that the total cost of producing 10 units of a good is $100 but that the tenth unit costs only $6 to produce. The average cost is $10, but the marginal cost is $6.

Adam Smith used marginalism to resolve the mystery of diamonds, which are only adornments, having much higher market values than water, which is essential to life. Diamonds have such high value because they are more scarce than water. If individuals were allowed to consume only one quart of water a week but they found jars full of diamonds each week, the price they would be willing to pay for one additional quart of water would be much higher than the price they would pay for an additional diamond. The principle of marginalism—which states that the value (and cost) of any good is determined at the margin—is easy to understand and memorize. It is not quite so simple to apply in practice.

Assume that the Army Corps of Engineers has recently completed a benefit-cost study of a 50-foot dam for a neighboring river and that the benefits of the dam are estimated to be $200 million and the costs $190 million. Are you inclined to approve the project because the benefits are greater than the costs? Gottcha?! If your initial reaction was approval, you would be wrong, because the study says nothing about those very important marginal costs and marginal benefits. Assume that you investigated further and discovered a listing of the marginal and total benefits and costs (see Table 2-1).

Assume that the dam could be built at alternative heights, as shown in the first column. The total costs of a 10-foot dam are $10 million, and the total benefits are $60 million. A 20-foot dam would cost an *additional*, or *marginal*, $30 million, which would bring total costs to $40 million.[5] The additional 10 feet would generate an *additional*, or *marginal*, increase of $50 million in benefits, for total benefits of $110. Certainly, we would want the dam to be *at least* 20 feet high. The marginal benefits of building a dam 10 feet higher (to 20 feet) are $50 million, but the marginal costs of these last 10 feet are only $30 million, so the dam should be built higher. On the other hand, the marginal benefits from increasing the dam height from 30 to 40 feet are only $30 million, while the marginal costs are $50 million. Since the marginal benefits generated by the additional 10 feet are less than the marginal costs, it doesn't make sense to build the dam

---

[5] Marginal benefits and costs are generally applied to single units in textbooks, but in the real world it is prohibitively costly to examine the marginal benefits and costs of every possible unit, and the "marginal" unit is defined as some convenient grouping of units. In this case, the marginal benefits and costs are examined at every 10 feet of dam height.

— TABLE 2-1 —
BENEFITS AND COSTS OF HYPOTHETICAL DAM
(IN MILLIONS OF DOLLARS)

Height (Feet)	Marginal Benefits	Marginal Costs	Total Benefits	Total Costs
10	$60	$10	$ 60	$ 10
20	50	30	110	40
30	40	40	150	80
40	30	50	180	130
50	20	60	200	190

as high as 40 feet. At a height of 30 feet, marginal benefits just equal marginal costs, which means that marginal benefits exceed marginal costs below a height of 30 feet and that marginal benefits are less than marginal costs above 30 feet. Notice that *total benefits* exceed *total costs* by the greatest amount at 30 feet. Net total benefits will always be maximized where marginal benefits equal marginal costs ($MB = MC$). A decision-making rule of equating marginal benefits and marginal costs will maximize welfare. In this example, it will result in the construction of the appropriate-size dam (30 feet). One must look at marginal benefits and costs and not whether total costs are greater than or less than total benefits. This simple example should illustrate the importance of marginalism and the costly mistakes that can be made when it is ignored. An important efficiency criterion in economics is that net social welfare is always maximized where marginal benefits equal marginal costs.

Postulate 5: Other factors constant, the lower the price of any good, the greater the quantity demanded.

Postulate 4 showed that the utility or satisfaction obtained from consuming an additional unit of some good decreases as the individual consumes more units of that good; hence, the individual would purchase additional units only if the price were lowered, thus illustrating the law of demand:

The Law of Demand

Other factors being equal, more of a good will be bought the lower its price, or less of a good will be bought the higher its price.[6]

---

[6] The "other factors equal" clause is another way of saying that economists are concerned about relative prices. For example, if the average price (or price index) of *all* consumer goods increases by 10 percent but the price of hamburger increases by only 6 percent, economists would say that the (relative) price of hamburgers has gone down. When economists mention price they almost always are referring to relative price.

The law of demand applies not only to such goods as clothes, computers, soap, and books but to dates, crime, studying, babies, national defense, and education. As the price of these goods goes down, individuals demand a greater quantity of them. Economists have found very few exceptions to this law.

Postulate 6: Economic costs are the other alternatives foregone when selecting one alternative.

The economic, or opportunity, costs of selecting one alternative are the opportunities foregone by not selecting the next best alternative. If there are no other alternatives available, then there is no opportunity cost, and cost has no meaning. When economists use the term *opportunity costs* they are generally referring to the costs to society (sometimes specifically calling them social opportunity costs) that are often different from the opportunity costs confronting the decision maker. In fact, one function performed by economists is pointing out those cases where the buyers or sellers of a good do not bear all the social opportunity costs. Although most goods are expressed in the common denominator of money prices, economists tend to think in real, as opposed to monetary, terms. Given the technology, resources, population, and culture of a particular country, there is a tradeoff that must be made in the production of one good as opposed to another. If a pair of shoes costs $60 to produce and shirts cost $20, then, *at the margin*, shoes are using resources valued at three times the resources used in making shirts. It also means that each pair of shoes produced is costing the country resources that could have been used to produce three shirts.

Economic costs include not only the explicit visible costs but also the implicit, or "invisible," costs. The costs of a college education, for example, include not only tuition and fees but also the income foregone over the time a student is at college and, if the student is one of those rare serious scholars, the leisure time sacrificed while studying evenings and weekends. Other examples of economic, or opportunity, costs include the following: the economic cost to an investor of committing his wealth to one investment alternative is the rate of return that could have been earned on the next best alternative; the cost of building a highway are fewer hospitals and schools; the cost of watching the late movie on TV are drowsiness and diminished performance the next morning.

Because the application of opportunity cost is more difficult than memorizing its definition, an example should help the student develop an appreciation for its application. The Red Cross and local community blood centers collect blood from donors and then send the blood to hospitals, where it is kept for future use. Donors are not paid for the blood, and the blood centers charge hospitals only for the processing, typing, and collection costs of the blood center, which generally total about $70.[7] Hospitals add their processing fees to their blood procurement costs (supplies and time of technicians in obtaining the blood) and then charge the patient or insurance company. The question is, Does the resulting price of blood represent the opportunity cost of blood? The answer is no, because it does not include the opportunity cost of the blood donor's time, which is socially valuable, even if the blood center does not pay for it. Most "volunteer" blood is obtained from employees of large and highly visible firms in the community that allow their employees to take the day off (sometimes two days) if they donate blood. If the average wage plus fringe benefits of the employee-donor total $200 a day, then the most significant component of the opportunity cost of blood procurement is being ignored. The true opportunity cost of blood procurement is not the explicit cost of $70 but the explicit costs of $70 *plus* the invisible but real cost of lost production of $200. When a unit of blood is obtained from the donor, the opportunity cost to the nation is $270. Note that the realization that the opportunity cost of blood procurement is $270 does not necessarily mean that patients must pay $270 for a unit of blood. The blood could be wholly or partially financed by the government or private insurance. However, efficiency in the use of the nation's blood resources cannot be obtained if blood centers, hospitals, insurance companies, doctors, and patients all believe that blood costs only about one-fourth of its true opportunity costs.

One additional note on opportunity costs. Economists include a "normal" return to capital in their cost calculations. Capital is a factor of production similar to any other factor, such as labor, land, or resources, and it needs a return to draw it into production. Hence, a rate of return on capital that is just sufficient to keep the marginal unit of capital in that industry is a cost of production. Profits that accrue to the capitalists, owners, directors that are greater than these opportunity costs are *economic profits*.

One of the fundamental functions of an efficient price and wage system is to reflect all opportunity costs. Once again, the concept of opportunity cost is simple, but its application can be troublesome to economic experts and novices. Because the concept of opportunity cost is simple, but its application difficult, one more example will be given before proceeding to other topics.

---

[7] The example is referring to whole blood and red cells collected from "voluntary" donors. Plasma is generally collected from donors who are paid money.

The peacetime military draft, first enacted in 1948 and ended in 1973, illustrates a disregard of opportunity costs. The draft was necessary because the wages and benefits paid new enlistees was insufficient to attract the required number of young men to staff the military services. When a draftee entered military service the opportunity cost to society was the lost value of the production by the draftee as a civilian. This production value, in turn, was approximately equal to the civilian wages and benefits earned by the draftee. Assume the marginal draftee could have earned $8,000 in the civilian sector, reflecting the value of the draftee's production, but his military pay and benefits amounted to only $3,000 per year. The Defense Department budget reflected the $3,000 annual budgetary cost of the draftee and military officials as well as Congress based their decisions about the size and use of military services on this artificially low cost. If the budget had reflected correctly the social opportunity cost of $8,000 (equal to lost production in the civilian sector), fewer young men would have been inducted into the armed forces, and those who were inducted would have been used more efficiently. Since the opportunity cost was $8,000 per soldier and taxpayers had to give up only $3,000 worth of goods and services to pay the wages and benefits of the soldiers, who paid the remaining $5,000? The answer is simple. Those who were drafted had to pay a tax-in-kind. They could have been earning $8,000, but they were now getting paid only $3,000, so they suffered a loss of $5,000.[8] The draft also illustrates another economic postulate, which will be discussed below. Since the military services simply did not need all of the young men coming of draft age, some system of discrimination had to be used to select those who would have the honor of paying the tax while serving their country and those who would stay home and pursue their education and careers. Until the mid-sixties, the discrimination was against those who did not go to undergraduate or graduate school, those whose parents had no influence with the local draft board, and those who remained single. After 1969, a lottery was used to select those young men who would pay the "tax" and go to Vietnam and those who would stay home and chase girls.[9]

---

[8] The numbers presented in this example were kept simple in order to illustrate the concept of opportunity cost. Actually, the opportunity cost would be higher because the average draftee would not have enlisted if the military paid him $8,000. The hardships of the military would have required a higher annual income, say $12,000, to enlist. The opportunity cost would have been $8,000 in goods and services plus $4,000 of additional hardship borne by the draftee.

[9] Note that the lottery actually increased the opportunity cost of the draft. While the previous system tended to exclude those with special skills and those pursuing advanced degrees, the lottery randomly selected from among young men regardless of skills or education.

The relationship between cost and production levels is very important in political economy. They are crucial variables affecting the optimal size of firms and governmental units and the efficiency of competitive suppliers in the private and political markets. If total costs increase at the same rate as total production, then average and marginal costs are the same and they do not change as output is changed. When average and marginal costs remain the same no matter what happens to output, economists say that the industry is a *constant cost industry.* Figure 2-1(a) shows a constant cost industry; the average and marginal costs per unit are the same no matter how much is produced each year. If the average and marginal costs per unit decrease as output increases, the industry is said to be characterized by decreasing costs, or increasing returns to scale, as shown in Figure 2-1(b).

FIGURE 2-1

CONSTANT, DECREASING, AND INCREASING COSTS OF PRODUCTION

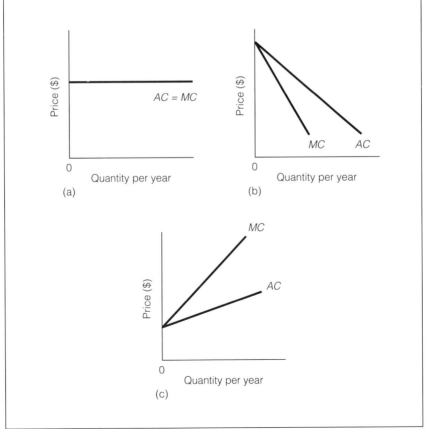

If the production of the firm is subject to *decreasing returns to scale,* the marginal and average cost curves increase, as shown in Figure 2-1(c).

Laymen recognize the decreasing cost case [Figure 2-1(b)] as "the economies of large scale" or "mass production." As production increases, the opportunities for specialization and division of labor increase, so average costs decrease. Production can be planned for smooth flows, and certain types of capital equipment that are not feasible at small production levels become feasible at large production levels. Decreasing average costs seldom continue throughout all feasible production levels because of the difficulties inherent in managing large operations. As the operation becomes larger it becomes increasingly difficult for the owner (or president, mayor, leader, etc.) to obtain accurate information from subordinates and to develop a set of incentives inducing subordinates to make the same decisions he would make based on the same information. Complicated decision-making procedures have to be enacted, audits and performance evaluations have to be made, and large departments have to be created to manage the flow of paper and decision making required to coordinate efforts. Unless all decisions are to be made unchallenged by first-level managers without any coordination among them, "red tape" and bureaucracy must be introduced.

The existence of increasing or decreasing costs is very important in the private and political markets. If there are decreasing average costs throughout the feasible range of production, then one firm, organization, agency, or governmental unit could produce the total output at lowest cost. Competition in the private or political markets would not be feasible since one firm, agency, or governmental unit could produce the entire output at the lowest cost per unit.

Based on extensive empirical research in both the private and political markets, most economists hold that the average cost curve of most organizations is a flat "U" or saucer-shaped curve, such as that shown in Figure 2-2. In the initial stages of production the average cost curve decreases, then it remains relatively flat for extended ranges of output, and then, as production is increased even further, the average cost curve begins to rise.

Very small and very large firms, agencies, governments, and departments tend to operate on the falling or rising portions of the cost curve, while most other firms and organizations tend to operate on the flat portion of the curve. A brief examination of many industries shows that small computer and software companies, large and small steel mills, large and small fast food restaurants, large and small government units, and large and small legal firms do exist and thrive in the real world. Hence, they must be operating on the flat portion of the average cost curve. The

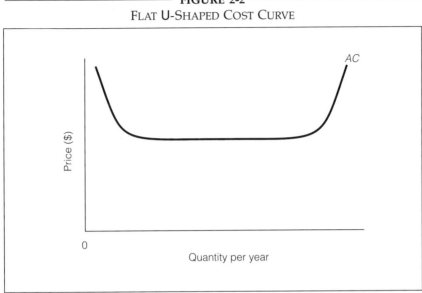

FIGURE 2-2

FLAT U-SHAPED COST CURVE

experiences of U.S. Steel, Woolco, Continental Illinois, United and Pan Am airlines, New York City, and the Soviet centralized government testify to the existence of diseconomies of scale inherent in large organizations.

Postulate 7: Competition and discrimination cannot be avoided in the allocation of scarce goods.

This last postulate is seldom discussed in economic textbooks, but ignorance of it makes learning economics difficult for those who, unknowingly, want to shoot the messenger bringing bad news. Many individuals immediately reject the price mechanism because it discriminates against those who are unwilling or unable to pay the market price for some goods. They don't realize that high prices reflect scarcities that cannot be eliminated by wishing or legislating away high prices. If the price mechanism cannot be used, some other form of competition and discrimination will have to be employed.

Assume that you had three Rembrandt paintings that you wanted to transfer to someone else, so you placed an ad in the Sunday classifieds announcing that you would distribute the paintings on Monday morning.[10]

---

[10] Note that we did not assume that you wanted to sell the paintings to the highest bidder, because that would limit your allocation choices to the price mechanism. You are a generous person who wants to allocate the paintings in the most ethical way. There is *no* issue of economic efficiency or supply here.

When you go to the front door on Monday morning you are likely to see thousands of individuals milling about on your front lawn. Each of these individuals is in competition with each of the other thousands of individuals, and you must now make a choice about which method of discrimination you will use in allocating the three paintings among these thousands of individuals. A few systems of discrimination available to you include the price mechanism—a first-come–first-served, or queuing, system—race, sex, age, physical stamina, religion, beauty, political and family connections, personal friendships, ancestral heritage, or a lottery. Each of these allocation criteria will result in some form of competition by the demanders and discrimination by you. For example, the queuing system discriminates against the elderly, handicapped, and those whose time (opportunity cost) is valuable; the beauty criterion discriminates against the plain looking; race discriminates against the minority (or majority); age discriminates against the young (or old); political connections discriminate against those who are politically inactive.

You might think that the lottery does not discriminate because each person has an equal chance of being selected and it appears to be a "fair" system of allocation. The easiest way to understand that discrimination occurs in a lottery is to imagine that instead of financing the federal government's $1 trillion annual budget through taxes and bond sales, we feed everyone's Social Security number into a computer and instruct it to randomly select one million names. Those whose names are selected would each have to pay $1 million to finance the $1 trillion budget. *Ex ante,* or before the drawing, the lottery appears to be equitable and nondiscriminatory because each person has an equal chance of having his or her name selected. But *ex post,* or after the drawing, some very unhappy individuals are going to have to pay $1 million to the federal government. Whether they are rich or poor, old or young, intelligent or stupid, good or bad, they did nothing to deserve such treatment except to have their Social Security number selected by the computer. Ex post, the lottery doesn't look to be so equitable and non-discriminatory. A few truly unfortunate people are being discriminated against, while the rest of the citizens are receiving favorable discrimination. Viewing the lottery ex ante it appears to be equitable and nondiscriminatory; viewing it ex post, it appears totally unacceptable.[11]

---

[11] Economists like to use hypothetical examples to illustrate general concepts, and such examples might appear to the reader to be totally unrealistic. You are probably thinking to yourself that this taxation example illustrates the difference between *ex ante* and *ex post* equity very well but that it is totally unrealistic to think that it, or anything similar, could happen in any civilized country, much less the United States. Reread the section above that discusses the military manpower procurement system that existed in the United States less than twenty years ago.

Let's return to our first example with the three paintings. If the paintings were allocated by lottery, some fortunate individuals would receive them even if they thought Mr. Rem Brandt dallied around the neighborhood tavern (their preferences for quality paintings not being intense), while the unfortunate ones not selected would have no chance to express the intensity of their love for fine art. No matter which allocation method is selected, competition and discrimination must result because there are only three Rembrandts and thousands of people wanting one. Some discriminatory criterion *must* be selected. If the Rembrandts are not allocated to those able and willing to pay the highest price, some other form of discrimination *must* be used.

Since discrimination is an ethical issue, we will leave you, the reader, to decide which method of discrimination, including the price mechanism, you would select for allocating the paintings as well as food, housing, automobiles, clothing, and other commodities. Before making a decision you might want to ask yourself which of these attributes you could most easily change if you had an intense preference for a particular good. You might also consider which criterion you would choose if you were an Arab living in Israel, an Israeli living in an Arab country, a black living in South Africa, a white South African living in Zimbabwe, a Catholic living in Northern Ireland, a Protestant living in the Republic of Ireland, a French-speaking Belgian (a Walloon) living in Flanders, or a Dutch-speaking Belgian (a Fleming) living in Brussels. What system of discrimination would your parents' grandparents or great-grandparents have selected when they arrived on the shores of the United States with little, if any, education and unable to speak or read English? Would they have preferred rent controls, price controls, and minimum wages? What would be your status in life today if your ancestors had migrated to a country that used a system of allocating goods and procuring laborers other than the price mechanism? These are questions to which only normative answers can be given, but a study of economics might provide information and analyses that might help you formulate your normative answers.

PARETO OPTIMALITY

Some normative criterion must be used to evaluate the desirability of alternative market mechanisms or specific policies. One criterion widely used in economic analysis is Pareto optimality, which is named after an Italian who was born in Paris and achieved academic fame while teaching in Lausanne, Switzerland.[12]

Definition of Pareto Optimality

A position, organization, or allocation is Pareto optimal only if there exists no change that will make one or more individuals better off without making someone else worse off.

A position is *not* Pareto optimal if a reallocation of resources would make at least one person better off without making anyone else worse off. Perhaps an example will make the concept of Pareto optimality more clear. Assume that Able has 100 apples and no oranges and is willing to sacrifice 10 apples to obtain 1 orange; Baker has 75 oranges and no apples and is willing to sacrifice 6 oranges to obtain 1 apple. The original distribution of commodities is *not* Pareto optimal because *both* individuals could be made better off through trade. As Able trades apples for Baker's oranges, the two are moving toward the Pareto frontier, that is, the welfare of both individuals is increasing. When Able and Baker have squeezed out all of the gains from trade, they will be at a Pareto optimal. Once Able and Baker have achieved Pareto optimality, the only way that Able's welfare can be increased is to decrease Baker's welfare, and the only way Baker's welfare can be increased is to decrease Able's welfare.

While the general concept of Pareto optimality is simple, confusion sometimes arises about certain specifics. Figure 2-3 is provided to eliminate some of the confusion. Assume that given the skills of Able and Baker and the resources available to them we could chart the maximum utility or welfare level that could be obtained by each individual.

This Pareto frontier, or line of Pareto optimality, is shown as the outermost curve, $W_1 - W_5$. At point W_1 all of the island's resources, including the time of Able and Baker, would be devoted to improving Able's welfare, and Baker's welfare would not be served at all. Presumably, he would soon die if this were the actual state of affairs. At W_5 the situation is reversed, and all of the island's resources would be devoted to Baker's welfare and none to Able's welfare. Of course, the island's resources could provide Able and Baker with various combinations of welfare, such as W_2, which would provide a relatively high level of welfare to Able and a relatively low level to Baker, or W_4, which would provide a relatively high level of

---

[12] Vilfredo Pareto entered the field of political economy at the age of 45, after abandoning an engineering profession. His most famous works, *Cours d'economie politique* (1896–97) and *Manuale d'economia politica* (1906), were completed while he was professor extraordinary at the University of Lausanne from 1893–1909. Pareto was a strong believer in the science of "pure economics," the application of mathematical tools to economics, and an originator of general equilibrium analysis.

FIGURE 2-3
PARETO FRONTIER

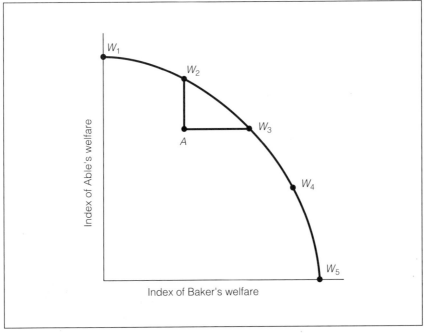

welfare for Baker and a relatively low level for Able. It is very important that the reader understands the meaning of the word "relatively." It *does not* mean relative to the other person's welfare. It *does* mean relative to some other level of that individual's welfare. For example, at W_2 we cannot say that Able would enjoy more welfare or happiness or satisfaction than Baker. We can only say that compared with his (Able's) situation at W_3, Able would be relatively more happy or more satisfied. One mistake we *don't* want to make is to say that we should divide the resources evenly so that Able and Baker "meet each other halfway at W_3," where their welfare levels would be equal. The halfway point has no such meaning, and we have absolutely no reason to assume that their welfare levels would be equal at W_3. If we could actually measure utils of welfare, we might find that at W_3 Able would have 5,432 utils of happiness and that Baker would have 276 utils. All we know is that Able would prefer W_3 to such less desirable distributions as W_4 and that Baker would prefer W_3 to such less desirable points such as W_2.

Point *A* represents an inefficient use of resources, such as when Able has 100 apples and Baker has 75 oranges. The welfare of both Able and Baker could be improved by redistributing the resources or utilizing resources more efficiently. If Able and Baker traded apples and oranges, they would be increasing the welfare of each of them. Such a move is called a Pareto optimal move (or one that meets the Paretian criterion) because the change in resources improves the welfare of all individuals in society without decreasing the welfare of anyone. If a policy of taking apples away from Able and giving them to Baker had been introduced, that policy would *not* have satisfied the criterion of a Pareto optimal move. The individuals might have ended up on the Pareto frontier (point W_4), but the policy that moved them there would not have satisfied the Pareto criterion. Baker's welfare would have been improved, while Able's welfare would have worsened.

When economists mention that some mechanism, system, or outcome is Pareto optimal, they mean that there is no reorganization that will make the private or political markets more efficient. It is often used to mean that all potential gains from trade have been squeezed out and no further mutual benefits are obtainable. Several modifications of the Paretian criterion have been made, such as accepting or approving a policy in which one or more individuals are harmed if these individuals are actually or potentially compensated for such harm. Pareto optimality is widely used by economists because it is a normative criterion that can be accepted by most individuals, and it forms a common denominator from which more specific normative judgments can be discussed. The important characteristic of Pareto optimality is that it does not compare the loss of one individual with the gain of the other; thus, interpersonal utility comparisons, which cannot be determined or weighed, are avoided.

CONSUMER BEHAVIOR

Economic or allocative efficiency is one of the most difficult concepts for the novice economist to grasp. Most textbooks utilize mathematics or graphs to illustrate the concept, but, in keeping with our commitment to avoid them as much as possible, we will use simple tables of costs, prices, and consumer preferences to illustrate the concept. We will begin by examining the logic of consumer decision making.

Although individuals engage in purchasing goods virtually every day, they do it so casually that they seldom reflect on the logic of their decisions. The most salient part of consumers' behavior is that, in the absence of rationing, consumers adjust the quantities of goods they purchase to the relative prices they observe in the marketplace. Refer to Table 2-2, which outlines the preference schedules for two individuals, named Able and Baker. Assume that income and the prices of other goods remain constant.

TABLE 2-2
PREFERENCES FOR SHIRTS

(a) Quantity of Shirts per Year	(b) Value of Able's Marginal Preferences for Shirts in $	(c) Value of Baker's Marginal Preferences for Shirts in $
1	$60	$100
2	50	90
3	40	85
4	30	75
5	25	65
6	15	50
7	10	40
8	7	25
9	5	15
10	0	10
11	0	5
12	0	0

Columns (b) and (c) represent the value of the marginal preferences, or taste patterns, for Able and Baker at alternative quantities, shown in column (a). As Able and Baker consume more shirts, the value they place on each additional shirt decreases. Each individual will adjust the purchases of shirts per year so that the market price of shirts equals his or her "internal" marginal preference value. At a market price of $25 Able will purchase the first shirt because it has a value of $60 to him; he will also purchase the second unit, which has a value of $50. Able, however, will not purchase the sixth unit, which yields only $15 worth of satisfaction but would cost $25. At a market price of $25, Able will purchase five shirts, because at any smaller quantity he will place more value on the marginal shirt than the market price, and at any quantity greater than five, the $25 market price will be higher than the value Able places on the marginal shirt. If the price is raised from $25 to $50, Able will want to purchase only two shirts, and he will once again be in equilibrium because the market price now equals his marginal value preference. If the price is lowered to $10, Able will purchase seven shirts.

Baker will have a similar schedule reflecting his preferences, except that he is a "shirt lover" and places higher marginal values on shirts. If the price of shirts is $25, Baker will purchase eight shirts. Both individuals are adjusting to the same price, but they reflect differences in their preference patterns by varying the *quantities* of shirts they purchase.

Refer to Table 2-3, which takes the data from Table 2-2 and reorganizes it to show the quantity each individual would demand at alternative prices. Table 2-3 also shows the market demand, which is obtained by aggregating the individual demands. At a market price of $50 the marginal preference value of Able ($50) will equal the marginal preference value of Baker ($50) but each will be purchasing a different quantity. Hence, individuals will purchase a quantity of shirts, or any other good, where the value of their marginal preferences is equal to the price of the good. Since each individual is adjusting to the same price, the marginal preference values of all consumers will be equal.

What would happen if Able could get shirts for $10, while Baker had to continue paying $50? Able would adjust his purchases until the marginal value he placed on the last shirt was $10, that is, he would purchase seven shirts. Baker would adjust his quantity of shirts purchased until the marginal value he placed on the last shirt was $50, that is, he would purchase six shirts. The value placed on the marginal (seventh) shirt by Able is now $10, but the value placed on the marginal (sixth) shirt by Baker is $50. Whenever the marginal values of individuals are not equal in a free market, we can expect them to engage in further trade. If Able can procure an unlimited amount of shirts at $10, he will continue to consume seven units, but he will buy additional units to sell to Baker at some price above $10 but below $50. If Able's supplier tells him he cannot resell the shirts, Able is likely to do so anyway, except that he will charge a higher price because of the risk of detection and the cost of the penalty. If the

---
TABLE 2-3
DERIVING MARKET DEMAND FOR SHIRTS

(a) Price	(b) Quantity Demanded by Abel	(c) Quantity Demanded by Baker	(d) Market Demand
$100	0	1	1
90	0	2	2
80	0	3	3
70	0	4	4
60	1	5	6
50	2	6	8
40	3	7	10
30	4	7	11
20	5	8	13
10	7	10	17

consumption of some good is subsidized for certain individuals, they will have an incentive to resell the good to other citizens, and such sales would take place so long as the nonsubsidized market price is higher than the subsidized price plus the expected penalty price for "cheating." Food stamps provide one example of individuals adjusting to subsidized prices and selling "excess" quantities of stamps in the gray or black market.[13]

If the price of shirts happens to be $10 but only ten units are supplied, the quantity demanded (17) would be greater than the quantity supplied (10). There are two ways to eliminate excess demand. One is to let prices increase; the other is to use a nonprice discrimination system to ration the goods. When nonprice rationing is effectively employed, individuals are unable to adjust the quantity of their purchases to the price, so their marginal values will not equal price and the marginal values of individuals will not be equal. Coupon rationing was used during World War II to lessen inflationary pressures. Congress decided that it was more equitable to keep prices low and ration certain goods than to permit prices to rise. Hence, coupons were distributed based on the size of a family and the "need" to drive an automobile. In certain circumstances, such as war, rationing is thought to be more equitable, but it is far less efficient than the price mechanism. Rationing does not permit individuals to reflect the intensities of their preferences through quantity adjustments, which means that some individuals with an intense marginal preference for the good are unable to get additional units, while other individuals with a low marginal preference are getting them.

Assume the government gives Able and Baker five coupons apiece per year to be used to buy shirts that are subject to price ceilings of $10. At this price Able would like to consume seven units and Baker ten units. However, each is only able to buy five units. At five units Able's marginal value is $25 and Baker's marginal value is $65 (refer to Table 2-2). This means that the fifth unit purchased by Able would increase Able's welfare by only $25, but if Baker received that unit instead, his welfare would increase by $65. Rationing is inefficient because it does not allocate goods to their most highly valued uses.

The equity of rationing is also questionable. The typical argument for rationing is that the poor will be unable to get any of the scarce goods in a free market. On the other hand, wealthy individuals might not have intense preferences for the rationed good: their closets might already be full of shirts or they might be able to obtain shirts by having a tailor make them. The poor, however, cannot "afford" to purchase tailor-made shirts,

---

[13] See the Questions and Answers section at the end of this chapter and the following chapter for exercises related to food stamps and other subsidized consumption goods.

that is, they would prefer to spend their income on other goods. The wealthy might be able to afford higher-priced substitutes (such as sweaters) that are not price controlled, or they might be able to procure shirts at higher prices on the black market. Without making a detailed investigation of available substitutes, black market options, and the relative preferences of rich and poor individuals, to list just a few variables, no conclusions can be made about the equity of rationing.

As long as there are no external constraints on the price system, rational consumers will *always* adjust the quantities of a good they purchase so that their individual *marginal* evaluations equal the market price. When consumers are not allowed to adjust to prices, we can expect distortions, inefficiencies, and black markets to emerge.

ALLOCATIVE EFFICIENCY

Efficiency has a specialized meaning to economists that differs from that of the layman who thinks it means that firms produce at the lowest possible average cost. Occasionally, economists are concerned about simple productive efficiency, but most economists focus their attention on allocative efficiency, which is concerned with the optimal combination of goods produced. Before discussing the meaning and significance of allocative efficiency we need to introduce costs into the example from Tables 2-2 and 2-3. Assume that the costs of production are those shown in Table 2-4. The first unit costs $205 because of start-up costs. After fixed costs are allocated to the first unit, marginal costs include only the cost of labor and materials necessary to produce each additional shirt. Each additional unit increases total costs by the amount shown in the marginal cost column (c). Note that marginal costs, which represent the addition to total costs, begin to rise with the production of the fifth unit.

Now we can integrate the consumer demand data from Table 2-3 and the cost data from Table 2-4 into Table 2-5, and we can examine the quantity of shirt production that will maximize the welfare of Able and Baker. If the market price is $60, the two individuals will purchase a total of six shirts, with Able demanding one unit and Baker five units. The marginal cost of producing the sixth shirt is only $20, but each individual places a value of $60 on the consumption of the marginal, or sixth, shirt. Hence, by sacrificing $20 of resources to produce one additional shirt, $60 worth of benefits are generated. If the price were lowered to $50, market demand would be eight shirts and each individual would have a $50 marginal preference value for the eighth, or marginal, shirt. Since the marginal shirt

--- TABLE 2-4 ---
COSTS OF PRODUCING SHIRTS

(a) Units Produced	(b) Total Cost	(c) Marginal Cost
1	$205	$205
2	220	15
3	230	10
4	235	5
5	250	15
6	270	20
7	295	25
8	325	30
9	360	35
10	400	40
11	445	45
12	495	50
13	550	55
14	610	60
15	675	65
16	745	70
17	825	80

now costs only $30 to produce, welfare would increase if more shirts were produced. If the market price fell to $20, Able and Baker would purchase a total of 13 shirts. Each would value the marginal shirt at only $20, whereas it would cost $55 to produce the thirteenth shirt. There are too many shirts now being produced. It doesn't make sense to use resources worth $55 to produce the thirteenth shirt, which individuals value at only $20.

It should now be obvious that the socially optimal quantity is ten shirts. The marginal cost of the tenth shirt equals the price of the shirt, which, in turn, means that the marginal value placed on the tenth shirt by both Able and Baker will be equal to the price and to the marginal cost. Able's welfare is increased by $40 when he consumes the third unit; Baker's welfare is increased by $40 when he consumes the seventh unit; and the cost of producing the marginal unit is $40. At a quantity of ten shirts, individuals will maximize their welfare, because the value each places on the marginal shirt is exactly equal to the cost of producing it. Resources are being allocated most efficiently, and Pareto optimality is achieved. No reallocation of resources

———————— TABLE 2-5 ————————
EFFICIENT QUANTITY OF SHIRTS
TO BE PRODUCED

(a) Price	(b) Market Demand	(c) Marginal Cost
$100	1	$205
90	2	15
80	3	10
70	4	5
60	6	20
50	8	30
40	10	40
30	11	45
20	13	55
10	17	80

could make both individuals better off. Able's welfare could be improved only by taking shirts away from Baker and giving them to Able. Baker's welfare could be improved only by taking shirts away from Able and giving them to Baker.

The above paragraphs can be summarized by stating that individuals always adjust the quantities of goods they purchase to the prices they observe in the marketplace, that is, the marginal value of the last unit consumed equals the price they pay for the good. If the market price is equal to marginal cost, then individuals' marginal preference values—the value each individual places on a marginal unit—will be equal to the additional cost to society of producing the marginal unit. When this occurs, no further improvements can be made in resource allocation. Thus, when economists talk about economic efficiency, they mean allocative efficiency, which is obtained when the price of a good equals the marginal cost of that good.

Efficiency Condition for a Private Good
price of a good = marginal cost of producing that good
or $P = MC$

When $P > MC$, an insufficient quantity of that good is being produced, because consumers have marginal preference values that are greater than the marginal cost. Their welfare could be increased by consuming more units.

Example: If the market price is $60, consumers will purchase six shirts while the marginal cost of the sixth shirt is only $20. The marginal shirt has a value of $60 to consumers but the opportunity cost to society of producing the marginal unit is only $20. Hence, welfare would increase if more shirts were produced.

When $P < MC$, too much of the good is being produced, because the value of the marginal unit to the consumer is less than the additional cost of producing it. Fewer units of the good should be produced if welfare is to be maximized.

Example: If the price of shirts is $20, consumers will purchase 13 shirts. The marginal cost of producing the thirteenth shirt is $55, which is much greater than the marginal benefit of $20. Hence, too many shirts are being produced, and $20 is not an efficient price. Fewer units of the good should be produced if welfare is to be maximized.

When $P = MC$, no further improvement can be made that would benefit at least one person without harming another and Pareto optimality has been achieved. If $P \neq MC$, then there is some change that could benefit Able, Baker, or both without causing harm to the other. However, once $P = MC$, no further improvements can be made without decreasing the welfare of either Able or Baker or both of them.

It is very important to note that we have said nothing about the economic or political system in which Able and Baker reside. The reason is that economic efficiency, $P = MC$, is preferable to inefficiency in *all* countries, whether they operate under capitalism, socialism, communism, or any other type of "ism." Various economic systems might try to achieve allocative efficiency in different ways, and the citizens of these countries might have radically different preferences, but the conditions for economic efficiency are the same. The following chapter will examine the ways in which efficiency is and is not achieved in the capitalistic system of private markets.

QUESTIONS AND ANSWERS

THE QUESTIONS

1. **a.** Which of the following competitive criteria does your college or university use in determining admission standards?

price	test scores
race	relatives who are alumni
sex	state or region of residence
age	religious beliefs
athletic ability	admittance of all applicants
high school record	

b. List the winners and the losers for each of the above criteria.

c. If you were dictator of the university, what criteria would you use? Why?

d. If you were an unborn spirit about to begin life and you were unaware of your future real-life family, race, intelligence, connections, religion, wealth, etc., which criteria would you select for admission to your state's university? Why? Would your answer change once you discovered that you had been born black, rich, or intelligent? Why?

e. If you were a taxpayer financing a state university, which of the above criteria would you select? Why?

f. If you were a professor at the university, which of the above would you select? Why?

g. Did you select the same answer for (c) through (d)? Why? Did any of your answers eliminate competition or discrimination? Why?

h. Why do you think it is acceptable to have competition for admission to a university based on the above criteria but not to have competition for grades in university courses based on the same criteria?

2. Do the following two statements have the same meaning? "There is a shortage of pencils" and "There is a scarcity of pencils."

3. **a.** Why is it acceptable for an accountant, but not a politician, to sell his services to the highest bidder?

b. A real estate company that promises to pay $100 if you visit a "secluded hideaway" and listen to a sales pitch must deliver on its promise or be sued in court. Why isn't it possible to sue a political party that promises it will "increase expenditures, decrease taxes, and eliminate corruption" if elected to office and then doesn't do so?

c. What's the difference between a political party competing for votes and a business firm competing for dollars?

d. Why do business firms that put misleading and inaccurate information in sales catalogs get prosecuted by the Federal Trade Commission while universities that put misleading and inaccurate information in their sales catalogs do not get prosecuted?

e. What do you think would be some major differences in content between a book entitled *Public Needs and Private Wants* and a book entitled *Private Needs and Public Wants*? Does your answer suggest anything about the use of the word "need"? Why?

4. When Arab members of OPEC put an embargo on the United States in 1973 to punish it for its support of Israel during the Yom Kippur War there was an oil "shortage," and the market price of imported crude oil quickly increased from about $3 per barrel to $10 per barrel. One reaction of the United States government was to impose price controls on oil by requiring all U.S. refineries to pay the same price for oil. Those refineries that obtained oil from Texas and Louisiana fields had to share their cheap oil with—or make payments to—those East Coast refineries that had to pay $10 per barrel for their imported oil. Refineries were not allowed to charge more for their products than warranted by the average cost of obtaining the oil plus processing costs. For example, assume that American refineries obtained imported crude oil at $10 per barrel, Texas crude oil at $4 per barrel, and that they used equal quantities of both imported and domestic oil. The controlled price of a barrel of refined crude passed on to a buyer could be only $7[($10 + 4)/2].

a. What was the marginal cost of oil in the United States before the embargo? Why? Ignore processing costs, tariffs, and taxes and assume a competitive market.

b. What was the marginal cost of oil after the embargo? Why?

c. What was the efficient, or Pareto optimal, price of oil before the embargo? Why?

d. What was the efficient, or Pareto optimal, price of oil after the embargo. Why?

e. If the market price had been allowed to increase to $10 per barrel, what would have happened to the income or capital gains of those who owned oil-producing land in Louisiana and Texas? Is this morally acceptable to you?

f. Did government oil policies after the embargo lead to efficient pricing, or Pareto optimality? Why?

g. Using simple words, can you explain how the government policy of average-cost pricing affected the welfare of the typical consumer in the United States?

h. Do you think the policy as outlined above stimulated oil-producing firms to search for and develop new oil fields in the United States? Why?

THE ANSWERS

1. All of the criteria listed in the question have been used by most universities in various degrees, whether they publish such criteria in their catalogs or not. The winners and losers in each criterion will depend upon the extent to which individuals possess the desired attributes. The price criterion will discriminate against the poor; academic criteria, against the stupid and lazy and applicants with poor secondary education. Obviously, competition and discrimination cannot be eliminated, and the type of discrimination we prefer to utilize will depend upon its anticipated effects on us. For example, a professor at a university might want to have admission based on price if she thinks it will increase her income. If she believes there is little or no relationship between tuition fees and her own salary, she would probably prefer some combination of test scores and GPAs because good students are more fun to teach than poor students and they require less time during office hours, fewer review sessions, etc.

A rational unborn spirit has no way of knowing which of the attributes he will possess, or whether he would even want to attend the university in his future life. Hence, his lack of a known vested interest provides him with an incentive to analyze the alternative criteria objectively. This objective unborn spirit would want a criterion that (a) he could work hard to satisfy if he found he had an intense desire to obtain an education and (b) improved the general level of welfare of the state in which he lived. The criteria that provide the most flexibility are the academic criteria, especially GPA, and the price mechanism. If the individual has an intense desire to attend college, he can compete hard for grades if the criterion is academic, or he can obtain full- or part-time employment or borrow the money to compete on a price basis. The unborn spirit realizes that he can improve his academic credentials and his monetary resources relatively easily. However, he realizes that the other criteria are very difficult. The unborn spirit might think of selecting black (or white) as a preferable color for college admission, but he knows that he might be born white (or black) and have an intense preference for a college education that he cannot satisfy. If he were born the wrong color, he simply would not qualify. The spirit also knows that sex, age, religious beliefs, and athletic ability are very difficult to change, so he would probably oppose them as well.

The unborn spirit would have to consider the possibility that he might not want to go to college or that the costs of meeting the admission criteria would be too high for him in the future life. Nevertheless, he would still be interested in the admission criteria because they would affect the general standard of living in the state. The unborn spirit, most probably, would see no need for wasting the state's resources on admitting everyone, so he would not select that criterion. Most noneconomists would probably argue that the unborn spirit would select GPA, test scores, high school courses taken, or some combination of these because such qualified individuals would benefit most from a college education and improve society the most with their skills and knowledge. This answer is not incorrect but it has some *very* ragged edges. Some economists would want to know how high the academic qualifications should be, that is, how many students should be admitted. Should the university admit the top 25 percent or the top 5 percent? How much should taxpayers have to pay to finance higher education? Also, who or what is to guide the students into the academic areas for which there is the greatest demand in society? Would there be too many philosophers and economists produced and not enough engineers and chemists. Some economists argue for the price mechanism because it would eliminate the marginal students who would rather use the annual $40,000 (approximately the unsubsidized cost of one year of a college education) for consumption or other investments such as starting their own business or going to chef school. The price mechanism would also guide students into the areas of critical scarcities, because students would have to consider the payoff from their education investments and financial institutions would make loans based on the future value of the borrower's profession. If a student wanted to borrow money to finance an education, a bank would be more likely to finance a student majoring in chemistry, where—reflecting the relative scarcities and marginal products—the average annual starting salary is $35,000, than a student majoring in philosophy, where the average annual starting salary is only $15,000.

2. No, a scarcity of pencils means that the production of pencils utilizes scarce resources, so there are not enough pencils, at a zero price, to satisfy everyone's wants. Scarcity implies that pencils are an economic good and that people would be willing to pay a positive price to obtain them. A shortage of pencils means that the price mechanism is not working. For some reason the price is below the market clearing level, and the quantity demanded is greater than the quantity supplied. At some price the shortage of pencils would be eliminated.

3. Read the questions and think about the answers for a few minutes. You might see some inconsistencies you had not thought about previously. Some of these issues will be discussed later in the book. Notice the use of the emotive term "need" in question (e) to convince the reader to agree with the author's values. Obviously the "author" wants you to conclude that public goods should have a higher claim on your preferences and pocketbook than those lower-class "wants" for private goods. Economists would say that individuals have wants or preferences for public and private goods.

4. **a.** Before the embargo, if domestic oil wells could have provided all the oil the country demanded at less than the imported price of oil, there would have been no need to import oil. Oil was imported only because at $3 per barrel, U. S. wells could not produce a sufficient quantity. Hence, imports provided the marginal quantity, which were priced at $3 per barrel. The marginal cost of oil to an American consumer was the world price of $3 per barrel.

b. Since the price of imported oil rose to $10 per barrel, the marginal cost also rose to $10, assuming that the U.S. continued to import at least some oil.

c. Allocative efficiency requires that $P = MC$. Since the marginal cost of oil was $3 per barrel, the optimal price was $3 per barrel. Remember that the normal profit (return to capital) is included in the cost of oil.

d. That's right, it was $10 per barrel. The marginal cost increased, so the efficient, or Pareto optimal, price increased.

e. Obviously, they would have increased significantly, and many American citizens viewed such increases as "unjust enrichments." Such views were a major cause of government policies that controlled the price of oil. Economists often use the term "economic rents" to indicate such increases in economic profits. Before you conclude that the increased profits or rents of oil land owners are unjust and should be taxed, ask yourself if you would also conclude that if the price of oil had fallen and the owners of oil lands had suffered an "unjust deprivation" you would approve a government subsidy?

f.   No, because the government required that oil be sold at the average cost ($7 per barrel), which was less than the marginal cost ($10). An efficient price would be one at which the price equalled the marginal cost.

g.   The government policy of establishing the price of oil at $7 per barrel means that consumers will adjust their quantity of oil consumed until the value (marginal preference value) they obtain from the last barrel of oil consumed is equal to $7. In order to get that marginal barrel of oil they have to pay $10 to the Arab exporting country, which means that the Arabs can buy $10 worth of goods from the United States. Thus, consumers are giving up $10 worth of the nation's resources to the Arabs in order to obtain a barrel of oil that consumers value at only $7. Giving up $10 worth of resources to obtain $7 worth of oil decreases the welfare of American consumers. That is why economists say that when $P > MC$, welfare is decreased.

   Note: The reader might be wondering why American firms would pay the Arabs $10 per barrel and then sell it for $7. The answer is that government policy required them to do it. Furthermore, those firms that paid $10 per barrel were subsidized by those who obtained oil at $4 per barrel. Hence, all firms continued to earn their "normal profits," but economic efficiency was not obtained and social welfare was not maximized.

h.   No, there would be little incentive for a firm to develop sources of low-cost domestic oil if it had to share the low-cost oil with a firm that had only high-cost oil imports. Consequently, the government had to establish a complicated program in which newly discovered oil could sell for higher prices than old oil.

CHAPTER THREE

THE PRIVATE MARKET

I am convinced that if the market system were the result of deliberate human design, . . . this mechanism would have been acclaimed as one of the greatest triumphs of the human mind.
—FRIEDRICH HAYEK, NOBEL LAUREATE IN ECONOMICS

An economist is one who knows the price of everything but the value of nothing.
—A POPULAR ADAPTATION OF OSCAR WILDE'S DEFINITION OF A CYNIC.

INTRODUCTION

The statistics on the American economy are staggering. The total population numbers about 250 million people, and nearly 130 million are in the labor force. There are more than 11 million proprietorships, 1.6 million partnerships, and 3.2 million corporations that produce $4 trillion of goods and services each year. About 700,000 new firms are started each year, and more than 65,000 fail. There are more than 14,000 banks, 14,000 credit unions, and 3,000 savings and loan associations. No individual, committee, or council directs the components of this massive economy, which produces and distributes more goods and services than any other country. To the dismay of dedicated hackers, there is no giant computer that issues digitized commands to human interfaces. Despite the absence of a human or digital "Big Brother," chaos and anarchy do not exist in the economy. The daily—and generally detailed, arduous, and boring—tasks of feeding, clothing, housing, transporting, and entertaining the population are accomplished without fanfare or centralized control. The source of this order is individual self-interest channeled by competitive supply and demand incentives. No individual spends time contemplating the effects of his or her actions on the total welfare of society. Rather, we individuals make decisions to improve our own welfare, but, in the process, our decisions benefit other individuals in society. A farmer considering the use of his 100 acres does not calculate the total quantities of various products required by the residents of a neighboring city, nor does he estimate the quantities that are likely to be supplied by other farmers. Instead, he looks at prices and costs and asks, "Will I increase my welfare more by planting corn, wheat, or soybeans?" He is concerned about that "little picture" over which he has some control, but the total of such "little pictures" forms the "big picture" of the economy. Economics, then, studies how the millions of "little pictures" form the mosaic of the "big picture" in the economy.

PURE COMPETITION: A BENCHMARK FOR ANALYSIS

The purely competitive model is a set of theoretical conditions that economists use to illuminate certain economic relationships and to evaluate and compare alternative market structures. At the other end of the continuum of markets is pure monopoly, which is a single-firm industry. The purely competitive model is characterized by a homogeneous commodity, by the existence of several firms—no one of which has a perceptible influence on price—by perfect knowledge, and by the freedom of entry and exit. Some economists assume flexible prices, although this is more correctly a conclusion of the competitive model unrestrained by external forces. Each firm in a competitive industry is a *price taker*, that is, it must take the price as given to it by all the factors affecting the general supply and demand forces in the marketplace. No single firm has a perceptible influence on price.

The market supply curve is the aggregation of the marginal supply curves of all firms in the industry, and the market demand curve is the aggregation of individual demand curves. This concept was illustrated in Table 2-3, where we aggregated Able's and Baker's demand for shirts. The intersection of supply and demand curves in Figure 3-1 determines the equilibrium price for shirts. Although supply and demand curves are widely used in basic economics, it is very important for the student to understand that the graphs represent certain interactions occurring in the marketplace and that they should be used as an aid in understanding the forces at work in the market and not as detached exercises in geometry. For example, a student asked to name the equilibrium price in Figure 3-1 might quickly respond that it is P_e, which is a correct but incomplete answer. Graphically, the equilibrium price could be nothing else but P_e. The economic explanation for P_e being the market equilibrium price is not quite so obvious. The best way to obtain an understanding of why P_e, or any other variable, is an equilibrium value is to ask what would happen if the observed price were different from the equilibrium price. What would happen, for example, if the observed price were above P_e, say at P_a? If the market price happened to be P_a, suppliers would be willing to supply X_2 quantity of the good but consumers would demand only X_1 quantity.

FIGURE 3-1
INDUSTRY SUPPLY AND DEMAND CURVES

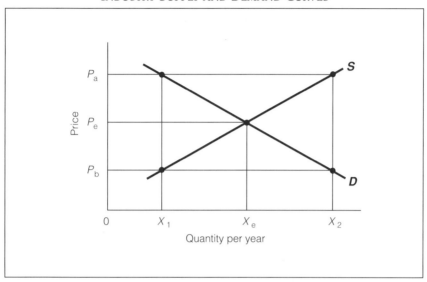

Hence, a surplus of shirts (equal to $X_2 - X_1$) for which some producers could find no buyers would exist in the market. Rather than accept a zero price for the surplus goods, producers would continue to reduce the price until the surplus were eliminated (a movement down the supply curve). As the price decreased, consumers would increase the quantity they demanded (a movement down the demand curve). Once the price were driven down to P_e, the surplus would disappear and there would be no motivation for sellers to lower the price any further. Hence, at P_e there would be no further pressures increasing or decreasing the price; it would be an equilibrium price.

If the market price happened to be below the equilibrium price of P_e, say P_b, consumers would demand a quantity of shirts greater than producers were supplying. There would be a shortage (equal to $X_2 - X_1$), and some consumers would be willing to pay a price higher than P_b rather than go without the shirts. Hence, they would bid the price up to P_e. As the price increased, some consumers would cut back on their quantity demanded (represented by a movement up the demand curve), and the higher price would induce suppliers to increase the quantity supplied (a movement up the supply curve). This process would continue until the equilibrium price of P_e were obtained.

The demand curve in Figure 3-2 is drawn assuming that incomes, tastes, and prices of other goods are held constant. Once P_e is obtained,

SHIFTS IN MARKET SUPPLY AND DEMAND

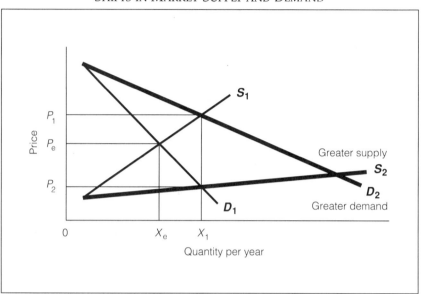

it will remain there until changes in one or more of many variables in the economy shift the supply curve (such as higher wages, strikes, new materials, or technology) or shift the demand curve (such as the introduction of competing goods, lower prices of substitute goods, or changing tastes, fashions, or income). Changes in any variable that could influence consumption other than the price are represented by a shift in the demand curve. If demand increases, the demand curve shifts upward and to the right, to D_2, and a higher equilibrium price (P_1) and quantity (X_1) are obtained. If supply increases the supply curve shifts downward and to the right, to S_2, and a lower equilibrium price (P_2) and greater equilibrium quantity (X_1) are obtained.

Since each firm in a competitive industry must take the price (P_e) as determined by the total market and no single firm can affect the price by its own production, the firm's marginal revenue is a constant (P_e). Assume the equilibrium market price (P_e) for shirts is $40 (see Table 3-1). Each firm knows that whether it sells 100 or 1,000 shirts a month, the price it receives for each shirt will remain constant at $40. Another way of saying this is that the firm's marginal revenue (change in revenue from producing one more unit) per shirt is a constant $40. Hence, the firm's marginal revenue [column (f)] will always equal the price [column (d)].

———————————————————— TABLE 3-1 ————————————————————
HYPOTHETICAL COSTS AND REVENUES IN A PURELY COMPETITIVE FIRM

(a) Output Sales	(b) Total Cost	(c) Marginal Cost	(d) Price	(e) Total Revenue	(f) Marginal Revenue	(g) Profit Loss
1	$205	$205	$40	$ 40	$40	$-165
2	220	15	40	80	40	-140
3	230	10	40	120	40	-110
4	235	5	40	160	40	-75
5	250	15	40	200	40	-50
6	270	20	40	240	40	-30
7	295	25	40	280	40	-15
8	325	30	40	320	40	-5
9	360	35	40	360	40	0
10	400	40	40	400	40	0
11	445	45	40	440	40	-5
12	495	50	40	480	40	-15
13	550	55	40	520	40	-30
14	610	60	40	560	40	-50

If the aggregate forces of supply and demand produce a market equilibrium price of $40 per shirt, each competitive firm will take that price as given because it cannot change it perceptibly. The only question confronting the firm is the quantity it should produce to maximize its profits or to minimize its losses. The firm will maximize profits by producing the quantity where the firm's marginal revenue is equal to its marginal costs. The profit-maximizing rule for *all* firms in *all* market structures follows:

Profit-Maximizing Rule
$$MC = MR$$

The firm has losses (remember that the normal returns on capital are part of costs) at all quantities except nine and ten units.[1] The marginal unit could be either of these quantities, but we know the firm will not produce the eleventh unit because it would cost more ($45) than the marginal or additional revenue ($40) the firm obtains from selling the unit. Hence, the firm would maximize its profits by producing ten units. The price charged by this and all other firms in the industry would be $40, which

———

[1] We are analyzing the long-run effects in this example, so economic profits are zero. During the short run, economic profits or losses can be earned because resources have not had time to enter or exit the industry.

is equal to the marginal cost of production. The firms are not interested in maximizing the welfare of individuals in the community; they are interested only in maximizing their profits (minimizing their losses), which they do by producing a quantity at which $MC = MR$. However, at this quantity $P = MC$, so we know that social welfare and economic efficiency are also being maximized.

Profit-Maximizing Rule or Condition for All Firms
$$MC = MR$$

Welfare-Maximizing Rule or Condition for Society
$$P = MC$$

In Pure Competition
$$MC = MR = P = MC$$

Economic profits can exist in the short run because of sudden decreases in costs or increases in demand, but the existence of such profits will entice new firms and resources into the industry, which in turn will push prices downward and costs upward until economic profits are eliminated. If there are economic losses, firms and resources will exit from the industry and move into other industries where they are more valuable. In the long run, firms will earn a rate of return on capital that is just necessary to keep that capital in the industry, and there will be normal profits but no economic profits. Firms will produce an output at which price equals marginal cost, and, as discussed in the previous section, consumers will adjust their purchases so that the marginal value they place on the good will equal its price. Since price equals marginal cost, the consumers' marginal value will also equal marginal cost and Pareto optimality will be obtained.

The significance of the competitive model is that firms pursuing their own self-interest and wanting only to maximize their own profits ($MC = MR$) will serve the public interest by producing at a rate where price equals marginal cost, which, as we have learned above, is where consumer welfare is maximized. No central planning agency, price controls, or central direction are necessary. The Invisible Hand of individual self-interest working in a competitive marketplace conceptually produces the optimal output at the optimal price. The key to this result, of course, is the proper functioning of the price mechanism, which performs both communicative and inducement functions. It communicates to producers and consumers correct information on relative resource and commodity scarcities, and it communicates to producers and resource owners shifts in relative consumer preferences. The price mechanism also induces consumers, producers, and resource owners to economize on the scarcest resources and products, it rewards those who produce the commodities when and where consumers want them, and it penalizes those who do not. Prices that equal marginal costs provide the correct information and incentives to consumers and producers while permitting a maximum degree of individual freedom by offering a large number of products and alternatives to consumers, workers, and resource owners.

The reader might wonder why economists spend so much time discussing the competitive market when there are so few, if any, competitive industries in the real world. Textbooks are fond of using agriculture as an example of an industry that comes closest to the competitive model, but an industry characterized by subsidies, price supports, cooperatives, and marketing boards is far from being a realistic example of a purely competitive industry. Indeed, there are few, if any, real-world examples of a purely competitive industry. The importance of the competitive model is that it provides an analytical benchmark for evaluating other industries, and it provides a working model for analyzing industries that do not meet all of the conditions for pure competition but function as though they did.

Most economists have come to the realization that the traditional competitive market assumptions are more restrictive than necessary to obtain nearly optimal pricing and output. So long as firms are able to enter and to leave industries freely and their fixed investments of plant and equipment can be recovered without undue loss, an industry of only a few firms might perform very much the same as a competitive industry. This is particularly true if other firms are waiting on the sidelines ready to enter the industry if existent firms begin to raise their prices, use inefficient technology, or pay unnecessarily high costs for resources, including labor.[2] A reasonably competitive price mechanism provides excellent coordination among millions of people producing and consuming millions of products without the necessity of having a coordinator or a central planning committee.

MARKET FACTORS AFFECTING INCOME DISTRIBUTION

The underlying explanation of income distribution in the unencumbered private market is the marginal productivity theory. If the price of a particular resource is below the value of its marginal product (the value that the resource adds to the good), a temporary shortage will exist and some employers will be unable to obtain the profit-maximizing quantity of that resource, so they will bid up its price in order to obtain a greater quantity. If, on the other hand, the price of a resource is above the value of its

---

[2] The possibility of a few firms producing competitive results has been explored for a few decades, but recently a new *theory of contestable markets* has arisen, which formalizes and consolidates much of the past research.

marginal product, a temporary surplus will exist and the price of the resource will be driven down. In pure competition a resource receives a price per unit equal to its contribution to the value of production.

Because resources in the private market receive payments approximating the value of their marginal product, individuals' incomes will depend upon the type and number of resources they own, the relative supply, competition, and reproducibility of these resources, and market demand. The individual's endowment of resources, in turn, is determined by many variables, including personal sacrifices, experiences, luck, education, and monetary, cultural, and genetic inheritance from parents.

Private Market Failures

Economic literature is full of detailed graphical, mathematical, and logical analyses of the idealized operation of the private market. Only a very brief outline of the competitive market was presented above, but, hopefully the reader now has some grasp of economic efficiency and the proper functioning of a price mechanism in a competitive market. Unfortunately, the private market in the real world does not always meet the competitive conditions. Many critics of the private market recognize the advantages of the competitive market model as taught in textbooks, but they justify their arguments for a greater reliance on the political market by referring to a number of market failures, which range from structural failures, such as monopolies, oligopolies, and cartels, to externalities, misleading advertising, ignorance, and the separation of corporate ownership and control.

PURE MONOPOLY: SINGLE SELLER

Heading the private market failure list of many critics is the "excessive monopolization" in the economy. Critics frequently comment that greedy monopolists and Big Business are squeezing out the "little guy" and charging prices that are simultaneously too high (gouging consumers) and too low (forcing "small firms" out of business). But the importance of monopoly in the American market is greatly exaggerated, and the monopoly powers that do exist are more frequently the result of government legislation and not the failure of the private market. A *monopoly* is at the opposite end of the market structure from pure competition and is defined as a single seller of a commodity for which there are no close substitutes. A pure monopoly can exist in the long run only if there are barriers to entry, the most significant of which are the control over resources and government regulations, including those pertaining to patents and licensing. A monopoly is a one-firm industry; therefore, it confronts the industry demand curve, which is negatively sloped to the right. A negatively sloped demand curve indicates that the firm's marginal revenue obtained from selling an additional unit is less than the price because the monopoly can sell additional units only by lowering the price for all previous units.[3]

With the exception of the first unit of output, marginal revenue is always less than price. For example, if the monopoly in Table 3-2 were to lower its price from $70 per shirt to $65 in order to sell five units, its marginal revenue would be only $45 instead of $65. The monopoly would receive $65 not only for the fifth shirt but for *all* shirts it sells, that is, it would have to reduce the price of the previous four shirts by $5 each. Hence, $65 minus the $20 in price reductions for the four shirts equals the marginal revenue of $45.[4]

TABLE 3-2

HYPOTHETICAL COSTS AND REVENUES IN A MONOPOLY SHIRT FIRM

(a) Shirt Output	(b) Total Cost	(c) Marginal Cost	(d) Price	(e) Total Revenue	(f) Marginal Revenue	(g) Profit or Loss
1	$205	$205	$85	$ 85	$ 85	$-120
2	220	15	80	160	75	-60
3	230	10	75	225	65	-5
4	235	5	70	280	55	45
5	250	15	65	325	45	75
6	270	20	60	360	35	90
7	295	25	55	385	25	90
8	325	30	50	400	15	75
9	360	35	45	405	5	45
10	400	40	40	400	-5	0
11	445	45	35	385	-15	-60
12	495	50	30	360	-25	-135
13	550	55	25	325	-35	-225
14	610	60	20	280	-45	-330

---

[3] A monopoly firm that cannot discriminate among its customers and must charge a single price to all customers is called a nondiscriminating monopoly. The discussion that follows pertains to a nondiscriminating monopoly. A discriminating monopoly is able to charge a higher price to those who have a more intensive demand for the commodity, and it does not produce the distortions that will be discussed below.

[4] *If* the monopoly had been able to sell the first shirt for $85, the second for $80, the third for $75, the fourth for $70, and the fifth for $60, marginal revenue would equal price and the monopoly would be called a price-discriminating monopoly. However, the non-discriminating monopoly will have to decrease the price of all units if it wants to lower the price to sell more.

The monopoly, just as the purely competitive firm, will maximize its profits by producing where $MC = MR$ and by charging a price that consumers are able and willing to pay at that quantity. The monopoly can maximize its profits (at $90) by producing seven shirts, where the marginal revenue of $25 equals the marginal cost of $25. The price the monopoly will charge for each shirt is $55. The purpose of this exercise is to show that the monopoly faces the entire industry demand curve, which means that it can sell additional units only by lowering its price. It selects its profit-maximizing quantity and price by producing where $MC = MR$. Compare Tables 3-1 and 3-2. The monopoly charges a higher price and produces a smaller quantity of shirts than the purely competitive firm. In the purely competitive industry the price was $40 and production was ten shirts. A monopoly with identical cost and demand conditions will produce only seven units and price them at $55 each. The monopoly's price is greater than its marginal costs, ($55 > $25). Hence, we know that the monopoly is misallocating resources, because the price it is charging is greater than the marginal cost ($P > MC$). Consumers will adjust their consumption of the monopoly's good until their marginal benefits equal the price, which means that consumers will receive $55 of benefits from having an additional unit produced and it will cost only $25 to produce it. The monopoly, in effect, drives a wedge between price ($55) and marginal cost ($25), which, as discussed previously, produces allocative inefficiency. A monopoly industry results in fewer resources being allocated to that particular industry than would result if the industry were competitively organized. Although the monopoly does not charge the highest price it could get (it would sell only one unit) and although it is constrained by a negatively sloping demand curve, the monopoly is termed a *price maker* because it sets the price rather than takes it as given by aggregate supply and demand forces.

Pure monopoly is said to be inefficient and non-Pareto optimal because it charges a price higher than marginal cost, which results in an underutilization of resources in that industry.[5] However, considerable caution must be exercised when applying this analysis in the real world. Identical cost curves were assumed in our comparison of competitive and

---

[5] Whereas economists emphasize the allocative inefficiency of monopolies, the noneconomist tends to emphasize the existence of monopoly profits. The layman's emphasis is misplaced however. First, *if* monopoly profits are earned, they constitute a redistribution from consumers to the monopoly's owners, workers, and suppliers, who are also members of society. Such distribution may be more or less desirable than that resulting from pure competition. Second, the existence of monopoly (economic) profits depends upon the demand and cost conditions confronting the monopoly industry and is not the inevitable result of monopoly organization.

monopoly firms. Monopoly organization, however, could shift the cost curves downward so far that the net result might be the production of a greater quantity at a lower price than could be produced by firms in a competitive industry. If marginal costs decreased throughout the feasible range of demand, the entire market demand could be supplied at the lowest cost by only one firm. Thus, there are many economists who would prefer a regulated monopoly or perhaps even an unregulated one to a competitive industry.

A monopoly may have less inducement to innovate than a competitive firm; however, a monopoly is more certain that it can recoup the benefits from those innovations it does make, and it can plan more efficiently for the future since it only has to predict market demand and costs without worrying about the decisions of its competitors. Monopolies that cannot restrict entry will face potential competition from firms that would enter the industry if the monopoly charged a monopoly price. Hence, the monopoly wishing to forestall entry would price at close to the competitive level. Even if there were only one firm in the industry, it might price at the competitive level if entry of other firms were virtually costless.

There are relatively few market-generated monopolies in the United States. Most monopolies, such as electric and gas utilities, that economists or laymen can identify are created and protected by government legislation. While such legislation may be justified, other legislation granting monopoly power to professional associations or licensing boards are less justified. Since most monopoly power in the United States can be traced to government legislation, monopolies are more properly an example of political market failure than private market failure.

OLIGOPOLY: FEW SELLERS

Many knowledgeable critics of capitalism admit that there are few, if any, national monopolies in the United States, but they point out that there are many oligopolistic industries—industries that contain a few sellers. They cite the automobile, farm machinery, steel, camera, and soft drink industries as a few examples of oligopolies. Oligopolistic industries contain some of the characteristics of pure monopoly, and they can produce economic problems. Oligopolies have some flexibility in setting their prices, but there is a great deal of uncertainty among oligopolistic firms because they have to estimate the pricing, output, innovation, and design decisions and reactions of their competitors when making their own decisions. If Ford Motor Company cuts its prices, it has to be concerned about the reactions of GM, Chrysler, Toyota, and Honda. It doesn't know what their decisions will be, so Ford must make its decisions with a considerable degree of uncertainty. Economists have developed a variety of models incorporating different assumptions about how competitors will react, but we need not examine them here.

Oligopolistic industries spend considerable resources on advertising in order to differentiate their products from competitors and to establish their "brand names" in the market so that it is difficult for new entrants to compete with them. However, if there is no collusion among oligopolistic firms and if there are no barriers to entry, they are reasonably competitive in their results. In fact, oligopolies are less numerous and less important than implied by attention paid to them, and most empirical studies have concluded that the social cost of oligopolies is not significant.[6] Oligopolistic industries receive much attention because they contain relatively large and well-known firms. The reader can probably identify the "Big Three" among the domestic automotive firms but not the "Big Three" in the construction industry or the wholesale industry. Even though these industries are very large, they are characterized by many relatively small and competitive firms.[7] We constantly hear references about the automobile and steel industries because the firms comprising them are few, large, and visible, but we seldom hear about the construction or wholesale industries because the firms comprising them are small and invisible. This popular emphasis on the large and visible industries distorts the relative importance of market power in the United States. Also, in this era of massive international trade, the existence of a few large domestic firms in an industry does not mean that the consumer market is oligopolistic, because imports provide significant competition in domestic markets.[8]

Firms that produce commodities in many different industries are termed conglomerates. A firm that produces shoes, pens, and electrical machinery is an example of a conglomerate. The textbook example of a multinational conglomerate is International Telephone and Telegraph, which a few year ago owned Avis, Aetna Finance, Continental Baking

---

[6] Arnold Harberger estimated the losses at one-tenth of 1 percent of GNP. "Monopoly and Resource Allocation," *American Economic Review* 44 (May 1954): 77–87. Also see F. M. Scherer, *Industrial Market Structure and Market Performance* (Chicago: Rand McNally, 1970) and D. A. Worcester, Jr., "New Estimates of the Welfare Loss to Monopoly: U.S. 1956–69," *Southern Economic Journal* 40 (October 1973): 234–46.

[7] The automotive industry has 726,000 employees, the wholesale industry has 4.4 million, and the construction industry has 7.5 million. Source: *The Statistical Abstract of the United States, 1989.*

[8] Economists sometimes list a fourth market structure called monopolistic competition, which, like oligopoly, is between pure competition and monopoly. It is characterized by many sellers, differentiated products, easy entry, and advertising. Since monopolistic competition contains many of the features of the other three market structures, it is not discussed in this summary review.

(Wonder Bread and Hostess Cakes), W. Atlee Burpee Seed Company, the Sheraton Hotel Corporation, Hartford Insurance Corporation, community development and real estate companies, Federal Electric Corporation, Eason Oil Corporation, and many retail stores. American Brands Corporation owned American Tobacco, Franklin Life Insurance, Master Lock Company, Swingline (staplers), Sunshine Biscuit, Wilson Jones (stationary stores), James Beam Distillers, Acushnet Company (golf equipment), Andrew Jergens Company (lotions), Ace Fastener Company, and Chemical By-Products, Ltd. General Mills owned Eddie Bauer (clothing), Monet Jewelers, Lark Luggage Corporation, Red Lobster Inns, Ship 'n Shore (clothing), Yoplait (yogurt), Saluto Foods, and Footjoy (shoes).

The noneconomist generally views conglomerates as barriers to competition, but such a priori conclusions are unjustified. A shoe manufacturer that expands into the electrical industry *increases* competition in the electrical industry without decreasing competition in the shoe industry. A conglomerate may obtain some "unjustified" advantage in the capital market, but these advantages generally reflect economies of scale, and most economists agree that capital markets are very competitive. Conglomerates increase competition by entering some industries and threatening to enter others if the firms within them are not competitive. Some critics complain that conglomerates are undesirable because they possess an undesirable amount of power in a democracy. On the other hand, one could argue that conglomerates provide checks on the overwhelming power of government in modern democracies. They have the resources and the incentives to gather evidence that government policies may be undesirable or inefficient. For example, it was not a small competitive newspaper that brought Watergate to the public's attention but the giant and noncompetitive Washington Post Company, which also owns *Newsweek* and numerous other papers and television stations.

CARTELS

A *cartel* exists when a number of independent firms or organizations coordinate their buying or selling decisions so they will earn monopsony, or monopoly profits. Economic cartels are both protected and prohibited by government laws. Antitrust laws prohibit firms from colluding or conspiring to set prices and production quotas. The most famous example of cartel collusion in the United States was the electrical equipment conspiracy during the latter 1950s involving more than two dozen manufacturers, including General Electric, Westinghouse, and Allis-Chalmers. Elaborate schemes, such as fake sealed bids, were concocted to set prices and divide markets. Twenty-nine manufacturers and 46 company executives were indicted in this conspiracy. Most cartels, however, are unsuccessful because price and market sharing agreements cannot be reached among the members or—if such agreements are made—they fall apart as each cartel member tries to improve its own position. Cartel members must agree on prices and quantities, which is difficult if each member has different cost and demand conditions. If product qualities differ, each member will try to hold out for higher "quality differentials" for its products and a common agreement on the proper differentials for cartel members will be difficult to reach. If an agreement to rig prices and divide markets is reached, each firm has an incentive to "cheat" on its fellow con-spirators by cutting prices and invading the territories of other members so long as its marginal revenue remains above marginal cost. A favorite technique is to publish an official price list that contains sanctioned cartel prices but to offer deep discounts to "special" customers. The difficulties of reaching and enforcing agreements are more responsible for the breakup of cartels than the antitrust laws.

The most spectacularly successful international cartel during the post–World War II era has been OPEC, which was able to raise prices from $2.50 to $10 per barrel of oil from 1973–74 and then to $32 by 1980. But economists performed a valuable public service during the mid-seventies when they constantly warned the nation not to commit itself to high-cost energy sources with large subsidies and tariffs in an attempt to make the country independent of oil imports. The arguments given by economists for expecting OPEC to lose some of its market power could have been applied to any cartel. One was that the long-run quantity demanded would react to the high cartel price as individuals purchased smaller and more fuel efficient cars and made their existing and new houses, offices, and plants more fuel efficient. Second, the higher prices set by the cartel would induce new sources (from inside and outside OPEC) of oil to come into the market. Third, the cartel was likely to suffer the same fate as other cartels when they had to reduce production to maintain cartel prices. This was especially true for OPEC, which was characterized by political dif-ferences among the countries and disparities between the oil reserves and wealth of OPEC countries.[9] Economists were proven correct when the cartel collapsed in the mid-eighties and prices dropped to $12 a barrel.

---

[9] Saudi Arabia, the key country with the largest oil reserves, a small population and, a high per capita income, had an incentive to keep cartel prices from getting so high that conserva-tion and other sources of energy decreased future demand for its oil. Other countries, such as Nigeria and Venezuela, were poor countries with heavy debts and a need for revenue, which induced "cheating."

When analyzing the competitiveness of the American economy, one should recall the words of Adam Smith:

> People of the same trade seldom meet together, even for merriment and diversion, but the conversation ends in a conspiracy against the public, or in some contrivance to raise prices. It is impossible indeed to prevent such meetings, by any law which either could be executed, or would be consistent with liberty and justice. But though the law cannot hinder people of the same trade from sometimes assembling together, it ought to do nothing to facilitate such assemblies; much less to render them necessary.[10]

Much of the noncompetitive behavior in the American economy has been caused by government. Licenses, tariffs, and regulations are responsible for more noncompetitive behavior than the market. Businessmen, as well as you and I, want to obtain more stability and higher income. Consequently, vigilance must be maintained and the rules of the competitive game enforced. On the other hand, one must determine in each case the existence of anticompetitive behavior and the probable cause of it. Perhaps a particular oligopolistic industry is quite competitive, or perhaps the existence of potential competitors forces a monopoly producer to price at, or close to, marginal cost. Even with many government restrictions on competition in certain industries and the existence of import duties, quotas, and other anticompetitive legislation, the American market remains surprisingly competitive.

EXTERNALITIES

The most widely recognized and most serious "failure" in the private market is the existence of spillover effects, or externalities. The private market works well when all costs and benefits involved in producing a good are reflected in costs and prices. Some costs, such as air and water pollution, are not internalized by firms and, thus, are not included in market costs and prices. Economists call such costs externalities. An *externality* exists when the decisions of one individual or firm affect the utility, costs, or profits of another individual or firm that are not normally reflected in market prices. Externalities may be positive (as in the case of a homeowner who paints his home each spring) or negative (as exemplified by the owner of a St. Bernard who fails to curb his dog). More serious externalities are air, water, and noise pollution, and their economic significance lies in the divergences they create between social and private costs. The use of land, labor, and capital to produce goods is part of the

---

[10] Adam Smith, *The Wealth of Nations* (New York: The Modern Library, 1937), 128.

social cost, which is normally reflected in the private costs of production and, thus, in the prices charged consumers. Hence, a consumer who buys an automobile for $10,000 is paying for the resources (decrease in provision of other goods) it cost society to produce and distribute that automobile. However, if a plant producing steel for the automobile dumps polluted water into a stream, which kills the fish or makes the water unsafe for swimming, there is a social cost that is paid by neither the automobile manufacturer nor the auto consumer. Thus, the marginal social cost of producing the automobile is greater than its price ($MC > P$), which means that there are too many automobiles being produced and too few fish and swimming opportunities left.[11]

Most externalities are not amenable to simple solutions. First, many externalities affect a large number of decision-making entities. Second, there are at least two parties to every externality: the party that generates the externality and the party that receives the externality. The externality could not exist without both parties, so it is not clear which party should be assigned the liability (or benefit) for the externality.

Assume that there are only two firms situated on a river. The upstream firm is discharging waste into the river, which degrades the quality of water used in the production process of the downstream firm. If there were no upstream firm discharging waste, there would be no externality. Similarly, if there were no downstream firm having to use clean water, there would be no externality. The traditional solution, and one accepted by generations of economists, would be to tax the output of the upstream firm. If each unit of output by the upstream plant caused a degradation of the water equal to 20 cents, the output of the upstream firm should be taxed at a rate of 20 cents. Hence, this would raise the cost of each unit of output by 20 cents, thus eliminating the divergence between private and social cost. It would force the consumers of the upstream production to cut back consumption until their marginal benefits from consuming the good equalled the marginal costs of production, including the pollution costs imposed on the downstream firm.[12] Economists now recognize that this excise tax solution may not be optimal. One reason is that the social value lost from the decreased production and consumption of the upstream firm's product might be greater than the value of the additional production

---

[11] This is the traditional analysis of externalities. It ignores the possibility that fish and swimming might not be optimally priced.

[12] The externality solution of taxing the output of a firm causing the externality is often called the Pigovian solution, named after British economist A. C. Pigou, who made important contributions to the externality theory. See A. C. Pigou, *The Economics of Welfare* (London: Macmillan, 1920).

by the downstream firm. Second, the least costly solution might be to have the downstream firm install cleaning devices, which it would have little incentive to do if the upstream firm decreased production.

For the past three decades economists have recognized that it is not always desirable to restrict the output of the firm producing the external cost. If the upstream firm were taxed or had to make payments to the downstream firm, there would be *less* than optimal production by the upstream firm and *more* than optimal production by the downstream firm. If the upstream firm were not liable and the downstream firm had to bear the costs of the polluted river, there would be *less* than optimal production by the downstream firm and *more* than optimal production by the upstream firm. Unless careful empirical studies are conducted, there is no way to determine which firm's production would be more valuable at the margin.

One solution to this problem follows:

The Coase Theorem
If transactions and bargaining costs are zero, then the economic outcome will be unaffected by an assignment of liability for any externality. Furthermore, the outcome resulting from an agreement between the parties will be Pareto optimal.[13]

Assume that it would cost the upstream firm $5,000 to clean up its discharged water to be acceptable to the downstream plant, whereas it would cost the downstream plant $3,000 to clean its water intake. Also assume initially that the upstream plant would be *legally liable* for damages done to the downstream plant. If bargaining costs were zero, the upstream plant would have an incentive to pay to the downstream plant something less than the $5,000, which the upstream plant would have had to pay to clean up its discharge. The downstream plant would be willing to accept any payment greater than $3,000. Hence, there would be room for a mutually acceptable agreement, say the upstream plant paying $4,000 to the downstream plant and the downstream plant employing the less expensive technology, which would cost society only $3,000. If the law assigned *no liability* to the upstream plant, the downstream plant would have to bear the costs and invest $3,000 in purifying the water. In either case, the low-cost technology would be used.

Now reverse the figures by assuming that it would cost the upstream plant $3,000 to clean its waste water and the downstream plant $5,000 to purify its intake. If the upstream plant were liable, it would invest $3,000 in cleaning its waste, and if there were no liability, the downstream plant

---

[13] R. H. Coase, "The Problem of Social Cost," *Journal of Law and Economics* (October 1960): 1–44.

would offer to pay the upstream plant between $3,000 and $5,000 (say $4,000) rather than clean it up by itself. Hence, no matter which plant were liable nor which plant had the lowest cost, the result would always be the same: the low-cost, socially optimal method ($3,000) would be utilized to clean up the river.[14]

If bargaining costs are zero, the externality-affected parties will always reach a socially optimal bargain. Unfortunately, when the number of affected parties is very large, such as is the case when thousands of automobiles produce smog that affects hundreds of thousands of people, bargaining among the affected parties is not feasible and the optimal solution cannot be obtained. Consequently, as will be shown in chapter 4, the existence of such pervasive externalities provides the basic argument for the existence of government.[15]

ADVERTISING

Many noneconomists as well as a few economists, frequently cite advertising as a cause of private market failure. They argue that it raises the cost to new firms thinking of entering an industry, provides little information, and subliminally seduces consumers to purchase goods they otherwise wouldn't want. This view is much less popular among economists today, because recent research has shown that most advertising is very useful and procompetitive. Advertising provides information about the product, informs consumers about its availability, and identifies a company with a particular product. Firms that produce high-priced but inferior goods have no incentive to advertise their firms' association with their products. Consumers know that a nationally advertised motel is unlikely to surprise them with dirty rooms and bedbugs, whereas they are more uncertain about the quality of the unadvertised Shady Lane

---

[14] Note that no matter which firm were liable nor which firm had the low-cost technology to clean the water, bargaining between the two firms would always result in the low-cost technology being used. However, legal liability would affect how much each firm paid, but this would be merely a transfer between the firms and would not represent a social cost. For example, when the upstream firm was liable for its effluent, it paid $4,000 to the downstream firm. It cost the downstream firm only $3,000 to clean the water, so the additional $1,000 was merely a transfer from one firm to another. Unlike the $3,000, which represented resources necessary to build the purifier, the additional $1,000 merely meant that the upstream firm had $1,000 less profits and the downstream firm had $1,000 more profits. If both firms were in competitive markets, the one that had to pay the liability might be forced out of the industry because its costs would be higher than its competitors.

[15] The literature on externalities is extensive. Some excellent reviews of the basic literature are contained in Ralph Turvey, "On Divergences between Social Cost and Private Cost," *Economica* and William J. Baumol, *Welfare Economics*, 2d ed. (Cambridge: Harvard University Press, 1965), 24–36.

Motel; when they are searching for toys they know that Fisher-Price produces high quality and safe toys but are more cautious about unknown brands. Advertising and brand name identification serve a social good, because those companies that advertise lay their reputations on the line and they have an incentive to live up to the expectations generated by the brand name identification. Contrary to the argument that advertising is a barrier to entry, most economists now view advertising as assisting competition and bans on advertising as constituting significant barriers to entry.

Assume that you and a few friends invented a new engine oil and were prohibited from advertising. Would you stand much chance of taking customers away from the visible and well-known companies such as Penn State, Quaker State, or Mobil Oil? Not likely. You would have no way of informing millions of consumers about your new oil and its advantages, and consumers would continue to buy the known brands. Despite a superior product you would soon be going into bankruptcy court. Numerous studies have shown that prices are higher when advertising is prohibited. A few years ago many states prohibited advertisements for eyeglasses, and those states that had such laws also had eyeglasses that were priced 20 percent to 100 percent higher than states that permitted advertisements.[16] One study found that the retail markup on toys that were heavily advertised were less than on those toys that were not heavily advertised.[17] Advertising does inform consumers about new products, and it might help create fads that sweep the country. But one of the benefits many consumers derive from a product is its faddishness. Guess jeans, Bartles and Jaymes coolers, Oleg Cassini shirts, Mercedes-Benz cars, Fisher-Price toys, Reebok shoes, Polo shorts, Corona beer, and a Princeton education might be indicators of both product quality and fads. Whatever the reason, status brands enable the consumer to increase his or her utility, and advertisements for these products increase competition in the marketplace.

The graveyard of products that "you couldn't do without" provides strong testimony to the inability of advertising to induce consumers to purchase products they don't want. The Edsel and New Coke are two good examples of well-financed advertising campaigns that could not make consumers buy products they didn't want. In the case of the short-lived abandonment of "Classic" Coke, there was outright indignation that a new

---

[16] Lee Benham, "The Effect of Advertising on the Price of Eyeglasses," *Journal of Law and Economics* (October 1972): 337–51.

[17] Robert L. Steiner, "Does Advertising Lower Consumer Prices?" *Journal of Marketing Research* (October 1973): 19–26.

product was replacing the preferred old Coke. While watching those tasteless and infantile advertisements, which you are certain reflect more upon the tastes of ad creators than upon the tastes of viewers, it takes a tough mental discipline to remember that advertisements generally *do* provide benefits to society. They are not a serious source of private market failure.[18]

LACK OF KNOWLEDGE

Another frequently mentioned private market failure is that individuals lack perfect knowledge of prices and products. While perfect knowledge is assumed in the purest theory of pure competition, no individual possesses perfect knowledge. Knowledge is costly because individuals must use their time and other resources to obtain it. Individuals will weigh the marginal benefits and costs of gathering information and becoming more knowledgeable. Some individuals, of course, can obtain information more cheaply than others, and some perceive more advantages from becoming educated. The important point is that in the private market there is a direct relationship between the effort expended on obtaining information and the benefits received. If you are going to purchase an automobile, the more you read about new automobiles, investigate repair records of previous models, discuss alternative cars with friends and relatives, and gather information about prices, the more likely you are to purchase a better automobile at a lower price. At some point, however, you will realize that while there remains much you don't know about automobiles, the additional efforts to become educated won't yield marginal benefits greater than marginal costs. A lack of knowledge may simply reflect optimal decisions about the allocation of the individual's time and other resources. Because knowledge is costly to obtain, individuals do not have perfect knowledge about the products they buy in the private market nor the politicians for whom they vote in the political market.[19]

DECREASING COSTS

The competitive model assumes that firms' cost curves are U-shaped—that is, marginal and average costs decrease as production increases—but, as discussed above, at some point marginal and average costs begin

---

[18] The comparative advantages of private and political market advertisements will be explored in chapters 5 and 9.

[19] See chapter 5 for a comparative analysis of incentives to seek knowledge about private and public goods.

to increase with additional production. If the cost curves decrease throughout the feasible range until the entire market demand is saturated, a single firm could supply the entire market output at the lowest cost. One firm could produce, say, 10,000 units more cheaply than ten firms each producing 1,000 units. Under these decreasing cost conditions only one firm would remain in the industry, and it might generate inefficient monopoly output and pricing. Apart from certain public utilities, most industries are characterized by the existence of both large and small firms, which suggests that the long-run cost curves are close to being horizontal. The relative decline of large production firms during the decades of the seventies and eighties suggests that the cost curves in some industries are upward sloping, as stressed in traditional economic theory. The American steel industry, which was dominated by large firms, is now having a resurgence because of the downsizing of the large firms and the emergence of new small, efficient firms. The conventional remedy for the public utility firms, which continue to have downward-sloping cost curves, is regulation by public service commissions. However, there is growing evidence that even large public electric utilities are not necessarily more efficient, and some localities are generating their own electricity or buying it from small firms. Once again, this is not a serious source of private market failure.

INDIVIDUALS, NOT FIRMS, MAKE DECISIONS

One potential private market failure is overlooked by many economists because they ignore the most fundamental postulate of economics. They analyze *individual* consumer behavior on the demand size of the market but then analyze *firm* behavior on the supply side. Firms do not make decisions, individuals do. In small firms, the owner-manager is the only significant decision maker, so defining the "firm" as decision maker causes no harm. However, when a firm has more than a couple dozen employees, other employees will be making major decisions, and there is less assurance that they will always decide to maximize profits or that they will make the same decisions as the owners if given the same information. This cleavage between "firm" and "individual" behavior is likely to be most significant in large corporations.

Corporations, which play major roles in modern market economies, are legal entities that are owned by stockholders and that have immense economic advantages because they are able to internalize market decision making, reduce uncertainty, amass large amounts of capital, take advantage of economies of scale, and shift labor and other resources quickly to their most profitable uses and locations. They have a continual existence, which should enable them to incorporate payoffs from long-run strategies and research investments. Their most serious disadvantage is the cleavage between rational "firm" and rational "individual" behavior, as noted by Adolf Berle and Gardiner Means, who wrote about the separation between corporate ownership and control more than 50 years ago.[20]

The owners-stockholders no longer manage the corporations and hire professional managers to run them. The fact that these managers are not responsible to a single owner but to thousands or millions of owning stockholders has produced divergences between the interests and goals of corporate managers and corporate stockholders. Corporate managers, however, do not operate without limits. The existence of capital markets places considerable constraints on the ability of managers to exploit stockholders. Investors would not provide capital to corporations in which the returns were lower than what they could earn from alternative investments. If the managers of a corporation pursued their own interests at the expense of stockholders, the rate of return would be lower than if the corporation were managed efficiently. This, in turn, would depress the market value of the corporation's stock and provide information that the corporation was not being managed efficiently, and this would provide an incentive for someone to gain control and manage the corporation more efficiently.

These constraints operate rather slowly and imperfectly in the real world, and corporations, like any large bureaucracy, are confronted with the problems of stimulating workers and managers to pursue the ultimate goals.[21] A typical, but hypothetical, criticism of modern corporations is given below:

> Most large corporations have entire divisions where the profit-loss criterion is so remote that it is impossible to measure performance on that basis, and corporate bureaucrats are able to take advantage of that distance by pursuing their personal goals of enjoying an easy life with many bureaucratic perks. The separation of management from stockholders-owners provides flexibility but little control over executives who seek security in the cocooned halls of the executive suite rather than on the risky streets of individual entrepreneurship. Corporate executives never exercise their creative imaginations more than when they are concocting fringe benefits and golden parachutes for themselves. Except for the level of their salaries and benefits and a very loose profit

---

[20] Adolf Berle and Gardiner Means, *The Modern Corporation and Private Property* (New York: Macmillan, 1934).

[21] The separation between ownership and control and the bureaucratic behavior it generates spawn even more problems in the political market. Some attention is devoted to corporate bureaucracy here because bureaucratic behavior in corporations and in government agencies have much in common. See chapter 10 for a thorough analysis of bureaucracy.

motivation to guide them, corporate executives are virtually indistinguishable from career bureaucrats in government. They call themselves executives instead of managers, supervisors, or capitalists and fight over such bureaucratic perks as a large office, a water-filled carafe, the size of convention hotel rooms, and an executive assistant or secretary instead of a typist. Vice presidencies multiply faster than corporate congeniality sessions, with a number of companies having more than one hundred vices. Middle-level managers are transferred from job to job every four or five years in order to broaden their management experiences, which means that the operating time horizon of most executive decisions is limited to less than a half-dozen years. During and after the sixties many executives put more emphasis on their reputation and progress within their profession than progress within the corporation employing them. They "served their time" in various corporations to enhance their reputation and to pad their resumes, but they did so at the cost of long-term commitment and responsibility to any corporation. Corporations became overmanaged by finance- and personnel-oriented MBAs from prestigious business schools who, unlike their predecessors, knew little about production, science, or engineering and had little devotion to the company that employed them. For all of these reasons there is considerable "organizational slack" in most corporations.

Many economists who emphasize the free rider problem in government legislatures and bureaucracies often fail to apply the same analysis to corporations. The autonomy of management in the large corporation and its ability to further its self-interests at the expense of stockholders is possible because of the free rider problem. Each stockholder wants the corporation to operate efficiently and to be managed well. However, the income of the corporation is a collective good to all stockholders, and any stockholder who holds only a minute percentage of the stock, like the member of any large group, has little incentive to work for the collective good by investing time and money in challenging management. The profit motive becomes a dim objective to individual managers and employees who are most concerned about their salaries, promotions, and bureaucratic perks.

Even profit sharing plans are unlikely to have much impact on the corporate bureaucracy, because the decisions of the individual worker in the corporation are not going to have a perceptible effect on the profits shared with the worker. The director of a corporate office attending a convention has a choice of staying at a $150 hotel room or an $80 room. If she were spending her own money, she would stay in the $80 room, if she went to the convention at all. However, if it were on the company account and she stayed in the $80 room, she would save $70 for the corporation, which might generate at most a penny or two of increased profit sharing funds to her, whereas staying in the more expensive room might decrease her profit sharing funds by, say, $5. Obviously, she would rather stay in the expensive room, which costs the corporation $150 but which she values at only $75. Individuals, including corporate bureaucrats, don't spend other people's money as carefully as they spend their own. Airlines, hotels, motels, and restaurants have profited from the realization of this timeless adage by establishing higher prices for business clients than for tourists.

Corporations have also suffered from an external view held by consumers, workers, regulators, and politicians that they have an irrevocable charter for eternity from Mother Nature and that they are unlimited sources of funds for charities, research projects, universities, governments, consumers, workers, and managers. Workers receive generous benefits while working, not working, and after retirement. Government regulation of competition in such industries as airlines, public utilities, trucking, and railroads protect inefficient but highly paid workers and managers against new competition. Government legislation protecting labor unions and enacting minimum wages force the unnecessary retirement of resources or channel them into areas of the economy where they are less productive. Antitrust laws prohibit corporations from performing collective research and innovations.

When some older economic regulations were relaxed in the latter sixties and seventies, new "social" regulations were laid upon corporations. It was widely thought that corporations could pay any wage, survive any tax or regulation, lower any product price, make any contribution, and pay any liability settlement. When it became obvious in the seventies that even the largest corporations were subject to limitations, it came as an unbelievable shock. Tax, environmental, safety, equal opportunity, and liability laws, supplemented by judicial decisions, put immense financial strains on corporations and required them to employ "nonproductive" staff in personnel, accounting, public relations, environmental, and legal departments. The costs of such legislation were not even considered because, it was thought, they fell on artificial legal entities called corporations.[22]

PRIVATE MARKET AND WELFARE: A SUMMARY

Competitive market forces in the commodity and resource markets will produce allocative efficiency (Pareto optimality) through the functioning of what Adam Smith termed the "Invisible Hand" of the marketplace. If

---

[22] An important principle of taxation is that corporations do not bear the burden of any tax. Stockholders, managers, workers, suppliers, or consumers bear the burden of taxes paid by corporations. The average citizen, of course, has no way of knowing what amount of the corporate income tax he or she pays. Thus, from a political perspective, a tax levied on a corporation is an ideal tax. Those who bear the burden of the tax don't even know it.

firms are free to enter and to exist in an industry, if resources are mobile, and if an optimal amount of knowledge exists, decentralized decision making by individual consumers and producers will result in the close approximation of Pareto optimality. However, one must always remember that the market mechanism that exists in the real world is not a *deus ex machina*. The complex models of economic theory often hide the fundamental fact that the "market" is not a frictionless body that one plugs into an equation to obtain definitive and unequivocal answers. The economy is composed of millions of individuals pursuing their perceived self-interests guided by prices, costs, income, and profits. The private market works amazingly well but not without friction, delays, information costs, oversights, market power, corporate bureaucracies, waste, externalities, and the pursuits of private interests, which do not always serve a social goal. Most importantly, externalities, which are very costly if not impossible to internalize through private market decision making, do exist. Market failures will continue to exist despite the efforts of free market apologetics to manipulate the King's English so as to exorcise them from conventional language or to avoid the problems by assuming away the richness of the real world that generates them. The best defense of the free market and the most intellectually honest approach is not to deny the existence of any "failures" in the private market but to construct a theory of the political market in which its failures are as thoroughly identified and analyzed as those in the private market. This is one of the roles of public choice.

Questions and Answers

The following three exercises apply economic analysis to certain government policies, both hypothetical and real. Though full of real-world complexities, they provide some insights into the economic effects of certain social programs, and they test the reader's ability to apply the concepts presented in the previous chapters.

EXERCISE 1: BREAD STAMPS

Assume the following facts:

Fact 1: The initial market price of bread is $1 per loaf, and the reference individual's (Baker's) annual consumption of bread before food stamps is 100 loaves.

Fact 2: Congress passes a bread stamp program in which stamps are sold to certain qualifying poor people for 20 cents per stamp, but the stamps have a retail value of $1 at the store. The store owner accepts these stamps, and they are redeemed by the government at their face value of $1 per stamp.

The reason Congress is passing this law is to increase bread consumption by the poor (Baker). After all, its supporters argue, the first law of demand states that as the price goes down, the quantity demanded increases. If the poor only have to pay 20 cents to get a loaf of bread, they will adjust the quantity they purchase until the marginal value they place on bread is equal to its price to them, which will be 20 cents.

Fact 3: Congress makes the resale of bread stamps a crime, but enforcement is nonexistent. Hence, a black market arises in which bread stamps are sold for 60 cents.

Fact 4: The maximum quantity of bread stamps the reference poor individual (Baker) can purchase is 200.

Fact 5: Because of the increased demand for bread caused by the bread stamp program, the market price of bread increases to $1.10, and Baker's annual consumption of bread is now 120 loaves. The *average* value Baker places on his consumption of bread beyond 100 loaves is 80 cents.

QUESTIONS FOR EXERCISE 1

1. What is the "price" or opportunity cost to which the bread stamp recipient (Baker) adjusts his consumption? What value does he place on the marginal unit?

2. How much food consumption among the poor (number of units and their market value) does the stamp legislation promote? What is the total quantity of bread stamps used by the poor?

3. Is Baker's real income increased by the stamp program? If so, by how much?

4. Is Baker's discretionary money income increased. If so, by how much?

5. What is the marginal cost of bread before and after the subsidy if the bread industry is competitive?

6. Is economic efficiency achieved in the distribution of bread? Why?

7. What is the opportunity cost to society of increasing bread consumption by the bread stamp recipients?

8. If one is concerned about a broader concept of efficiency, is it possible that economic efficiency is promoted by the stamp program? What value would taxpayers have to place on Baker's marginal consumption of bread to have such efficiency?

9. Who wins and who loses from this bread stamp program?

ANSWERS TO EXERCISE 1

1. In a free market system without bread stamps, each individual adjusts to the market price of $1.00. Because the bread stamp program increases aggregate demand, the price rises to $1.10, and those individuals who do not receive bread stamps adjust their quantity to the higher market price. The marginal preference value normal consumers place on the last loaf purchased is $1.10. The stamp recipients, such as Baker, adjust to a much lower price. If the black market for stamps did not exist, Baker would adjust his purchases to the price he had to pay for the marginal loaf of bread, which is 22 cents (20 cents × 1.1 stamps). However, since stamp recipients can sell bread stamps at 60 cents each and since it takes 1.1 stamps to buy one loaf of bread, Baker adjusts the quantity of bread he consumes to the black market price he can get for his food stamps, or 66 cents (1.1 stamps × 60 cents). Baker consumes 120 loaves, and his marginal preference value of the 120th loaf is his opportunity cost of 66 cents.

2. The additional bread consumption by the poor made possible by the food stamp legislation is 20 loaves. Baker purchases a total of 120 loaves and he uses 132 stamps (1.1 × 120). The total value of his additional bread consumption is $22 ($1.10 × 20). Baker is allowed to purchase 200 stamps, he uses 132, and sells 68 stamps on the black market. Though the stamps sold are not used by the poor they are used by someone. Hence, 182 loaves (200 stamps with a value of $200/$1.10) are purchased with the 200 stamps. Since 120 loaves are purchased by Baker, the nonpoor who purchase the 68 stamps in the black market consume 62 loaves.

3. and 4. When individuals obtain goods at subsidized prices, their real incomes are increased. Baker's income is increased in three ways. First, the stamp program enables Baker to reduce expenditures on his *previous consumption* of bread. Prior to the program, Baker was spending $100 on 100 loaves each year. Now he can purchase 100 loaves by buying $22 in coupons (each loaf now costs $1.10 or 110 coupons at 20 cents each = $22). So Baker's real income increases by $78 ($100 – $22). Second, because of the subsidy Baker consumes 20 additional loaves of bread. We know the value of the 20 additional loaves is worth less than $1 (or he would have been purchasing them before the stamp program) and more than 66 cents (or he would have decreased his bread consumption and sold 1.1 stamps for 66 cents). *Fact 5* states that Baker's average preference value for each of the additional 20 loaves is 80 cents. Since Baker pays 22 cents for the coupons required for each loaf, the total increase in his real income from the consumption of the 20 additional loaves is $11.60 [(.80 – .22) × 20]. The third increase in Baker's real income is obtained by his sale of stamps on the black market. We know that Baker will buy the maximum number of stamps (200) from the government because Baker can get 60 cents for a stamp while only paying 20 cents. Since he is consuming 120 loaves at $1.10, we know that he is using 132 stamps, which leaves 68 stamps for sale at a profit of 40 cents (.60 – .20) per stamp for a total revenue of $27.20.

Thus, the total *increase in Baker's real income* as a result of the bread stamp program is $116.80 ($78 + $11.60 + $27.20). The *increase in his discretionary money income* is only $105.20 ($78 + $27.20).

5.   In a competitive industry the marginal cost of bread is always equal to the market price. The market price was $1 prior to the stamp legislation and $1.10 after the program was in effect.

6.   We know that efficiency in the bread industry is not obtained, because the marginal value placed on a loaf of bread by Baker and other stamp recipients is only 66 cents (1.1 stamps × .60) whereas the marginal cost is $1.10. It is costing society $1.10 in resources to provide a marginal loaf of bread, which Baker values at only 66 cents. Thus, *MC > ME*.

7.   The net increase in the consumption of bread by the poor is only 20 loaves. The cost of the stamp program to the taxpayers is $176 [($1.10 − .22) × 200] or an average of $8.80 for each additional loaf purchased by the poor.

8.   Because of the nature of the program, we have to properly interpret marginal costs of achieving the social goal of increasing the consumption of bread by the poor. The marginal increase in Baker's consumption is 20 loaves, but the program requires the financing of inframarginal consumption (the 100 loaves Baker was consuming before the program). Hence, these costs become part of the marginal costs of procuring the additional 20 units of consumption. The cost of providing the poor with 20 additional units of bread is the entire $176, including the stamps obtained by the nonpoor through the black market. If the additional consumption of 20 loaves of bread by Baker is worth at least $176 to taxpayers, then it could be said that the stamp program is generally efficient.

9.   Winners include bread stamp recipients, bread producers and retailers, black marketeers, and possibly government workers in the food stamp agency. Losers include nonpoor bread consumers, and, if citizens are not aware of the various costs and benefits, all individuals in society because of the misallocation of resources.

SUMMARY TO EXERCISE 1

Economists prefer providing direct grants to the poor rather than specific subsidies. It is almost always true that the value placed on the specific subsidy by the recipient is much less than the cost to the taxpayer of providing the subsidy. If Baker were unable to sell the stamps, the marginal value to him of consuming the last loaf of bread would equal the price that Baker had to pay for the bread, or 20 cents. The cost to society (taxpayers) of providing that last unit however, was $1.10. Baker would have much preferred a cash grant of, say, $140, and taxpayers could have saved $36.

One counterpoint to the argument that cash grants are preferable to specific grants is that taxpayers want the poor to consume specific goods, such as bread, rather than booze and tobacco, which taxpayers fear they will purchase with their cash grants. These assumed preferences of taxpayers are clearly possible, if somewhat elitist, and there is nothing wrong with taxpayers wanting to subsidize bread rather than redistribute income. However, it is the function of economists to point out that what taxpayers think they are doing is not always what is actually happening. In this example, Baker was able to convert a specific subsidy into a general increase ($105.20) in his discretionary income. Thus, taxpayers thought they were subsidizing Baker's consumption of bread by offering him low-cost bread stamps. However, Baker substituted the low-cost stamps for his normal expenditures on bread, and he sold some stamps on the black market. Although surveys of bread consumption would show that Baker was using his stamps to purchase 120 loaves of bread, we know that the stamp program increased Baker's consumption of bread by only 20 loaves. A specific grant was converted into a partial cash grant with minimal increases in specific consumption.

There has been no discussion of the costs of administering the program, identifying the poor, and checking for fraud by store owners, which would increase the costs of the stamp program. Although the program and the data are purely hypothetical, the reader might apply this general analysis to subsidies of merchant marine ships, wheat, college educations, and, of course, food stamps.

EXERCISE 2: RENT CONTROLS

Background: During World War II the extreme shortage of housing caused by shifting populations and wartime restrictions drove up apartment rents in many cities. A few cities reacted to the higher rents by enacting rent controls that limited the amount landlords could charge for certain apartments. New York was the only major city to continue these controls after the war, but during the 1970s a large number of cities initiated rent controls, and by 1985 more than 200 localities, including Boston, New York, Los Angeles, and Washington, D.C., were using some form of rent control. Arguments supporting rent controls are generally based on equity considerations:

> When demand for housing increases, rental prices are driven up, which means that the poor cannot afford decent housing and landlords are unjustly enriched. It is morally acceptable to have the pricing system work for such goods as VCRs because, unlike housing, they are not necessary for life, and when

the prices of VCRs increase, a greater quantity of VCRs will be forthcoming and price increases will be moderated. However, when housing rentals are driven up by increased demand, the result is higher rentals without any increase in the quantity supplied. As a result, landlords get richer and tenants get poorer. Unless rent controls are enacted, only the rich will be able to afford housing.

Facts: Assume that the competitive apartment market had settled down to an equilibrium rental price and quantity of apartments. Now assume that the central business district of the city experiences an economic renaissance, which increases the demand for housing in the city. The city council, reacting to arguments such as those above, places a rent ceiling on apartments equal to the original equilibrium rental rate.

QUESTIONS FOR EXERCISE 2

1. Show the effects of the increase in demand for rental housing in a competitive market. Explain what is causing the uncontrolled rental price to move from the old equilibrium to the new equilibrium rental. Show your analysis in a supply and demand graph.

2. Analyze the direct economic effects of rent controls in the short run (say a few weeks or months), and then contrast that with a similar analysis for the long run (a couple of years). Show your analysis in supply and demand graphs. Who wins and who loses in the short run?

3. Analyze the indirect economic effects of the rent control, such as the impacts on (a) black and gray market activities, (b) maintenance of rental housing, (c) creation of slums, (d) property tax base in the city, (e) sub-urbanization, (f) traffic congestion on freeways, (g) condominium conversions, (h) rents in non-rent-controlled housing, and (i) demand for lawyers and accountants.

4. Who wins and who loses in the long run from rent controls?

ANSWERS TO EXERCISE 2

1. The increased demand for housing is shown in Figure 3-3 by an outward shift in the demand curve from D_1 to D_2. At the old equilibrium rental price of P_1 there is now a temporary shortage of apartments (equal to $Q_3 - Q_1$) and those unable to obtain rental housing will bid up rental prices to a higher equilibrium price, P_2. During the short run the supply of housing will be relatively fixed, but some increased quantity of housing units can be expected as landlords and homeowners, reacting to the inducement of higher rents, convert basements, attics, and spare bedrooms into apartments. The new market equilibrium values will be at P_2 and Q_2. Those obtaining the rental units will be the individuals able and willing to pay the highest rents.

FIGURE 3-3
SHORT-RUN SUPPLY AND DEMAND CURVES FOR RENTAL UNITS

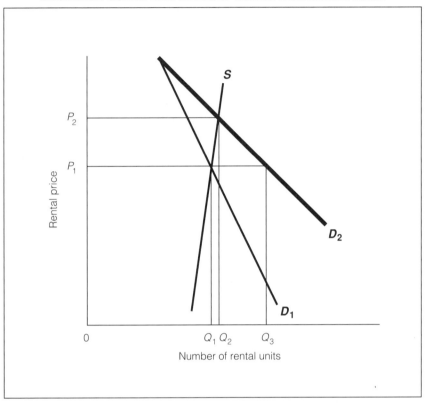

2. Rent controls always involve setting a rent ceiling below the market equilibrium rent. Since the city council wants to keep rents at the old rent, the rent-controlled price is P_1 and the rental price is *not* permitted to increase to P_2. Landlords can no longer accept the higher rental bids of tenants, so the quantity demanded will be Q_3 in Figure 3-3, while the supply of housing units will be only Q_1. A housing shortage of $Q_3 - Q_1$ will result, and the landlords will have to employ some non-price-discrimination criteria to allocate the available housing units.

During the short run individuals do not have many alternatives to housing in the city, and investors are unable to increase the supply of housing by very much. In the long run consumers have more time to react to the higher rents by searching out low-cost alternatives, moving to the suburbs, buying their own homes, or living with friends or parents. Thus, the long-run demand curve becomes slightly flatter (economists would say it is more elastic) to reflect the wider variety of housing alternatives in the long run (see Figure 3-4). The impact of time in this case, however, will be greatest on the supply side of the market. The long-run supply curve is flatter, or more elastic, to reflect the fact that investors have an

FIGURE 3-4
LONG-RUN SUPPLY AND DEMAND CURVES FOR RENTAL UNITS

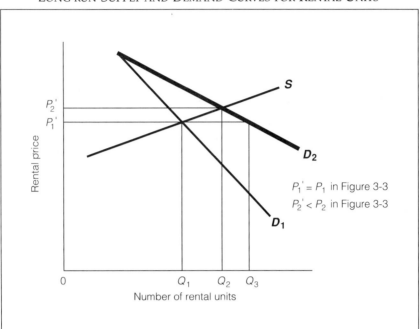

incentive to build more apartment buildings, possibly destroying old and small apartment units and constructing newer and larger apartment buildings. Investors who keep their older apartment buildings have an incentive to maintain them and to make additions where possible. Thus, the increased supply and the greater opportunities among consumers will result in the long-run free market rental price (P_2' in Figure 3-4) being lower than the short-run rental price (P_2 in Figure 3-3).

When rent controls are first enacted, their effects are not immediately noticeable. Tenants will occupy the same units they occupied before the rent controls, and there will be a transfer of real income from the landlords to the tenants. The tenants become better off and the landlords become worse off. There is little landlords can do to escape the effects of rent control in the short run. They are unlikely to sell because the market values of their apartment buildings will have decreased due to the decrease in rental revenues. Whether they sell or not, current landlords are clearly hurt by the rent controls and current tenants are clearly benefitted. Another group of losers are those potential tenants who have recently moved to the city and are searching for an apartment. Many of them would gladly pay the market price of P_2 to get an apartment in the city, but they are forced into alternative housing, which is less desirable to them than living in the city and paying the higher rents. In the long run, however, various adjustments will be made that enlarge the effects of rent controls and the groups impacted by rent controls (see answer 4 below).

3. **a.** Black and gray market activities will increase, but this will be only part of an ever-expanding effort by landlords to "get around" rent controls and the city council to shut down such an alternative. The inevitable history of *all* legislation that interferes with the market processes can be summarized as follows. Some legislative body reacts to an initial set of complaints from a group of citizens that wants "protection" from some market process. A simple law providing such "protection" is then passed, but shortly thereafter it is noticed that certain "activities" are occurring to thwart the intent of the legislation. The legislative body then passes a law prohibiting or restricting that new activity. Then it discovers other activities that are thwarting the intent of the first two pieces of legislation, and it has to pass yet another legislative act. . . . And so the process continues. This process happens so frequently that it might be elevated to a political-economic "law," call it Johnson's law of ever-increasing government legislation.

Johnson's law can be applied in this housing example. After rent control laws are passed, the inevitable initial impact is explicit or implicit bribery. Some landlords accept monetary bribes from potential tenants, or they make "side," or "unofficial," agreements in which tenants agree to help maintain the apartment building. City councils react by passing laws prohibiting such agreements, and the councils create a new department such as an office of rent control compliance. Faced with a continual shortage of housing units, landlords require tenants to pay a nonrefundable deposit of, say, $200. The city council becomes aware of this attempt to circumvent previous laws, and it promptly prohibits nonrefundable deposits. Landlords then require a refundable deposit of $500, but they pay no interest on these deposits. The city council then passes a law prohibiting refundable deposits unless the landlords pay interest. Landlords react by requiring an $800 deposit, and they pay only 2-percent interest on such deposits. The city council now places a ceiling on the deposits that landlords can require, and they create an interest-determination subagency in the office of rent control compliance that has the power to regulate interest rates that landlords must pay on the deposits. Johnson's law of ever-increasing government legislation continues as landlords try to devise new ways of increasing the effective price of housing while the city council reacts by trying to close the ingenious loopholes through legislation or regulations. Soon the district attorney's office creates a separate division to prosecute violations of the numerous laws and regulations that have been passed by the council.

Assuming that the office of rent control compliance and the district attorney are able to enforce these laws, the landlords will eventually have to turn to other criteria to select the individuals who will be allowed to become tenants. They might decide to rent only to families without children, to white families, to men, to women, to those without handicaps, or to those with college degrees. The city council, responding to charges of discrimination against certain groups, then passes a basket of antidiscrimination laws, and the landlords are forced to use new discriminatory criteria such as the queuing system, which harms those who cannot stand in long lines. A major cost of rent controls is the cost of administering the additional legislation created by the rent control laws. Lawyers, accountants, and civil rights investigators are hired by the city, landlords, and tenants (see chapter 12 for a discussion of such social costs).

b. and c.   Landlords build their rental units with the expectation that they will be allowed to adjust prices to reflect estimated future trends in market demand, inflation, and costs. One way they try to recoup the difference between the market price and the rent-controlled price is to reduce maintenance expenses, and the building begins to deteriorate. As the building deteriorates, the tenant who has the apartment begins to lose some of the benefits initially gained through rent control. The renter can be expected to complain to the city council, which will pass various laws designed to force landlords to maintain certain physical appearances and services such as heat, water, and electricity. Johnson's law takes on new dimensions as the office of rent control compliance and the district attorney's office grow by leaps and bounds. These maintenance laws pertain to more arbitrary variables (is a temperature of 68 degrees in winter a reasonable minimal temperature all landlords should provide?), and the buildings begin a trend to seediness and diminished services. At some point, the costs of maintenance, compliance with the hundreds of detailed laws passed to reinforce rent control laws, and the hiring of attorneys to defend landlords in court become so high that the buildings are simply abandoned and slums are expanded. The city council, of course, will attempt to prohibit such abandonment.

d.   The property tax base in the city is likely to be reduced for at least two reasons. The first is that the reduced rental payments generated by rent controls will immediately reduce the value of the building, which is based upon the capitalization—determining the present value—of future rental payments. The second reason is that the disincentive to maintain rent-controlled apartments will result in a deterioration of the building, which will decrease its property value and, hence, property taxes.

e. and f.   In the absence of rent controls, investors would have a tendency to expand the supply of housing units in the city. However, after rent controls are enacted they will quickly see the capital losses incurred by those who invested in apartment housing, and they will begin constructing apartments and houses in the suburbs. The process of decentralization of residential housing will be further encouraged, and freeway congestion will increase as workers who could not find acceptable housing in the city move to the suburbs.

g.   Apartment owners who are seeing the value of their investments decrease and their rate of return shrink to levels far below other investments will take actions designed to rescue their investments and, hopefully, make a profit. These landowners can expect to be strong supporters of slum clearance projects and the construction of public housing, stadiums, or industrial parks on the sites of their buildings. They hope they will have enough influence to get above market payments from the city, state, or federal governments for their low-valued property. If that fails or appears unlikely, they will try to convert their apartment buildings to condominiums because the sale price of condominiums is not controlled. It should not be surprising that cities that have rent controls are also the cities that have problems with many apartments being converted to condominiums. Many of these cities, of course, react by passing laws restricting the conversion of apartments to condos, and a new branch of Johnson's law is begun.

h.   Most rent control laws do not cover all apartments in the city. They cover only apartments in certain sections, apartments of a certain size, or more likely, apartments within certain rental limits. Apartments with rents of $200–$500 per month will almost always be subject to rent controls, while those with rental prices of $2,000 per month will almost always be excluded. One effect of rent control is to force some families who cannot find rent-controlled apartments to move up to non-rent-controlled apartments, thus raising the rents of these apartments. A working-class family that cannot find a rent controlled apartment might be forced to rent a larger or higher quality apartment than it would prefer because rent controls have made their preferred type of apartment unavailable.

i.   The answer to this question should now be obvious. All new legislation increases the demand for lawyers and accountants, but legislation that interferes with the market's price mechanism is likely to produce very significant shifts in the demand for lawyers and accountants. The initial legislation will generate second, third, and fourth rounds of legislation, and the governmental unit will have to hire lawyers and accountants to interpret and enforce the new legislation. Those on both sides of the market—landlords and tenants in this example—will also have incentives to hire lawyers to argue over the interpretations and enforcement of these laws.

4.   The initial winners are those who are able to obtain or retain apartments. However, over time these renters, or those who replace them, will have fewer services and poorly maintained facilities. Fewer rent-controlled apartments will be available as fewer, if any, new housing units are built and older ones fall into decay and abandonment. Tenants will be net gainers in the short run, but many, if not most, of their gains will be eradicated over time as their buildings and neighborhoods deteriorate. Other winners include lawyers, accountants, court reporters, politicians (at least in the short run), city bureaucrats, landowners in the suburbs, housing and highway contractors, apartment finders, and, at least at the margin, all those, such as drug pushers, who thrive in slums.

The losers are those who owned the apartments and land at the time the rent-control laws were passed, those who are unable to find apartments in the city because of the induced shortage, contractors who build city apartment buildings, city maintenance firms, and those, such as small grocery store owners, who thrive in a better-maintained neighborhood. Apartment seekers unable to find apartments are likely to suffer the most from non-price-discrimination: the elderly, blacks, hispanics, families with children, the handicapped, and those socially and politically unconnected. Those who possess the abilities or attributes utilized in the allocation scheme might win initially because they will pay a lower rent than in the unregulated market. Those who do not possess these abilities or attributes will lose because they cannot find housing.

SUMMARY TO EXERCISE 2

Are rent control laws desirable? Unexpected events do increase the demand for housing, which increases rents for apartment owners and enriches the landlord at the expense of the renter. Perhaps the rent-control laws do benefit current tenants, even if their buildings do deteriorate some. Perhaps the rent-control laws give tenants some time to adjust until the buildings deteriorate so much that they have to move.

The reader might view the "unfair enrichment" of the landlord as a justification for rent controls. So be it! Test your values and your economics by going through the same exercise as above, but assume that unexpected events decreased the demand for apartments. The resulting lower rents would lead to the "unfair enrichment" of renters and the deprivation of landlords. Assume that landlords were able to convince the city council that rent floors—no renter would be allowed to pay *less* than a certain amount—were passed. Would you support such laws? Why? Are you really concerned about unjust enrichment caused by unexpected events or about overall income and wealth distribution?

EXERCISE 3: DOWN ON THE FARM

Background: The golden age of American agriculture occurred during the first two decades of this century. During World War I American farmers fed not only the civilians and soldiers of the United States but many of the civilians and soldiers of Allied countries. Prices of American farm products were high not only because of high world demand but also because the Wilson administration adopted hefty price supports to encourage farm production. The high prices induced many farmers to expand their cultivated land and mechanization with the expectation that these price supports would continue after the war. When price supports were allowed to expire in 1919, agricultural prices plummeted, and many farmers found themselves unable to pay off their large debts. The golden age of agriculture had ended, and farmers never again enjoyed the relative prosperity they enjoyed between 1900 and 1920. Farmers began lobbying Congress for various forms of agricultural aid during the twenties; their efforts were intensified during the thirties, and they continue today.

The political activities of farmers and their supporters have produced a patchwork array of programs designed to provide assistance to farmers. These major programs are outlined in the following questions, and the reader who worked through the previous questions and answers should have enough skill in economics to at least begin analyzing these policies.

QUESTIONS FOR EXERCISE 3

1. *Price Supports* One way the government supports farm income is through price supports. Government targets a certain support price for a specific commodity and then buys the agricultural product if its price drops below that support price. Outright purchases of some commodities are made by the government, but the more usual method is the price support loan. Farmers use their crops as collateral to obtain loans from the Commodity Credit Corporation, a government corporation, and the collateral value placed on each bushel of wheat is the official support price. Let's say the official support price is $3 per bushel. If the actual market price at the time the wheat is harvested is above the support price of $3 per bushel, farmers will sell the wheat in the market and pay off their loan to the CCC. If the market price is less than $3, farmers will default on the loan and let the government take the wheat. The farmer is guaranteed a price of at least $3 per bushel no matter what happens.

   a. Using a simple supply and demand graph, show the effects of wheat support prices set at prices above the free market level.

   b. Analyze some other effects of this price support program. (*Hint:* consumer prices, storage costs.)

2. *Acreage Restriction* Periodically since the 1930s the government has sought to *restrict* agricultural production in order to limit costly purchases and storage of the commodities. The government wanted to reduce both the government and private resource costs associated with producing farm goods that were simply placed in storage to rot. It was thought that if the farmer could be paid not to produce surplus goods the government and the farmers would benefit, hence, the origin of the soil bank programs in which the federal government pays farmers to place their land in "soil banks" that cannot be used to produce crops. More than 25 percent of American farmland was in "soil banks" during the mid-eighties.

a. Assume that the quantity of agricultural production exceeds the quantity demanded by 20 percent and the Department of Agriculture reduces the quantity of land available by 20 percent, say from 50 million acres to 40 million acres. It pays farmers to put 10 million acres in the soil bank. Using a simple supply and demand graph, show the effects of government restricting the amount of land available for consumption so that at the support price of $3 the quantity supplied will just equal the quantity demanded.

b. Analyze some further effects of this soil bank program? Do you think that a withdrawal of 20 percent of American farmland from agricultural production results in a 20-percent decrease in agricultural production? Why? Do you think that the cost per unit of farm output is affected? Why?

3. *Target Price Subsidies* A relatively new farm subsidy program is the target price subsidy program. The Department of Agriculture simply targets a particular price, say $3 per bushel of wheat. If the market price is at or above that price, the government does nothing. However, if the price is below $3, it pays the difference to the farmers. For example, if the market price is $2, it will pay $1 per bushel to the farmers.

a. Analyze the effects of this program with a simple supply and demand graph.

b. Analyze some further effects of this program.

4. *Impact of Domestic Agricultural Subsidy Programs on International Trade*
As mentioned in the rent-control exercise above, the passage of one law that attempts to alter the market process usually requires other legislation. One repercussion of the domestic subsidies programs for agricultural products is reflected in international trade.

Analyze the impact of the price support and soil bank programs on international trade. (*Hint:* If government policy is to increase the domestic price of farm products, what happens to exports?)

ANSWERS TO EXERCISE 3

1. a. Refer to Figure 3-5. Price supports are placed above the expected market level. If the government's wheat support price is $3 per bushel and the free market price is $2, the higher guaranteed price brings forth a greater quantity supplied to Q_3 while decreasing the quantity demanded to Q_2. The result is a surplus ($Q_3 - Q_2$) of wheat, which is purchased and stored by the government.

b. If support prices are higher than market prices, farmers are induced to produce more wheat while consumers are encouraged to consume less. Taxpayers not only have to pay higher prices to buy the wheat but they also have to pay the subsidies to the farmer for wheat not consumed as well as the costs of storing it. Part of the

-- **FIGURE 3-5** --

PRICE SUPPORTS ON WHEAT

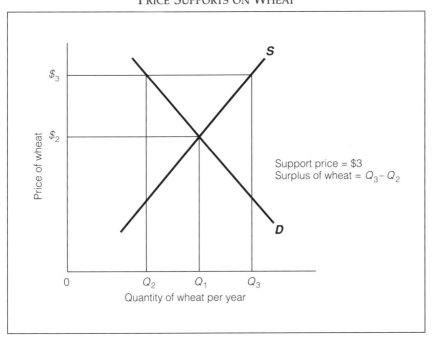

Support price = $3
Surplus of wheat = $Q_3 - Q_2$

country's real resources will have to be diverted from producing other goods to building and maintaining storage silos. Much of the wheat will rot in storage. The United States actually has more than an entire year's consumption of wheat in storage.

2. **a.** Refer to Figure 3-6. The free market price is P_1, and quantity con-sumed is Q_1. If government establishes a target price of P_2 and calculates that production will be Q_3, it will have to take out of pro-duction an amount of land necessary to reduce output to Q_2. If government pays farmers to soil bank the requisite amount of land, the supply curve will become vertical at Q_2. This curve assumes that the amount of production per acre is fixed and that farmers cannot vary the mix of inputs on their remaining land. The supply curve, in effect, becomes vertical at that quantity (Q_2) of production that can be supported by 40 million acres. Price is driven to the target level of P_2, and farmers produce and sell Q_2, which costs them only P_3 per unit to produce. Consumers pay a higher price for a smaller quantity.

b. The problem with the analysis in 2.a. is that farmers are much better economists than assumed in that answer. Farmers are not going to take out of production a random 10 million acres and see their pro-duction drop by 20 percent (from Q_3 to Q_2). They will place in the

---
FIGURE 3-6 ---
SOIL BANK PROGRAM ASSUMING FIXED INPUT RATIOS

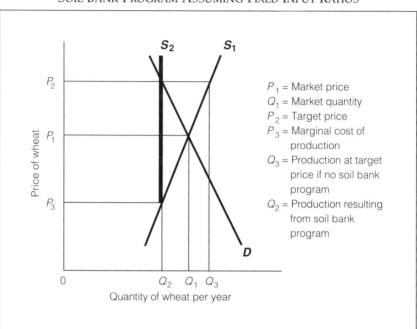

P_1 = Market price
Q_1 = Market quantity
P_2 = Target price
P_3 = Marginal cost of
     production
Q_3 = Production at target
     price if no soil bank
     program
Q_2 = Production resulting
     from soil bank
     program

soil bank the acres that are the least productive and the most time-consuming to maintain. Since they no longer have to use their other inputs, such as labor and fertilizer, to farm the "soil bank" land, they will use some of that labor and fertilizer on the 40 million acres remaining in cultivation. These more realistic assumptions are shown in Figure 3-7. The supply curve is no longer vertical because farmers can take 10 million acres out of production but farm the remaining 40 million acres more intensively. The higher the support price of wheat, the more fertilizer and labor the farmers will devote to the 40 million acres and, thus, the greater the production will be. At the target price of P_2, farmers will supply Q_4 units while the quantity demanded by consumers will be only Q_2. The government will have to purchase and store ($Q_4 - Q_2$) in order to maintain the support price. Each cultivated acre will now produce more wheat, and the quantity supplied under the soil bank program will be only, say, 10 percent less than without the soil bank program. If the Department of Agriculture wanted to decrease production by 20 percent they would have to reduce the land available by, say, 30 percent.

Consumers pay the same price for wheat as they did in 2.a. but the quantity produced is greater than consumers want, so the government must pay to store the surplus of $Q_4 - Q_2$. Taxpayers have to pay

FIGURE 3-7

SOIL BANK PROGRAM ASSUMING VARIABLE INPUT RATIOS

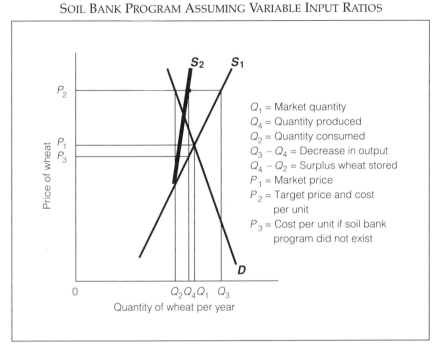

Q_1 = Market quantity
Q_4 = Quantity produced
Q_2 = Quantity consumed
$Q_3 - Q_4$ = Decrease in output
$Q_4 - Q_2$ = Surplus wheat stored
P_1 = Market price
P_2 = Target price and cost
per unit
P_3 = Cost per unit if soil bank
program did not exist

the farmers for the land they put into the soil bank and for purchasing and storing the surplus produced. Another effect of this soil bank program is to increase the per unit cost of wheat. The cost per unit of output has increased from P_3 to P_2 because farmers are unable to use the preferred cost-minimizing combination of resources. They would prefer to use more land and less fertilizer and labor to produce Q_3, but the soil bank "forces" them to use a less preferred and more costly combination.

3. **a.**   Refer to Figure 3-8. Farmers know that the minimum price they will receive for their wheat is $3 per bushel, so they will plan on producing at least that amount. If no government program existed, farmers would produce Q_1 at price P_1, say $2.50. However, since they expect to receive a price of $3, they will produce Q_2. When they sell the quantity Q_2, consumers will pay only $2 per bushel. Hence the amount of the subsidy provided to farmers is ($3 – $2) × Q_2.

b.   Previous programs required taxpayers to pay storage or land payment costs and higher prices for the commodity. This program requires consumers to pay subsidies to the farmers, but it also enables consumers to pay lower prices for the product. In addition to farmers, the target price subsidy tends to benefit those who have intensive

---
FIGURE 3-8
TARGET PRICE SUBSIDIES

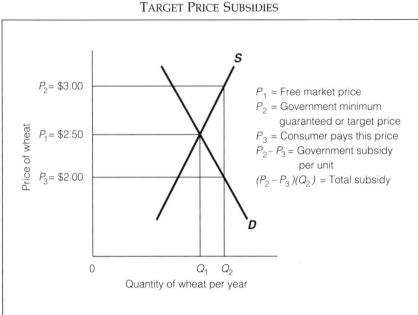

P_1 = Free market price
P_2 = Government minimum
       guaranteed or target price
P_3 = Consumer pays this price
$P_2 - P_3$ = Government subsidy
       per unit
$(P_2 - P_3)(Q_2)$ = Total subsidy

P_2= $3.00

P_1= $2.50

P_3= $2.00

Price of wheat

0   Q_1 Q_2
Quantity of wheat per year

preferences for the supported product because the price they pay is subsidized by taxpayers. They pay $2 per bushel rather than the free market price of $2.50.

4. Price supports and soil bank programs result in higher prices of agricultural products in the United States than in other countries. These higher prices would encourage an inflow of foreign products to the United States until the world price has been brought up to the American price level. If there were no import restrictions, the Department of Agriculture would, in effect, be supporting or subsidizing the world prices of agricultural products. This would entail enormous and unacceptable budgetary expenditures for the government. Consequently, the United States has placed limits, or quotas, on the importation of many agricultural products. One of the results of our domestic agricultural subsidy programs is the limitation on international free trade and the benefits that it could provide consumers. Many European countries also subsidize agricultural products, so it is not surprising that free trade negotiations often fail because the parties cannot agree on the treatment of agricultural imports.

Another implication of our agricultural policy is its effect on American agricultural exports. Foreign consumers will not purchase agricultural products from the United States if they have to pay the high prices that exist in the United States because of price supports. Consequently, prices for exported products are "subsidized," or sold for lower prices in foreign countries than they are in the United States. If these exports are taken from government storage bins where the products would otherwise have rotted, clearly the low export price is better than no price at all. However, very often these products are shipped from current production, and support prices are determined, at least in part, on the premise that certain quantities of an agricultural product will be exported. If the support price is $3 per bushel, no farmer is going to export his wheat if the international price is $1.70 per bushel. Hence, the government provides a subsidy of $1.30 per bushel to the farmer who exports. The farmer is going to produce a quantity of wheat up to the point where $MC = MR$. Hence, we know that the marginal value of resources used in producing the last bushel of wheat is $3, but that unit is provided to foreigners at only $1.70. In effect, the combination of domestic price supports and export subsidies has resulted in Americans expending $3 worth of resources to produce a good to send to a foreign country in return for goods or services worth $1.70. American politicians and the media spend much time discussing whether the prices that foreigners charge us for their products are "fair"; such time might be better spent examining whether the prices of American exports accurately reflect their real marginal costs to American residents.

SUMMARY TO EXERCISE 3

The fundamental problem of American agriculture is that too many resources are committed to its production. The tremendous expansion in technology has enabled American farmers to produce more than Americans want to consume at prices that are necessary to retain these resources in agriculture. Obviously, the simple answer is that farmers, land, and other agricultural resources should exit from the farming industry and move into other industries where their returns would be higher. Such mobility happens routinely in most other industries when demand decreases (blacksmiths) or technology changes (telephone operators). It has also happened in agriculture, but at a slower pace than required to avoid surpluses. During World War I, when the population of the United States was about 100 million, there were about 7 million farmers (owners, tenants, and workers). Today, the population is 245 million, and there are about 2 million farmers.

Despite their dwindling numbers, farmers have worked hard to get Congress to establish and maintain special subsidies. They view farming as a way of life that would be altered drastically if they had to leave their farms and search for other employment (their supply is relatively inelastic). They also have a considerable investment in their land, buildings, and machinery, which would lose considerable value if the subsidies were eliminated. They have used many arguments to convince congressional representatives that these subsidies should be continued. A few of these arguments are the following: "the family farm should be maintained as an American institution"; "farm surpluses should be stored to cover uncertainties in future production"; "economic and social forces are pulling people off the farms, and unless the trend is stabilized, agricultural production will decrease sharply within a few decades"; "it's easy to destroy the human and physical capital that has been invested in agriculture over the past 200 years, but it's very difficult to put such withdrawn resources back into farming." This is not the place to analyze each of these arguments, but the reader might want to apply the economic analysis learned in this chapter to them. The following analysis of the winners and losers of agricultural subsidies might provide some assistance.

Soil bank payments are based on the quantity of land placed in the soil bank. While there are many regulations governing such banked land, the more land owned by the farmer, the greater the amount can be placed in the soil bank. The more wheat produced by the farmer, the greater the total subsidy received by the farmer in price supports. Hence, large and productive farms receive large payments; small and unproductive farms receive small payments. It is not surprising that the 5 percent of the farms with the greatest sales received more than one-third of the $30 billion of agricultural subsidies in the mid-eighties. Statistics even worse than these motivated Congress to pass limits on the payments made to individual farmers in certain subsidy programs. As one might expect, farmers quickly formed separate corporate entities and entered joint ventures with family members or "subdivided" their farms so that the maximum could be paid to each "owner."

The large payments made to farmers did not produce such increases in their net incomes. Some of the inefficient farms used these payments to cover the real expenses of the resources associated with production. All farmers had to pay somewhat higher prices for certain resources associated with production because the subsidized production drove up demand and prices for the inputs. The resources that increased most in price were those that were inelastic in supply. A cursory examination of the agricultural industry suggests that the resource with the most inelastic supply is cultivatable land. Most of the fertile land is already in cultivation, and adding more would require bidding it away from residential, commercial, or industrial uses or converting infertile land into fertile land. Much higher prices would be required to bring forth this additional land. Hence, one resource that has received higher payments as a result of agricultural subsidies is fertile land. Owners of farm land benefit, but those who currently own the land are not necessarily those who benefit. When the current owners purchased the land, they paid a price that included expectations that agriculture products would be subsidized. Hence, those who benefitted the most were those who owned the land when the agricultural subsidies were announced. Many owners of farm land in the fertile Midwest who purchased their land in the twenties or thirties and sold it in the early seventies made large capital gains. They were the ones who benefitted most from the country's farm subsidies. Others who gained slight benefits (because of more elastic demands) from farm support policies were the suppliers of services, goods, and equipment to the farmers, such as feed and farm implement companies. The losers were the taxpayers who paid the subsidies, consumers who paid higher prices, and businesses—breweries, for example—whose productive processes utilized inputs of agricultural products.

CHAPTER FOUR

THE POLITICAL MARKET AND PUBLIC GOODS

*Society in every state is a blessing, but Government, even in its best state,
is but a necessary evil; in its worse state, an intolerable one.*
—THOMAS PAINE, *COMMON SENSE*

The happiness of society is the end of governments.
—JOHN ADAMS, *THOUGHTS ON GOVERNMENT*

GROWTH OF THE POLITICAL MARKET

At the beginning of the century federal government employees accounted
for only 1 percent of the civilian labor force, and federal expenditures were
less than 3 percent of the GNP. Both ratios rose during World War I but
decreased to the low prewar levels during the Coolidge years of the
twenties. The Depression stimulated increases in federal government
expenditures, but these changes were miniscule compared with the growth
in federal expenditures during World War II, when they accounted for a
whopping 45 percent of the GNP. Federal expenditures represented a
smaller proportion of the GNP in the latter forties, but they remained at
relative levels nearly three times higher than in the twenties. Starting in
the latter fifties federal expenditures continued to increase steadily until
they accounted for nearly one-quarter of the GNP in 1985. Contrary to
expectations, federal government employment has been *decreasing* as a
percent of the civilian labor force. In fact, in relative importance it has
decreased by nearly 30 percent since 1955, and federal employment was
a smaller percent of the civilian labor force in 1985 than in any year since
1940 (see Table 4-1). Federal employment has grown much less rapidly
than federal expenditures, primarily because much of the increase in
government expenditures consists of transfer payments to individuals and
expenditures for goods and services provided directly by firms.

The federal government has been the most important but certainly
not the only source of government expenditure growth; while local government expenditures as a percentage of the GNP have only doubled since

──────────────────── **TABLE 4-1** ────────────────────
GOVERNMENT GROWTH: FEDERAL, STATE, AND LOCAL GOVERNMENT GROWTH
EMPLOYMENT AS A PERCENT OF THE CIVILIAN LABOR FORCE

	Total Government	Federal Civilian	State	Local
1910		1.1%		
1920		1.6		
1930		1.2		
1935		1.5		
1940	8.0%	2.0	1.2%	4.8%
1945	12.7	6.3	1.4	5.0
1950	10.3	3.4	1.7	5.2
1955	11.4	3.7	1.8	5.9
1960	12.7	3.5	2.2	7.0
1965	14.2	3.5	2.7	8.0
1970	15.8	3.5	3.3	8.9
1975	16.0	3.1	3.5	9.4
1980	15.2	2.7	3.5	8.9
1985	14.5	2.6	3.4	8.4

SOURCE: U.S. Bureau of Labor Statistics

the beginning of the century, state government expenditures have grown almost as fast as federal government expenditures (see Table 4-2), and the growth in the number of state employees since 1940 has been much greater. The net result is that in the latter eighties total government employees accounted for nearly 15 percent of the total labor force and total government expenditures were nearly 40 percent of the GNP. Since government purchases most of its goods from the private market, this 40 percent doesn't mean that the private market produces only 60 percent of the GNP. However, it does mean that decisions about the initial allocation of 40 percent of the GNP is made through the political mechanism rather than through the private market mechanism.

A few decades ago some economists thought that government expenditures equal to about 25 percent of the GNP were the maximum the economy could tolerate during peacetime. Less than twenty years ago economists thought that government could grow no larger than 33 percent of the GNP. We now know, as we should have known then, that there was nothing magical about the 25-percent or 33-percent levels. However, many economists still worry that government is too large and that, while the economy might not collapse if it becomes even larger, it could become

--------------------------------- TABLE 4-2 ---------------------------------
GOVERNMENT GROWTH: FEDERAL, STATE, AND LOCAL GOVERNMENT
EXPENDITURES AS A PERCENT OF THE GNP*

	Total Government	Federal	State	Local
1902	7.7%	2.6%	0.6%	4.4%
1913	8.2	2.4	0.8	5.1
1922	12.6	4.9	1.5	6.2
1927	11.9	3.6	1.6	6.7
1936	20.4	10.1	2.9	7.4
1940	20.6	9.2	3.6	7.7
1945	51.6	44.9	2.3	4.3
1950	24.7	14.9	3.8	6.0
1955	27.8	17.7	3.6	6.5
1960	30.0	17.9	4.4	7.7
1965	30.0	17.4	4.6	8.1
1970	32.8	18.2	5.5	9.0
1975	35.0	18.3	6.7	10.1
1980	35.1	19.3	6.3	9.5
1985	39.4	23.1	6.7	9.7
1986	40.0	23.1	6.9	10.0

* Intergovernment transfers are excluded.

SOURCES: *Historical Statistics of the United States* and *Statistical Abstracts of the United States*

increasingly less efficient and more difficult to control. At the beginning
of the century the federal government obtained virtually all of its revenue
from custom duties, and local governments obtained their revenues from
property taxes and fees (see Table 4-3). There was no income tax in the
early 1900s. (The United States had adopted an income tax in 1861 as a
temporary measure to help finance the Civil War, but the tax was repealed
in 1871.) When Congress tried to reinstate the income tax a couple of
decades later, the Supreme Court declared it unconstitutional. The
Sixteenth Amendment to the U.S. Constitution, ratified in 1913, enabled
Congress to levy an income tax. The initial income tax legislation exempted
the first $3,000 from taxation and taxed the remainder of income at
graduated rates, ranging from 1 percent for incomes up to $20,000 to as
high as 7 percent for incomes over $500,000. These brackets were so high
relative to income levels at the time that less than 1 percent of the population actually paid income taxes. The top rate was increased to 77 percent
to help finance World War I, but it was reduced to 25 percent during the
twenties. Roosevelt's New Deal program increased the top rate to 78 percent

TABLE 4-3

SOURCES OF ALL GOVERNMENT REVENUE

	Total Revenue	Individual Income Tax	Corporate Income Tax	Sales & Custom Taxes	Property Taxes	Charges	Other	Trust Funds
1902	$ 1.7	7.8%		30.3%	41.5%	15.2%	12.6%	0.0%
1927	12.2	7.8%	11.1%	12.8	38.8	17.2	10.4	1.9
1936	13.6	6.0	6.3	24.9	30.1	14.4	16.0	2.3
1946	61.5	26.9	20.0	16.2	8.1	14.2	7.5	7.1
1960	153.1	28.2	14.8	16.0	10.7	11.4	7.4	11.5
1970	333.8	30.3	11.0	14.6	10.2	11.9	6.3	15.8
1980	932.2	30.7	8.4	12.0	7.3	15.3	5.9	20.4
1985	1,418.0	28.3	5.6	12.3	7.3	17.3	6.2	22.8
1986	1,516.0	27.9	5.5	12.0	7.4	17.3	6.0	23.9

SOURCES: *Historical Statistics of the United States* and *Statistical Abstracts of the United States.*

by 1936, it was further increased to 94 percent during World War II, and it remained above 90 percent until 1964, when it was reduced to 70 percent. In 1981 the top rate was reduced to 50 percent and was further reduced to 33 percent by the Tax Reform Act of 1986. The practice of withholding income tax payments on payday was instituted during World War II.

By the end of World War II, the personal income tax had become the most important revenue producer for the federal government. It accounted for about 45 percent of all federal revenue and nearly 28 percent of all government revenue in 1986. The corporate income tax accounted for 17 percent of federal revenue and 11 percent of all government revenue in 1970, but its relative importance gradually diminished to only 9 percent of federal government revenue and less than 6 percent of all government revenue in 1986. Despite its slightly decreasing importance during the past few years, the United States relies more heavily upon the income tax to finance public goods than most other countries. New Zealand is one glaring exception. It obtains about 60 percent of its tax revenue from the personal income tax and another 7 percent through corporate income taxes. Canada raises 37 percent of its revenue from personal and 14 percent from corporate income taxes. The personal income tax is responsible for 32 percent of tax revenue in Britain, 25 percent in Italy, and about 15 percent in West Germany, Norway, and Sweden. Throughout the world, countries raise an average of only 10 percent of their revenues from income taxes, because less developed nations rely primarily on import and export taxes.

Custom duties collected by the federal government were important sources of revenue through the twenties, but with the exception of a few excise taxes, sales taxes did not exist in the United States until cities and states began introducing them during the twenties and thirties. Then local sales taxes began increasing as federal tariff revenues fell off. Retail sales and excise taxes now account for nearly one-half of state tax revenue and about one-eighth of all government revenue. The relative importance of property tax revenue fell the most among the sources of government revenue. Property taxes accounted for nearly three-fourths of all state and local government revenue at the beginning of the century, decreasing to 30 percent of state and local revenue by the mid-fifties and to only 15 percent by the mid-eighties. Property tax revenues dropped from more than 40 percent of all government revenues in 1902 to less than 8 percent in 1985. The most significant growth in government revenues occurred in trust fund revenues, particularly among retirement and Social Security revenues.

Table 4-4 presents a short but interesting overview of shifting government priorities during the century. Education expenditures remained fairly constant in relative terms; defense and foreign affairs increased during World War II, decreased after the end of the conflict, but remained high during the cold war and the Vietnam years. They fell rapidly during the latter

TABLE 4-4
GOVERNMENT EXPENDITURES

	1902	1927	1936	1946	1960	1970	1980	1985
Total (in billions)	$1.7	$11.2	$16.8	$79.7	$151.2	$333.0	$958.7	$1,581.0
Defense/Foreign*	9.9%	5.5%	5.6%	63.3%	32.3%	25.3%	15.6%	16.5%
Education	15.5%	20.0%	14.1%	4.7%	12.8%	16.7%	15.0%	13.0%
Streets/Highways	10.5%	16.2%	11.6%	2.1%	6.3%	5.0%	3.5%	2.9%
Welfare	2.5%	1.4%	5.9%	1.8%	2.9%	5.3%	6.8%	6.0%
Health/Hospitals	3.8%	3.8%	3.5%	1.4%	3.5%	4.1%	4.5%	4.0%
Police/Fire	5.4%	4.4%	3.2%	1.1%	2.0%	2.1%	2.2%	2.1%
Sewerage	3.1%	2.8%	1.2%	0.5%	1.1%	1.0%	1.4%	1.1%
National Resources**	2.8%	3.2%	13.5%	4.1%	5.2%	4.0%	4.5%	4.5%
Housing	0.0%	0.0%	0.4%	0.3%	0.8%	1.0%	1.3%	1.2%
Interest	5.8%	12.0%	8.7%	5.4%	6.2%	5.5%	7.9%	10.9%
Veterans	8.5%	5.2%	4.2%	3.2%	2.5%	1.6%	1.3%	1.1%
Utilities	4.9%	4.4%	4.2%	2.2%	3.4%	2.8%	3.8%	3.8%
Social Security, etc.	0.0%	1.2%	1.3%	3.0%	11.6%	14.6%	20.8%	20.8%
Other	27.2%	19.7%	22.8%	7.0%	9.3%	10.9%	11.5%	12.0%

* Includes expenditures for defense and foreign affairs.
** Includes expenditures for parks and recreation and for farm price and income supports.
SOURCES: *Historical Statistics of the United States* and *Statistical Abstracts of the United States.*

seventies and stabilized during the eighties. Social Security expenditures grew the most rapidly, followed by welfare and interest payments. The growth in the size of post–World War II governments, as well as shifts in revenue and expenditures, was the primary motivation for economists to begin analyzing the political market. When governments' major sources of revenue were custom duties and when its expenditures—a small percentage of the GNP— went to finance such public goods as national defense and streets, which benefitted all citizens, there was little interest in government efficiency or limits on government discretionary powers. Because today's governments spend 40 percent of the GNP, raise revenues from many sources, and provide valuable benefits to specific groups of individuals, they have become too significant and powerful for economists to ignore.

PUBLIC GOODS

Microeconomic theory of the private market is composed of three major stages: (1) a determination of the efficiency conditions ($P = MC$), (2) an examination of systems that, under certain assumptions, can satisfy the efficiency conditions (such as pure competition), and (3) a discussion of the effects on efficiency produced by the introduction of various impediments and distortions (such as monopolies, externalities, and ignorance). Microeconomic theory of the political market will be developed in the same three stages, but first we need to discuss the reasons a political market is necessary in a free society. Even if the private market functioned perfectly and even if everyone in society were satisfied with the distribution of income generated by the private market, there would still be a need for the political market to provide a certain class of goods for which efficiency can be approximated only through collective provision. Collectivization is not synonymous with the political market, because there is a third market—the charity market—in which goods are collectively, but voluntarily, provided without intervention by government institutions. This third market presents an interesting and formidable challenge to social scientists, and some analytical and empirical work has been done on the charity market. However, it is still relatively undeveloped and will not be discussed here.[1] This chapter will explore the

---

[1] The nature of public goods and the free rider problem suggest that public goods be provided through a collective mechanism. Most economists believe this collective mechanism to be the political market. However, a third market—the charity market—is a collective mechanism that can and does provide public goods. Its decision-making mechanism and its selective incentives to ameliorate the free rider problem differ from those in the political market and are discussed in Thomas R. Ireland and David B. Johnson, *The Economies of Charity* (Blacksburg, VA: Center for the Study of Public Choice, 1970); in Art Seldon, ed., *Economics of Charity* (London: Hobart Papers [Institute of Economic Affairs], 1973); and Harold M. Hockman and James D. Rodgers, "Pareto Optimal Redistribution," *American Economic Review* (September 1969): 542–57.

characteristics of public goods and examine the reasons they cannot be provided efficiently through the private market.

David Hume (1711–1776) began the discussion of a class of goods that economists now call public goods,[2] and he provided the argument for the existence of government in a society of free persons.

> Two neighbors may agree to drain a meadow, which they possess in common; because it is easy for them to know each other's mind; and each must perceive, that the immediate consequences of his failing in his part, is the abandoning of the whole project. But it is very difficult, and indeed impossible, that a thousand persons should agree in any such action; it being difficult for them to concert so complicated a design, and still more difficult for them to execute it; while each seeks a pretext to free himself of the trouble and expense, and would lay the whole burden on others. . . . [3]

The sentences are complex, but Hume's concept is simple. Hume recognized a fundamental principle in collective decision making. If there were only a few farmers bordering the watershed, it would be relatively easy for neighbors to get together and say, "I'll clear the stumps if Clem will build the earthen dam and Zeke will plow the terraces." The costs of collective decision making are low when only a few individuals are involved, and the identification of the *free rider*—the person who attempts to enjoy the benefits without contributing to the project—is easy. However, when there are a thousand individuals benefitting from the drainage project, it is difficult to get them to agree to the design of the project and to contribute their share of time or materials. The identification of the free rider is now much more difficult, and many farmers can "hide" in the anonymity of large numbers. Each farmer can attempt a free ride on the efforts of others, and the meadow will not be drained. Hence, Hume recommended the use of government to finance the construction of the drainage project.

During the past few decades political economists have formalized Hume's analysis by clearly separating the concepts of private and public goods. An essential characteristic of *private goods* is that individuals can be excluded from enjoying their benefits, and the consumption of a private good by one individual means that another individual cannot consume that same good. Bread is a good example of a private good. If an individual does not pay for a loaf of bread, the seller can exclude that individual from

---

[2] The terms "collective good" and "public good" are used interchangeably by most economists. Note that "public good" does not imply a moral or value judgment about that good. Public good is a technical term used to differentiate a certain class of goods (public) from other goods (private). As always, one individual's public good might be another's public bad.

[3] David Hume, *A Treatise of Human Nature* (1740), ed. L. A. Selby-Bigge (Oxford: Clarendon Press, 1960), 538.

consuming it; if an individual pays for it and eats it, other individuals are not able to consume that same loaf of bread. This characteristic of excludability is important because if individuals can be excluded from enjoying the benefits of a private good, then the seller can say to the potential consumer, "If you want to enjoy the benefits of this good, you must pay for it. If you don't pay, you don't enjoy." As shown in chapter 3, the private market can provide such private goods quite nicely.

The private market, however, cannot provide *public goods*, because individuals feasibly cannot be excluded from enjoying their benefits. When economists search through their bag of examples to illustrate a public good they invariably come up with national defense. The benefits provided by a nuclear submarine patrolling the oceans are available to all citizens in the country, and the submarine cannot be divided or segmented to benefit some citizens and not others. National defense is a public good, regardless of the preferences of particular citizens for defense expenditures. A "hawk" enjoys the benefits of a submarine keeping potential enemies at bay, while a "dove" suffers the disutility of a "militaristic" policy. Both hawks and doves, however, cannot be excluded from "consuming" these public costs and benefits. This nonexclusion is what makes the submarine a public good. The hawk cannot be excluded from enjoying the protection offered by the submarine, and the dove cannot be excluded from suffering the humiliation. Another example of a public good is the elimination or reduction of a *public bad* such as air pollution. A person who does not pay to reduce air pollution cannot be excluded from enjoying the resulting cleaner air. The polluted air, which affects all citizens, is a public bad, and the cleaning of the polluted air is a public good.

Externalities, which were discussed in chapter 3, are one of the major causes of private market failure. When externalities in production or consumption are pervasive, they define a purely public good. For example, the provision of a submarine by one individual will create significant positive externalities for other citizens, because such a provision will increase the welfare of all other individuals in the country (assuming there are no doves). The existence of such extensive and pervasive externalities in the provision of a submarine suggests that submarines are pure public goods. Few externalities, however, are so pervasive. The household that manicures its front lawn, the firm that emits smoke that falls on a neighbor's laundry, the teenager whose record player induces insomnia in the neighborhood, and the automobile owner who drives with faulty brakes are examples of activities that produce externalities, or public goods or bads, of a more limited nature. Quasi public goods are private goods that generate some externalities.

A common mistake made by beginning students in political economy is to identify goods according to the classification of the provider of the goods. They classify those goods provided by private firms and sold through the price mechanism as private goods, and they classify those goods provided by government or through the political mechanism as public goods. However, this is *not* the correct way to classify private and public goods. A good does not become a public good simply because it is provided by government.

A city park, for example, is *not* a public good because it is financed by city taxes and administered by the city's park and recreation department. It is quite feasible for the city to construct a fence around the park and to charge admission. Disney World, African Safari, various private "gardens," and government-owned and -operated parks, zoos, and museums that charge admission testify to the fact that nonpayers can be excluded from enjoying a park's attractions. A city park is essentially a private good that is provided by government. However, it is possible that a park may generate some genuine public good benefits. For example, a park with many trees and vegetation may generate oxygen, purify the air, and lower the temperature of the surrounding area on a hot, sunny day. These "goods" are genuine public goods (they emit significant externalities) because it is not possible to exclude city residents from enjoying these benefits. They can enjoy these benefits whether or not they pay a park fee or even enter a park. Hence, a park provides many benefits to city residents. It provides a refuge from the turmoil of the city and an opportunity to see flowers blooming, to ride a boat in the lagoon, to enjoy a brown bag lunch under a tree, or to play a game of baseball with friends. These are the private goods provided by the park, because it is feasible to exclude nonpayers from enjoying these benefits just as nonpayers are excluded from enjoying the benefits of Yellowstone or Yosemite, which charge entrance fees and deny entrance to those who do not pay. A park also generates such benefits as clean air, higher values of private property located along its edges, and cooler temperatures. These are public goods from which nonpaying individuals cannot be excluded.

So far the discussion of public goods has proceeded quite logically and clearly. (If it is not clear, reread the above three paragraphs). However, there is a gray area in the conceptualization of public goods that has bedeviled neophytes and professionals. Let's sneak up on this gray area by assuming that our city park has facilities for baseball, basketball, tennis, soccer, and other sports. Clearly—or is it clear?—these facilities are private goods. Fences could exclude those who do not pay to use them. However, assume that gangs of teenagers have been roaming residential streets and roughing up citizens, stealing from stores, and generally making a "public" nuisance of themselves. Let's further assume that several social science studies have proven conclusively that boys who participate in sports are less likely to belong to such gangs. Assume that if the facilities of the park could be made readily available to these youth, the city's crime rate would go down. Is the park with such facilities a private or a public good? It is a private good because citizens could be excluded from enjoying its facilities. *It is also a private good to the young gang members who use it.* However, the use of the facilities by young men who might otherwise be participating in gang activities would be a public good to citizens of the city. If the city crime rate were reduced because young men were utilizing the park's facilities, all citizens would benefit (fewer crimes, lower insurance rates, more secure feelings). Citizens would enjoy these crime-reduction benefits from the park whether they used the park or not or whether they ever paid an admission fee or not. Hence, this use of the park would generate the genuine public good of increasing the quality of life for the citizens of the city.

Let's take another example. Education is clearly a private good because the benefits of education accrue primarily to those who are educated and those who do not pay tuition can be excluded from classrooms. Those who provide public education services (administrators and faculty) frequently claim that education should be supported by generous public expenditures because it is a public good. Education, they argue, provides a public good by training young men and women to become engineers, journalists, doctors, and lawyers (economists are never mentioned). However, this justification for classifying education as a public good is fallacious. The country would have engineers, journalists, doctors, or lawyers even if there were no public schools. Shortages in such occupations would very quickly drive up salaries in these occupations, and it would profit a young person (or his or her parents) to pay for a private education or to borrow money to pay tuition. Many skilled chefs, for example, have received little formal public education but have gone to private chef schools and, shortly after leaving these schools, are earning substantial incomes that reflect the value of their services to their fellow citizens. When confronted with this argument, the providers of education say that education is a public good because those who receive the education will repay the public through higher tax payments later in their lives. This, too, is a fallacious argument because it assumes (1) that education is necessary to earn a high income and to pay high taxes and (2) that only individuals educated in subsidized public schools will earn high incomes and pay high taxes.

Assume that a young woman does not go to college and works part-time and saves $30,000 to open a business that soon becomes a successful national firm. Ten years later she is earning an income of $200,000 a year, and other members of society are benefitting from the services her business is providing. A second young woman receives a "free" public education worth $30,000 and becomes a lawyer earning $200,000 a year. Both the woman who invested her own money in a business and the woman who received a subsidized education will pay the same taxes later in life. If taxes are viewed as paying for public education received in earlier years, why should the businesswoman be taxed at the same rate as the lawyer? Why should one who financed his or her own education in a private school be taxed at all? Why should the state permit those young people who received an education to move to another state before repaying their debt to the state that financed their education?[4] In fact, the woman who forsook an education to start her own business will end up paying more taxes because she will have had to pay taxes on the income she earned as a youth.

Distribution of the tax burdens and the benefits from education are not conceptually related, and each issue should be decided on its own merits. Education is not a public good because students become brain surgeons, paper shufflers, or economists who write books few people read. The country could obtain these skills from individuals educated in private institutions. Education is not a public good because students may pay higher taxes later in life. Education is a quasi public good because, presumably, it makes these students better persons and citizens in society, that is, they are more pleasant to live with. Individuals who have received an education *presumably* take more interest in public affairs, vote more often and intelligently, and develop more collegial social attitudes. These are public good benefits (positive externalities) from which nonpayers cannot be excluded. Even childless citizens benefit from the education of others' children because they enjoy some of the social benefits of having better-educated citizens.

Some economists have used the term "merit goods" to describe some private goods such as education, subsidized school lunches, subsidized

---

[4] The concept that public education is provided because the beneficiaries will repay their education subsidy through higher tax payments in the future is not only poor logic, it can also produce problems for a democratic society. The justification that Eastern European countries used to prohibit the emigration of their citizens is that the émigrés had not repaid their debt to the society that educated them. It is a completely logical argument once one accepts the premise that education is an investment in human capital made by the state. In fact, the prohibition of emigration by those educated in public institutions would have even greater support in societies where private and public education coexist. The Jewish scientist denied emigration papers by the Soviet government because he has not repaid his debt to the Soviet people for educating him could always say that he had no choice about where he got his education. He had to go to a publicly financed university because there were no private ones available. A person educated in a publicly financed university in Britain or the United States could not use this argument—if the British or the American government prohibited emigration—because private schools are available.

low-cost housing, and food stamps.[5] *Merit goods* are private goods that could be offered through the private market but are offered or financed through the political market because citizens believe that if they are left solely to private market provision, some people would not consume a sufficient quantity of such goods. Hence, many textbooks state that the public sector provides public goods and merit goods. However, a closer examination of merit goods reveals that they are merely a subclass of public goods. Merit goods are private goods to those whose consumption is subsidized, but they are public goods to citizens who are financing them. Education is a quasi public good because the provision of education provides some public benefits to all citizens, and the beneficiaries cannot be excluded from these benefits. The same is true of welfare programs.

Assume that the Poore family lives in a dilapidated shack and that 50,000 citizens in the city would prefer to see the Poore family have better housing. "Better housing for the Poores" is now a public good. If public housing is provided for the Poores, none of the 50,000 citizens can be excluded from enjoying the very real benefits of seeing the Poores live in improved housing. It is also a merit good because it is a private good to the Poores, who consume it directly, but a public good to all other citizens. In addition to national defense, foreign policy, and certain environmental issues, the elimination of slums, hunger, and ignorance are excellent examples of pure public goods. They potentially benefit all citizens.

FREE RIDERS

The reason government, rather than the private sector, must provide public goods is the existence of the free rider problem. If a private firm were to attempt to "sell" a public good or service, individuals would not "buy" it because they would know that they could not be excluded from enjoying the benefits whether they purchased it or not. If the public good were to be financed by voluntary contributions, rational individuals would say to themselves, "Why should I contribute to the provision of the public good when I am able to enjoy the benefits whether or not I contribute?" Thus, each individual would expect "George" to finance the public good, and "George," of course, would expect others to finance it. This is known as the free rider problem. In its most extreme version, each individual will attempt to free ride on the efforts of others, no one will finance the public good, and the public good will not be provided.

---

[5] See Richard Musgrave, *The Theory of Public Finance* (New York: McGraw-Hill, 1969).

As recognized by Hume, the significance of the free rider problem is affected by the number of people benefiting from the public good. If a small number of individuals will benefit from a public good, each individual must consider that his or her own behavior will exert some influence on the decisions of other members in the group. Also, individuals living in a small society or group will be able to identify and put social pressure on the free rider to contribute his "fair share." Thus, small communities are more likely to voluntarily finance the provision of public goods. However, if a large number of individuals will benefit from a public good, it will be difficult to identify the free rider, and each individual will passively accept the decision of all others as a given, unaffected by his or her own decision. Thus, individuals in large communities will more likely select the free rider alternative, and private provision will fail. Public goods will have to be financed by government.

Economists frequently use simple game theory to illustrate the free rider problem. This particular version of game theory is called the *prisoner's dilemma* because when it was formulated by A. W. Tucker during the 1950s, it related the story of a district attorney offering various sentences (payoffs) to two suspects who depended upon the pleas entered by each other. A typical prisoner's dilemma payoff matrix is shown in Figure 4-1.

Two men are accused of armed robbery, and the district attorney is attempting to procure a confession from them. The district attorney offers payoff alternatives to Able (which are shown in the *top* row of each payoff cell) and to Baker (which are shown in the *bottom* rows). The arrows point

FIGURE 4-1
ABLE'S ALTERNATIVES

Baker's alternatives	Able's alternatives: Confess	Able's alternatives: Don't confess
Confess	↑ 5 yrs ← 5 yrs	↑ 20 yrs ← 6 mos
Don't confess	↑ 6 mos ← 20 yrs	↑ 2 yrs ← 2 yrs

to the individual affected by each payoff. The district attorney tells Able that if he confesses *and* if Baker confesses, both will get 5 years in prison (shown in the northwest cell); if Able confesses and Baker doesn't confess, then Able will get 6 months and Baker will get 20 years (shown in the southwest cell); if Able doesn't confess and Baker confesses, Able will get 20 years and Baker will get 6 months; and if both don't confess, they both will get 2 years. The district attorney tells Baker the same information he told Able.

The strategy that minimizes the prison sentences of *both* individuals is to remain silent and not confess. Each would then receive only 2 years. However, the dominant strategy for each individual is to confess. Able will say to himself, "If Baker confesses, I can minimize my sentence by also confessing because I will get 5 years instead of 20 years. If Baker doesn't confess, then I can minimize my sentence by confessing because I will get 6 months instead of two years." Hence, the dominant strategy for Able is to confess, regardless of what Baker does. Baker will reason in the same way, and he will confess. Thus, both individuals will end up with a 5-year sentence, although they would be better off if each selected the "Don't Confess" alternative with prison terms of only 2 years. The significance of the prisoner's dilemma is that each individual attempting to minimize his prison term actually ends up with a longer prison term. Note that the same results would be obtained if the prisoners were able to make an agreement that they would not squeal on each other: after sealing the bargain with a firm handshake, each would go into the district attorney's office and squeal.[6]

The prisoner's dilemma analysis has been applied to many decision-making environments, including the financing of a public good through voluntary contributions (see Figure 4-2). Assume that a public good costs $10,000 to produce and yields benefits valued at $30 to each of 1,000 individuals living in a community. Each person's pro rata share of the cost is $10. If Able, as one member of this group, contributes $10 and the other 999 individuals also contribute their pro rata share, the *net* monetary benefit to Able will be $20 ($30 in benefits minus the $10 contribution); if others do not contribute, the payoff to Able will be -$10 because the public good will not be provided and Able will be out his $10 contribution. If Able does

---

[6] Some external force or selective incentive is required to keep the prisoners quiet, and this is one of the conceptual roles played by the Mafia. If the two prisoners were members, each would know that if he informed on the other, the organization would find some appropriate punishment for the "squealer." The threat of this "ultimate tax" imposed by the Mafia would actually produce a public good for the criminals. Each prisoner would refuse to confess, knowing that the other also would not confess because the punishment by the Mafia would be worse than the reduction in the prison sentence.

FIGURE 4-2
ALL OTHER INDIVIDUALS

FIGURE 4-2
ALL OTHER INDIVIDUALS

All other individuals

	Contribute	Don't contribute
Contribute	$20	- $10
Don't contribute	$30	$0

Able's alternatives

not contribute but the others do contribute, the public good will be provided and Able's payoff will be $30. If the others do not contribute and Able does not contribute, then the net benefits will be zero. Hence, the optimal strategy for Able, regardless of what other individuals do, is not to contribute. Since all individuals are rational, they would tend to behave the same way, and they would end up in the southeast cell, which means that the public good would not be provided.

The vital role performed by government is to compel individuals to contribute toward the costs of public goods. Thus, individuals can use the political-governmental mechanism to make decisions about the types and quantities of the public goods they want provided and then agree to tax themselves to finance these public goods. When each individual makes a tax "contribution" for a public good, he knows that other individuals are also being required to make theirs. Governments are necessary in a society of free individuals because of (1) the existence of public goods and (2) the free rider problem.

SOME CHARACTERISTICS OF THE DEMAND FOR PUBLIC GOOD

Individuals have preferences and demands for public goods just as they do for private goods. They demand national defense, highways, and low-income housing in the political market just as they demand shoes, stereos, and sauerkraut in the private market. There is no fundamental difference between an individual's demand curve for private goods and his demand curve for public goods, because both reflect individual preferences about quantities demanded based on perceived prices.

Refer to Figure 4-3. The individual will demand a greater quantity of shoes at a lower price and a greater quantity of submarines at a lower price. In order to make a rational decision about the quantity of shoes to purchase, the individual must know the price of shoes. The same is true for submarines and all other public goods: In order to make an effective decision about the preferred quantity of a public good, the individual must know the price he will have to pay for marginal quantities of the public good.

The price paid for shoes is obviously the price that is posted at the shoe store, but the price for submarines is not so obvious. It is the additional tax that the individual will have to pay in order to provide some additional quantity of submarines—or any other public good. The reader's well-developed common sense might be agitated by the concept that effective political market decision making requires knowledge of public good prices. Few, if any, American citizens, you might argue, know the price they pay for each submarine. Undoubtedly, this is true, and there are many reasons for such lack of knowledge, which will be discussed in chapter 5. However, *the fact that citizens don't know the prices they pay for marginal quantities of the public goods does not invalidate the requirement that effective decision making requires that they have such information.* The absence of such information constitutes one of the "failures" of the political market.

Ignorance about the price of public goods confronting each individual is a glaring failure of the political market, which will be discussed below,

---

FIGURE 4-3

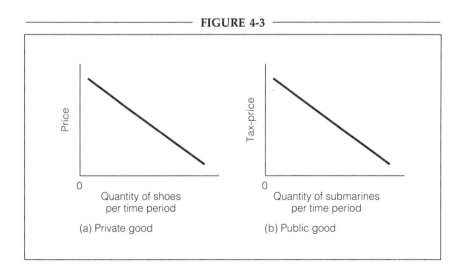

(a) Private good

(b) Public good

but in order to proceed with the analysis, assume that individuals do have certain knowledge of the prices they will be charged for additional units of a public good. The tax, or price, that the individual has to pay for a unit of a public good—say a submarine—is known as a tax-price, and in order to simplify the analysis, assume that this tax-price is the same for each unit. This means that the individual will have to pay a constant tax-price, TP_1, per unit. At a tax-price of TP_1 the individual will demand X_1 units of the public good. Although there are no differences between an individual demanding public and private goods and making choices based on the price of each good, the market conditions in which private goods are provided differ from the conditions in which public goods are provided. The most obvious difference in the provision of public and private goods is that decisions on public goods have to be made through a collective choice mechanism such as voting. Another characteristic of public goods that differentiates them from private goods is the construction of their aggregate demand curves.

As discussed in chapter 3, the market demand curves for private goods are simply the horizontal additions of individual demand curves (see Figure 4-4). They are added horizontally because when one individual buys a unit of a private good, that same unit is no longer available for other individuals to consume.

If Able buys a pair of shoes, that same pair of shoes is not available for anyone else to buy. Thus, if shoes are priced at $20 per pair and Able demands 5 pairs and Baker demands 5 pairs, the total market demand for shoes at a price of $20 per pair is 10 pairs. Each individual can independently adjust to the price of private goods. If the price is high, he can purchase fewer pairs of shoes; if it is low, more shoes.

FIGURE 4-4

DEMAND CURVES FOR PRIVATE GOODS

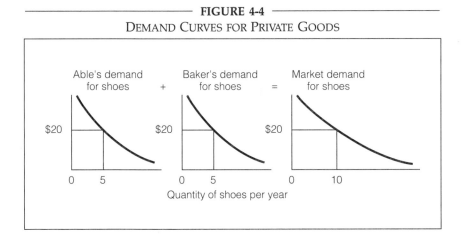

Demand curves for public goods are added vertically to reflect the fact that individuals can consume public goods without decreasing the quantity available to others (see Figure 4-5). Both Able and Baker can benefit from submarines patrolling the oceans, and if an additional submarine is provided by Able, it will also benefit Baker. Unlike private goods, individuals cannot independently adjust to the price of a public good, because all individuals must "consume" the same quantity. If there are 5 nuclear submarines patrolling the Pacific Ocean, every citizen in the

---
FIGURE 4-5 ---

DEMAND CURVES FOR PUBLIC GOODS

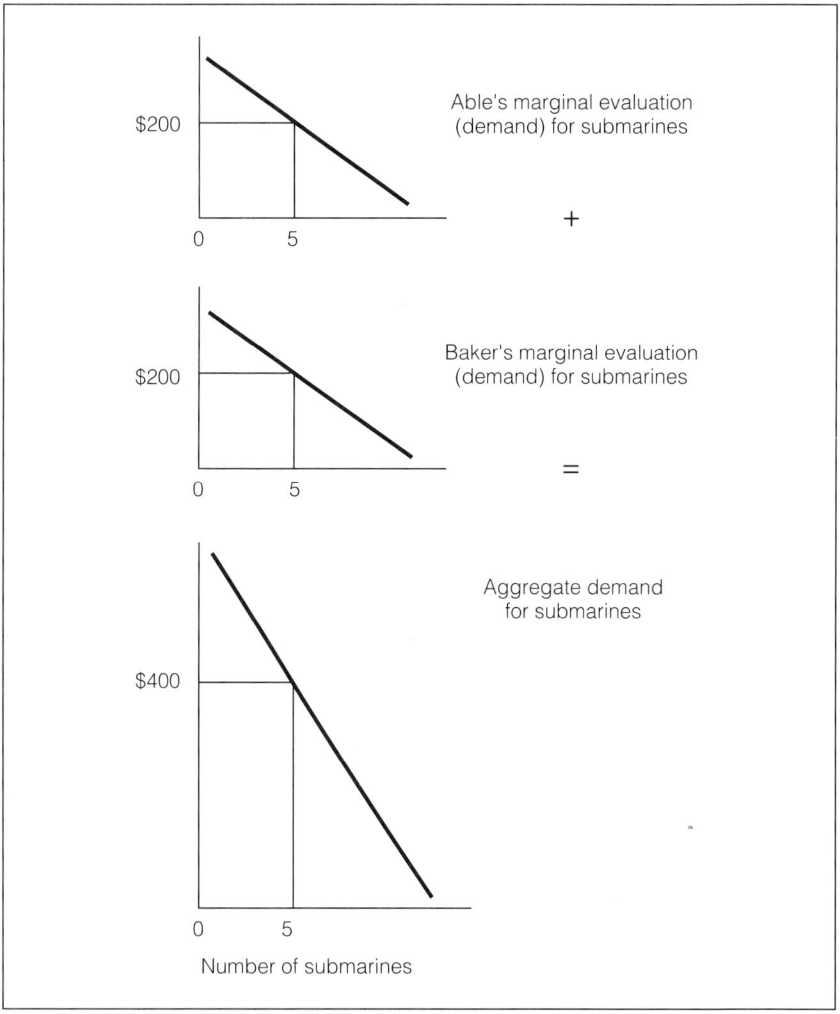

country is "consuming" the services of these 5 submarines, and no single individual can independently adjust to, say, 3 submarines. Like it or not, those 5 submarines are providing benefits that each individual must "consume."

Assume that Able and Baker have identical preferences for submarines and that each places a $200 value on the fifth submarine. When determining "society's" total marginal benefits provided by the fifth submarine, the benefits are added vertically to obtain total social benefits of $400. For reasons we need not discuss here, the demand curve for public goods is generally called the marginal evaluation curve.[7] The marginal evaluation curves for public goods are normally drawn on a single graph, as shown in Figure 4-6. Since each individual's marginal evaluation curve is identical to the other's, the aggregate, or market, demand curve will be charted twice as high on the vertical axis as a single individual's

---

FIGURE 4-6

AGGREGATE DEMAND (MARGINAL EVALUATION) CURVE FOR A PUBLIC GOOD

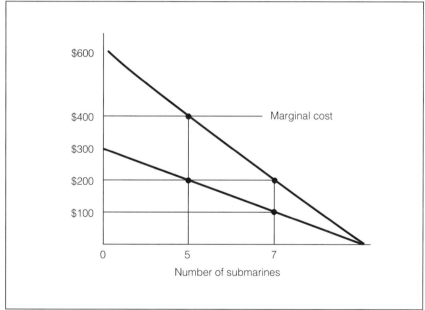

---

[7] For the purposes of this introductory text, marginal benefits and marginal evaluations have the same meaning. However, we will use the more technically correct term of marginal evaluation when discussing the efficiency conditions for public goods. The aggregate marginal evaluation curve can be considered to be the aggregate demand curve.

marginal evaluation, or demand, curve. For example, if Able's marginal evaluation curve (which is the same as Baker's) intercepts the vertical axis at $300, the aggregate marginal evaluation curve will intercept the vertical axis at $600.

Each individual places a marginal evaluation of $200 on the fifth submarine, and the aggregate (society's) marginal evaluation of the fifth submarine is $400. Assume that the cost of producing each submarine is $400, so that marginal cost equals average cost at 5 submarines. The optimal quantity of submarines for this two-person society is 5 because that is where the sum of the marginal benefits (ΣME) provided by the fifth submarine equals the marginal cost (MC) of producing the fifth submarine. A sixth submarine would cost $400 to produce, but it would yield lower social marginal benefits of, say, $300. Hence, it would not make economic sense to produce the sixth submarine when the benefits of the sixth submarine are $300 while the cost of producing it is $400. On the other hand, if only 4 submarines are provided, the marginal benefits, say $500, will be greater than the marginal costs of $400, and an additional submarine should be provided. The efficient or optimal quantity of submarines is obtained only at 5 submarines. The efficient quantity of a public good that maximizes the welfare of society is where the sum of all individuals' marginal evaluations equals the marginal cost of producing the last unit of the public good, or:

(1) *Aggregate Condition for Public Goods Efficiency (Pareto Optimality)*
$$\Sigma ME = MC$$

(a) If $\Sigma ME > MC$, marginal benefits of the last unit of the public good are greater than the marginal costs of producing the marginal unit, so more units should be provided.
(b) If $\Sigma ME < MC$, the marginal benefits of the last unit of the public good are less than the marginal costs of producing it, so fewer units of the public good should be provided.

Although most economists use only this aggregate statement to express the efficiency condition for public goods, some economists specify a second condition, which relates to the tax-prices charged each citizen. There are many ways in which the costs of providing the public good can be divided between the two individuals. Able could pay $100 for the fifth submarine, and Baker could pay $300; Baker could pay $100 and Able $300; or they could each pay $200. The cost-sharing provisions would impact on the quantity preferred by each individual. Assume the individuals agree to share the total costs of the submarines equally (each individual will pay

$200 for each submarine).[8] At a quantity of 5 submarines, each individual's marginal evaluation will equal the marginal tax-price. That is, each individual will obtain $200 in benefits from the fifth submarine, and each will pay $200 for the fifth submarine. Each individual's marginal tax-price will be equal to his marginal evaluation, and he will not want to alter the quantity being provided. Thus, the individual condition for public goods efficiency states that the marginal tax-price paid by each individual should equal the individual's marginal evaluation.

(2) *Individual Condition for Public Goods Efficiency*
$$MTP^i = ME^i$$

The marginal tax-price paid by each individual should be equal to the marginal evaluation of each individual.

As mentioned above, some economists argue that only the aggregate condition is relevant for efficiency conditions, because the individual condition deals only with welfare transfers: one taxpayer pays more and another taxpayer pays less. However, if the individual condition is not satisfied, equilibrium does not exist, because the individual who is taxed less than his marginal evaluation will want an increase in the quantity of the public good; the one who is taxed more than his marginal evaluation will want a decrease in the quantity of the public good.

One of these two conditions may be satisfied without the other being satisfied. For example, if each individual's marginal tax-price were $100 and the quantity of the public good supplied were 7 submarines, the individual condition would be satisfied because each individual's marginal tax-price would equal his marginal evaluation but the aggregate condition would be violated because the sum of the marginal evaluations ($200) would be less than the marginal cost ($400). On the other hand, if the efficient quantity of 5 submarines is provided but Able is taxed $100 and Baker is charged $300, the aggregate condition, but not the individual condition, will be satisfied.

---

[8] We are assuming that the submarines are produced under conditions of constant cost, which means that average costs will equal marginal costs for all conceivable quantities of submarines produced. If the submarines were produced under conditions of increasing or decreasing costs, there would be some income effects on the marginal evaluation curves and the geometry would become more messy. The basic conclusions would not be altered, however.

COOPERATIVE PROVISION BY INDIVIDUALS
WITH DIFFERENT PREFERENCES

Although the identical preference model is useful to illustrate the nature of public goods and the efficiency conditions in public goods provision, it is very unrealistic. Hence, we will now assume that Able and Baker have different preferences for the public good.

In Figure 4-7 the marginal evaluation curves for Able (ME^A) and Baker (ME^B) are drawn to reflect different tastes for submarines. Note that one cannot state which individual has the greater demand for the public good without specifying the marginal tax-price. At a low marginal tax-price Baker demands a greater quantity than Able, but at a high marginal tax-price Able wants more units provided than Baker. This illustrates an important analytical consideration. One cannot conclude that an individual is a "hawk" or a "dove" on national defense, welfare transfers, or other public goods unless that individual knows his or her marginal tax-price. At a low marginal tax-price the individual might be a hawk (wants a larger defense or welfare budget than the majority of citizens), whereas

―――――――――――――――――――― **FIGURE 4-7** ――――――――――――――――――――
DEMAND CURVES FOR SUBMARINES ASSUMING DIFFERENT PREFERENCES

at a high marginal tax-price the same individual might be a dove (wants a smaller defense or welfare budget than the majority of citizens). Vertically summing the two curves yields the aggregate demand curve (ΣME) for submarines. Since the marginal cost of producing submarines is $400, the aggregate efficiency condition for public goods is satisfied at 5 units, where the aggregate marginal evaluation curve is equal to marginal cost. At this quantity, however, each individual places a different marginal value on the public good; Able places a marginal value of $250 on the fifth sub-marine, whereas Baker's marginal evaluation is $150. Obviously, if individuals with different preferences are charged the same marginal tax-price, say $200, efficiency will not be obtained, because neither individual will be in equilibrium; Able will want a larger quantity provided, whereas Baker will prefer a smaller quantity. Hence, if individuals have different marginal evaluation schedules for the public good, they must be charged *different* marginal tax-prices. In this example Able must be charged a tax-price of $150, and Baker must be charged a tax-price of $250.

Prices in the private market are determined by aggregate supply and demand forces, and the individual reflects his or her marginal evaluation by adjusting the *quantity* of private goods consumed; in the case of public goods, however, each individual cannot independently adjust his or her quantity, because the number of units available to one citizen is, by defini-tion, also available to all other citizens. If 5 nuclear submarines are patrol-ling the oceans, each American is provided with that quantity of defense services and cannot adjust individually to a larger or smaller amount. Hence, given the nature of public goods, individual quantity adjustments cannot be made and the tax-price must be adjusted to the individual's marginal evaluation at the quantity that satisfies the aggregate condition.

SUMMARY

Goods can be classified on a continuum, with pure private goods located on one end of the spectrum and pure public goods on the other end. Private goods are divisible because nonpayers can be excluded from con-suming these goods, and consumption of a single unit by one individual means that another individual cannot consume that same unit. The private market demand curve is derived by the horizontal summation of individual demand curves; the quantities individuals want to consume at a given price are summed to obtain the market demand.

Private provision of a public good is possible when the number of individuals in the community is small, but as the size of the community increases, it becomes more difficult to provide public goods through the private or charity markets. Public goods cannot be sold by private firms because of the nonexclusion property of public goods and because of the free rider, or prisoner's dilemma, problem. Hence, the free rider problem and the costs of decision making require a mechanism in which taxes can be levied and collected and in which decisions about the public good can be made. According to almost all political economists, the only viable alternative is the political market or government.

Pareto optimal efficiency conditions are satisfied when individuals adjust their purchases to the point where their marginal evaluations of a particular private good are equal to each other's marginal evaluations and these marginal evaluations, in turn, are equal to the marginal cost of producing the private good. In terms of a simple two-man economy this is expressed as:

$$ME^A = ME^B = MC$$

If the conditions described in chapter 3 are met, private goods can be efficiently provided through the free market price mechanism.

Public goods are nondivisible because nonpayers cannot be excluded from consuming these goods, and one individual's consumption does not decrease the consumption by other individuals. Individual demand curves must be summed vertically to obtain the aggregate or market demand curve for public goods.

There are two parts in the efficiency conditions for public goods:

(1) *Aggregate condition:* The optimal quantity of a public good is that quantity at which the sum of the individuals' marginal evaluations equal the marginal cost.
(2) *Individual condition:* The tax-price paid by the individual must be adjusted to equate it with the individual's marginal evaluation at the quantity specified by the aggregate condition.

This chapter has discussed the fundamental theory of public goods. The alert student should be questioning the relevance of this theory to the real world. How, she might ask, is this theory applied? Certainly, no government attempts to charge citizens by their marginal evaluations for public goods. Citizens, in fact, would not reveal their true preferences for public goods intensely desired by them for fear of being taxed accordingly. *The fact that the two-part optimality condition cannot be achieved because preferences are not revealed or because of any other reason does not affect the validity of these conditions.* These conditions, as well as those for the private market, are useful as logically developed criteria based on the postulate that individuals should obtain what they want and that resources should not be wasted. These optimality conditions are not destroyed if there are no social, political, or economic institutions capable of satisfying these conditions. It would be useless, however, to develop the efficiency conditions without examining the institutions that might satisfy these conditions. Private market price theory analyzes the ability of the free market mechanism to satisfy the efficiency, or Pareto optimality, conditions in private goods provision. The following chapter examines the applicability of the political mechanism in satisfying the efficiency conditions in public goods provision.

QUESTIONS AND ANSWERS

THE QUESTIONS

1.   Most large towns and cities have private and public golf courses.

   a.   Is the public golf course a public good and the private course a private good? Why?

   b.   Which of the golf courses do you think has the lowest prices and which has the longest waiting lines or reservation lists?

   c.   Who benefits more from public golf courses, and who benefits more from private courses.

   d.   Why do city governments provide public golf courses when the private market also provides them?

2.   Most states provide public parks with camping facilities that are often located near private campgrounds.

   a.   Which campgrounds do you believe will fill up first? Why? What factors would cause you to alter your conclusion?

   b.   The state of Florida recently increased the fees for its public campgrounds so that they were higher than the fees charged by most private campgrounds? Why would Florida charge higher fees, and why would campers pay them rather than go to the private campgrounds?

   c.   If a state passed a law requiring that camping fees reflect the full cost of public campgrounds, what factors would you include in your list of costs?

   d.   If your local newspaper began an editorial campaign for more public campgrounds because there was a shortage of campgrounds, what questions might you raise in a letter to the editor? Why?

3.   Able, Baker, and Charlie have varying preferences for public housing for the poor. Assume that we can aggregate their marginal evaluation curves and discover that at the quantity of public housing where the sum of the marginal evaluations (aggregate demand) equals the marginal cost

of providing public housing the marginal evaluations for public housing for each of the individuals are:

Able $200
Baker $100
Charlie   –$100

a. Is public housing a public good? Why?

b. What marginal tax-prices should be paid by Able, Baker, and Charlie? Why?

c. From the above information can you describe Able as pro-public housing and Charlie as anti-public housing? Why?

4.   Which of the following are public goods? Why?

a. Mosquito eradication
b. The Apollo (moon landing) space program
c. Agricultural research on a new seed
d. Bridge over the Mississippi River
e. The knowledge and skills you obtain from this book.

THE ANSWERS

1.   **a.**   Both golf courses provide private goods or services since those who don't pay can be excluded from either course.

b.   Generally, the private course would have the higher prices and the shortest lines.

c.   The private courses use the price system as an allocating mechanism, while the city courses tend to use the queuing system. Hence, those whose opportunity costs are high, such as brain surgeons and trial lawyers, will be willing to pay the higher prices charged by the private courses. Also, those who do not wish to associate with individuals whose opportunity costs are low will benefit from the private courses. Those whose opportunity costs are low, such as economic and political science professors, will tend to use the public golf courses. Also, those who do not wish to associate with individuals who have high opportunity costs will use the public courses.

d.   This is not an easy question to answer because golf courses clearly are primarily private goods. Generally, one can expect the parks and recreation department to push for the development of public golf courses, since doing so enlarges the bureaucracy and provides control over more resources and increased promotion opportunities (see chapter 10 for a discussion of bureaucracy). Customers of private courses may support the development of public parks to reduce potential congestion at private parks and siphon off those individuals with low opportunity costs. Mayors often believe that they will be evaluated by the number of city projects begun during their administration, so they support the construction of golf courses, among other public projects.

2. **a.** Because of the low price we would expect public campgrounds to fill up early. However, one has to consider the relative attractiveness and quality of public and private campgrounds (as well as golf courses in the previous question). Many public campgrounds are located on large tracts of land next to streams and lakes, while private campgrounds are located in flat fields. Hence, many campers would prefer the state campgrounds even if they charged the same, or even higher, prices as the private campgrounds.

b. The Florida Department of Recreation said that it raised fees because the state legislature did not provide enough funds to the department to "carry out its functions." Thus, the department tried to recoup losses of budgeted revenues by charging higher fees for its campgrounds. Also, the department might have been playing political games with the legislature by stimulating a backlash from campground users, which they might have hoped would result in future increases in its budget. Although the Florida Association of Private Campgrounds denied any role in the price increase, legislatures in other states have been subjected to pressures by private campground owners to increase fees in public campgrounds.

The department also quietly mentioned that the demand for its campgrounds had been increasing, so it felt "justified" in raising its prices; in fact, it raised prices the most at those campgrounds that had the greatest and most inelastic demand. It was, in effect, acting like a rational, profit-maximizing private firm, and rather than allocating scarce campsites by a queuing system, it decided to use the price mechanism. Also, as many private firms have discovered, higher prices do not always mean higher revenues. Because the prices at some parks more than doubled, many consumers avoided the public campgrounds, and the department subsequently had to lower its fees. Public agencies, like private firms, must pay attention to the first law of demand.

c. Some states have required that public campgrounds charge fees that cover "all related costs." Most states have included in "all related costs" the costs of labor, lighting, maintenance, and other variable costs. However, most states do *not* include an implicit rental cost of the land, which is the largest component of campground costs. Many states do *not* include fringe benefits or the administrative overhead costs of the department in "related costs." Thus, even in states that require full cost pricing, the fees in public parks are lower than in private campgrounds, and they are not market-clearing prices.

d. You should ask what fees the public campgrounds charge and how they determine the level of these fees. You might ask what would happen to the "shortage of public campgrounds" if a higher and more cost-reflective price were charged. Finally, you might point out that the existence of campgrounds that charge a low or zero price means that there are too many, and not too few, campgrounds.

3. **a.** Yes, it is a private good for those who live in public housing, but it is a public good to citizens who cannot be excluded from enjoying the benefits of having their neighbors live in better housing.

    b. Each individual should pay an amount equal to his marginal evaluation. Able should pay $200, Baker should pay $100, and Charlie should *receive* a payment from the government of $100. Charlie not only does not want the marginal unit of public housing provided, he gets negative utility from it. Hence, he needs to be subsidized for undergoing this loss in utility.

    c. No, because the data describe only the marginal evaluation of the individuals. At fewer units of public housing, Charlie might have the highest marginal evaluation.

4. **a.** It is a public good because you cannot exclude individuals from enjoying the benefits. Furthermore, if I spray my property, I provide benefits to my neighbors, and if they don't spray their property, I will get bitten by their mosquitoes.

    b. Yes, presumably because it provided some basic research, prestige, esteem, and entertainment for all American citizens. However, further developments in space tended to be more private than public.

    c. No, private firms could conduct the research and sell the seeds only to those farmers willing to pay the price.

    d. No, tolls could be charged, and those who did not pay could not cross the bridge.

    e. To the extent that it makes you more witty and entertaining at cocktail parties or teaches you skills that you can sell to private firms or governments, it is a private good. To the extent that it makes you a better citizen, it is a public good.

CHAPTER FIVE

VOTING, RATIONAL ABSTENTION, AND RATIONAL IGNORANCE

Here each individual is interested not only in his own affairs but in the affairs of the state as well: even those who are mostly occupied with their own business are extremely well informed on general politics— this is a peculiarity of ours: we do not say that a man who takes no interest in politics is a man who minds his own business; we say that he has no business here at all.

—PERICLES' FUNERAL ORATION, THUCYDIDES

Born as I was the citizen of a free state and a member of its sovereign body, the very right to vote imposes on me the duty to instruct myself in public affairs, however little influence my voice may have in them.

—JEAN-JACQUES ROUSSEAU

As long as I count the votes, what are you going to do about it?

—WILLIAM TWEED, "BOSS" OF TAMMANY HALL, COMMENTING ON CHARGES OF VOTING IRREGULARITIES IN NEW YORK, 1871

INTRODUCTION

Free markets and free governments imply that individuals are allowed to express their preferences freely, efficiently, and without coercion. People living in a capitalistic economy express their preferences for the provision and allocation of private goods by casting their dollar votes in the private market. Those living in a democracy express their preferences for the provision and allocation of public goods by casting their political votes in the ballot box. The idealized version of free private markets, along with its many market failures, was discussed in chapter 3. The idealized version of democracy is one in which individuals can effectively determine the rules by which they will live, the public goods and services they will enjoy, and the taxes they must endure by informing themselves about issues and candidates and by entering the voting booth committed to casting their votes for the common good of all. "Let the People Govern," "The Will of the People," "Every Vote Counts", and "Majority Rule" are shouted in classrooms, street demonstrations, and legislative assemblies from Calcutta to Charlotte to the Cotswolds. Voting has been called "a sacred trust," a "priceless right," and an "obligation" of every citizen in a democracy. Scholars write, students learn, and politicians talk about voting and democracy, but there has been surprisingly little analysis of the efficiency of alternative voting rules or even of the incentives to vote or to become informed about public issues. While thousands of books have been written about politics, political theory, political parties, government, public administration, and voting behavior, there have been only a few written on *the* most important issues in democracies: voting incentives and alternative voting procedures. One would think that much intellectual and academic inquiry would have been devoted to these subjects and that these efforts would have sifted down through the academy into the ranks of practical individuals concerned with reforming the political process. While some scholarly work has been done on voting within the past three decades, much of this work has not sifted down to the classroom, and even less has oozed into legislative halls or the offices of journalists and editorial writers.

AMERICAN DEMOCRACY: MANY ELECTIONS BUT FEW VOTERS

The United States is committed to the primacy of elections in the political decision-making process. It was the first nation to conduct regular elections involving large numbers of voters, and it was the first nation to have modern political parties contesting these elections. Nevertheless, the United States has been criticized for not having extended the franchise to many classes of citizens sooner than it did. But the universal franchise is a remarkably recent phenomenon, even within the strongest democracies. Australian aborigines were not fully enfranchised until 1967. Women were not given the vote on equal terms with men until 1944 in France, 1946 in Italy, Japan, and Venezuela, 1948 in Belgium, and 1971 in Switzerland. Prohibited from voting in some countries are vagrants and drunkards (Finland and the Netherlands), prostitutes (Italy and Belgium), members of the armed forces (Venezuela and Columbia), and judges and election officials (Canada), and most countries deny voting rights to criminals and the mentally ill. Disfranchisement aside, there were fewer than a dozen democracies during the first two decades of the twentieth century; despite the proliferation of independent countries and social consciousness since World War II, there are fewer than 40 working democracies today, which means that more than 75 percent of the world's countries are governed by some form of dictatorship. Democracy is preached, discussed, and debated more than it is practiced.[1]

Democracy involves citizens revealing their preferences through voting, and Americans tended to vote in comparatively large percentages during most of the nineteenth century, when about 80 to 85 percent of the eligible population voted in presidential elections. Around the turn of the century the percentage of eligible individuals exercising their franchise began to drop and continued dropping throughout most of this century until only about one-half of the eligible population went to the polls during the 1980s (see Table 5-1).

The percentage of the eligible voting-age population that actually voted in presidential elections dropped by nearly one-third between 1900 and 1984. The turnout for elections of U.S. representatives in nonpresidential election years tells a different, but not entirely encouraging story. As shown in Table 5-2, the percentage of the voting-age population voting in non-presidential election years has always been much lower than the percentage

───────────── **TABLE 5-1** ─────────────
PERCENTAGE OF THE ELIGIBLE
VOTING-AGE POPLULATION VOTING IN
PRESIDENTIAL ELECTIONS

1900	73.2%	1948	53.0%
1904	65.2	1952	63.3
1908	65.4	1956	60.6
1912	58.8	1960	62.8
1916	61.6	1964	61.9
1920	49.2	1968	60.9
1924	48.9	1972	55.2
1928	56.9	1976	53.5
1932	56.9	1980	52.6
1936	61.0	1984	53.1
1940	62.5	1988	50.2
1944	55.9		

SOURCES: *Statistical Abstract of the United States,*
1989, and *Historical Statistics of the United States.*

---

[1] Robert A. Dahl estimated that more than 80 percent of the world's countries were dictatorships in 1971. [Robert A. Dahl, *Polyarchy Participation and Opposition* (New Haven: Yale University Press, 1971)]. The rapid changes occurring in Eastern Europe while this book was being written resulted in a few more very welcomed democracies being added to the list.

――――――― **TABLE 5-2** ―――――――

PERCENTAGE OF THE VOTING-AGE
POPULATION VOTING FOR
U.S. REPRESENTATIVES IN
NONPRESIDENTIAL ELECTION YEARS

1922	32.1%	1958	43.6%
1926	30.1	1962	45.4
1930	33.7	1966	45.4
1934	41.8	1970	43.5
1938	41.1	1974	35.9
1942	33.9	1978	34.9
1946	37.4	1982	38.0
1950	41.7	1986	33.4
1954	42.5		

SOURCES: *Statistical Abstract of the United States,*
1960 and 1988.

turnout for presidential elections. Apart from the war years, the turnout
increased during mid-century but then decreased during the seventies
and eighties. The idealized textbook version of democratic self-rule is
obviously tarnished by the fact that only one of three individuals of the
voting-age population voted in congressional races in 1986, and one of
two voted in the 1988 presidential election.

A comparison of average voter participation in major democracies for
the period 1958 to 1976 is shown in Table 5-3. One interesting sidelight
to this table is that one respected study has shown that interest in politics,
feelings of civic duty, and trust in political institutions are highest in
Switzerland and the United States, followed by Britain, Germany, and
Italy—exactly the reverse of their rank order of voting turnout.

The only country with a voting turnout lower than the United States
is Switzerland. The low turnout in Switzerland, which has been steadily
dropping since World War II, is often explained by the lack of competition among the four major national parties that share cartel-like political
power in an executive council selected by the legislature. Another possible reason for the low turnout in Switzerland is the lack of major changes
when one party succeeds another. By all the traditional political criteria,
Switzerland should have a high voter turnout. It has automatic registration of eligible voters, and four cantons have compulsory voting. It also
has an informed, educated, and prosperous citizenry, which most scholars
claim ought to increase voter turnout. Perhaps, as we shall discuss below,
the Swiss are too intelligent to vote, or perhaps their lack of voting indicates

—————————————— **TABLE 5-3** ——————————————

AVERAGE VOTER PARTICIPATION IN SELECTED COUNTRIES
BETWEEN 1958 AND 1976

Switzerland	53%	Israel	81%
United States	59	Norway	82
India	60	Finland	84
France	70	West Germany	84
Canada	71	Greece	85
Japan	71	Australia	86
United Kingdom	74	Sweden	86
Ireland	75	Denmark	87
Philippines	77	Austria	89
Venezuela	80	Italy	94

SOURCE: G. Bingham Powell, Jr., *Contemporary Democracy* (Cambridge: Harvard University Press, 1982), 14. Also see David Butler, Howard R. Penniman, and Austin Ranney, *Democracy at the Polls*, (Washington, DC: American Enterprise Institute for Public Policy Research, 1981).

that they have such a stable democracy that they see no reason to be disturbed by elections. The poor turnout by the Swiss on election day, like that by Americans, may not be a cause for concern at all. It might merely reflect contentment with a constrained and limited government that has relatively little influence in the daily lives of citizens. The Philippines has had a much better voting record than either the United States or Switzerland, but its democracy, while certainly colorful and exciting, cannot be described as exceptionally healthy or stable.

Many countries, such as Australia, Greece, Costa Rica, Belgium, Uruguay, and Venezuela, have high turnouts because citizens who do not vote are subjected to fines, special taxes, or other penalties. Italy records nonvoting on citizens' official work and identification papers (*Did not vote* is stamped on the papers), and it is widely believed that they are discriminated against in employment and other benefits.[2] Several studies have shown that such penalties do increase voter participation. The Netherlands, for example, abandoned compulsory voting in 1967, and the average turnout fell from 95 percent to 83 percent.

The sharp decrease in the voting percentages in the American presidential campaign years of 1920 and 1972 might be partially explained

———————————————————————————————

[2] Italy also has polling stations open two days from 6 A.M. to 10 P.M., elections are held on public holidays, and low train fares are given to those who return to their local constituencies to vote and to spend a few days with family during the election holidays.

by the fact that all women could vote for the first time in 1920[3] and persons between 18 and 21 could vote for the first time in 1972. Moreover, there is some evidence that election day turnouts during the turn of the century were not as large as the data indicate. Voting records were not kept as fastidiously as they are today, and fraudulent voting and straight party ballots probably produced a larger number of "cemetery votes" and "repeaters." However, the general trend throughout the century has been to make voting easier, less restrictive, and more convenient. Poll taxes, literacy tests, and many registration restrictions that lowered the turnout in the early part of the century were gradually eliminated during the latter part of the century. In 1789 only about 1 of every 30 adult Americans (mostly propertied white males) was legally eligible to vote. Today only a few adult Americans are legally barred from voting: convicted felons, inmates of correctional institutions, persons judged to be mentally incompetent, and aliens.

Blacks were first given the right to vote throughout the nation with the passage of the Fifteenth Amendment in 1870, but many southern legislatures passed laws that discouraged or limited black voting. These limitations included poll taxes, tests for literacy and knowledge of the Constitution, rigorous residency and registration requirements, and the use of all-white primary elections. The Twenty-fourth Amendment, adopted in 1964, eliminated the poll tax for national elections, and the Voting Rights Act of 1965 eliminated poll taxes for state and local elections. That same act and its amendments in 1970 also eliminated literacy tests in local, state, and national elections. Despite intense federal efforts to sponsor black voter registration and efforts by community and political parties to get blacks to the polls, fewer than 37 percent of eligible blacks vote in congressional elections, compared with a white turnout of 47 percent. Special efforts have been made to get hispanics to the polls, even to the extent that bilingual ballots are required in areas of the country that have significant non-English-speaking populations.

ˋ Voter registration was enacted around the turn of the century as part of reform efforts to eliminate voting fraud. While registration was restricted during the first half of the century, the Civil Rights Acts of 1957 and 1960 and the Voting Rights Acts of 1965, 1970, and 1975 significantly relaxed registration and residency requirements for all citizens and eventually established a residency requirement of 30 days for presidential elections. The Supreme Court in 1972 expanded the requirement for a reasonable

---

[3] The Nineteenth Amendment, which gave the vote to women, was ratified in 1920, and female turnout at the polls is now just slightly less than that for men.

registration deadline to all elections. The Voting Rights Act of 1970 and the Twenty-sixth Amendment ratified in 1971 made all persons 18 years or older eligible to vote in local, state, and national elections. Generally, fewer than one-fourth of those under age 25 vote in congressional elections, and fewer than 40 percent vote in presidential elections. The turnout among these young voters has decreased since 1972.

If you looked solely at the easing of voting and registration laws and the efforts devoted to get minorities to vote, you could conclude that voting turnout should have increased significantly during the past three decades. If you looked at recent trends in those variables that are supposed to promote voting—educational attainment, expansion of media coverage, increases in real income—you could conclude that voting turnout also should have increased. Actual data (as shown in Tables 5-1 and 5-2) indicate that voting turnout in all elections has continued to drop, and most presidential primaries attract no more than about 10 to 15 percent of the eligible electorate. There are some institutional changes that might promote marginal increases in voting among Americans. The United States could follow the example of most other countries and hold elections on public holidays or weekends instead of on weekdays, and it could automatically register people to vote. Changes in the day of elections and in registration, however, cannot be expected to increase voting significantly.

Perhaps American citizens have just gotten tired of voting. They are called upon to vote more often than the citizens of any other country. No country even comes close to the United States in the frequency and variety of elections. No other major democracy elects its lower house as often as every two years or its president as frequently as every four years. No other country popularly elects its state governors and town mayors. No other country has such a wide variety of offices (judges, sheriffs, attorneys general, secretaries of state, city treasurers, registrars of voters, dog catchers, education superintendents, school boards, city councils, mayors, tax assessors, and town marshals) subject to elections. Only Switzerland can compete in the number of referendums, and only Belgium and Turkey also hold party primaries. Americans might have grown tired of voting so often for so many offices, or perhaps they have become educated to the real-world fact that their individual vote truly doesn't count.

PUBLIC RATIONALITY AND PRIVATE IRRATIONALITY OF VOTING

One of the most unwarranted assumptions in traditional democratic theory is that the voting franchise is valuable to the individual citizen. According to popular folklore, men and women have sacrificed their resources and lives for the right to vote, and it is one of the most treasured possessions of American citizens. Collectively, the right to vote is extremely valuable, but the value of the entire populace electing the government or making decisions on public issues should not be confused with the value of the voting right to the individual. The right to vote has little operational value to the individual, because a single vote has little probability of affecting the outcome of any election.

If a single individual in society had the *sole* right to cast a vote for the president, this vote would have an extremely high value, and there is no doubt that the rational individual would exercise his or her franchise. However, as more individuals share in the decision-making process, the vote becomes less important to the individual. Assume there are five individuals in the country with the right to vote for the president. The reference voter knows that her vote will now count only in the case of a tie among the other four voters. Assume she knows nothing about the preferences of the other voters. She knows that there are two alternatives, x and y, and five voters; thus, there are five possible voting outcomes among the other four voters:

Alternatives	x	y	
Possible Vote Combinations	4	0	
	3	1	
	2	2	One tie vote among five
	1	3	possible outcomes
	0	4	

If the reference voter has no knowledge about the likely voting patterns of the other voters, each of these five voting combinations is equally possible, so the probability of a tie is one in five. Thus, the reference voter would reason that there is a one-in-five chance that the votes cast by the other voters would result in a tie and that her vote would determine the outcome. It is clearly possible that the reference voter might have reason to expect that the voting outcome will not range over all of the above combinations. For example, the reference voter might know that at least one individual is going to vote for y. The possible outcomes are now reduced to:

Alternatives	x	y	
Possible Vote Combinations	3	1	
	2	2	One tie vote among
	1	3	four possible outcomes
	0	4	

The reference voter now knows that she has one chance out of four of determining the outcome. If she also knows at least one voter who is going to vote for alternative x, then she will have a one-in-three chance of determining the outcome. If she is certain that two voters would vote for x and two for y, the reference voter would know that her vote would determine the outcome, and the probability of her vote affecting the outcome would be 1.0. If there are more than two alternatives, the combinations increase exponentially and the math becomes messy. However, the lower bound of the probability that a single individual's vote will affect the outcome is $\frac{1}{v}$, where v is the number of voters. The upper bound is 1.0, or complete certainty that a single vote will affect the outcome.

Thus, the probability that a single vote will affect the outcome is determined by the number of voters, the number of available alternatives for which to vote, and the individual voter's expectations about the distribution of votes among the issues.[4] The voter's expectations about the distribution of the vote will depend upon poll results, news reports, and interviews. Nevertheless, the reference individual would expect that his single vote would have an infinitesimally small probability of affecting the outcome of most elections. However, the individual would still vote if the act of voting were costless. Unfortunately, voting is *not* costless. Each individual must devote time and effort to go to the polls, stand in line, cast the vote, and then return to home or to work. This time allocated to voting has an opportunity cost of income or leisure foregone. For an individual living in all but the smallest political units, the cost of voting will almost always be greater than the benefits obtained from voting. Hence, the rational voter would *not* vote.

This analysis of rational voter abstention can be cast in more formal terms. Assume that each individual places some value on the outcome of an election in which there are two possible outcomes: V_1 is the value placed by the individual on x winning, and V_2 is the value placed on y winning. Assume that the individual is not apathetic and believes that he would be better off by $100,000 if candidate x won and only $40,000 better off if candidate y won. Therefore, the net value of a successful outcome to the individual is:

$$(1) \quad V_1 - V_2 = \text{Outcome Differential}$$
$$\$100,000 - \$40,000 = \$60,000$$

If the individual is the *sole* decision maker, the outcome differential will equal the individual's net benefit from voting. However, if there are

---

[4] The probabilities are also affected by the meaning of a tie vote.

five voters, the outcome differential has to be discounted by the probability that the individual's vote will determine the outcome. If the voter has no information about the probable distribution of votes and a random distribution is assumed:

$$(2) \ B = p(V_1 - V_2) \ \text{where}$$
$$\$12{,}000 = .20(60{,}000)$$

B is the expected benefit of voting to the individual, p is the probability of the individual's vote affecting the outcome, and V_1 and V_2 are the values the individual places on the outcomes. The net benefit of voting to the individual in this example is a healthy $12,000. Now assume that the number of voters is increased to 100. If the reference voter has no information about the likely voting behavior of the other 99 voters, then the expected benefit of voting has been reduced to:

$$(3) \ \$600 = .01(\$60{,}000)$$

Though only a fraction of its previous value, the benefit is probably still greater than the cost of voting, and the individual would vote. Lastly, assume that there are 100 million voters, which is the approximate number of voters in the country. The *lower bound* of the value of voting is only:

$$(4) \ \$0.0006 = .00000001(\$60{,}000)$$

The expected benefit of voting has been reduced to less than one-tenth of one cent. If the voter values his time at $4 per hour, approximately the minimum wage, and it takes two hours to go to the polls, vote, and return home, the opportunity cost of voting is $8 while the individual's expected net benefit from voting is less than one cent. These probabilities have been based on the assumption that the individual's vote would have the lowest possible chance of affecting the outcome. In most cases the individual would expect the chances of a tied vote to be higher, but it is clear that in virtually all real-world elections the rational voter would stay home and watch a rerun of the "Beverly Hillbillies."

Voting is rational if the voter's time costs are valued at an infinitesimally low value, if the outcome differential is very large, if little personal time is required to vote, or if the individual expects the race to be an extremely close one so that his vote could be the deciding one. Seldom are these conditions met in political voting. Voting at work and at club or lodge meetings is rational because the costs are virtually zero, few decision makers are involved, and the individual generally has some personal knowledge about the preferences of the other voters. However, in virtually all political elections the number of voters is quite large and the costs significant. For example, there are about 300,000 voters in each congressional district. If the individual's outcome differential is $60,000, the *minimum* expected benefits from voting in a congressional election are only 20 cents. There are very few local, state, or national elections in which expected benefits from voting would exceed the average individual's voting cost, although some small-town elections that are expected to be very close might qualify. Hence, one must conclude that it is the rational voter who stays home and refuses to vote and the irrational one who votes.

This conclusion is so disagreeable to those who have not thought about it that they immediately react with various criticisms. One frequent comment is that the individual who does not vote is an apathetic bum who has no interest in public affairs. The critic is supported by most traditional social science studies and innumerable newspaper editorials that equate nonvoting with apathy.[5] However, the cause of rational abstention is not apathy. The voter in our example feels very strongly about the election results, as reflected in his maximum outcome differential of $60,000. He simply realizes that despite his strong preferences, the outcome of the election will be the same whether he votes or not. In virtually all cases the probability that his vote will affect the outcome is so infinitesimally small that his abstention will have no meaningful impact on the outcome. He wishes his vote could influence the outcome, but he realizes his single vote will change nothing.

Another reaction of the critic is to state that if every individual in society thought this way, decisions would not be made. The statement is correct but meaningless. Each individual realizes that his decision to vote will not influence others to vote and that the voting decisions of others are totally independent of his own decision. Others will or will not vote regardless of whether a particular individual votes or not.

A third reaction of the critic is the proclamation that the individual has a moral obligation to vote and that the rational individual would act on this moral obligation. The source of this obligation is not clear, nor is it evident why an individual would believe he has a moral obligation to vote. Undoubtedly, some individuals do vote because they believe they have a moral obligation to do so, although individuals frequently state they have a moral obligation to do something that they are doing for other reasons. Moral obligations are not part of the analysis, because they can explain everything, thereby explaining nothing. Furthermore, it is not

---

[5] See, for example, Gordon M. Connelly and H. H. Field, "The Non-Voter—Who He Is, What He Thinks," *Public Opinion Quarterly* 8 (1944): 175–87 and David Riesman and Nathan B. Glazer, "Criteria for Political Apathy" in *Studies in Leadership,* ed. Alvin W. Gouldner (New York: Harper & Brothers, 1975), 505–59.

clear that a moral obligation actually exists, because even the morality of an act will be influenced by the probable outcome of that act.[6]

Another criticism of the rational abstention analysis is that the individual who does not vote does not have a "right" to criticize the outcome. Without discussing the nature of rights of nonvoting citizens, it is readily apparent that this argument has no merit. If the individual could have changed the outcome with his vote, then he might be said to have given up his right to criticize the outcome. However, it is clear that the individual could not have changed the outcome with a single vote and that the outcome would have been the same whether that individual voted or not. Hence, an individual has every right to criticize that outcome whether he voted or not, since the outcome would have been the same.

Rational abstention is very damaging to the theory of democratic self-rule. The foundation of the democratic decision-making structure, based on individuals reflecting their preferences about candidates and issues, is destroyed. Second, the analysis clearly shows that an individual is at the mercy of a political decision-making process over which he has no control. The political outcome will always be the same, whether an individual places a high or a low value on the outcome and whether he votes or not. This inability to influence the outcome is, to the individual, virtually no different from that which would exist in a dictatorship. It suggests that the institutions and rules that exist in a country might be far more important than whether the operational rules are determined by a dictator or by the aggregation of the votes of other people. The individual has two defenses in a constitutional democracy that are generally not available in a dictatorship. First, the constitution narrows the area in which the political unit can interfere in the individual's life. The second defense, though very costly in time and other resources, is the ability of an aggrieved citizen to bring a perceived plight—and the probability that it could happen to

---

[6] Analysis cannot impart moral principles, but it can clarify moral boundaries. Assume that an infant falls off a bridge into a river with a swift current. Does a bystander on the bridge, knowing that he can't swim and would drown along with the infant, have a moral obligation to jump into the river and attempt to save the infant? Most people would probably answer no. Similarly, does an individual, knowing that he can't affect the outcome of an election, have an obligation to vote? The reader might object to the analogy by claiming that the cost to the bystander of attempting to rescue the infant is his life, whereas the cost of voting is only a hour or two of time. Okay, assume that the bystander knows he will waste two hours of his time by attempting a *futile* rescue. Does the reader believe that the bystander now has a moral obligation to attempt the rescue? As the probability of a successful outcome gets larger and the cost of the rescue gets smaller, more people would probably believe that a moral obligaton exists. The point is that it is difficult to argue that a moral obligation of some action exists when the probability of that action effecting a favorable outcome is zero or close to zero.

others—to the attention of other individuals whose collective voting power might affect the outcome. This ability depends to a great extent on the willingness of the media to report the individual's complaints.

A third problem revealed by the rational abstention theory is that the preferences of nonvoters are not reflected in the outcome. If congressional representatives are elected by one-half of the 30 percent who voted, then only 15 percent of the citizens have affirmed their support for these candidates. It is difficult to interpret this as the "consent of the governed." A fourth problem is that those individuals who voted probably do not constitute a random selection of the population. Certain classes of citizens tend to vote more often than others, and the preferences of these classes tend to be reflected in Congress, while the preferences of those who abstain are not reflected. The voting outcome reflects not the will of the majority—however that might be defined—rather it reflects the preferences of those who, for some reason, actually went to the polls.

We have seen that the theory of rational abstention is damaging to the theory of democracy. We can now turn the worm around and conclude that the millions of voters who *do* go to the polls are damaging to political economic theory. One of the continuing mysteries in public choice theory is why some individuals bother to vote when it is clear that their individual votes will not affect the outcome.[7] Why, for example, do more than one-half of the eligible citizens vote in presidential elections? Survey respondents generally state that they voted because they believed they had a civic or moral obligation or because they wanted to express their preference for a particular candidate or party. However, economists have always been more inclined to investigate how people really acted rather than how they said they acted. All of us tend to explain our actions by saying what we expect others to approve, and we try to hide our real motivations if, indeed, we even know them. Economists become snug and smug in their theoretical cocoons when they see data, such as those from a recent University of Michigan poll, that reveal that 91 percent of those surveyed believe that it is important to vote even when their own party has no chance to win; 87 percent believe that every single vote matters, though it may be only one of millions cast; 84 percent think that everyone

---

[7] Some empirical studies on voting motivations include W. H. Riker and P. C. Ordeshook, "A Theory of the Calculus of Voting," *American Political Review* (March 1968): 25–42; Y. Barzel and E. Silderberg, "Is the Act of Voting Rational?" *Public Choice* (Fall 1973): 51–58; H. Rosenthal and S. Sen, "Electoral Participation in the French Fifth Republic," *American Political Science Review* (March 1973): 29–54; J. Silberman and G. Durden, "The Rational Behavior Theory of Voter Participation," *Public Choice* (Fall 1975): 101–8; and B. S. Frey, "Why Do High Income People Participate More in Politics," *Public Choice* (Fall 1971): 101–5. For a survey of traditional social science explanations and empirical studies of nonvoting see Stephen Earl Bennett, *Apathy in America* (Dobbs Ferry, NY: Transnational Publishers, Inc., 1984).

should vote, even in apparently unimportant local elections. But, economists gleefully point out, only 33 percent voted in the last congressional election. Obviously, people say one thing and do another. Based on incentives widely assumed *and* observed in the private market, economists know that individuals are motivated by selective incentives, including monetary prices, costs, income, recognition, public esteem, and social approval.

Although the selective incentives prodding individuals to the polls are many, the role of social pressures probably plays a role much larger than has been recognized. The social pressure hypothesis is entirely consistent with the self-interest motivation used in other aspects of human behavior, and it explains voting turnout as well as other political phenomena. The social pressure thesis states that individuals vote in order to avoid the social pressures their friends, family, neighbors, and professional, philosophical, or political colleagues would place upon them if they did not. It is postulated that individuals vote not to influence the outcome—since they can't—but to avoid having to tell their friends that they failed to vote, to avoid embarrassing questions from their children, and to please their boss, their friends, or their union or professional colleagues who have strong political views and would view nonvoting as a betrayal of one's class. Those individuals whose social, political, or economic positions could be damaged by nonvoting will tend to vote, not to influence the election but to avoid the social and/or economic costs that could be levied upon them by others if they did not. Such pressures are particularly high among political or class reference groups, politically active blacks and hispanics, conservationists, feminists, union members, chamber of commerce members, and those groups where voting is thought to be a professional or class imperative. It is difficult to isolate this motivation because of complex interrelationships and the tendency of poll respondents to hide their real motivations. However, there is indirect evidence that the social pressure thesis is important. Some studies have found a high correlation between social class memberships, in which social pressures can be applied most strongly, and voting turnout. Many other studies have shown that individuals with high incomes and high education, professionals, older residents of a community, and members of organizations are more likely to vote.[8]

The figures are pretty much what one would expect. The upper-class occupations vote more heavily than lower-class occupations, although

---

[8] See, for example, Ivor Crewe, "Electoral Participation, in *Democracy at the Polls*, eds. David Butler et al. (Washington, DC: American Enterprise Institute, 1985), 216–63; Raymond E. Wolfinger and Steven J. Rosenstone, *Who Votes?* (New Haven: Yale University Press, 1980); and Roy A. Teixeira, *Why Americans Don't Vote, Turnout Decline in the United States, 1960–1984* (New York: Greenwood Press, 1987).

clerks and salespeople had nearly the same turnout as the first two levels of occupations. However, when occupation was adjusted for education, the effect of occupation was more modest. When income was adjusted for the level of education, it had a weaker effect on voting behavior, but income was still an important determinant for those who did not go to college. The effect of occupation was greatest for farmers, clerks, and salespeople and least for those with college degrees. The high turnout of farmers was probably caused by their keen political awareness due to farm support programs and the high social pressure that farmers place on their neighbors to vote so these programs will be continued. Also farmers tend to vote in small precincts, where one's absence is noted by other voters and poll watchers.

Those in the 18- to 24-year age bracket voted the least and the percentage rose as age increased until the 70- to 78-year age bracket. Those older than 78 had a higher percentage turnout than the 18- to 24-year age bracket (62 versus 53 percent). Women voted at the same rate as men until they reached 70 years, when their participation rates dropped significantly below men. Blacks had a lower turnout rate than whites, but when adjusted for education, occupation, and income, blacks voted at about the same rate as whites. Generally, an individual was more likely to vote if he or she had received a college education, was married, less mobile, older, and engaged in a professional occupation.

All of these characteristics are compatible with the social pressure theory. Anonymous individuals, or those who socialize with friends who do not discuss politics, will suffer little social costs if they do not vote. Most likely to vote are those who are well established in their neighborhoods and who have personal friends and professional colleagues who take politics seriously. If this social pressure hypothesis is correct, then rational individuals will not vote unless they are potentially subjected to selective incentives such as social pressure. One explanation of the declining voter participation is the increasing urbanization and mobility in the country. An individual living in a small town or rural area who is known by his neighbors is likely to be "pegged" as a laggard or un-American if he does not appear at the polling place, whereas an individual living in an apartment house in a large city can hide in anonymity. Voting turnout in the future is likely to be affected by variables producing opposing pressures. On the one hand, increasing urbanization, mobility, and the realization that no individual vote has an effect is likely to lead to less voting. However, as more workers enter professions in which collegial pressures can be applied more effectively, voting turnout should increase. Whatever the future trends of voting participation, democracy takes on a much different meaning when voting is based not on the inherent responsibilities of every citizen but the vagaries of membership in social-economic classes in which social pressure can be applied most effectively.

One obvious solution to the poor voting turnout is to tax those individuals who do not vote. A fixed monetary levy on nonvoters would send to the polls those who value their time relatively low and their disposable income relatively high. This would complement nicely the social pressure thesis, which already places high social costs on nonvoting individuals in the high-income professions, and the public record and receipt of a nonvoting citation would "shame" into voting those nonvoters who might otherwise be unaffected by the monetary fine. A very attractive remedy to the low voter turnout might be found in the new electronic and communication technology. It is technically possible for individuals to register and to cast their vote on the telephone from their office or home. Electronic voting would significantly lower the costs of voting and, thus, encourage more voting.

RATIONAL IGNORANCE

The bad news for democracy does not end with the argument that rational individuals vote not to affect the outcome—as is assumed by virtually every political science book and analyst featured on election night television—but to avoid social pressures. Even if individuals could be driven to the polls by social pressures, by fines, or by "costless" electronic voting, there is no assurance that those individuals who did vote would have sufficient knowledge to vote their own interests. The traditional assumption is that voters are familiar with the issues and are able to formulate informed preferences about alternative issues and candidates. However, when an ignorant voter casts a vote, it is relatively meaningless from both a social and an individual point of view. With more knowledge about issues or candidates the individual might have voted much differently. In order to cast a meaningful vote for a proposed government expenditure—or the candidate who espouses such expenditures—the individual must know both the marginal costs that he will bear as well as the marginal benefits that will accrue to him from the expenditure. Given the complexities of modern tax systems, it is virtually impossible to determine the total amount of taxes paid by any single citizen to support government, much less the marginal tax costs associated with a specific government program. A citizen may have somewhat greater knowledge of the personal benefits of specific government programs, but only if he has a selective incentive to gather such information. There is even less incentive for the individual to obtain information about political issues or candidates than there is to vote.

An individual considering the purchase of a car can be expected to read automotive literature and *Consumers' Report,* to talk to friends who own different models, to take test drives, and to obtain information on prices and quality. This search for information takes a considerable amount of time, but the consumer is willing to bear these costs because he will personally enjoy the benefits of better quality and/or lower price. The consumer will continue to ferret out information until the marginal cost of an additional hour of search is equal to the expected marginal benefits. He will not have all of the relevant information, but he will have an optimal amount of information, as he views it, on which to make a decision.

Now assume that instead of the individual purchasing the car the municipal government announces that it will provide identical automobiles to all families in the city after it holds an election to decide which particular automobile the "people want." In order to be an informed voter, the individual should go through the same search process as when purchasing a car in the private market. But there is a major distinction in the decision-making process in the two markets. When the car-selection process occurs in the political market, the individual realizes that the amount of information obtained by him will be of no value, since the probability of his vote affecting the outcome is close to zero. He hopes that all citizens will obtain as much information about the merits of various automobiles as he did when purchasing the car in the private market. He also realizes that if voters don't obtain this information, they will make a poor choice in the ballot box, and they, as well as he, will have to pay higher taxes or have a lower-quality car. However, since he realizes that his individual vote will not determine the outcome, he will not invest in costly information search activities. Individuals simply have no incentive to invest their time and other resources in obtaining and sorting out information on public sector issues *in order to make more informed voting decisions.* They will remain rationally ignorant.

In order to illustrate the theory of rational ignorance, the author asked students in his political economy class whether they possessed any knowledge about specific public issues. During the seventies and early eighties, the United States was engaged in Law of the Sea negotiations to determine wide-ranging property rights in the world's oceans. They were among the most important international negotiations since World War II, but less than 5 percent of the more than 1,000 students majoring in political science, public administration, economics, history, and business had even heard of the negotiations. Not more than 1 percent could mention more than two issues involved in the negotiations, and not one student could discuss the pros and cons in any depth. I congratulated the students for being rationally ignorant and told them that they would now have a selective incentive (that is, grades) to learn about Law of the Sea issues and analyses of the alternatives.

The reader should think about how much he or she knows about Law of the Sea, SALT treaties, energy policies, MIRV missiles, acid rain, farm subsidies, maritime subsidies, or mass transit subsidies. Exactly what does the Gramm-Rudman balanced budget law mandate? Last year Congress passed more than 400 pieces of legislation. List eight—which is less than 2 percent of the 400 pieces of legislation—and state how your representative and senators voted on each of these issues (you do know if they voted, don't you?). Each year the Supreme Court makes about 150 to 200 decisions of which about 10 percent are notable for setting precedents. Name five of these decisions made last year. Congratulations! You are rationally ignorant.

Political theorists inform us that in a representative democracy, individual citizens need not concern themselves with these details because they employ representatives who specialize in obtaining information about issues and making political decisions. Our representatives in Congress do free us from the burden of obtaining detailed information about hundreds of issues each year, but the theory of rational ignorance applies to voters' knowledge about their representatives as well. First, numerous empirical studies have shown that voters often do not know the name of their congressional representative and have even less knowledge about their representative's voting record or positions on the major issues.[9]

Second, competing politicians are very much like competing automobile dealers. Each realizes that information about his or her products or positions is costly for the consumer-voter to obtain. Hence, both the car dealer and the politician says, "Trust me," "You can't go wrong with honest John," "I'll give you a fair, better, super, deal!" Their advertisements provide little useful information. But the car buyer does have an incentive to search out further information about competing car dealers' service, reputation, and products because he will personally reap the benefits of such search. The voter has no incentive to search out information about competing politicians because the individual's vote does not make the determination, and the outcome will be the same whether much or little is known about the candidates. Hence, the rational individual is

---

[9] See, for example, Thomas E. Mann and Raymond E. Wolfinger, "Candidates and Parties in Congressional Elections," *American Political Science Review* 74 (1980): 617–32 and Thomas E. Mann, *Unsafe at Any Margin: Interpreting Congressional Elections,* (Washington, DC: American Enterprise Institute, 1978).

uninformed about political candidates as well as the issues.[10] Because they have little, if any, incentive to invest time and other resources in gathering information about public issues, most voters obtain their information from low-cost sources such as casual conversations with friends, candidates' advertisements, and the media, especially television. These sources seldom provide much depth, and when they do, most voters do not want to waste their time (their opportunity costs are too high) listening to an in-depth discussion of the issues. The most widely covered political campaign is that for president of the United States, but television coverage is dominated by the campaign hoopla—the description of the candidates' travel schedules, the handshaking, the crowds, the pictures of balloons and motorcades. More than 80 percent of campaign stories discuss which candidate is nosing out the other (the horse-race question), whereas half make no mention whatsoever of any policy questions.[11] Three-quarters of the newspaper coverage focuses on the presidential candidates' personal qualities and general competence rather than their issue positions and the substance of their speeches.[12] Only 4 percent of the coverage deals with economic policy and only 5 percent with foreign policy.

Some critics argue that the most serious problem with the media is that those working within it assume that viewers or readers are as analytically weak as they are. However, the lack of substance in the media is not the result of reporter ignorance or a conspiracy among journalists to keep the public ill informed. It is just that viewers want to remain rationally ignorant and are not interested in coverage of substance because they see no personal benefits in it. The "McNeil Lehrer Newshour" covers political issues in greater depth than other evening news broadcasts, but its "ratings" are so low that they cannot be calculated by the usual statistical procedures. Many media critics thought the advent of cable television would result in a greater diversity of offerings so that "public-spirited" citizens could dial a channel that provided public-issue broadcasting. However, the advent of cable has resulted in less, rather than more, political information. Prior to cable, viewers were captured by the simultaneous

---

[10] For additional information on lack of participation in the political market see Sidney Verba and Norman H. Nie, *Participation in America: Political Democracy and Social Equality* (New York: Harper and Row, 1972) and Marvin E. Olsen, "A Model of Political Participation Stratification," *Journal of Political and Military Sociology* 1 (Fall 1973): 183–200.

[11] See, for example, Michael J. Robinson and Margaret A. Sheehan, *Over the Wire and on TV: CBS and UPI in Campaign '80* (New York: Russell Sage Foundation, 1983) and Doris Graber, *Mass Media and American Politics* (Washington, DC: Congressional Quarterly Press, 1984).

[12] Such general coverage, however, might enable the voter to make more intelligent decisions. See the discussion on political personalities below.

broadcasting of the evening news on the three major—and only—networks, but now viewers can escape becoming "informed" by turning to the counter-programming cable networks' reruns of those delightful fifties' and sixties' situation comedies. The proportion of the television audience watching the news has gone down. Many public affairs programs required for license renewal purposes are scheduled for the "intellectual ghetto," which is Sunday afternoon, or for the "dead weeks," when the Nielsen and Arbitron audience ratings are not collected.[13] The beloved media caricature of a working man coming home, taking a can of beer from the refrigerator, walking to the TV set, and turning off "The Pros and Cons of Multiple-Reentry Missiles" to watch a "Gilligan's Island" rerun is depicting not the actions of an ignorant slob but the decisions of a very rational person.

DISTORTIONS PRODUCED BY RATIONAL IGNORANCE

The human propensity to remain rationally ignorant about public issues produces several distortions in the political market's decision-making process. One of the most serious is the dominance of narrow producer interests over the broader general interests of consumers in political decision making. Most, if not all, of a person's income is derived from a single-producer role, whereas a consumer's expenditures are spread over an enormous range of goods and services, no one of which constitutes a significant proportion of his or her total expenditures. Accordingly, the average voter is much more sensitized to factors affecting his work and personal income than to factors affecting any particular consumption activity. One well-known example of greater sensitivity to work-related issues than to consumption-related activities is the import tariff. Individuals may be dimly aware that free trade is beneficial to them as consumers, but if the imported product proposed for tariff reduction is one that they produce, they will become acutely aware of it and will oppose it strongly. Thus, total social benefits from free trade may be much greater than the costs, but the benefits are widely distributed among millions of consumers who have little incentive to become informed while the costs are borne by a relatively small group of producers and workers who have strong incentives to obtain such information and to protect their income levels. Consumers may not know there is a tariff on shoe imports, but

---

[13] Until recently the British Broadcasting Corporation attempted to thwart the human propensity to remain rationally ignorant by broadcasting the campaign speeches of parliamentary candidates at a specified hour of prime time on *all* channels throughout Britain.

managers, stockholders, and employees in domestic shoe-producing firms will surely know it and work to keep it. Thus, producer interest groups, which include labor unions, employee and employer organizations, and trade and professional associations, form more readily than do consumer organizations, and they exercise more active political influence.[14] Once again, there is nothing sinister or conspiratorial about such activities. They merely reflect individual incentives to obtain information about their producer interests in protecting their sole source of income while they remain ignorant and blasé about each of their many sources of consumption. When voters ask their politicians, "What can you do for me?" they mean, "What can you do to restrict my competitors, raise my wages, protect me from foreign producers, or provide more subsidies for my products?" Successful politicians understand this, of course, and act accordingly. They support producer interest groups such as the farming industry, the oil industry, the education industry, the legal industry, the sugar cane industry, the car manufacturers, and the unions. They give speeches to producer groups, solicit campaign funds from them, and logroll with other politicians who are representing still other producer groups: "I'll support your sugar bill if you support my pork bill."

A second distortion produced by rational ignorance in the political market is that certain individuals, by virtue of their role in the division of labor, have a disproportionate influence on public policy. Individuals have no incentive to gather information about public issues in order to become more informed voters, but they do have an incentive to gather information related to their profession or occupation. Journalists, editorial writers, teachers, lawyers, professors, and lobbyists have job-related incentives to gather information about policies and candidates. A political science or economics professor has an incentive to gather information about public policy alternatives, while an automobile mechanic has an incentive to gather information about automobiles. The mechanic obtains his rewards for becoming educated through the private market mechanism increasing the value of his human capital. The professor can publish more papers and obtain her private reward through promotion and salary increases. However, unlike the mechanic, the professor also has an impact on decision making in the political market. She teaches students, gives lectures to groups, and is interviewed on television. She is a dispenser of low-cost information to other citizens and, thus, occupies an important choke point in the distribution of information and attitudes about policy issues. She has a disproportionate influence on public policy solely

---

[14] For a more thorough examination of special interest groups see chapter 9.

because of her occupation. Reporters, journalists, TV commentators and writers, and others in the media possess even more influence. Every observer reporting an event must select some facts to pass on and others to omit; hence, all reporting is inherently biased. The selection and arrangement of facts are inevitably tinged by the viewpoint of the reporter. Thus, to a great extent the nation's political agenda is set, debated, and influenced by a relatively small percentage of the populace who have professional incentives to obtain information and who occupy positions in which they can dispense low-cost information. Those engaged in other occupations do not have such opportunities to dispense their ideas and prejudices, and they have little influence on public opinion or policies.

As a result of rational ignorance, voters in a democracy do not have equal influence on policy formation, even though each person has one vote. In spite of the universal franchise, politicians cannot regard each voter as being of the same importance as every other. Because some citizens have more political influence than others, rational politicians and bureaucrats must give them more consideration in forming policy than they give other citizens who do not have such influence. Note that this difference in political influence is not caused by differences in income, wealth, or campaign contributions. It is caused by the fact that some individuals occupy choke points in the dispensing of information and values, while others do not.

A third distortion produced by rational ignorance is the poor quality of issue-related information provided by politicians and political campaigns. Politicians realize that most individuals have no incentive to gather or to retain information about issues, so they provide very little of it. They are afraid that if they take a strong public position on some issue they will lose votes among individuals in their producer roles while not attracting support or even notice among the general public. Most political advertisements provide no information other than such clichés as "Vote for _____, a man of the people" or "Vote for me and I'll work for you." Those who complain about vacuous, misleading, and false advertisements in the private market might well turn their attention to advertisements in the political market.

The following chapters on voting and political parties assume that individuals do vote and that they do obtain relevant information about public issues. However, the reader should not neglect the material presented in this chapter, because despite the increasingly sophisticated analyses of voting and political parties, some of the most serious distortions in the political market arise from rational abstention and rational ignorance. The most sophisticated models of voting and political behavior are virtually worthless if rational men and women have no incentive to vote or to obtain information about issues and candidates. Though not without problems, rational abstention from voting might be "cured" through a system of fines or other penalties, and easier voting and registration procedures. There are no acceptable remedies for rational ignorance in a free society, and we might have to conclude that the political market will continue to be plagued by fundamental distortions and that, other factors remaining equal, this is an additional argument for placing more reliance on private market decision making, where individuals do have an incentive to gather at least some information about competing products and distribution channels.

QUESTIONS AND ANSWERS

THE QUESTIONS

1. **a.** Did you vote in the last presidential election? Why?

    b. Do you have a guilty conscience because you did not vote? Why?

    c. Would you have a guilty conscience if no one knew you didn't vote?

    d. Did you vote in the past couple of congressional elections in which there was no presidential election (1986, 1990)? Why? Do you have a "right" to criticize congressional legislation if you didn't vote? Why?

    e. Can you offer any explanation why millions of people vote in presidential election years and not in the nonpresidential elections? Perhaps you are one of these individuals. What were your real reasons for not voting in the last congressional race?

2. Assume that before the election campaign in your community you drove around your neighborhood and compared billboard advertisements for political parties and politicians with billboard advertisements for private market firms.

    a. Do you think the political market advertisements or the private market advertisements would provide more useful information to you when you had to make a decision as a consumer or a voter? Why?

    b. Assume you made a similar comparison of TV advertisements. Which would provide you with more useful information? Why?

3. **a.** Have you ever donated blood without being paid or without having received special favors or treatment of any kind—such as time off from work, tickets to sport events, or blood assurance plans? Why?

    b. Do you know any friends or relatives who donated blood without receiving some form of compensation or a special request from someone who needed to have a blood transfusion?

c. What is the analytical connection between donating blood and voting?

d. What would be your ethical reaction if you heard an economist recommend that blood could be obtained in greater quantities and more efficiently if blood donors were paid? Why?

4. Assume that you are in a public choice class of 100 students, and the professor assigns a paper topic: "An Analytical Comparison of Advertising in the Private and Political Markets." Would you spend more time and effort researching and writing this paper if (a) the professor required each student to submit a paper or (b) assigned the paper to four working groups of 25 students, with each group submitting a single but much more lengthy paper? The grade received on the group paper would be the grade assigned to each student. Explain your answers.

5. "Jeez! Economists are a cynical and uncaring lot," might be your reaction to this and previous chapters. You might be thinking, "If the world had fewer cynics and economists and more optimists, it would be a much better place." Your reaction to the material presented in these first five chapters is normal. In fact, although most textbooks seldom discuss such reactions, they constitute the major reasons people ignore the analyses and recommendations of economists. Before you reach your final conclusion, read the following set of questions and answers on a topic that, more than most other topics, elicits much criticism about the cynicism and lack of human concern on the part of economists.

Does the concept of buying and selling used body parts (lungs, kidneys, eyes, bones) sicken you? Would you agree that it is morally reprehensible to sell parts of the human body? Would you prefer to see people who have damaged body parts live longer? Are you aware that modern surgical techniques have made it possible to replace many body organs and tissues and that the only factor keeping hundreds of thousands of individuals from having successful transplants and returning to a normal life is a lack of such body parts?

a. Assume an economist told you that it is possible to procure thousands of kidneys, eyes, lungs, and other body parts by paying people an appropriate price to have one or more of such body parts surgically removed and implanted in another individual. Would you reject the economist's recommendation because it was morally reprehensible to you?

b. Assume that the same cynical and morally reprehensible economist told you that thousands of individuals could have their lives prolonged or could be taken off dialysis machines or other intensive care treatment if healthy individuals were offered, say, $200 to sign a contract that when they died certain of their body parts could be removed and expressed to hospitals where patients were waiting to receive those body parts. Would you find such contracts morally undesirable? Would you vote to prohibit such contracts? Why?

c. Assume that you could simply sign a "will" that, upon your death, would authorize the removal of certain body parts to be given to some person who would die if he or she did not receive them. You would *not* be paid for signing the contract. You would simply be asked to sign the contract out of your concern for a fellow human being. Would you sign such a contract? Do you think others would sign it? Since such contracts would not involve "an exchange of body parts for money" would they be morally acceptable to you? Why?

d. If people could sell body parts for money, would rich patients be able to obtain the body parts and live longer lives while poor patients, who could not "afford" to pay for the used body parts, would simply die?

e. Do you believe that the economist who suggests the possibility of paying for used body organs is cynical, immoral, and without any concern for human values? Why?

THE ANSWERS

1. Perhaps your "guilty conscience" might be quieted if you realized that the outcome would have been the same whether you voted or not. Sure, you can criticize legislation if you didn't vote, because the election results and the legislation would have been the same whether you voted or not. There are many reasons people don't vote in the "off-year" elections, including the fact that there is less media hype to vote and individuals suffer less social pressure if they don't vote during the off-year elections. Also, many individuals probably place a lower value on the voting outcome differential during off-year elections.

2. **a.** You would probably find that both types of billboards provided you with little useful information. However, the billboards of politicians might have provided you with just a little less information. Politicians have an incentive not to take strong public positions that might alienate voters who have a strong preference intensity on the opposing side without attracting voters who have low intensities on the supporting side. If a politician is in favor of granting construction subsidies to the American maritime industry, she will state her position at the annual convention of the maritime industry and not on billboards. Thus, you would likely see political ads containing the candidate's name, picture, and, possibly, one or two meaningless clichés.

b. Television enables political and private market advertisers to provide more information. Although neither might provide much explicit information, you could obtain some valuable information from political ads. Since you would not want to invest much time in obtaining knowledge about public issues, you would be very interested in the values of the politician so that you could vote for a candidate who came closest to sharing your values. Television ads do provide some information on the "kind of person" the candidate is, which is useful to the voter. Candidates know this, and they try hard to sell themselves without being explicit on specific issues.

3. Only you know the answer to the first three questions. A very small percentage of the American population has "donated" blood, and most of those have done so for money (money is paid for plasma) or other incentives, such as a day or two off from work, prizes of various sorts, or because the boss "suggested" it. Blood is technically a private good because we can exclude nonpayers from receiving it. However, most individuals would not want to deny blood to those who "needed" it and could not afford to pay for it, so a sufficient blood supply takes on many attributes of a public good. Similarly, electing politicians to office is a public good. Individuals need some selective incentive to vote and to donate blood, and the free rider problem is applicable to both. If there is not an appropriate individual incentive, the country will be unable to procure a sufficient quantity of blood and a sufficient number of voters.

4. If you are solely responsible for the paper, you know that there is a direct relationship between your efforts and the grade received. Hence, you have an incentive to spend some time on it. However, in a group even as small as 25 students you would have an incentive to "free ride" on the efforts of others, and the quality of the group paper would likely reflect the "free rider" problem. Can you think of one or more ways the professor might reduce these "free rider" effects?

5. **a.** Some individuals would be willing to part with one kidney if, say, they received $10,000 for it. Thousands of individuals with total kidney failure would be willing to pay more than $10,000. Why would you want to keep these two sets of individuals from engaging in mutually beneficial trades? Are you willing to accept the moral responsibility of denying life to thousands of individuals who cannot obtain these body parts because you and others believe such trades are immoral? Perhaps you are concerned that the poor, but not the rich, would sell their body parts for money, and you view this as discrimination against the poor. As many other neophytes in economics, you are unnecessarily mixing issues. If you're concerned about the poor, the issue is unequal income distribution, which is totally different from the issue of procuring used body parts. It might be unfortunate that there are poor people who are willing to sell their body parts, but their welfare, as they view it, would be increased by selling them. Just as some individuals are willing to pick crops for $4 per hour, work on tall skyscrapers, be policeman or firemen, there are others who believe that their welfare would be increased if they could sell a kidney for $10,000. The poor are better off and not worse off as a result.

b. You can, of course, view such contracts as morally undesirable and refuse to sign one. However, if you voted or lobbied to prohibit such contracts because you believed that only a "sick" or immoral society would permit such contracts, you should realize that you would be prohibiting individuals, some very poor, from increasing their income by $200. Most importantly, you would be condemning some individuals to death, blindness, or a life on a dialysis machine. That is the moral trade-off with which you are confronted. The issue is not simply determining whether such contracts violate moral principles about the sanctity of the human body. You have to examine the *moral effects* of your decision. Is the sanctity of the human body a higher moral goal than the life and quality of life of the recipients?

c. "Sure," you say, "I would sign such a contract because it does not involve trading body parts for money." Take out your driver's license and turn it over. Does it contain the following statement or one similar to it: "I, the undersigned, hereby consent to the donation of my _____ as an anatomical gift at the time of my death under the provision of Act _____ . Signature _____ Date _____ Witness _____"

Have you signed this "will of life" which many states provide on the back of driver's licenses? Why? Do you know anyone who has signed it? Would you sign it if you received $200 . . . $500 . . . $1,000? Why?

d. If you answered yes, you are confusing issues once again. The issue being discussed is how a society should procure used body parts and not how a society should allocate the body parts that are procured. Body parts procured through a price mechanism could be allocated by a private firm, a nonprofit institution, or a government agency using the price mechanism, a queuing system, professional opinion, age, sex, income, race, or any of the other discriminatory mechanisms that were discussed in previous chapters. There is no reason why body parts have to be *allocated* by the price system if they are *procured* by the price mechanism. The services of doctors and nurses are procured through the price-wage mechanism, but many of their services are allocated to the poor through various other mechanisms, including subsidies, grants, and Medicare. A serious and stressful task confronting those in the medical profession is deciding which of the many patients should receive one of the very few body parts the present system happens to provide.

e. An economist is concerned about the efficient procurement and allocation of resources. If Able has two apples and wants to sell one for 10 cents and Baker has no apples and places a value of 20 cents on one apple, the economist wants to investigate why trade is not occurring. He will point out that if trade does occur, the welfare of both individuals will be improved. Moralists might argue that Able *should* be willing to give that apple to Baker without charge. If Able gives Baker an apple without expecting anything in return, the economist will applaud Able's humanity and keep quiet. However, if a considerable period of time passes and Able does not give the apple to Baker, the economist must conclude that Able is not sufficiently motivated by considerations of Baker's welfare and he will suggest the use of the price mechanism as a way to improve human welfare. The same approach can be applied to used body parts. If individuals would freely and willingly donate blood and other body parts in sufficient quantities, the economist would happily keep quiet and applaud the humanity of the donors. Unfortunately, the economist has to deal with people as they really are rather than as he wishes they would be. Sufficient quantities of apples, bread, clothing, housing, Bibles, text-books, and used body parts are simply not provided by those who are motivated by a concern for humanity. Hence, the price incentive (or some other incentive, such as physical force or social pressure) has to be used to procure these goods, or shortages will persist and difficult decisions will have to be made about how such shortages are to be shared. The economist does not claim that the use of the price system is morally inferior or superior to any other system, including one that generates severe shortages. He does not conclude that voting or becoming informed about public issues is moral or immoral or that people should act in certain ways. He takes peoples' decisions and actions as he sees them and tries to point out the benefits and costs and, occasionally, the moral trade-offs.

Obviously, the more valuable a good is to consumers, the more concerned the economist will be that the good is efficiently procured and allocated. The economist knows that there are few, if any, goods that have a higher marginal value to consumers than those that pro-long life and reduce suffering. Hence, it is both professionally and morally disturbing to economists—certainly to this author—that thousands of people die each year and additional thousands despair because of the shortage of used body parts. While not wanting to dictate morality or to criticize the moral values of others, the economist who points out that the price mechanism could reduce or eliminate shortages of used body parts or the economist who concludes that individuals require an incentive to vote and to obtain information on public issues is simply trying to improve the welfare of fellow citizens. Do you think the economist's analyses should be rejected because it appears to some that he is immoral, cynical, crass, and uncaring?

CHAPTER SIX

THE WILL OF THE PEOPLE

The people's government, made for the people, made by the people and answerable to the people.
—DANIEL WEBSTER, 1830

Democracy is the worst form of government, except for all the rest.
—WINSTON CHURCHILL

PREFERENCE INDICATORS

Individuals have varying preferences and intensities of preferences for public and private goods. The function of a preference indicator is to provide information on individuals' preferences so that scarce resources can be allocated efficiently. The larger and more complex a society becomes, the greater the social importance of these indicators. Preference indicators are not needed for a few individuals living on an island, but as population increases, as political power tends to gravitate toward larger political units, and as goods, services, and externalities proliferate, the science of political economy—which studies preference indicators and their relative efficiency in the political and private markets—becomes increasingly important.

Prices constitute aggregate preference indicators in the free private market. They provide signals to producers, informing them of the preference patterns of individuals, and they supply information to consumers, informing them of the relative scarcities of goods. Prices also induce suppliers to increase their provision of the scarcest resources and goods and reward consumers for conserving the scarcest resources and goods. Preference indicators are needed in the political market to perform similar functions, and the type of such indicators will depend upon the political framework of the country. If a dictator exercises complete control over all subjects, the only preference that counts is that of the dictator, and his dictates will be a reliable indicator of his preference orderings and intensities. Preference indicators in a weak dictatorship would be the preferences of the dictator constrained by the preferences of powerful political revolutionaries. Similar indicators would exist in oligarchic or elitist political frameworks. Such preference indicators are inappropriate, however, in a democracy, in which the preferences of all citizens are supposed to count.

A very useful framework for examining the efficiency of preference indicators and understanding political markets in Western democracies is the individualistic model, which clearly illustrates the obvious fact that the state is a collection of individuals and not a separate organic entity that exists apart from the individuals who comprise it. It accepts the view that the preference indicator most appropriate and realistic for a democracy is the individual's vote and that the individual voter is motivated by his or her own preferences. As mentioned in chapter 5, it also assumes that citizens possess information about issues or candidates and that they do vote.

MAJORITY VOTING AND DISCRIMINATION

Preference indicators in the political market are revealed by the collective outcome produced when individuals cast their votes. Later in this chapter we will examine the efficiency of alternative voting mechanisms, but first we need to examine some problems that can arise when majority voting is used to reveal individual preferences and to make collective choices. Assume the following:

1. Government provides some service, say national defense, to a community of 300 individuals divided, according to marginal evaluation, into groups A and B.

2. The marginal cost (equal to the average cost) of producing the public good is a constant $25,000 per unit.

3. Group A voters pay $50 per unit of the public good, and Group B voters pay $100.[1]

4. Initially, all fiscal decisions are made unanimously, that is, all voters must approve all fiscal bills before they can become law.

If this were a private good, we know that each individual would want to equate his marginal evaluation with the market price. This is also true for public goods. Each voter will prefer a quantity of public goods at which his own marginal evaluation equals the marginal tax-price. Confronting the fixed tax-prices given in assumption 3, *all* voters will vote for the provision of 5 units of the public good. Group A voters will vote for 5 units because the marginal tax-price (MTP) they will pay for the fifth unit ($50) is equal to the marginal benefits they obtain from the fifth unit ($50). At a quantity

---

[1] The assumptions that the individual's marginal tax-price is constant over all quantities of the public good and that the public good is produced under constant cost conditions are used to simplify the analysis, but the essential equilibrium and efficiency properties would not change if these assumptions were relaxed. See James Buchanan, *Demand and Supply of Public Goods* (Chicago: Rand McNally, 1968) for a discussion of the effects of alternative assumptions.

—————————————— **TABLE 6-1** ——————————————
MARGINAL EVALUATION OF PUBLIC GOODS

Units of the Public Good	Group A 100 Voters	Group B 200 Voters
1	$150	$200
2	125	175
3	100	150
4	60	120
5	50	100
6	25	75
7	0	50
8	0	25
9	0	0

smaller than 5 units, their marginal evaluation would be greater than their marginal tax-price, and they would want to have more units provided. At a quantity greater than 5 units their marginal tax-price would be greater than the marginal benefits obtained, so they would want fewer units provided. Since voters in Group B are being charged $100 per unit of the public good, they will vote for the provision of 5 units, at which their marginal tax-prices equal their marginal evaluations ($100).

The individual's decision-making process for public goods is essentially the same as it is for private goods. Each individual tries to adjust to the quantity where his marginal evaluation for the good is equal to the price he has to pay for it. In this hypothetical and severely constrained example, there is a unanimous decision that 5 units should be provided. Also, the democratic voting mechanism has produced an efficient, or optimal, outcome:

Efficiency Conditions for a Public Good and Pareto Optimality Are Satisfied at 5 Units:

(1) The Aggregate Condition: ΣME = MC
    Sum of Marginal Evaluations   = Marginal Cost of Public Good
    ($50 × 100) + ($100 × 200)   = $25,000

(2) The Individual Condition: $ME^i = MTP^i$
    (a) $ME^{\text{Group A Voter}}$ = $MTP^{\text{Group A Voter}}$
             $50   = $50
    (b) $ME^{\text{Group B Voter}}$ = $MTP^{\text{Group B Voter}}$
             $100   = $100

The use of a unanimity voting system satisfies the two efficiency conditions for public goods and produces Pareto optimality.

Let's now shift from a fixed-price unanimous voting model to one where a simple majority determines the outcome and the majority can place the tax burden on whomever it chooses, that is, assumptions 3 and 4 are relaxed. If there are no constitutional restrictions on the ability of the majority to practice tax discrimination, the 200 voters in Group B will vote for their preferred quantity of the public good and place the entire tax burden on the members of Group A. Since Group B voters will pay no costs for the public good, they will vote for a quantity of public goods where their marginal value for the public good equals zero, which occurs at 9 units. The political unit will provide 9 units, the total cost of the public good will be $225,000 (9 × $25,000), and the tax-price for each member in Group A will be $250 per unit of the public good, for a total of $2,250 for 9 units. Thus, each member of Group A will be paying $250 for the ninth unit of the public good, which he values at zero. The simple majority voting system has enabled the majority to shift the tax burden to the minority. In addition to this equity problem of the majority discriminating against the minority, majority voting will most likely produce economic inefficiency or a misallocation of resources.

Efficiency Conditions and Pareto Optimality Are Not Satisfied at 9 Units:

(1) The Aggregate Condition: $\Sigma ME = MC$
       Sum of Marginal Evaluations   < Marginal Cost of Public
                                                       Good
                  $0   < $25,000

(2) The Individual Condition: $ME^i = MTP^i$
       (a) $ME^{\text{Group A Voter}}$ < $MTP^{\text{Group A Voter}}$
                  $0   < $250
       (b) $ME^{\text{Group B Voter}}$ = $MTP^{\text{Group B Voter}}$
                  $0   = $0

The marginal evaluations of all individuals for the ninth unit of the public good is zero but the social cost of providing the ninth unit is $25,000, or $\Sigma ME < MC$. Obviously, simple majority voting has led to an excessive supply of public goods and a waste of the country's resources. This is to be expected if the majority of voters can determine the quantity of the public good while placing the burden of financing the public good on the minority. Since the majority pay no cost for the public good, they will always want to extend the quantity of public goods until their own marginal values are zero. Blatant tax discrimination such as this violates the commonly accepted principle of horizontal equity—that taxes should be applied on a uniform and nondiscriminatory basis. It is unconstitutional in the United States and most Western democracies.[2] Hence, the majority of voters are constrained from practicing such egregious discrimination, but majority voting can produce other problems.

One realistic problem in the political market arises when the majority of voters enact taxes to finance public goods that benefit the majority more than the minority. Individuals are required to pay an identical tax-price per unit of the public good, but their marginal evaluations differ. Assume the same set of data as in Table 6-1, except that the cost of the public good is $30,000 per unit. Assume that individuals are each taxed $100 per unit, which is equal to the cost of the public good divided by the number of citizens.

The majority of voters, who are in Group B, will vote for the provision of 5 units, at which their marginal evaluation ($100) equals their marginal tax-price ($100). However, members in Group A will also have to pay $100 per unit for 5 units, even though their marginal evaluation for the fifth unit is only $50.

Efficiency Conditions and Pareto Optimality Are Not Satisfied at 5 Units:

(1) The Aggregate Condition: $\Sigma ME = MC$
     Sum of Marginal Evaluations   < Marginal Cost of Public
                                          Good
            $25,000   < $30,000

(2) The Individual Condition: $ME^i = MTP^i$
     (a) $ME^{\text{Group A Voter}}$ < $MTP^{\text{Group A Voter}}$
                $50   < $100
     (b) $ME^{\text{Group B Voter}}$ = $MTP^{\text{Group B Voter}}$
                $100   = $100

The marginal cost of the fifth unit is $30,000, but the community's total marginal evaluation is only $25,000 ($100 × 200 + $50 × 100); the community will sacrifice $30,000 worth of resources to obtain marginal benefits of $25,000. Hence, majority voting results in a waste of resources by providing too many units of the public good.

Budget decisions in a democracy are made by the majority who vote for the quantity of the public good at which their marginal evaluation is equal to their marginal tax-price. The majority of voters ignore the marginal social cost of providing the public good, and they base their decisions

---

[2] Such obvious tax discrimination is not possible, but the majority might come close to achieving similar results if the minority (Group A) consumed certain goods that the majority did not. The majority could then place excise taxes on those goods and still meet the non-discriminatory criterion.

solely on the tax-price that they confront. In the above example the majority coalition voted to provide an inefficiently large quantity of the public good. If the distribution of preferences had been reversed—200 voters in Group A and 100 in Group B—only 3 units would have been produced and *less* than the optimal quantity of public goods would have been provided by majority voting, $\Sigma ME > MC$. Thus, an informed majority can vote to provide too much or too little of the public good. Furthermore, majority voting produces a serious equity problem. In our example the voters in Group A were forced to pay $100 for the fourth and fifth units of the public good, even though they valued the units at $60 and $50, respectively. The example could have been easily changed so that Group A, the minority, had a zero marginal evaluation for the first unit. The public expenditures then would have benefited only those in the majority, Group B, while those not benefiting at all would have had to pay for the public good.

While constitutional constraints place limits on the degree of tax discrimination that a majority can levy on the minority, there are no such constitutional constraints on the expenditure side. The Supreme Court has ruled that Congress can make whatever expenditures it desires.[3] Consequently, Congress and most legislative bodies, which are prohibited from practicing tax discrimination, can establish programs to benefit certain regions, occupations, industries, or races and deny them to others who, nevertheless, must share in the financing of the expenditures.

WICKSELL'S UNANIMITY RULE

The first economist to recognize that simple majority voting could result in the majority passing expenditure bills to benefit themselves while placing the tax burden on the minority was Knut Wicksell, a Swedish economist who wrote around the turn of the century.[4] He recommended a "new principle of taxation" based on two fundamental proposals. The first proposal was intended to change the common legislative practice—then and now—of considering revenue and expenditure bills separately.

---

[3] 262 U.S. 447 (1923).

[4] Johann Gustav Wicksell (1851-1926) was 49 years old before he received his first academic appointment, which was the chair of political economy and fiscal law at Lund University in Sweden. He is most widely known for his pioneering theoretical works in money, marginal productivity, and capital. Wicksell's relative unanimity theory is often criticized as being reactionary because, according to its critics, it enables a minority to veto changes favored by the majority. Actually, Wicksell was a radical reformer who championed such causes as universal suffrage, workers' rights, birth control, and a stationary population. It was his interest in the latter that led him to Malthus's work on population and, subsequently, into economics.

Wicksell proposed that each government expenditure bill be accompanied by a related tax bill to finance that expenditure, which would enable the benefits and costs of the expenditure to be considered simultaneously. Second, to avoid tax and expenditure discrimination by the majority, Wicksell proposed that this joint expenditure-tax package be passed unanimously by the legislature.[5] One hundred percent approval makes fiscal decision making analogous to the voluntary exchange mechanism in the private market in which no individual can be forced to pay for unwanted public goods. By his single negative vote, an individual, or representative, could veto any tax-expenditure proposal and, thus, could not be forced to pay for or to consume unwanted public goods. The unanimity rule is the only voting rule certain to lead to Pareto optimality, in which all individuals benefit from government fiscal decisions. Wicksell and his supporters recognized that democracies permit expenditure discrimination that enables the majority to vote for expenditures that provide benefits to themselves. They also recognized that majority voting may generate either too much or too little of the public good, because the majority of voters will equate their estimated tax-price with their marginal evaluation without any consideration for the preferences of the minority. It was to ensure against such possibilities that Wicksell argued that a unanimous voting rule be adopted.

There are two major problems with Wicksell's unanimity rule. First, it could take so much time and other resources to reach a unanimous decision that citizens might prefer the risk of being exploited by the majority rather than bearing the costs of reaching a unanimous decision. Second, strategic behavior is encouraged by Wicksellian unanimity. Since each individual would know that a single vote could veto any proposal desired by everyone else, he would be placed in a strong bargaining position. Even though a particular tax-expenditure proposal might benefit him, the individual could engage in strategic behavior and hold out for even lower taxes or greater benefits. At the extreme, an individual would attempt to garner all of the gains from trade for himself. With each individual engaging in strategic behavior for himself or his constituents, few tax-expenditure packages would be enacted by the legislature. Wicksell recognized this possibility and agreed to a qualified or relative unanimity between 75 and 90 percent of the legislature. This meant that each individual would know that his single negative vote could not veto a budget proposal and that if he held out for a large portion of the benefits, other voters could make

---

[5] Knut Wicksell, "A New Principle of Just Taxation," in *Classics in the Theory of Public Finance*, eds. R. T. Musgrave and A. T. Peacock (New York: Martin's Press, 1967).

a deal without him. Thus, strategic behavior would be lessened considerably by relative unanimity while offering the minority some protection against the majority.

Although Wicksell didn't realize it at the time, he initiated the basic theory of interaction costs, later formalized by Buchanan and Tullock.[6] An individual in society is confronted with two types of cost related to collective decision making. The first type of cost is the bargaining cost required to reach a group decision. Decision-making costs include the time and other resources that are used in bargaining with others, reaching agreements, and making decisions. If 100 percent of the vote were required to make a decision, bargaining costs would be substantial because of the time required to inform and bargain with all citizens and the extensive strategic behavior of the votes. Voters attempting to hold out for greater gains would make it difficult to arrive at any decision. Holding the number of voters constant, the higher the percentage of the group required to approve a political decision, the higher the costs, because more effort would be required to secure cooperation from, say, 70 percent of the group than from 30 percent. Curve BC in Figure 6-1 shows the increasing costs to the individual as the percentage required for approval increases from 1 to 100 percent.

The individual also confronts an externality cost, which is the expected cost borne by him if he disapproves of the decision. For example, if 1 percent of the electorate can enact a budget policy and require the other 99 percent to abide by its decision, the costs resulting from such a rule could be quite high to the individual. As the percentage of voters required to approve a budget increases, these externality costs go down. At the extreme of 100 percent, or unanimity, the individual does not have to worry about externality costs because his own approval is required. Externality costs would then be zero. Curve VE represents these voter externality costs as the percentage of the group required for approval increases.

Curve AA is a simple vertical summation of these two costs. Given the way the curves are drawn, the political interaction costs are minimized when approval by 70 percent of the group is required for all budget decisions. Economists have not been able to obtain data to quantify these curves, but they shouldn't be expected to do so. The analysis merely enables us to conceptualize the variables involved and to illustrate that 50-percent approval has no magic or scientific superiority.

---

[6] James M. Buchanan and Gordon Tullock, *The Calculus of Consent* (Ann Arbor: University of Michigan Press, 1962).

FIGURE 6-1
PERCENTAGE OF GROUP REQUIRED TO REACH A DECISION

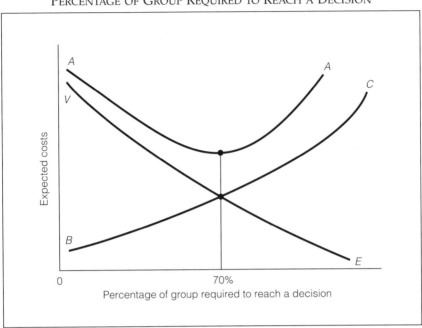

FIGURE 6-1
PERCENTAGE OF GROUP REQUIRED TO REACH A DECISION

ANALYSES OF ALTERNATIVE VOTING SYSTEMS

The very nature of public goods requires that decisions about their provision be made collectively. There can be no national will, agenda, or goals apart from the preferences of individuals comprising the nation. Thus, an important task of any democracy is finding an efficient means of transferring the preferences of individual citizens into a single, collective preference and a national program. Although voters have little incentive to vote and to obtain knowledge about issues and candidates, there is no acceptable alternative to counting the preferences of those individuals who do vote. Hence, the foundation of all voting analyses must begin with the individual. As stated above, the individual voter wishing to make a rational decision must know the tax-prices for marginal units of the public good and the alternative quantities of the public good that are potentially available. We will assume that the individual possesses this information, and we will begin the analysis by assuming that each individual will vote directly—rather than through a representative—for the quantity of the public good, although the analysis will later be applied to a vote for representatives.

RANKING OF PREFERENCES

Assume that Individual A knows that each unit of the public good, say a nuclear submarine, will cost some constant tax-price, and, consequently, she is able to rank her preferences for alternative quantities of submarines. Based on Individual A's perceived tax-prices, assume her first preference is to have 4 submarines; if she cannot have 4 submarines, she prefers to have 3; if she cannot have 3, she prefers to have 5; followed by 2 and then 1 submarine. This order of preferences can be represented by a simple vertical or horizontal preference ranking [see Figure 6-2(a) and (b)]. A third method of representing Individual A's preferences is shown in Figure 6-2(c). The public good alternatives are placed on the horizontal axis in ascending order of magnitude, while the preference ranking is shown on the vertical axis. The vertical spaces between the rankings have no meaning; only the relative levels are important. Thus, starting at the peak of the curve we can see that Individual A prefers 4 submarines; her next

---

FIGURE 6-2

INDIVIDUAL A'S RANK ORDER OF PREFERENCE FOR NUMBER OF SUBMARINES

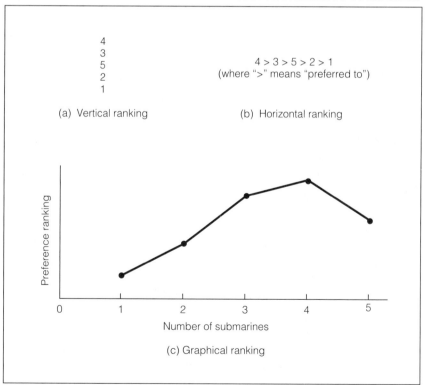

highest ranked preference is 3 submarines, followed by 5, then 2 submarines; and her least preferred alternative is 1 submarine. An important characteristic of Figure 6-2(c) is that the preference curve is *single peaked*, which means that it does not change direction at all, or if it does change direction, it moves from up to down only once.[7] The preference curve in Figure 6-3(a) is single peaked because it does not change direction at all,

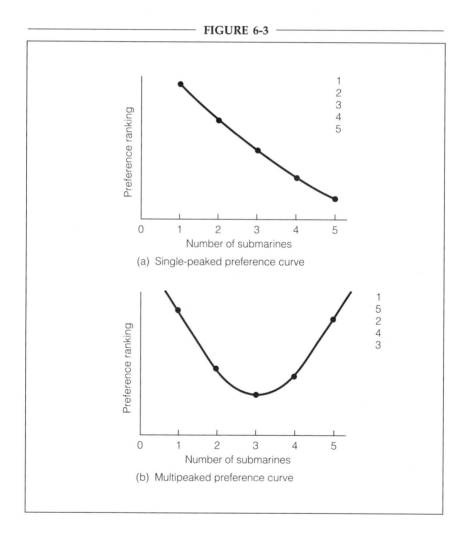

FIGURE 6-3

(a) Single-peaked preference curve

(b) Multipeaked preference curve

---

[7] Starting at the origin the curve can go up and then turn downward once and still be a single-peaked curve. If it descends and then turns upward, there are two peaks, or one at each extremity.

and the preference curve in Figure 6-3(b) is multipeaked because it goes down then up. It has a peak at 1 unit and at 5 units. Single peaks occur when voters believe that there is an optimum (their preferred choice) amount of the public good, and the further away the quantity of the public good is from that optimum, the worse off the individual becomes.

The preference curves and associated single-peaked rankings shown in Figure 6-2(c) and 6-3(a) make obvious sense. The preference ordering in Figure 6-2(c) reflects a first preference for 4 submarines (a moderate militarist); the second preference of this voter is 3 submarines; and the third preference is 5 submarines. This individual's preference ranking suggests a preference for a moderate defense position (4 or 3 submarines), but if he can't get that, he would prefer to have a militant policy (5 submarines), and his lowest preferences are for a dovish 1 or 2 submarines. The preferences of the voter in Figure 6-3(a) can be described as those of a pacifist who prefers the country to build only 1 submarine; next he prefers having 2 submarines, then 3 submarines, and so on. The multipeaked preferences represented in Figure 6-3(b) are more difficult to understand. The individual's highest preference is 1 submarine (a pacifist preference), but his next highest preference is 5 submarines (a hawkish preference), then the next highest preference is 2 submarines (a moderate pacifist preference).

The preferences reflected in Figure 6-3(b) *are* rational and transitive, and there have been periods in American history when a considerable number of voters apparently had multipeaked preferences. During the Vietnam War, for example, the first preference of many voters apparently was an aggressive policy of invading and bombing North Vietnam, while their second preference was pulling the troops out. Their third, fourth, and fifth preferences were some combination of gradual escalation or gradual withdrawal. This "win or get out" preference function was multipeaked, similar to Figure 6-3(b). Such multipeaked preferences are clearly possible and are rational, but they are not common. As will be explained below, the significance of multipeaked preferences is that they can lead to inconsistent aggregate voting behavior. These methods of expressing the preference rankings of individuals will be used to analyze voting behavior and the efficiency of alternative voting systems.

SIMPLE MAJORITY VOTING SYSTEM

One of the most easily understood voting methods is a *simple majority,* in which each voter casts a single vote for his or her most preferred alternative, and that alternative or candidate receiving more than 50 percent of the votes is elected. When there are more than two alternatives, there may be no alternative that receives more than one-half of the votes. Thus, there is no winner. Simple majority elections can be used efficiently in direct referendums, in which the voters approve or disapprove some proposal, or in elections in which a number of alternatives have been narrowed to only two through some other voting system. In the latter case, the efficiency of the simple majority system is determined by the efficiency of the voting methods that narrowed the field to two alternatives.

SINGLE VOTE PLURALITY

One of the most commonly used election systems in corporate board rooms and parent-teacher associations as well as in political elections in English-speaking countries is the single vote plurality. *Single vote plurality* permits each elector to cast one vote, and the alternative or candidate receiving the most votes (a plurality) is the winner. Assume that there are a total of 25 voters with varying preference rankings among the 5 alternatives v, w, x, y, and z, which represent left-to-right positions on the political spectrum (see Table 6-2).

The 8 voters who prefer alternative v constitute a plurality, so v wins the election. However, an overwhelming majority (15) of the voters view v as the least desired alternative. This illustrates a very serious deficiency in the single vote plurality system. A minority of voters can elect a much hated alternative or candidate because single vote plurality reveals only the first preferences of voters while suppressing all indications of lower preferences. A single vote plurality, in effect, assumes that voters are indifferent to all but their first preferences. It assumes, incorrectly, the preference rankings illustrated in Table 6-3. If all voters actually have such preference rankings, then the single vote plurality will accurately reflect the rankings, but it is highly unlikely that voters have one preferred alternative and are indifferent to all other alternatives.

————————————————TABLE 6-2 ————————————————

Group A 8 Voters	Group B 7 Voters	Group C 5 Voters	Group D 3 Voters	Group E 2 Voters
v	z	w	y	x
y	y	x	z	w
x	x	y	x	v
w	w	z	w	y
z	v	v	v	z

TABLE 6-3

Group A 8 Voters	Group B 7 Voters	Group C 5 Voters	Group D 3 Voters	Group E 2 Voters
v	z	w	y	x
w, x, y, z	v, x, y, w	v, x, y, z	v, w, x, z	v, w, y, z

Single vote plurality is a grossly inefficient and dangerous voting scheme, which highlights the importance of analyzing the characteristics of an efficient voting system. The most important criterion for an efficient voting system is that the entire preference ordering of voters must be represented and the alternative or candidate with the highest average standing on the voters' preference ranking should be elected.[8] A candidate or alternative meeting this criterion is called the efficient candidate or alternative. A real-world danger of single vote plurality is that radical minorities are able to garner a plurality of votes, even though the radical alternative may be highly detested by the majority of voters. As the number of alternatives increase, the greater the likelihood that minority groups located at one end of the political spectrum could win a plurality.

There have been many notable real-world examples of voter preferences being distorted by the single vote plurality. James Buckley was elected United States senator from New York in 1970 with only 39 percent of the vote, and John Lindsay was reelected mayor of New York City in 1969 with 42 percent of the vote. Both candidates most probably would have lost if a more efficient voting system had been utilized. In the 1980 New York senatorial race Alphonse D'Amato (Republican) received 45 percent of the vote, Elizabeth Holtzman (Democrat) received 44 percent, and Jacob Javits (Liberal) received 11 percent. An ABC exit poll revealed that if Javits had not been in the race, Holtzman would have won. Nixon won the 1968 presidential election with 43.4 percent of the vote, while Humphrey received 42.7 percent and Wallace 14 percent.[9] Adolph Hitler never received more than 40 percent of the vote, but he was fairly elected by the Weimar Republic's use of the single vote plurality and by the existence of 15 parties in the Reichstag between 1928 and 1932.

---

[8] Duncan Black was the first economist to analyze the efficiency properties of alternative voting systems. He refused to further narrow the average criterion by specifying mode, median, or mean, because it was impossible to prove that, say, the arithmetic mean was superior as a measure of average to the mode or median. This is a normative criterion for evaluating voting systems that is based on the premise that every voter's entire preference schedule should be reflected. Such rankings for private goods are reflected in the private market.

[9] The following presidents in this century were elected with less than 50 percent of the popular vote: Wilson (1912 and 1916), Truman, Kennedy, and Nixon. Wilson, who won the election in 1912, received less than 42 percent of the popular vote.

SINGLE VOTE PRIMARY (DOUBLE ELECTION)

Primary systems, widely utilized in the United States, involve two or more successive elections to determine the winning candidate or alternative. Generally, the primary system is related to the selection of candidates, but it can be applied to the selection of issues as well. A single vote primary is the same as a double election, in which all alternatives are presented to voters in a first election and the two alternatives with the greatest pluralities are then placed against each other in a second (general) election. The alternative that receives the most votes in the second election wins. Another primary system involves groups of voters or political parties nominating a candidate in a primary election and then the party candidates compete in the general election. The candidate with the plurality of votes wins the general election.

The serious deficiency in the double election is that it is clearly possible for the alternative that, on the average, ranks highest in the voters' preferences to be eliminated in the first round. In Table 6-2, alternatives v and z would win the primary election and would face each other in the final election, which would be won by z (Groups B, C, and D would vote for z). Alternative y—the alternative that, on the average, ranks highest in the voters' preference ordering—is eliminated in the first round. The single vote primary, or double election, is not much more efficient than a single vote plurality, because only the first preferences of voters are revealed in the first election, and the most efficient alternative could be eliminated in the first election.

Most voting systems are likely to induce some degree of strategic behavior by voters. Strategic behavior occurs when voters do not actually vote according to their true preference ranking, because they hope that voting for a slightly less preferred alternative will keep an even less preferred alternative from winning the election. If individuals engage in strategic behavior, the voting outcome can be distorted. One frequent way of engaging in strategic behavior in the double election is to vote for a less preferred candidate in the primary because the voter believes that his preferred candidate has no chance of winning the second election. If a significant number of voters preferred w to v to x but voted for v because they thought that w didn't have a chance of winning in the second election, alternative v would win the election.

Voting theorists call a situation in which voters change their preferences in favor of a particular alternative that consequently loses the election a *monotonicity paradox*. This monotonicity paradox is often associated with a primary election employing a simple plurality voting system. Refer to the preference rankings listed in Table 6-4.

―――――――――――――――――――――TABLE 6-4 ―――――――――――――――――

Group A 800 Voters	Group B 700 Voters	Group C 600 Voters	Group D 300 Voters
v	x	w	w
w	v	x	v
x	w	v	x

If individuals voted their actual preference rankings in the first election of a double-election system, candidates v and w would get into the runoff and v would win the second, or general, election by 900 to 1,500 votes. Now let us change the assumptions to reflect the fact that Group D voters hear a rumor that their preferred candidate, w, has little chance of entering the second election. Consequently, Group D voters reorder their revealed preferences to $v > w > x$, and candidate v picks up another 300 first-place votes. Consequently, the top two vote getters in the first election would be candidates v (1,100 votes) and x (700 votes). In the second election, candidate v would receive 1,100 votes, while candidate x would receive 1,300 votes. Hence, v would get more first-place supporters and end up losing the double election. The reason, of course, is that the change in preferences resulted in candidate v facing candidate x in the second election and losing to x, whereas v would not have lost to w. When some voters change their preferences *in favor* of a candidate and this change causes the candidate or alternative to lose the election, a monotonicity paradox exists. It should more correctly be called the nonmonotonicity paradox because monotonicity exists when the candidate can be helped but not hurt by a favorable change in preferences. *Monotonicity simply means that an alternative cannot be hurt by being raised in the preference rankings of some voters while remaining the same in the rankings of all other voters.* The monotonicity paradox is most likely to occur in multistage election systems that use the single vote plurality to select the winners who will compete in subsequent elections. It also arises in some of the proportional representation methods discussed below.

The double election is used, with modifications, to elect the president in the United States and in France, where it is known as the second-ballot system. Most primary elections in the United States use a single vote plurality system, which can easily return inefficient winners in the primary and, thus, distort the selection of candidates nominated to run in the general election. A plurality primary system is a two-party democracy in which the overwhelming majority of members of both parties are moderates could nominate a left-wing radical in one party and a right-wing radical in the other party. The public would then be confronted with having to select one of the radicals for president in the general election. This has already happened in a few congressional districts but has not yet happened in the presidential primary. However, the selection of presidential delegates by popular votes in primary elections is relatively new, and one might contemplate the frustration of moderate voters if Barry Goldwater and George McGovern had been nominated by the Republican and Democratic parties in the same year. This is one of many examples of the practical impacts of inefficient voting systems.[10] Apart from the rational abstention and rational ignorance problems, the use of the single vote plurality to select presidential and congressional nominees is the most significant and dangerous problem in American politics.

ALTERNATIVE VOTE

The alternative vote, which is used in Australia, is more efficient than the single vote plurality or the single vote primary and would be an improvement over the current nomination voting system used in the United States. In the *alternative vote* system, individuals rank the candidates by marking on the ballot their preferences as first, second, third, fourth, and so on. The first preference votes are counted, and if any candidate receives more than one-half of the votes, he is declared the winner. If not, the candidate with the fewest first preference votes is eliminated, and all his votes are transferred to the candidates listed as second preferences. If one candidate now has a majority of votes, he is elected. If no one has a majority, the candidate with the fewest total votes is eliminated and second preferences are distributed among the remaining candidates. This process continues until one candidate emerges with more than 50 percent of the total votes cast. The preferences used in the example on page 167 have been reprinted in Table 6-5 to illustrate the alternative vote.

---

[10] A better-known inefficiency in the selection of the American president is the use of the electoral college. The electoral college consists of representatives from the 50 states (plus the District of Columbia) equal to each state's total congressional delegation. The smallest states have three electoral votes, while the largest (California) has 47. Because the representatives elected to the electoral college in each state give their votes *en bloc* for one presidential team, the clear possibility exists that the candidate winning the largest number of popular votes will obtain fewer electoral college votes and, thus, lose the election. Andrew Jackson led three challengers in the popular vote for the 1824 presidential election, but he was unable to obtain a majority in the electoral college. Hence, the election was thrown into the House of Representatives where Jackson lost. Rutherford B. Hayes in 1876 and Benjamin Harrison in 1888 were elected president even though they received fewer popular votes than their leading challengers.

--------------------------------------- TABLE 6-5 ---------------------------------------

Group A 8 Voters	Group B 7 Voters	Group C 5 Voters	Group D 3 Voters	Group E 2 Voters
v	z	w	y	x
y	y	x	z	w
x	x	y	x	v
w	w	z	w	y
z	v	v	v	z

On the first count, no alternative wins a majority of the votes, so alternative x, which received the fewest votes, would be eliminated (see Table 6-6). Alternative w, which is the second preference of the Group E voters, whose first preference was x, would receive 2 additional votes. No alternative has a majority on this second count, so alternative y would be eliminated, and Group D's second preference, z, would receive 3 more votes for a total of 10. No alternative has a majority of the votes, so w, which now has the fewest votes, would be eliminated. Alternative v would pick up 2 votes from Group E. Group C's first, second, and third choices have already been eliminated so its 5 votes would go to alternative z, which now has 15 votes, a majority of the 25 votes.

The alternative vote ensures that a radical candidate who appeals to a plurality of voters but is detested by the majority will not get elected. It does enable voters a limited opportunity to express the range of their preferences, but its major weakness is eliminating the candidate who receives the fewest first-preference votes. A candidate who is everyone's second choice, but the first choice of only a few, would be eliminated in the first round. Alternative x, for example, ranks fairly high on the average voters' preference rankings but is eliminated in the first round because only 2 voters listed x as their first preference. Alternative z, which is the winner of the alternative vote, ranks much lower on the voters' preferences than alternatives y or x. It wins because the other alternatives (x and y)

--------------------------------------- TABLE 6-6 ---------------------------------------

	v	w	x	y	z
First Count	8	5	2	3	7
Second Count	8	7	eliminated	3	7
Third Count	8	7		eliminated	10
Fourth Count	10	eliminated			15

on Group C's rankings were already eliminated. Hence, the efficient candidate could be eliminated in the first or second round.

EXHAUSTIVE PRIMARY SYSTEM

Exhaustive primaries involve the gradual elimination of alternatives through a series of elections. If there are 5 alternatives, each voter is given 4 votes to cast for all but the least preferred candidate. The alternative receiving the fewest votes in the first round is eliminated. A second election is held, with each voter getting 3 votes to cast among the remaining 4 alternatives. Once again, the alternative receiving the fewest votes is eliminated. Additional elections are held until only 2 alternatives remain, and the one receiving the most votes in the final election is declared the winner.

Since there are 5 alternatives in our continuing example (refer again to Table 6-5) each of the 25 voters would receive 4 votes, and Groups A and E would cast a vote for all alternatives but z; Groups B, C, and D would cast a vote for all alternatives but v. Hence, alternative v would be eliminated in the first round. In the second round alternative z, the winner of the alternative vote, would get only 10 votes (from Groups B and D), and it would be eliminated. Alternative w would receive only 7 votes in the third round, and it would be eliminated, leaving alternatives x and y to fight it out in the final election. Alternative y would win handily by 7 to 18 votes. Alternative y is the alternative that, on the average, stands highest in the preference ranking of all voters. Hence, by enabling voters to express their entire preference orderings, the lowest-ranking alternatives are gradually eliminated. Whenever voting preferences are single peaked, the exhaustive primary system will result in an efficient outcome and will almost always return the same winner as the exhaustive majority and the weighted ranking method.[11]

Voters could engage in strategic behavior in the exhaustive primary system by voting against their second most preferred candidate if they believed that their second preference was the most serious threat to their preferred candidate winning the election. For example, Group D voters who prefer alternative y to all other alternatives except v, may place y low on their preference rankings when they vote and, thus, eliminate y in the second round.

---

[11] If the voters' preferences are not single peaked, it is possible that the efficient alternative will be eliminated in the first elections. This is most likely to happen if the efficient alternative is the least preferred alternative of the requisite number of voters.

EXHAUSTIVE MAJORITY SYSTEM (CONDORCET CRITERION)

Condorcet, a French mathematician, philosopher, economist, and revolutionary, was one of the first persons to apply rigorous analysis to voting procedures.[12] Condorcet suggested that the most efficient alternative is the one that would defeat each of the other alternatives in a direct election. Some modern political economists, notably Duncan Black,[13] use the Condorcet method as a criterion to evaluate other voting systems. However, Condorcet's plan is also a viable voting scheme in itself; in the *exhaustive majority system*, voters are presented with a list of alternatives, and each alternative is placed against *each* of the other alternatives. The alternative that receives a simple majority over *each* of the other alternatives is selected. In our continuing example from Table 6-5, the winner of the exhaustive majority election is alternative y. If y is placed in a direct election against v, Groups A and E will vote for v but Groups B, C, and D will vote for y, which will defeat v. Thus, $y > v$. If y is placed against w in a direct election, only Groups C and E will vote for w, and $y > w$. Similarly, $y > x$, and $y > z$. Hence, alternative y is the only alternative that obtains a majority of votes when placed against each of the other alternatives. Therefore, it is declared to be the exhaustive majority winner.

The exhaustive majority system is far superior to the single vote plurality, double election, or alternative vote systems because it reflects the entire preference orderings of individuals and not merely the first preference. The alternative selected by the exhaustive majority system may not rank the highest on any voter's preference schedules, but it will rank relatively high on the average of all voters' preference schedules. In our example, alternative y would be selected by the exhaustive majority system even though it is the first preference of only 3 out of 25 voters. Alternatives located on the extremes tend to be eliminated by the exhaustive majority system unless, of course, the winning alternative is located on the extremity.

Strategic behavior is minimized in the exhaustive majority system. Voters cannot improve the winning chances of their most preferred alternative, but their strategy may result in the selection of their least preferred alternative. Because strategy is unlikely to be profitable but likely to be costly, it does not pose a very significant problem in the exhaustive majority system. The major deficiency of the exhaustive majority system is the possibility that no alternative will be able to obtain a majority over each

---

[12] See footnote on page 8 for a brief discussion of Condorcet.

[13] Duncan Black, *Theory of Committees and Elections* (Cambridge: Cambridge University Press, 1958). Students interested in voting theory should study Black's book because it is a modern classic in the field. This section is heavily indebted to Black's methodology and analysis.

of the other alternatives. In this case, the outcome would be indecisive, and some other voting system would have to supplement it. If there is a winner, however, that alternative generally will, on the average, stand highest on the voters' preferences.[14]

WEIGHTED RANKING VOTE

The *weighted ranking vote,* first suggested by Jean-Charles de Borda[15] in 1781, requires individuals to rank their preferences. Weights are assigned to the rankings by election commissioners or computers, and the alternative with the most weighted votes wins. Refer again to Table 6-5. The first-ranked preference would receive 5 weights; the second-ranked alternative would receive 4 weights; the third-ranked alternative would receive 3 weights; and so forth (see Table 6-7).

One can casually observe that alternative y stands highest on the voters' preferences on the average, and it is the one that receives the greatest number of weighted votes and is declared the winner. Notice that the winner of the weighted ranking vote is the same as the winner of the exhaustive majority vote, and it is the efficient alternative. Usually, but not always, the two voting systems will select the same winner if the exhaustive majority system selects a winner. One advantage of the weighted ranking method is that it will generally select a winner even if the exhaustive majority system does not.

The weighted ranking method is very attractive. It is simple, easy to understand and to calculate, and it returns the efficient alternative by counting the entire preference rankings of the votes. Once again, however, strategic behavior may be employed by the voters. For example, Group A voters, who have alternative y ranked second, may place alternative y

---

[14] The exhaustive majority winner might not always be the efficient winner. Assume that there are 41 voters with the following preferences:

Group A 21 Voters	Group B 20 Voters
a	b
b	c
c	a

Note that the Condorcet majority winner would be candidate a. This is one example where it appears that the Condorcet winner is not the efficient candidate. Candidate a is the preferred candidate of the majority of voters but the least preferred of the minority. Candidate b would be the efficient candidate.

[15]"Memoire sur les Elections au Scrutin," *Histoire de l'Academie Royale des Sciences,* 1781. Borda was a French mathematician and astronomer who spent a considerable part of his adult life in the French military. His paper on elections presented to the French Academy of Sciences was the first attempt to apply mathematical theory to voting.

TABLE 6-7

Group A 8 Voters	Group B 7 Voters	Group C 5 Voters
$v = 5 \times 8 = 40$	$z = 5 \times 7 = 35$	$w = 5 \times 5 = 25$
$y = 4 \times 8 = 32$	$y = 4 \times 7 = 28$	$x = 4 \times 5 = 20$
$x = 3 \times 8 = 24$	$x = 3 \times 7 = 21$	$y = 3 \times 5 = 15$
$w = 2 \times 8 = 16$	$w = 2 \times 7 = 14$	$z = 2 \times 5 = 10$
$z = 1 \times 8 = 8$	$v = 1 \times 7 = 7$	$v = 1 \times 5 = 5$

Group D 3 Voters	Group E 2 Voters
$y = 5 \times 3 = 15$	$x = 5 \times 2 = 10$
$z = 4 \times 3 = 12$	$w = 4 \times 2 = 8$
$x = 3 \times 3 = 9$	$v = 3 \times 2 = 6$
$w = 2 \times 3 = 6$	$y = 2 \times 2 = 4$
$v = 1 \times 3 = 3$	$z = 1 \times 2 = 2$

Final Weighted Votes

$v = 61; w = 69; x = 84; y = 94; z = 67$

---

at the bottom of their ballots, where it will receive a low weight, if they believe that alternative v, their most preferred alternative, and alternative y are the most likely to win the election. When such strategy is played, the outcome of the weighted ranking vote election will not correctly reflect the real preferences of individuals. The advantages of the weighted ranking vote are that it considers the ranked positions of all preference alternatives of all voters, it tends to eliminate extremist alternatives, and it is more likely to return alternatives identical or close to those returned by the exhaustive majority system.

APPROVAL VOTING

Approval voting is a newcomer to the list of voting mechanisms and has received serious scholarly interest only since the latter 1970s.[16] In *approval voting*, individuals are not restricted to voting for just one candidate. In fact, they can cast votes for all the candidates they approve. Each candidate gets a full vote from each voter who votes for him. The candidate with the most votes, and presumably acceptable to the most voters, wins the election.

---

[16] The most thorough examination of approval voting is provided in Steven J. Brams and Peter C. Fishburn, *Approval Voting* (Boston: Birkhauser, 1983).

Approval voting is more likely to return the efficient candidate than simple plurality and is likely to reduce the probability that an extremist candidate would win, but not much more can be said for it. It is subject to the vagaries that are produced by strategic behavior if voters fail to approve the alternative that ranks high on their preferences but is thought to be a close competitor of a preference that is more preferred. Approval voting assumes that there are considerable gaps in the intensity of preferences for the various candidates, and it is more efficient when voters can clearly group their "good alternatives" in one set and their "bad alternatives" in another set. If the intensity of the differences among the alternatives is about the same, there will exist no obvious division line between the good alternatives and the bad alternatives and the voter could just as easily cast one vote for v and none for w, x, or y. Or the voter could cast one vote for v and w and none for x or y, or one vote for v, w, and x and none for y.

For example, assume that the 25 voters in our example (see Table 6-5) have entered the voting booth and they have to decide which alternatives they will approve and which they will ignore. If they approved of their first three preferences we would have the results shown in Table 6-8. The winner would be alternative x, but if the voters approved of only their first two preferences, alternative y would win. If they approved of their first four preferences the election would result in a tie between alternatives w, x, and y. Many other outcomes are possible because some voters might approve of their first four preferences whereas others would approve of only their first choice.

POINT DISTRIBUTION METHOD

One advantage of the private market is that individuals can express the intensities of their preferences as well as their ranking of preferences. Individuals express the intensity of their preferences for private goods by adjusting the quantity they purchase. An individual who has an intense

—————— **TABLE 6-8** ——————

Alternatives	Votes
v	10
w	7
x	25
y	23
z	10

desire for mystery novels adjusts her annual consumption to the price of these novels. If the market price is $4 per novel, the individual may purchase and read 50 novels per year; if the price is lowered to $3, she may increase her consumption to 70 novels per year. If the individual is attending an auction, she will express her preference for an antique Shaker chair by the price she is willing to pay for it. Because of the nature of public goods, the individual cannot express the intensity of her preference by adjusting the quantity of the public good since, by definition, the public good is equally available to all citizens. She cannot directly adjust the price she is willing to pay because there is no direct price mechanism or quid pro quo for public goods. Since individuals express their preferences for public goods through a voting mechanism, any expression of intensity of preference has to occur through the ballot box. The previous discussion on voting was confined to individuals reflecting their preference rankings, but none of them reflected intensities of voter preferences. If an individual can express only the ranking of his preferences for public goods but not the intensity of these preferences, then, at least on this criterion, it must be concluded that the political market compares quite unfavorably with the private market.

Some scholars have suggested that individuals can express their intensities of preference for political alternatives through a point distribution system of voting. The numbers in Table 6-9 represent the relative intensities of the voters for the 5 alternatives. Groups A, C, and E have preferences that vary little in intensity, whereas Groups B and D have fairly strong feelings for some alternatives and against others. B voters strongly prefer alternative z, whereas D voters have strong tastes for y and z but have little desire for the other alternatives.

Assume that each voter is allowed 100 points to be distributed among the 5 alternatives and does not engage in strategic behavior. Each voter will distribute the points in exactly the same proportion as their preferences (see Table 6-10).

--- TABLE 6-9 ---

Group A 8 Voters		Group B 7 Voters		Group C 5 Voters		Group D 3 Voters		Group E 2 Voters	
v	25	z	70	w	26	y	38	x	27
y	23	y	10	x	23	z	37	w	20
x	20	x	9	y	19	x	15	v	19
w	17	w	8	z	17	w	6	y	18
z	15	v	3	v	15	v	4	z	16

TABLE 6-10

Group A 8 Voters	Group B 7 Voters	Group C 5 Voters
v $25 \times 8 = 200$	z $70 \times 7 = 490$	w $26 \times 5 = 130$
y $23 \times 8 = 184$	y $10 \times 7 = 70$	x $23 \times 5 = 115$
x $20 \times 8 = 160$	x $9 \times 7 = 63$	y $19 \times 5 = 95$
w $17 \times 8 = 136$	w $8 \times 7 = 56$	z $17 \times 5 = 85$
z $15 \times 8 = 120$	v $3 \times 7 = 21$	v $15 \times 5 = 75$

Group D 3 Voters	Group E 2 Voters
y $38 \times 3 = 114$	x $27 \times 2 = 54$
z $37 \times 3 = 111$	w $20 \times 2 = 40$
x $15 \times 3 = 45$	v $19 \times 2 = 38$
w $6 \times 3 = 18$	y $18 \times 2 = 36$
v $4 \times 3 = 12$	z $16 \times 2 = 32$

$$v = 346; \ w = 380; \ x = 437; \ y = 499; \ z = 838$$

The winner is z with 838 points

If individuals honestly voted their actual preferences, the point distribution voting system would enable relative preferences to be reflected, but voters are very likely to engage in strategic behavior. Since each voter wants his most preferred alternative to win, there is a strong incentive to cast all 100 points for the most preferred alternative. If this happens, and the probability is high that it would, the point distribution method deteriorates into the equivalence of the single vote plurality method. Thus, there is no effective system for voters to express the intensity of their preferences, and the best that an efficient voting system can do is to reflect the preference rankings of voters.

CYCLICAL MAJORITIES, NONTRANSITIVE SOCIAL PREFERENCES, OR MUCH ADO ABOUT LITTLE

Cyclical majorities have occupied the attention of voting scholars for nearly 200 years but especially during the past 30 years. Although they have little practical impact in the real world, they will be discussed here because the reader needs to recognize them in the voting literature. A cyclical majority exists when there is no alternative that is able to obtain a simple majority over each of the other alternatives and the outcome is indeterminate. Table 6-11 shows the preference rankings of three voters. The

——— **TABLE 6-11** ———

A	B	C
v	w	x
w	x	v
x	v	w

preference ranking of each voter is transitive, that is, each voter has a consistent preference ordering, and no cycles exist. Individual A, for example, prefers v to w and w to x. Thus, he also prefers v to x. If Individual A preferred x to v, his preferences would be intransitive, or inconsistent. Individual B prefers w to x and x to v. His preferences are transitive and consistent. Individual C prefers x to v and v to w, and his preferences are consistent and transitive. There are no transitivity problems with the preference rankings of individual voters. However, when the three individuals vote according to the exhaustive majority system (Condorcet Criterion), strange results are produced. If v is placed in a direct election against w, alternative v will win with the votes of A and C. If w is placed in a direct election against x, A and B will vote for w, and w will win. Now comes the surprise. When x is placed against v, B and C will vote for x, and x will win. Hence, there is no clear winner of the election because there is a cycle:

$$v > w > x > v$$

This result is known by many names: nontransitivity, cyclical majority, impossibility theorem, voting paradox, or the Arrow problem, named after Professor Kenneth Arrow, who was incorrectly given credit for discovering it.[17] The cyclical majority is generally shown with the exhaustive majority system (Condorcet Criterion), but it shows up in other voting methods as well. A plurality system applied to the above preferences would yield no winner because each of the alternatives has 1 vote; no alternative can obtain a simple majority, the weighted vote system would result in each alternative having the same number of weighted votes,[18] and the exhaustive primary would not eliminate any alternative because they would all have the same number of votes. The significance of the

---

[17] Kenneth Arrow, *Social Choice and Individual Values* (New York: John Wiley & Sons, 1951). As we have discussed elsewhere, Condorcet, Borda, Dodgson, and Duncan Black were aware of the cyclical majority problem, but Arrow formalized and popularized it.

[18] If the voters' first preference received 3 weights, the second preference 2 weights, and the last preference 1 weight, each of the alternatives would receive a total of 6 weighted votes.

cyclical majority problem is that the outcome of the election depends upon the sequence in which voting occurs or where the voting process is stopped. The existence of the impossibility theorem results in an arbitrary outcome, but the cyclical majority has received far more attention than warranted by its practical implications.

Nontransitivity occurs because some of the voters' preferences are multipeaked (see Figure 6-4). Voter C's preference is transitive, but his preference ordering is the cause of the nontransitivity. He has a multipeaked preference ranking because his two most preferred alternatives are at opposite extremes. Although it is clearly possible for voters to have such preferences, they are rather unlikely to exist among many voters. Assume that alternatives v, w, and x represent policy alternatives of 1, 2 or 3 submarines, respectively. Voter C's most preferred alternative is the extreme position of x, or 3 subs. His next preferred position is not w (2 submarines) but v, or 1 submarine. His least preferred position is w, which is a moderate number of two submarines. If C had normal preference rankings in which two submarines (alternative w) would be his second preference, the transitivity problem would disappear (see Table 6-12).

FIGURE 6-4

MULTIPEAKED PREFERENCE RANKINGS

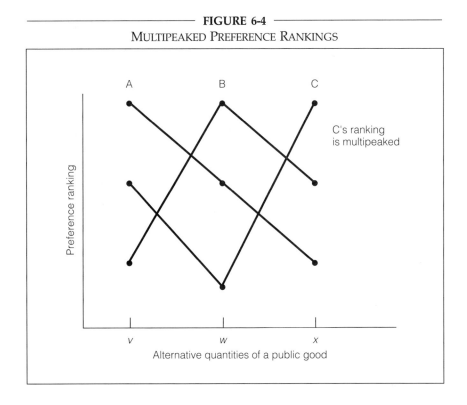

—— **TABLE 6-12** ——

A	B	C
v	w	x
w	x	w
x	v	v

Alternative w would clearly defeat both v and x, and it would be the winner. Now, $w > x > v$, and there is no cycle.

Even *if* C's preference ranking is multipeaked in this highly restricted example, one cannot conclude that nontransitivity will occur. For example, if B's second and third preferences were reversed, we would have the preference rankings shown in Table 6-13. Voter C's ranking is multipeaked, but B's second preference is now v instead of x. Instead of having a cyclical majority, alternative v is the clear winner and we have a normal outcome: $v > w > x$. Hence, even if some voters have multipeaked preferences, social nontransitivity will occur only if other voters with single-peaked preferences have particular preference rankings.

To summarize, nontransitivity and its associated arbitrary outcome in an election process can occur only if a significant percentage of voters have multipeaked preference orderings. Multipeaked preference curves reflect an unusual ranking of preferences, which only a few voters are likely to have. However, even if the requisite percentage of voters do have these unusual preferences, other voters must have a specific ordering of preferences (such as B's in Table 6-11) that enable the multipeaked preferences to produce collective nontransitivity. The coupled occurrences of these two events are highly unlikely, although the probability of their occurrence is sensitive to the type of issues, number of alternatives, and voters. If all possible preference orderings are equally likely, the probability of a cycle occurring increases as the number of alternatives and issues

—— **TABLE 6-13** ——

A	B	C
v	w	x
w	v	v
x ·	x	w

--------------------------------- TABLE 6-14 ---------------------------------

Radical Left	Center	Radical Right
Leftist	Moderate	Rightist
Rightist	Leftist	Moderate
Moderate	Rightist	Leftist

being voted on increases. However, the real-world significance of the cyclical majority decreases as the number of voters increases.[19]

Although cyclical majority has received much attention in the literature, a real-world example is seldom given. One example of the practical significance of the cyclical majority is the instability that it can produce in a legislative vote. Assume that a parliament is divided into three political groups of an equal number of members: radical right, radical left, and center. It has to select the prime minister from among three candidates who are a leftist, rightist, and moderate (see Table 6-14). The individual preferences of the members of Parliament are consistent and transitive, but rankings of the radical left are multipeaked. The collective result is that a moderate defeats a leftist, a leftist defeats a rightist, and a rightist defeats a moderate. Some analysts have stated that this collective non-transitivity characterized the French Fourth Republic (1946–59), when there were continuous cabinet crises and various coalitions had to organize the government.[20] There is no empirical evidence that a cyclical majority actually existed, and the political chaos in the Fourth Republic was more likely due to voting rules, multiple parties, and shifting allegiances and coalitions.

QUESTIONS AND ANSWERS

THE QUESTIONS

1.   Assuming you are a radical leftist (or rightist) running for an office where the overwhelming percentage of voters are moderates, what type of voting system would you prefer?

---

[19] M. B. Garman and M. I. Kamien, "The Paradox of Voting: Probability Calculations," *Behavioral Science* 13 (July 1968): 306–17; R. G. Niemi and H. F. Weisberg, "A Mathematical Solution for the Probability of the Paradox of Voting," *Behavioral Science* 13 (July 1968): 317–23; W. H. Riker and P. C. Ordeshook, *An Introduction to Positive Political Theory* (Englewood Cliffs, NJ: Prentice-Hall, 1973), 94–97.

[20] See Hans Van Den Doel, *Democracy and Welfare Economics* (Cambridge: Cambridge University Press, 1979).

2. Assume you are a supporter of a radical (leftist) candidate in the Democratic party and that you are a member of the committee to select delegates for the national nominating convention.

   a. What rules would you like to see the committee adopt for electing delegates to the convention? Why?

   b. What rules would you like to see the rival Republican party adopt for selecting its delegates? Why?

3. Assume that there are three voters with the following preference rankings with the associated relative intensities of preferences.

A	B	C
x 85	y 35	y 45
y 8	x 33	x 28
z 7	z 32	z 27

   a. Who would win a simple majority election?

   b. Will the election of this candidate maximize welfare in the community?

   c. If voters did not engage in strategic behavior, what voting system would return the candidate that would maximize the welfare of the voters?

   d. If voters did engage in strategic behavior, what voting system would you recommend to maximize welfare in the community.

   e. If voters were permitted to buy the votes of other voters who would win? Why?

   f. Would you approve of a system in which votes could be sold to the highest bidders? Why?

4. If you were an Arab living in Israel or a Jew living in Libya, would you prefer that your parliament employ simple majority voting or Wicksellian relative unanimity? Why?

5. Democracy is sometimes defined as rule by the majority. Can you give examples where democracy means rule by the minority? Can you give examples where rule by the majority would not be desirable?

6. Assume that you have to decide whether some good or service should be provided through the political market or through the private market. How would your decision be affected by whether you lived in one of the following countries?

   Country A, with a large population and area composed of many races, nationalities, and religions.

   or

   Country B, with a relatively small population and area composed of one race, nationality, and religion.

THE ANSWERS

1. You would prefer a single election with a single vote plurality system. You would want there to be many moderate candidates who would split the moderate votes among themselves so that you would have enough dedicated followers to achieve a plurality.

2. a. You would not want current political leaders to nominate the delegates because they would have an incentive to select candidates whose political philosophy was closer to the center and, thus, had a better chance of winning. You would want all of the delegates to be elected by a primary election system with single vote plurality with a winner-take-all-delegates, that is, the plurality winner would take all of the state's delegates.

b. If you were nominated by the Democratic party, you would want a rightist radical to win the Republican nomination. Hence, you would want the Republican party to have the same delegate selection rules as you recommended to the Democratic party and hope that a rightist, rather than a leftist, Republican would be nominated by such rules.

3. a. Candidate y would receive the votes of B and C and, thus, win the election.

b. Voter A feels very strongly about his preference for x, while B is almost indifferent among the candidates, and C slightly prefers candidate y. Hence, A loses much more (77 utils) by candidate y winning the election than B and C gain. Total welfare in the community is decreased by the majority victory of x. *Note of caution:* there is no way that anyone can directly measure levels of voter welfare. However, we do know that voters do have varied intensities of preferences and the hypothetical preference intensities listed in the parenthesis merely illustrate such varying intensities.

c. The point distribution method, in which voters are given points to distribute among the candidates to reflect their relative intensity of preferences, would result in the welfare-maximizing candidate winning. If the voters were given 100 points to distribute among the candidates in the same ratio as their intensity of preferences, candidate x would win the election by 80 to 85 points.

d. If voters engaged in strategic behavior they would cast all of their points for their preferred candidate, and candidate y would win the election by 100 to 200 points. Thus, the point distribution system would produce the same results as the simple majority system. There simply is *no* other voting system that would reflect voter intensities. *All* other voting systems—single vote plurality, weighted ranking, approval, exhaustive majority, and exhaustive primary—would produce candidate y as the winner. One of the serious problems of democracy is that those who have intense preferences about issues and candidates cannot reflect these intensities through the ballot box.

e.   Voter A feels very strongly about x winning, and Voter C has a slight preference for y to win. If Voter B could publicly state "I slightly prefer candidate y but I am willing to offer my vote to the highest bidder," Voter A would obviously outbid Voter C, and the welfare-maximizing candidate (x) would win. Thus, the selling of votes appears to accomplish what "honest" voting systems are unable to achieve: it ensures the election of the welfare-maximizing candidate.

f.   The expected and perfectly reasonable answer is that votes should not be sold, because this would give the rich an "unfair" advantage in the political market. "One-man-one-vote" would quickly deteriorate to "one-dollar-one-vote." You could illustrate this argument by using the data presented in this example. If Voter A were rich, he could outbid Voter C in bribing Voter B, and x would win. However, if Voter A were very poor and Voter C were very rich, Voter C might well be able to outbid Voter A, despite the fact that Voter A felt more strongly about his first preference, and candidate y would win. The income effect is stronger than the preference intensity effect. In other words, the poor would not have as many dollars as the rich in reflecting the intensities of their preferences, and they would be repeatedly outbid by the rich. While this is a strong and, perhaps, a compelling reason for prohibiting vote buying there are some other considerations:

1.   One cannot conclude too quickly that the poor would always be hurt by vote buying. First, many of the poor would benefit from the income generated by selling their votes. Second, there would be many issues in which organizations of the poor and others who sympathized with them could collect revenues and bid for votes. For example, there are many individuals—poor and nonpoor—who would be willing to contribute money to buy votes to support candidates who advocate housing for the homeless, while there are many rich who would not have intense opposition to this policy.

2.   The rich currently do influence votes through their expenditures for advertising, economic and political research centers, and campaign contributions.

3.   Expenditures on pamphlets, advertising, and lobbying utilize real resources of society and, thus, may be less socially desirable than outright transfers of money to vote sellers. See chapter 12 for a discussion of the differences between utilizing the resources of society for lobbying purposes and making transfer payments.

4.   Assuming that there were at least a substantial number of minorities living in each country, you would want parliament to use Wicksellian unanimity, because fiscal programs could not pass without the consent of the minority block. The purpose of Wicksellian unanimity is to protect minorities from majority dictatorships.

5. The fact that individuals can elect their representatives does not mean that the preferences of the majority will be reflected in the government. Those who actually cast their votes may not be representative of the voting-age population; certain occupations and income classes will have more influence on the selection of candidates and legislation; and the voting system may enable minority parties to win the election. Logrolling enables a minority of voters with intense preferences to achieve their preferences even though the majority oppose them. Other impediments to majority voting will be discussed in the following chapters.

6. In deciding whether some good should be provided through the political or private markets you have to consider that in the political market your own decision will not determine the outcome. In fact, it is possible that a minority of citizens with whom you disagree will make the operating decisions in the political market. Hence, you would be more favorably disposed toward the political market if the overwhelming majority of citizens in the political unit shared your own tastes and values. You would reason that in Country B the decisions made through the political mechanisms would be very close to the decisions that you would make. Hence, a small and homogeneous political market (Country B) would be more efficient for you than a large and heterogeneous one (Country A).

CHAPTER SEVEN

PROPORTIONAL REPRESENTATION

Under every stone lurks a politician.
—ARISTOPHANES, 400 B.C.

Preserve the sweetness of proportion.
—BEN JONSON, 1600

INTRODUCTION

Electoral systems vary widely among the world's democratic countries, not only in the voting systems they employ but in the size of the constituencies (election districts) and the number of representatives elected from each constituency. Most English-speaking countries and France have geographically based constituencies represented by one person, whereas most of the rest of the world's democracies have multimember districts with many elected representatives. The American and British system of electing a single representative from each district means that the minority of voters in that district have no representation in the Congress or Parliament. The United States inherited the single-vote, single-member district form of government, also known as the first-past-the-post system, from Britain, and it has retained that form of government at the local, state, and national levels for more than 200 years. About 20 American cities have experimented with *proportional representation,* in which a certain number of representatives are elected from a single district based on the percentage of votes they or their party receive, but all except Cambridge, Massachusetts, had abandoned it by the mid-1960s.[1] The school board in New York City is elected by proportional representation in order to obtain balanced representation of racial and ethnic minorities. Following the Civil War, the state of Illinois was deeply divided, with Republicans dominating in the north and Democrats in the south but with significant minorities in each section. In order to reflect the wide divergences of views,

---

[1] Some of the cities that had proportional representation for a considerable period of time include Boulder, Colorado, and Cincinnati and Hamilton, Ohio.

each district was allowed three representatives to the lower house and each voter could cast 3 votes. All 3 votes could be given to one candidate, 1½ votes to two candidates, 2 votes to one candidate, and 1 to another, or 1 vote to each of three candidates. Illinois's system of cumulative voting, which existed from 1870 to 1980, gave representation to the weaker major party and tended to smooth out sectional differences.[2] The major reason for the lack of proportional representation in the United States is that while Democrats and Republicans may disagree on many issues, they readily agree on their opposition to proportional representation and multimember districts that encourage the emergence of new political parties.

The English-American system of single-member districts is based on the concept that individuals living in different parts of the country have varying preferences that can be best represented by individuals who are personally responsible to voters in those areas. Another advantage is that information and communication costs are minimized when a single delegate represents a particular district. A major deficiency of single-member districts is that representatives elected from various districts may not proportionally represent political opinion in the country. More precisely, there need be no relationship between the distribution of votes among parties in recent elections and the distribution of seats in the legislature. Even *if* only two parties existed and even *if* all districts were equal in population, the election results could range from one party winning every seat in the legislature with just over half of the vote to a small minority of seats held by a party that received a large majority of the popular vote.[3] The following examples shows these two extremes:

(1) One party gets slightly more than one-half of the votes but 100 percent of the legislative seats.

	District 1	District 2	District 3	Total Votes	Seats Won
Party A	50,001	50,001	50,001	150,003	3
Party B	50,000	50,000	50,000	150,000	0

---

[2] For a more thorough discussion of Illinois's system of cumulative voting see Charles W. Dunn, "Cumulative Voting in Illinois Legislative Elections," *Harvard Journal on Legislation* 9, no. 4 (May 1972): 627ff. and George S. Blair, *Cumulative Voting* (Urbana: University of Illinois Press, 1960).

[3] The results could be even more disproportionate if there were more than two parties or if the districts had unequal populations.

(2) One party gets a large majority of the votes but a minority of the legislative seats.

	District 1	District 2	District 3	Total Votes	Seats Won
Party A	50,000	50,000	95,000	195,000	1
Party B	50,001	50,001	5,001	105,003	2

Single-member districts encourage gerrymandering,[4] because a party getting 50.1 percent of the vote or 100 percent of the vote gets the same representation in the legislature. A party can maximize its seats in the legislature by drawing district boundary lines so its opponents are grouped in a single district or two while its supporters have a safe but not exceptionally large majority in many of the neighboring districts. This is what Party B in example (2) might have done prior to the election. If Party A could have redrawn the boundary lines to gerrymander just a few of its supporters from District 3 into Districts 1 and 2 and get in return a few of its opponents into District 3, Party A would have won all three seats. Proponents of proportionality argue that if multimember districts existed, there would be relatively little incentive for gerrymandering.

One of the remarkable characteristics of American electoral experience with single-member districts is that, despite the potential of disproportionate representation, the percentage of Republicans and Democrats serving in Congress very closely approximates the percentage of votes cast for their parties in the last election. After making adjustments for those candidates who ran unopposed, the Democrats received 55 percent of the popular vote in 1986 and captured 56 percent of the seats. This left the Republicans with 45 percent of the vote and 44 percent of the seats. This was not an isolated event occurring only in one election year. Between 1966 and 1986 the adjusted percentage of votes obtained by the two parties varied by less than 5 percent from the relative proportions of the party affiliations of congressional representatives. This is an extraordinary degree of proportionality for a country that eschews proportional representation and multimember districts for single-member districts. Not only do the relative numbers of total Republicans and Democrats in Congress proportionally represent the country's votes for the two major parties, but

---

[4] A gerrymander is an election district whose boundaries have been redrawn by the party in power for its own political advantage, usually by excluding areas in which the opposing party is strong or including areas in which it is weak. The term originated in 1812 when Elbridge Gerry was governor of Massachusetts and the legislature redistricted the state. One of the new senatorial districts was particularly sprawling, resembling a salamander; thus, a newspaper editor said that redistricting was a Gerry-mander. The Supreme Court has ruled that legislative districts must have roughly equal populations, but state legislatures are still permitted to draw district lines so as to give a particular party an electoral advantage.

individual states tend to have a high degree of proportionality between the number of congressional representatives in each party and the relative party vote in the last election. Apart from those states with only one congressional representative[5] only *two* small states had a serious disparity between the relative votes received by the parties in the 1986 congressional elections and their relative representation in Congress.[6]

Critics of single-member districts point out that even though two parties might have *de facto* proportional representation in Congress and in state legislatures, the minority members of particular districts are not represented. For example, a Democrat in Illinois's Twenty-first Congressional District received 65,722 votes in 1986, while his Republican opponent received 64,779. According to these critics the 49.6 percent minority received no representation in Congress, whereas a multimember district with a proportional system would have ensured them proportional representation. But these critics ignore the fact that most issues with which representatives have to deal are national ones, where the parties do have proportional representation. Minority voters in the Twenty-first District may have felt frustrated because they lacked direct representation, but they could take solace in the knowledge that in other congressional districts their preferred party won a few elections by a narrow margin and the composition of Congress *did* proportionally represent their party.

A more serious problem with single-member districts is the difficulty they produce for potential minority parties to get a toehold in the political market. Even if these new parties were to receive a respectable percentage of the votes in a single-member district election—say 25 percent— they would fail to send any representatives to Congress if one of the major parties received over 50 percent. If they could obtain a visible toehold in Congress, they might be able to win elections in other districts after a few years, but they would be unable to achieve this toehold because the winner-take-all elections in single-member districts are effective barriers to entry. This would be similar to firms in the private market having to obtain 50 percent of the market before they could enter it. Supporters of single-member districts argue that a large number of parties are socially and politically disruptive and that single-member districts tend to produce an electorate whose political values are distributed closely around the center.

---

[5] Delaware, Wyoming, North Dakota, South Dakota, and Alaska.

[6] Thirty-five percent of the electorate voted for Democratic candidates in Nebraska, but all three representative seats from Nebraska were won by Republicans. About 35 percent of the voters in New Hampshire cast their votes for Democratic candidates, but both New Hampshire seats went to Republicans.

Many scholars have recommended a voting system known as proportional representation, which attempts to remedy the perceived problems of single-member districts. Proportional representation involves electing several representatives to Congress or Parliament from each district. Presumably, these several representatives would better reflect the broad range of political views held throughout the voting districts. Single-member districts support broadly based political parties and discourage the emergence of weak ones, so that, other variables remaining constant, two parties are likely to dominate. Proportional representation enables minority preferences to be reflected in the legislature, but it encourages the fractionalization of political parties over time. On the other hand, the two-party system can be maintained by single-member districts but at the expense of less than proportional outcomes and the discouragement of new and weak parties.

POPULAR SYSTEMS OF PROPORTIONAL REPRESENTATION

There are many variations of proportional representation, but the two basic types are the single transferable vote system and the party list. The first proportional voting system, known as the *single transferable vote*, was devised around 1850 by a Danish politician, G. G. Andrae, and by a London barrister, Thomas Hare. It was popularized and championed by John Stuart Mill in his *Representative Democracy*, published in 1861. The single transferable vote system has been tried in the United States—it was used in Cincinnati from 1925 until 1951, and it is still used in Cambridge, Massachusetts, and in New York City's school board elections—but, by now, it has been almost completely abandoned. It continues to be used in countries such as Malta, the Republic of Ireland, South Africa, and in elections to the second chambers in the Commonwealth of Australia and its states of New South Wales and Tasmania. The single transferable vote system requires (1) multimember districts in which each voter has only one vote, no matter how many legislative seats are to be filled, (2) that each voter list the candidates in order of personal preference, (3) that election officials determine a quota or the minimum number of votes needed to win a seat, and (4) that excess votes be allocated to other candidates until all seats are filled. The number of votes a candidate needs to obtain a seat is determined by the *Droop quota,* which is the total number of votes cast divided by the number of seats to be filled plus one and then adding one to the quotient:

$$\text{Droop Quota} = \frac{\text{Votes Cast}}{\text{Number of Seats} + 1} + 1$$

Assume there are 4 seats to be filled in an election district and the total number of votes cast is 100,000. The Droop quota would be:

$$\text{Droop Quota} = \frac{100,000}{4 + 1} = 20,000 + 1 = 20,001$$

Any candidate receiving more than the Droop quota is assured a seat in the legislature. The difficulty with the single transferable vote system arises not from the calculation of the Droop quota but from the treatment of the excess votes (more than the quota) the winning candidates receive. Basically, these excess votes are distributed according to the second preferences of those voters whose first preference won a seat. These excess votes are then added to the first-preference votes received by the other candidates. If no candidate receives more than the Droop quota, the one receiving the fewest first-place votes is eliminated and the second preferences of those who voted for the eliminated candidate are then distributed among the remaining candidates. This process continues until the requisite number of winners are selected.[7]

Advantages of the single transferable vote system include the following: marginal representation of political minorities increases, compared with single-member districts; voters can vote directly for their preferred candidates, unlike most other forms of proportional representation; and voters can rank their preferences across party lines. For example, a voter's first preference might be a candidate from the leftist party; his second choice, a candidate from the moderate party; and his third, a candidate from the rightist party. Despite these advantages, the popularity of the single transferable vote system among many scholars is difficult to comprehend. First, it does not ensure proportional representation over the entire range of political beliefs in a district. It is very possible that the three candidates receiving seats will come entirely from the middle of the political spectrum. Second, and most seriously, the single transferable vote system lacks analytical justification. The literature mentions only that it is likely to "make each elector's vote count," and that "fewer votes are wasted." By using the second and third preferences of voters whose first choice is elected or eliminated, the single transferable vote system does reveal *part* of the preference rankings of *some* voters, but it does not reveal nor count *all* preferences of *all* voters. Because it does not systematically examine or count all preferences of all voters, there is no assurance that the efficient candidate will win. In fact, it is quite possible that the efficient

---

[7] Examples of the single transferable vote and party list systems of proportional representation are shown in Appendix A to this chapter. Since an example is worth more than a thousand words of instructions, the reader is encouraged to work through the appendix.

candidate will be eliminated in one of the early countings. The single transferable vote system is also subject to the monotonicity paradox, discussed in chapter 6, in which a potential winner is displaced after one or more voters change their preferences in a way favorable to that candidate without changing the order in which they prefer other candidates. The single transferable vote system tends to weaken the influence of parties, since the individual can vote for any candidate who wants to run, whether he or she is affiliated with a major or minor party or no party at all. Thus, those who believe that a strong two-party system is necessary for political stability and legislative action are opposed to the single transferable vote system.

The most popular alternative to the single transferable vote version of proportional representation is the *party list system*, in which voters choose not among individual candidates but among lists of candidates sponsored by political parties. The list-proportional system was introduced in Belgium in 1899 to remedy some of the irreconcilable differences between the Walloons and the Flemish and was later adopted in Switzerland, Holland, Israel, Denmark, Norway, Sweden, and Finland. In the pure party list system, each party in a multimember district selects a number of candidates equal to the number of seats to be filled in the district. Voters are allowed to cast only one vote for one list, or party, and no second, third, or lower preferences are allowed. The available seats in that district are then distributed among the parties in proportion to the votes cast for each.

The positions of the candidates on the party lists are very important. Each party is entitled only to a number of seats proportional to its share of the popular votes, and those seats go to the candidates in sequence, beginning at the top of its list until the party's quota is filled. Hence, each party list has some safe slots near the top and a few marginal slots just below, while those at the bottom are considered to be hopeless. Generally, the regional or national party has the power to determine the order in which the candidates' names appear on the party's list in each constituency. Parties that have strong factions must ensure that the various factions are represented among the safe seats as well as among the hopeless ones.

Problems with the party list system revolve around allocating the number of legislative seats to fairly reflect the actual distribution of votes for the various parties. Assume there are four parties and five seats available and that the votes are distributed as shown in Table 7-1. The voters in this example were considerate enough to make the calculation simple and direct. Party D gets no seats, while Party A gets three seats and parties B and C get one each. The proportion of seats exactly matches

---
TABLE 7-1

Party	Votes	Number of Seats
A	60,000	3
B	20,000	1
C	20,000	1
D	0	0

---

the proportion of votes (3:1:1). But the outcome of elections in the real world are never so simple. Table 7-2 assumes a more realistic distribution of votes.

The fantasies of the electorate notwithstanding, the candidates cannot be sliced, cut, or diced to reflect each party's proportional share of the seats. Consequently, two popular methods are used to solve such a messy distribution of votes while keeping the candidates whole. The most popular method of calculating proportional representation in multimember districts in Europe is the *d'Hondt method*—named after its Belgian "inventor," Victor d'Hondt[8] —which allocates seats based on the average number of votes received per seat obtained. The d'Hondt method tends to favor larger parties, which creates an incentive for minor parties to make alliances with other parties that are not justified by political similarities, a practice called *apparentement*. Also, it can produce results that are far from being proportional.

While the d'Hondt method focuses on the average votes per seat, another method focuses on the marginal votes outstanding after the last seat is allocated. This system is known as the *"greatest remainder" method*,

---
TABLE 7-2

Party	Votes	Number of Seats
A	35,000	1.75
B	28,000	1.40
C	24,000	1.20
D	13,000	0.65
	100,000	5.00

---

[8] d'Hondt was not its original inventor, but he was mainly responsible for its adoption in Europe during the latter part of the nineteenth century.

which is used in Italy and Denmark. A simple vote quota (a larger quota than the Droop quota used for the single transferable vote) is calculated by dividing total votes by the number of seats available. Each party is given a seat for every vote quotient it receives. The remaining seats, if any, are allocated to parties by the number of votes remaining after deducting the votes used for the quotas. The "greatest remainder" system tends to award seats at the margin, which, as we have pointed out many times, is more efficient. Those parties with the largest number of votes outstanding at the margin—after awarding the quotas—have the available seats awarded to them. The advantage of the party list system with the "greatest remainder" calculation is that it tends to reflect a broader range of political views. However, there is no guarantee that it will proportionally reflect political opinions on the extremes. If political opinions are clustered around the middle of the spectrum, all seats could be captured by moderate parties, leaving radical parties unrepresented. Furthermore, depending upon the number of seats to be awarded, the number of votes, and the party's support, it is possible for a party to gain additional seats by splitting into two parties.

The most frequent criticism of the party list system is that it gives too much power to party machines and "bosses" by permitting them to determine the candidates who will appear on the list. Consequently, various modifications of the party list system have been made to allow each individual to vote for the preferred party as well as to rank his or her preferences for the candidates. Some countries use a system of proportional representation with panachage and cumulation in order to avoid party control. Each voter may cast one vote for the preferred party or he may cast votes for individual candidates. These votes may be given to candidates from more than one list (*panachage*), and two votes may be given to the same individual (*cumulation*). In Belgium and Italy the individual can vote for the party by checking a circle at the top of the party list —indicating that he votes for that party and accepts its candidates in the order the party has placed them—or he can place a check next to a candidate's name or write in a name. This latter vote will count as a vote for the party but will change the rank order of the candidates. Seats are divided among the parties in proportion to the total number of votes received by the candidates on each party's lists and among the candidates on each list in order of the number of votes they receive personally.

EVALUATION OF PROPORTIONAL REPRESENTATION

Proportional representation is supposed to remedy the problems associated with the "winner-take-all" aspects of single-member districts by enabling a number of delegates to represent a broader spectrum of political opinion and to lessen the domination of politics by major parties. Compared with single-member districts, proportional representation tends to encourage the proliferation of parties, thus weakening the power of major parties, and, in the case of *the single transferable vote*, it reduces the power of all parties because electors cast their votes for individual candidates regardless of party affiliation. In parliamentary systems, the government —that is, the cabinet and chief executive—is chosen by the majority party or a coalition of parties. Hence, critics charge that proportional representation's encouragement of multiple and weaker parties can lead to unstable majority coalitions and government instability.[9] However, in the United States, France, and some cantons in Switzerland—where chief executives are elected in a separate national election—the stability of the executive branch can be maintained independently of the method used to select members of the legislature. The evaluation of proportional representation in these countries need not be confused with the issue of stable governments.

Another argument against proportional representation is that it encourages multiple parties and coalition governments, which leads to a reduction in the voters' control of government and the accountability of the government to the electorate.[10] A coalition government is most likely to be determined by a process of back-room bargaining between party leaders from which the electorate is excluded. If government is in the hands of a single majority party, that party cannot escape responsibility for what has gone wrong during its term of office. Parties in a coalition government, however, can always lay the blame on their partners, or at least cause uncertainty in the minds of the voters. Furthermore, severe inefficiencies can result from the bargaining process. Assume the following distribution of votes in the legislature among three political parties:

Liberal Party	46%
Conservative Party	47%
Radical Party	7%

The two major parties will compete to get the votes of the radical party, and, in the process, each party will offer major policy and staffing

---

[9] For evidence supporting the thesis that proportional representation leads to instability, see M. J. Taylor and V. M. Herman, "Party Systems and Government Stability," *American Political Science Review* (March 1971): 28–37.

[10] Coalition governments are necessary whenever no single party has more than 50 percent of the members of the legislative body. Although the mechanisms vary, legislatures select their prime ministers and the cabinets by simple majority voting, and if there is no majority winner, parties must enter into coalitions with other parties in order to secure a simple majority of the votes in the legislature.

concessions to the radicals to get them to join with it in forming a government. It is possible that the policies of the coalition will reflect the radical platform more closely than the platforms of either major party, even though 93 percent of the voters rejected the radical party. If a legislature has more than three parties, there are many combinations possible, but the net result is that the coalition's policies may not come close to reflecting the preferences of the average voter. The voter may have some knowledge about the position of his preferred party on major issues, but he cannot know what deals the party will make in the legislature. By increasing the number of parties in parliament, proportional representation greatly increases the level of uncertainty among voters. They simply do not know the deals that certain parties might make with other parties after the election. It is possible that a voter might prefer the platform of Party A to the platform of Party B, but if he knew the deals that each party would strike with other parties in an effort to obtain a coalition, the voter may prefer Party B to Party A.

Proportional representation also places additional information and decision-making costs on voters. Chapter 5 showed that the voter has little incentive to gather information about the relative merits of two or three candidates running for a single seat in a first-past-the-post system. The incentive to gather information about many candidates running for three to six seats would be even less. We would expect voters to know more about two or three candidates running for one seat in a single-member district than about each of the many candidates running for numerous seats in a multimember district.

It appears impossible to design an election system that serves the goals of proportional representation and efficient representation of the voters' entire preference schedules. Proportional representation gives minority parties a better chance of obtaining seats in the legislature, but it does not follow that it always helps extremist minority parties. A move from first-past-the-post to a proportional electoral system lowers the electoral threshold, but it lowers it for moderates as well as extremists. If most voters are moderates, new moderate parties will arise to run their own candidates in order to capture some of the numerous votes in the center. One system that would reflect a broader range of the political spectrum would involve dividing voters into, say, four groups along the political spectrum and to allow each group to elect its own representative. A weighted ranking or exhaustive majority voting system could be used to select the winning candidate in each group. The winning candidates would represent a broad range of political constituencies, but they most probably would not represent the mass of voters, nor would they rank high on the average voter's preference ranking.

Lastly, there is no practical system for dividing voters along the political spectrum.[11]

The proportional representation methods do not examine the entire preference rankings of individuals. Thus, they are not efficient voting systems, and candidates or parties that stand high on the average voter's preference may be eliminated in the early rounds. The methods of allocating seats in proportional representation systems is clumsy, arbitrary, and inefficient. A weighted ranking method could be used to select the candidates (whatever their party) with the greatest number of points. It would be far more efficient than single vote plurality or party lists since it would reflect the entire preference schedules of voters. However, the candidates elected might still come from the middle of the spectrum and, thus, fail to reflect the broad range of political opinion, which the advocates of proportional representation are striving to obtain.

QUESTIONS AND ANSWERS

THE QUESTIONS

1. If you were forming a new political party, would you prefer the American-English first-past-the-post system or proportional representation? Why?

2. Assume once again that you are forming a new political party.

a. If the country's parliament or congress had proportional representation with a fixed number of members, would you prefer a small number of election districts or a large number? Why?

b. If the country had a first-past-the-post system would you strive to concentrate your party's activities in a particular region of the country, or would you try to establish the party on a national level?

3. Assume your country had a parliamentary form of government and you viewed it desirable that the executive/ministerial branch of government be strong and stable.

a. Would you prefer a single-member district form of representation or proportional representation? Why?

b. If the country had proportional representation, would you prefer a large number or small number of election districts? Why?

c. If the country had proportional representation, would you prefer a single transferable vote or a party list system of election? Why?

---

[11] A few countries such as Cyprus, West Germany, Belgium, New Zealand, and Zimbabwe have special election districts or party lists for ethnic minorities, which guarantees them minimum representation in Parliament. Only members of the minorities vote for their candidates in these special election districts.

THE ANSWERS

1. You would prefer proportional representation system because if there were, say, five seats from each district, your party could win some representation in Congress if you received at least 20 percent of the vote. With single-member districts you would have to get more that 50 percent of the vote in one or more districts to obtain representation in Congress. Such voting strength would be difficult for a new party to obtain. Small or new parties prefer proportional representation, and large and established parties prefer single-member districts.

2. **a.** The fewer the election districts, the greater the number of members elected from each district and the smaller the percentage of votes necessary to obtain some representation in congress or parliament. If there were 600 members in congress/parliament and 200 districts, then there would be only 3 members elected from each district and your candidate would have to win at least 33 percent of the votes to get a seat. If there were only 60 election districts, then each district would elect 10 members and a single candidate would need only 10 percent of the vote to get a seat. Thus, a small party would always prefer to have a few election districts with a large number of representatives elected from each district.

b. Minor parties or candidates can most easily emerge out of single-member plurality systems if they have concentrated, *local* strength. In 1948 two Democrats broke away from the Truman administration and ran their own campaigns for president. Both Henry Wallace, who disliked Truman's anticommunism, and Strom Thurmond, who disliked Truman's civil rights, received 1.2 million votes apiece. Thurmond won 39 electoral votes and Wallace none; Thurmond's votes were concentrated in the South, where he won a couple of states, whereas Wallace's votes were scattered, and he was not able to win any state. Minority parties in Britain have had the same experience. The Scottish and Welsh nationalistic parties have consistently been able to win seats in Parliament because their votes are concentrated in particular geographical areas. The Liberals and Social Democrats in Britain suffered electoral difficulties until the leftward drift of the Labor party resuscitated both parties a few years ago, which shows that minor parties with diffused strength do not do well.

3. **a.** A single-member district tends to encourage two major parties, so you would prefer it. Minority parties have little chance of winning representation in most districts, so one of the two major parties would have a majority in parliament.

b. You would prefer a large number of districts because this would mean that fewer representatives would be elected in each district. For reasons explained in the answers to question 2, that would mean that major parties would have an advantage.

c.   You would prefer a party list system because the party machinery would determine the individuals who would be awarded the seats won by the party. The single transferable vote would require electors to vote directly for individual candidates, so the party would have much less control. Thus, parties could exercise much more control over their members in parliament with the party list system.

APPENDIX A: DETAILS ON PROPORTIONAL VOTING

CALCULATING THE SINGLE TRANSFERABLE VOTE

The first task in selecting the winners of a single transferable vote is to determine the quota of votes necessary to select a winning candidate. This is determined by calculating the Droop quota:

$$\text{Droop Quota} = \frac{\text{Votes Cast}}{\text{Number of Seats} + 1} + 1$$

If a candidate receives more votes than the Droop quota, the second preferences of those voters who listed this candidate as a first preference are allocated to other candidates who did not receive a quota in the first count. These second, or allocated, preferences are "discounted" to reflect the relative number of excess votes received by the winning candidate. The formula for discounting these second-preference votes allocated to each of the other candidates is:

$$\frac{(\text{Total Vote for Elected Candidate}) - (\text{Quota})}{\text{Total Vote for Elected Candidate}} \times \begin{array}{c}\text{Second Preferences}\\ \text{for Each Remaining}\\ \text{Candidate}\end{array}$$

These prorated second-preference votes are added to the first-preference votes received by the remaining candidates, and those candidates, if any, who now obtain a quota are awarded a seat. If all the seats have not been awarded, the candidate having the fewest votes is eliminated, and the second preferences on his or her ballots are distributed (undiscounted) to the second-preference candidates. Candidates now having a quota are declared to be elected, and the second preferences of these winning candidates are distributed in the same way as above. This cycle is continued until all of the seats have been awarded. There is no simple explanation of the single transferable vote or the Droop quota, so, hopefully, an example will clarify the process.

Assume 10,000 voters have the following preferences:

Group	A	B	C	D	E	F	G	H
Voters	2,000	1,200	2,000	1,500	1,300	1,000	400	600
	v	w	x	x	y	z	y	w
	w	v	y	w	z	y	x	x
	x	x	v	z	x	x	z	v
	y	y	y	v	w	w	w	y
	z	z	z	w	v	v	v	z

Five candidates are vying for three seats. On election day voters list their preferences for the five candidates shown in the preceding table. After counting the number of ballots, the election officials determine the Droop quota.

Step 1: Calculating the Droop Quota

$$(10,000) / (3 + 1) = 2,500 + 1 = 2,501 \text{ votes}$$

The election officials then count the first preferences of all voters.

Step 2: Counting of First Preferences

v	2,000	Candidate x wins because he or she received 3,500 votes
w	1,800	and only 2,501 are necessary.
x	3,500	
y	1,700	
z	1,000	

Since candidate x received 999 more votes than necessary to win, those voters who listed x as their first preference will have their second preferences "discounted" by .2854 (or 999 / 3,500). Candidate y was the second preference of the 2,000 voters in Group C, so he will receive 571 votes (or .2854 × 2,000). Candidate w was the second preference of the 1,500 voters in Group D, so she will receive 428 votes (or .2854 × 1,500).

Step 3: Counting of Second Preferences

	First-Preference Votes		Allocated Votes		
v	2,000	+	0	= 2,000	No candidate has received a
w	2,000	+	428	= 2,428	Droop quota, which is 2,501
x	elected				votes.
y	1,700	+	571	= 2,271	
z	1,000	+	0	= 1,000	
Total Allocated			999		

Since no candidate received the quota of 2,501 votes in the second counting, the candidate with the fewest votes (z) is eliminated, and those voters who listed candidate z as their first preference will now have their second preferences distributed among the remaining candidates. The second preference of all those who voted for candidate z is candidate y. Hence, candidate y, who received the 1,000 votes of Group F and now has a total of 3,271 votes, will become the second person to represent the district.

Step 4: Counting of Third Preferences

v	2,000	Candidate y is elected.
w	2,428	
x	elected	
y	2,271 + 1,000 = 3,271	
z	eliminated	

Since only 2,501 votes are needed for the quota and candidate y received 3,271 votes, there are 770 votes to distribute among the two remaining candidates. The preference rankings of the four groups of electors whose votes constitute the 3,271 votes for y are discounted by .185 [or (3,271 – 2,501) / 3271]. Group E, numbering 1,300 individuals, voted for y in the first counting. Their second preference is z, which has already been eliminated. Group E's third preference, x, has been elected, so we need to go to their fourth preference, which is w. We do the same for Group G's 400 voters, whose first preference was y and whose next relevant preference is w. In addition to the 1,700 first-preference voters in Groups E and G, there are 1,571 second-preference voters included in y's 3,271 voters. There are 571 voters from group C in the second counting and 1,000 voters from Group F in the third counting. The next relevant, or third, preference of Group C voters is v; the next relevant preference of Group F voters is w (their third preference, x, has already been elected). The calculations are summarized below:

Step 5: Counting of Fourth Preferences

Group	Votes	Discount Factor	Relevant Preference	Number of Votes
E	1,300	.185	w	307
G	400	.185	w	94
C	571	.185	v	134
F	1,000	.185	w	235
			Total	770

	Previous Votes		Allocated Votes		
v	2,000	+	134	= 2,134	
w	2,428	+	636	= 3,064	Candidate w is elected.
x	elected				
y	elected				
z	eliminated		___		
Total Allocated			770		

This is the process by which the three candidates are selected by the single transferable vote process and, if worked through slowly, should be understandable. Although the process of selecting the winners is complicated, the voter has only to list his or her preferences. The rest can be calculated by computer.

THE D'HONDT RULE: HIGHEST AVERAGE METHOD OF CALCULATING THE PARTY LIST SYSTEM OF PROPORTIONAL REPRESENTATION

The d'Hondt rule states that available seats are allocated one at a time to the party that gets the highest average number of votes, assuming it gets the seat in question. When the first seat is allocated, the party's average number of votes is simply the number of votes cast for it.

Party	Votes	
A	35,000	Party A gets the first seat.
B	28,000	
C	24,000	
D	13,000	
	100,000	

Since Party A has the largest number of votes (35,000), it is awarded the first seat. When the second seat is allocated, Party A already has one seat and is competing for a second, while the other parties are competing for their first seat. The votes and averages are the following:

Party	Votes	Seats	Average	
A	35,000	2	17,500	
B	28,000	1	28,000	Party B gets the second seat.
C	24,000	1	24,000	
D	13,000	1	13,000	

Since Party B has the highest average, it gets the second seat. The third seat allocation now takes place:

Party	Votes	Seats	Average	
A	35,000	2	17,500	
B	28,000	2	14,000	
C	24,000	1	24,000	Party C gets the third seat.
D	13,000	1	13,000	

Party C clearly gets the third seat. But which party gets the fourth and fifth seats? Party D does *not* get the fourth seat because Party A now has a higher average of voter per seat:

Party	Votes	Seats	Average	
A	35,000	2	17,500	Party A gets the fourth seat.
B	28,000	2	14,000	
C	24,000	2	12,000	
D	13,000	1	13,000	

Party B gets the fifth seat because its average number of voters is also higher than Party D:

Party	Votes	Seats	Average	
A	35,000	3	11,667	
B	28,000	2	14,000	Party B gets the fifth seat.
C	24,000	2	12,000	
D	13,000	1	13,000	

After all the seats have been allocated, the total votes, the number of seats, and the average number of votes per seat are:

Party	Votes	Seats	Average
A	35,000	2	17,500
B	28,000	2	14,000
C	24,000	1	24,000
D	13,000	0	

As mentioned in this chapter, the d'Hondt method tends to favor larger parties. For example, if parties C and D merged, the resulting single party would receive two seats instead of one. The new CD party would get 37,000 votes, and it would receive the first and fourth seats, while Party A would receive the second and fifth seats and Party B would receive only the third seat.

The d'Hondt method does not produce proportional results. Party B, which has 20 percent fewer votes than Party A, gets the same number of seats as Party A, while the smallest party gets none. Anyone trained in marginalism should recognize that this average-based system is undesirable because it focuses attention on the average number of voters rather than on the number of marginal voters left without representation. This "highest average" system is used in Belgium, Finland, Israel, and Luxembourg and was used in France's Fourth Republic after World War II.

THE "GREATEST REMAINDER" METHOD OF CALCULATING THE PARTY LIST SYSTEM OF PROPORTIONAL REPRESENTATION

The "greatest remainder" method, which is used in Italy and Denmark, focuses attention on the marginal remainder of voters without representation. A simple vote quota (a larger quota than the Droop quota used for the single transferable vote) is calculated by dividing total votes by the number of seats available, and each party is given a seat for every vote quotient it receives. The remaining seats, if any, are allocated to parties by the number of votes remaining after deducting the votes used for the quotas. The following example utilizes the same data as the "highest average" method outlined above.

Step 1: Calculation of the Vote Quota

Quota = 100,000 / 5 = 20,000 votes

Step 2: Determining the Quotient Seats Won

Party A, with 35,000 votes, wins one seat and has 15,000 votes remaining; parties B and C each win one seat and have 8,000 and 4,000 votes remaining, respectively. Party D doesn't have enough votes to reach the quota, so it doesn't win a seat yet.

Party	Votes	Quotient Seat Won	Votes Used by Quotient	Remaining Votes	Remainder Seats Won
A	35,000	1	20,000	15,000	1
B	28,000	1	20,000	8,000	
C	24,000	1	20,000	4,000	
D	13,000	0	13,000	13,000	1

Step 3: Determining the Remainder Seats Won

The seats remaining after the quotient seats are awarded are distributed to those parties having the largest number of remaining, or "left-over" votes. Party A—with the largest number of remaining votes—gets one additional seat, and Party D gets its first seat. Compared with the "highest average method," Party D's candidate takes a seat at the expense of Party B.

APPENDIX B: PROPORTIONAL REPRESENTATION IN OTHER COUNTRIES

Americans have little knowledge about the electoral systems of other countries, and while students of public choice need not become experts in these alternative systems, they should be aware that they differ considerably from our own and that there exists a wide variety of electoral systems among democratic nations. Most non-English–speaking Western countries use some form of proportional representation, but the rules for determining proportionality and the effects of proportional representation on the number of parties and the frequency of new governments vary widely.[1] The Swiss were the first to use proportional representation in local elections in 1892, but they did not adopt it for federal elections until 1918. Today the Swiss officially use a party list system, but voters do not vote for parties. The Swiss voter is given as many votes as there are positions to be filled and casts those votes among the candidates as he or she wishes without regard to party affiliation. The individual may cast *two* votes (cumulation) for one candidate. The election commission then totals the votes cast for the candidates of each party and awards the seats to the *parties* in proportion to these totals. The party's seats are awarded to the candidates with the greatest number of votes, regardless of the official order of the candidates on the ballot. The Swiss have eight parties, but about 90 percent of the votes are cast for the four largest parties. No single party ever approaches 50 percent of the vote, and the Swiss government has consistently been ruled by coalitions of the major parties with minor representation from the linguistic and religious parties.

A reform movement led by Victor d'Hondt in the 1880s resulted in Belgium becoming the first country to use proportional representation at the national level and the first to use the d'Hondt method of proportional representation. As one might expect, Belgium introduced this method in order to defuse the volatile situation produced by the population split between the Catholic Flemish and the Protestant and French-speaking Walloons. Today there are about a dozen parties in Belgium, and it is rare for one party to get 50 percent of the seats in the Belgian Parliament. Coalition governments are the rule, and changes in government are frequent. Another early adopter of proportional representation was Finland, where candidates are listed by party with a number next to each candidate's name.

---

[1] For a remarkably thorough description of voting systems in Europe see Andrew McLaren Carstairs, *A Short History of Electoral Systems in Western Europe* (London: George Allen & Unwin, 1980).

The voter places the preferred candidate's number in a circle. The party affiliations of the candidates are totaled, and seats are allocated by the d'Hondt method. The candidates receiving the most votes in each party are then selected to represent that multimember district. Finland has about ten parties, but its coalition governments have been remarkably stable. Sweden, which adopted proportional representation in 1907, is divided into 28 districts, each electing from 2 to 33 members, depending upon the population. Swedes vote for a party list, and seats are allocated by the Saint Lague formula of the d'Hondt method, which gives an advantage to small parties. The voter is not allowed to indicate a preference for a particular candidate, but if a segment of a party is unhappy with the party's list of candidates it can submit an alternative party list, which is printed on the ballot alongside the official party list. Voters can then select between the two alternative party lists as well as among the other parties. The two lists for a particular party are treated as one for the allocation of the party's seats. The system of proportional representation is very accurate in Sweden. When one of the two major parties received only 8,000 votes more than the other major party in 1979, it ended up with one more parliamentary seat. Sweden has about a half dozen parties, but the Social Democrats have been the dominant party for most of the post–World War II years.

The Australians have experimented with many different electoral arrangements. The alternative vote was used for the longest period of time and is still used for electing members to the Federal House of Representatives and most state parliaments. Until 1949 the alternative vote was even used in multimember districts to elect members of the Senate. After the first senator was elected by a clear majority, his name was eliminated from the preference ranking and the papers were counted again to elect the second by a clear majority, and then the third, and so on. Hence, if 51 percent of the people voted for three candidates of one party, all three representatives of that party went to the legislature. This system of electing senators was changed to a proportional representation system in 1949.[2] Each state constitutes a single election district that can return ten senators selected by the single transferable vote. New South Wales and South

---

[2] Major parties are normally reluctant to change voting methods for reasons given above. However, in this case the Australian Labor party constituted the government, and it expected to lose a number of votes in the next election. Under the old nonproportional representation system it would have won less than 50 percent of the votes and, thus, would have lost many seats in the Senate. It figured it would do better with proportional representation. Hence, it voted to change the system, and in the next election it received 45 percent of the vote and slightly more than 45 percent of the seats. In the House of Representatives, where the alternative vote was maintained, it retained less than 39 percent of the seats.

Australia had used party lists to elect members to their upper houses, but they recently adopted the single transferable vote system.

The single transferable vote was specified in the legislation that set up the Irish Free State in 1918, and it was written into the Irish Constitution in 1937, which meant that it could not be changed except through a popular referendum. When the dominant Fianna Fail party attempted to abandon the single transferable vote in 1958, it was defeated by a close vote. The party tried to change it in 1968, but this time it was defeated by a clear 3-to-2 majority, and the single transferable vote appears to be institutionalized now. Irish voters are given a ballot with the names of various candidates and affiliated parties and are asked to rank their candidate preferences. Most voters in Ireland vote strictly along party lines, so there is a proportional result similar to the party list system, but occasionally voters will elect a member who has been rejected as a candidate by the party. Until 1981, the constituencies were very small, many with only three members, which meant that the major party was overrepresented in the Dial.[3] Since then the number of members in the constituencies has been increased, and the results have become more proportional.

The most extreme form of the party list system is used in Israel. The voter has no choice among the candidates—the name of the candidate is not even listed on the ballot—and the entire country constitutes one election district. As expected, there are many political parties in Israel (about 30), but only a dozen have consistent representation in Parliament, so, generally, no party wins a majority of the seats in Parliament and governments are formed by coalitions. Israel had fairly stable coalitions until the 1980s, when elections became more divisive and bitterly fought. Israel does not have the problems that bedevil electoral systems based on geographical election districts such as gerrymandering, differences in the relative number of voters in each constituency, or a lack of connection between votes received by a political party and seats obtained in the legislature. The disadvantages of this extreme system of proportional representation include a proliferation of parties and the delays and uncertainty associated with forming a coalition to constitute a government.

The Netherlands combines some features of the Israeli party list system and some features of those countries that permit the voter to express a preference for particular candidates. The voter casts a ballot for a party, list and the seats are awarded to each party by the d'Hondt method, in

---

[3] In districts with only three members and five parties, a minority party getting 10 percent of the vote would probably not get a seat. In a ten-member district the minority party would be assured of a seat. Thus, large member districts tend to give more proportional results than small member districts.

proportion to the party's *national* total of votes. The voter also casts a vote for an individual candidate on his party's list. The party's list votes are divided by its allocated seats, and any candidate that gets this amount is elected. The surplus votes are transferred to the unelected candidates the party has placed highest on its list, but those candidates—whatever their place on the party list—whose personal votes are less than half the list quota are eliminated.

Italy has had proportional representation since 1919. It uses party lists with some personal choice of candidates. The voter can vote for a party and for up to four candidates; most voters do not designate a candidate whose name they have to write in, and their votes are assumed to have been given to the first candidates at the top of the party's list. The Christian Democrats have been the dominant, but not the majority, party in Italy since 1946, with the Communist party a close second.

Greece permits voters to select their preferred party and to cast one vote for their preferred candidate. Seats are allocated according to the Droop quota within each district, and then the 56 districts are grouped into nine large ones, where the seats left unallocated in the first stage are allocated proportionally to the votes, subject to the condition that the parties must have polled at least 17 percent of the votes in the whole country. A third count divides the remaining seats among those parties that shared in the second allocation. Generally, the candidates who fill a party's seat are those who receive the largest number of personal votes, but some parliamentary leaders receive all of the votes cast for their party in their district. The Greek system favors large parties, and in 1981 only three among a dozen parties were represented in the legislature.

The Federal Republic of Germany uses a mixed single-member and proportional representation system. One-half of the members of the Bundestag are elected from single-member districts with a plurality first-past-the-post voting. The other half are elected by proportional party lists in multimember districts. Any party must win three single-member constituencies and obtain 5 percent of the national vote to benefit from proportionality. A German voter receives a ballot with the list of the candidates on the left side and the list of the parties on the right side. The voter selects the preferred candidate (party affiliation is identified) and the preferred party. He can vote for a candidate of one party and then vote for another party on the party list. The Bundestag consistently has been made up of three parties, the Social Democrats, the Christian Democrats, and the much smaller Free Democrats, and most governments have been coalitions.

Austria has a proportional voting system in which the seats are divided among the nation's nine provinces based on population, and the quotient is divided into each party's votes to determine the number of seats that party wins. The seats awarded go to the candidates at the top of the party's list. The remainder of the votes and seats not filled are pooled over two regions and awarded to the parties based on the d'Hondt rule. Austria is one country that has proportional representation but only two parties. One party dominated during the fifties and sixties and the other during the seventies and eighties.

Japan has multimember districts but does not officially have proportional representation for the 511-member Diet. Each voter casts one vote for the preferred candidate, and those candidates receiving the most votes are elected to the two to five seats in that district. Since many competing candidates run for office in each district, it is not uncommon for a winning candidate to receive less than 10 percent of the total votes. Japan uses a single vote plurality system with a vengeance, and it is certain to elect at least some extremist members to the Diet.

During the life of the French Fourth Republic, from 1947 to 1958, there were more than 20 governments, averaging less than seven months each. Fifteen different persons held the position of premier, and no single party was particularly successful at obtaining a legislative majority. As a result, French governments were based on unstable party coalitions, with the various ministries allocated to different parties in the coalition. If one party within a coalition thought that its policies were not receiving sufficient attention, it would withdraw its support from the coalition, thereby precipitating a new round of bargaining and coalition making. The Fifth Republic strengthened the powers of the president by making the position directly electable by the people and independent of the French legislature. The president may now bypass the legislature by taking issues directly to the voters in the form of referenda. The French cabinet (the Council of Ministers) is largely independent of Parliament, and the executive branch now more closely resembles the American executive branch and is considerably more powerful than in previous republics.

CHAPTER EIGHT

OTHER PREFERENCE INDICATORS

The cure for the ills of democracy is more democracy!
—SLOGAN OF LATTER-NINETEENTH-CENTURY PROGRESSIVES

You roll my log, and I will roll yours.
—LUCIUS SENECA, A.D. 50

THE REFERENDUM

Voting for candidates or parties is not the only way individuals can express their preferences on political issues. They can make a direct decision on public issues by voting in a referendum, which is the oldest device for registering citizen preferences. It was used in ancient Greece, in Switzerland since the sixteenth century, and in some parts of the United States since the eighteenth century. A referendum involves referring a political issue or a legislative bill to the direct vote of the citizens without intermediation by political representatives. Referenda can find their way to the voters in many different ways, depending upon the constitutional provisions of the political unit. A few of such provisions are one or more of the following:[1]

1. *Obligatory referendum:* all legislation, or designated types of legislation such as certain expenditures or treaties, must be approved by a referendum.

2. *Optional (approval) initiative:* a certain percentage of the voters may petition for a referendum to be held on some recent bill passed by the legislature.

3. *Popular initiative:* a certain percentage of the voters may petition for a referendum to be held on an issue that was submitted to the legislature but on which the legislature has taken no action.

4. *Direct referendum:* a certain percentage of the citizens may petition for a referendum on some issue that was not considered by or submitted to the legislature.

---

[1] For a thorough and excellent discussion of referenda see David Butler and Austin Ranney, eds., *Referendums: A Comparative Study of Practice and Theory* (Washington, DC: American Institute for Public Policy Research, 1978).

Referenda may be consultative (which the government or legislative body may ignore if they wish) or compulsory (where the voters' decisions become the law). Some countries permit one or more of the above referenda at the national but not at the local level or at the local but not at the national level. Switzerland permits referenda at the local and national levels, but the United States permits referenda at the local level only.[2] Switzerland has held more than 300 referenda during the past 130 years, which account for more than one-half of the national referenda held during the past century. All changes in the Swiss federal constitution and certain international treaties must be submitted for referendum approval (obligatory referendum) by *both* a majority of all voters in the country *and* by a majority of the voters in the majority of the 22 cantons. Laws that will last longer than one year can be subjected to a referendum (optional initiative) petitioned by 50,000 or more citizens.[3] If the people vote no to a bill passed by the legislature, the legislation cannot be put into force.[4] Initiatives to amend the constitution can be brought to a referendum (direct referendum) by the signatures of 100,000 citizens, and approval requires the majority of the citizens and the majority of the cantons. Since citizen-initiated referenda can be brought only on constitutional changes, those who want to change a simple law must propose a constitutional amendment. Swiss citizens, but not the government, can initiate popular initiatives, and all referenda decisions are mandatory. However, citizen initiatives are normally made by small minorities and, in fact, are almost always defeated. Yet, the distinct possibility that some group of citizens may mount a successful drive against a piece of legislation induces the legislature to draft laws that consider the preferences of all blocs.

The British held their first national referendum in 1974, when voters were asked to vote yes or no to continuing membership in the Common Market. Although the United States has never held a national referendum, about 15,000 state referendums have been held in the United States since 1900. The referendum is an important political institution in California, and the most celebrated referendum was Proposition 13 on limiting property taxes, which was passed in 1978. Mandatory constitutional referenda exist in all states but Delaware. About 20 states require that certain policies—bond issues or debt authorizations—be submitted by the

---

[2] The United States and the Netherlands are the only Western democracies that have never held a national referendum.

[3] Neither the legislature nor the government can initiate a referendum, except for a constitutional referendum.

[4] Only a majority of the citizens are required to approve legislation; the approval of the majority of the cantons is not required.

legislature to the voters. Twenty-four states permit voters to use a protest, or petition, referendum to force an issue passed by the legislature onto the ballot, where it must receive majority approval before the legislation can take effect.

Referenda offer an alternative political decision-making mechanism to those who have become cynical and suspicious about representative government. Because of many imperfections in the political market (including the power of information choke points), individuals' preferences on many issues seem to get watered down, altered, or ignored. Referenda are one way for citizens to directly reflect their preferences on issues and to lessen the role of interest groups and political oligarchies. The disadvantages of referenda include a weakening of the powers of elected authorities, the lack of a systematic way of selecting from among many possible options, and the inability of voters to reflect intensities of preferences. Even when many referenda are held on the same day, logrolling is discouraged because there is no assurance that voters will honor their bargains.

LOGROLLING

Most physical and mental attributes in society, including beauty, intelligence, knowledge, athletic talent, minerals, and plots of land are allocated by monetary payments. Political market votes are not . . . at least not openly. This inability to bribe other voters with money often means that individuals who are in the political minority are not able to realize their preferences even if they are more intense than those of the majority. Assume that 100 farmers in Wyoming want the county government to enact a coyote eradication program because coyotes are killing their chickens, which is costing the farmers $50,000 a year. However, there are 200 coyote lovers living in the city. The farmers have an intense preference to eradicate the coyotes, but the 200 city dwellers have only a slight preference to preserve the coyotes, say $100 per individual. If vote selling were allowed, the farmers could pay each city dweller $200 (for a total of $40,000) to vote for coyote eradication. All 300 persons in the county would be better off, because each city dweller would be $200 richer, and the farmers would no longer have the coyotes killing their stock. Such trades of votes for money is prohibited by law, custom, and morality, but a trade of votes for votes—though frequently viewed as undesirable by many citizens—is almost universally practiced. A trade of votes, like a trade of money, should benefit all parties *involved* in the trading.

Trading votes is called logrolling, and it can occur whenever two or more issues are being considered and the relative intensities of preference among the voters are different. Assume three voters have the indicated utility payoffs from two separate issues, x and y, as shown in Table 8-1. Individual A is opposed to both because he receives negative utility from both; B approves y but opposes x; and C favors x but opposes y. The total social gain from each issue passing is 300 for x and 100 for y.

Both issues would be defeated by a majority voting rule without logrolling. However, B and C could make an agreement to trade votes: B would be willing to vote in favor of x if C would vote in favor of y. Both issues would now be approved to the benefit of B and C and to the detriment of A. Beneficial trading of votes is possible only if there is a difference in the intensity or the preferences held by each voter. If B's gain from issue y were 200 or less, she would not trade votes because she would lose as much from the passage of x as she would gain from the passage of y.

In the absence of logrolling, a simple majority of citizens who have less intense preferences are able to dominate, even though the minority of citizens may feel much more strongly about their preferences. Logrolling enables individuals to exchange their less urgent preferences for their more urgent preferences. Minorities are able to express the intensity of their preferences through vote trading and, thus, improve the community's net welfare; however, those who prefer the outcome without logrolling lose. In our example from Table 8-1, without vote trading both issues would be defeated; with vote trading both issues would be approved. Individual A, who disapproved of both x and y would obviously lose if B and C traded votes. Those who criticize logrolling generally focus on the harm done to such nonparticipants as A. However, in this case B and C would gain more than A would lose, and the community would be better off. If we assume that Individual A would lose 800 rather than 100 on both issues, A would lose more than B and C would gain, and community welfare

---
TABLE 8-1
UTILITY PAYOFFS FROM POLITICAL ISSUES

Voters	Issues	
	x	y
A	−100	−100
B	−200	+500
C	+600	−300
Net Social Gain	+300	+100

would be decreased by logrolling. This last example strengthens the argument of logrolling critics: not only do the nontraders lose from logrolling, but they lose more than the traders gain, therefore reducing the overall level of welfare in the community.

Logrolling can easily lead to overspending by government, because voters can trade off votes for expenditures while placing the tax burden on others.[5] Assume that A, B, and C live on separate rural county roads, that the costs of repaving *each* road is $6,000 while the benefits are $5,000, and that the three individuals share taxes equally. Since the marginal cost of paving each road is greater than the marginal benefits, no individual would want to pave his own road, and the three individuals would not collectively agree to pave all three roads. However, two of the individuals could agree to vote for paving their roads and then split the tax burden among all three citizens. A and B, for example, could benefit by trading votes in which A would vote for paving the road to B's house if B would vote for paving the road to A's house. A and B would each receive $5,000 in benefits, but since taxes are split evenly among the three individuals, A and B would each pay only $4,000 in taxes. Voter C would be left out of the vote trading but would get to share in providing one-third of the revenues. Hence, C's road would not be paved, but he would have to pay taxes of $4,000 while voters A and B would each get a repaved road, which they value at $5,000 while paying taxes of only $4,000 each. Total benefits to society are $10,000, while total costs are $12,000.

This is a clear example of logrolling increasing government expenditures beyond the optimal by enabling certain groups of citizens to vote for each other's preferred projects and then spreading the tax bill among all citizens. The example is not merely a hypothetical one. There are many real-world cases of logrolling yielding potentially negative sums to society each year. The pork barrel projects—you vote for my pork or port and I'll vote for your sugar or silo—are a familiar part of every congressional session. Various minority groups benefit by voting for each other's projects while the tax bills are shared by the majority of citizens.

PUBLIC OPINION POLLS' EFFECTS ON VOTING BEHAVIOR

Political polling and the media's wide disclosure of the results of such polls are increasingly mentioned as sources of distortions in voting. The

---

[5] The following example is taken from an article from Gordon Tullock, who first wrote about the tendency of logrolling to increase the size of government. See Gordon Tullock, "Some Problems of Majority Voting," *Journal of Political Economy* 67 (December 1959): 571–79.

extensive use of polls in political races is a relatively new phenomenon. Political polling began in the twenties but achieved respectability when the Gallup and Elmo Roper polls correctly predicted the outcome of the Roosevelt-Landon contest in 1936. Political polls were still not very popular until pollsters improved their sampling procedures following their incorrect predictions that Dewey would win the presidential election in 1948. During the past 30 years public polls on the presidential election have been remarkably accurate, and their results have been widely reported by the media since the early sixties.

One important criterion for a good poll is that every voter should have an equal probability of being selected in the sample. Probability theory can then be used to estimate how close the sample results are to those for the entire population. A sample of about 1,500 people will give results 95 percent of the time that are within 3 percent of what would be obtained by asking the same question of all members of the population. Thus, a survey finding that 60 percent of the population supports candidate x means that we can be 95 percent certain that between 57 and 63 percent of the voters support candidate x. The 3-percent margin of error can be reduced by increasing the sample size (the margin of error can be cut in half by tripling the size of the sample). The size of the sample rather than the size of the population is what counts most, so a 1,500 sample size should work about as well for the United States as for California. If the pollster wants to use subsets of the population (for example, hispanic females) the sampling error would be greater than 3 percent because a much smaller number of such people would be included in the sample. Hence, pollsters often oversample to correct for this problem. Polls may give wrong results for a number of other reasons. People may lie about their preferences, the questions may be confusing or biased, clerical errors may be made, or the respondents may not be truly representative of the total population for many unknown reasons.

Public controversy about political polls did not arise until the sixties, when many politicians and some political scientists began to argue that the early release of election day exit polls and projections of results from early counts influenced the turnout and the outcome of the election, especially where the polls had not yet closed. The evidence of such influence is mixed.[6] But a potentially more serious problem is that information provided by polls prior to, as well as on, election day can induce

---

[6] See Harold Mendelssohn, "Election-Day Broadcasts and Terminal Voting Decisions," *Public Opinion Quarterly* 30, 2 (Summer 1966): 212–25 and Laurily K. Epstein and Gerald Strom, "Election Night Projections and West Coast Turnout," *American Politics Quarterly* 9, 4 (October 1981): 479–91.

—————————— **TABLE 8-2** ——————————

Group A 100 Voters	Group B 75 Voters	Group C 50 Voters
v	w	x
x	x	w
w	v	v

strategic voting behavior. Polls can produce "bandwagon," "underdog," or "hopeless" candidates, which may easily result in the efficient candidate being eliminated as voters adjust their strategies to the information provided by the polls. This is especially true during the early stages of primary elections, in which there are many candidates. The following example shows how polls can affect primary outcomes (refer to Table 8-2). Candidate x is the efficient candidate, but he has only 50 first-preference votes. If early polls revealed only the first preference of voters (which is the custom) and if they reported that v and w were the "front-runners," the voters in Group C might think that their preferred candidate, x, had little chance of winning and they would cast their primary votes for their second preferred candidate, w. Thus, not only would candidate x receive no votes in the election, but w—the least preferred candidate of the largest group of voters—would win. Strategic behavior induced by early polling may result not only in a shifting plurality but it can also give a candidate a majority of votes just as it did in this example. The least preferred candidate won by a solid majority, whereas the candidate who, on the average, is the most preferred candidate received no votes at all. It is easy for efficient candidates who are not front-runners to be harmed by the early announcement of leaders through polling information or through "news articles" or editorials.

Publication of polling results can also produce cyclical behavior on the part of voters adjusting their preferences as they engage in strategic behavior. Assume that voters can be aligned into four groups and that their real preference rankings are unaffected by strategic behavior (see Table 8-3).

—————————— **TABLE 8-3** ——————————

Group A 800 Voters	Group B 700 Voters	Group C 600 Voters	Group D 300 Voters
v	x	w	w
w	v	x	v
x	w	v	x

If a poll were conducted a couple of weeks before the election, v and w would be the top two leaders. This information might induce Group B voters, who prefer candidate x, to plan on voting for v in order to ensure the election of candidate v rather than their least preferred candidate, w. If another poll were taken a few days later, the results would show v to be the front-runner. This latest information might induce Group C voters to plan on voting for x instead of w because they don't want v, their least preferred candidate, to win. Thus, in the next poll, v would receive 1,500 votes from Groups A and B, x would get 600 votes from Group C, and w would get only 300 votes from Group D. This new poll might lead Group B voters to think that candidate x was indeed a viable up-and-coming candidate, and they might switch their first preference back to x. The next poll then would reveal that candidate x was winning with 1,300 votes from Groups B and C. The cycle, which is similar to the cyclical majority, would continue right up to election day. There would be a definite winner on election day, but the actual winner would be determined by the latest polling information obtained by the voters and the extent to which they were or were not engaging in strategic behavior.

Another problem produced by releasing poll results before elections is that they can have the same effect on voters as a primary election. They, like the information obtained from primary elections, can produce the monotonicity problem discussed in chapter 7. For example, assume that Group D learned from the polls that candidate w was trailing in the polls and they decided to act strategically by voting for candidate v. This would result in v receiving 1,100 votes, x receiving 700 votes, and w only 600 votes. Candidates v and x would face each other in the general election, which x would win by 1,300 votes (Groups B and C) to 1,000 votes (Groups A and D). If poll results had not been announced and all voters had cast their votes based on their original preference rankings, the two winners in the primary would have been v and w and v would have won in the general election. Thus, there would have been a monotonicity problem (a more correct way of saying this is that there is nonmonotonicity) because candidate v was placed higher on some voters' preferences because of the polls and he lost the election as a result of this upward movement.

Some countries such as France, West Germany, Brazil, and South Africa permit the free reporting of opinion and political polls during most of the year, but poll results cannot be reported during the official political campaign period. A number of developing countries in Africa, the Middle East, and Southeast Asia prohibit political and even opinion polls at all times.

EXIT AND VOICE

THE INVISIBLE FOOT

Voting for representatives and voting in referenda are not the only mechanisms through which individuals can express their preferences for public goods. When economic or political entities fail to perform efficiently or to satisfy preferences, individuals can express their displeasure by complaining or moving to other products or political units. Economists have traditionally relied upon a mechanism that Albert Hirschman has termed "exit" to discipline and guide market forces.[7] A customer dissatisfied with the quality or price of one firm's product simply buys another product. If other customers have similar views, that firm begins to lose revenues and either improves the quality of its product, lowers its price, or eventually goes out of business. Political scientists, on the other hand, have traditionally focused upon "voice" behavior in which citizens express disagreement and criticism by changing those policies with which they disagree. Voice behavior includes complaints expressed in letters, boycotts, lobbying, marches, and protests as individuals attempt to change management or bureaucratic decisions. The exit option is normally thought to be excessively costly to members of a family, church, or political unit while relatively less costly to consumers of private goods who, generally, have many substitutes. This difference in mobility costs explains why individuals use exit reactions in the private market and voice reactions in the political market.

However, the exit option may have been too quickly dismissed by political scientists, because individuals can and do transfer membership among governments by moving to different political jurisdictions. In fact, the United States owes its very existence to millions of individuals who favored exit behavior over voice behavior and migrated to the United States. The "Invisible Foot" organized the individual efforts of 18 million immigrants (one-fourth of the entire population in 1901) who entered the United States between 1901 and 1925 in the most massive migration in world history. It is no accident that the most centralized and bureaucratic states have the most restrictions on emigration and that international population flows are uniformly in the direction from more centralized and controlled economies to less centralized and free market nations.

One way citizens in a free market society can express their displeasure with public policies on certain goods is to switch to private provision. For example, those unhappy with the quality of public education can take

---

[7] Albert O. Hirschman, *Exit, Voice and Loyalty* (Cambridge: Harvard University Press, 1970).

their children out of public schools and put them into private schools. They can hire private detectives to track down lost persons, employ private police to patrol their businesses or neighborhoods, or create units such as shopping malls or office parks, which offer many of the services otherwise provided by municipal governments. Individuals can also express their displeasure with the public policies of a community by leaving it. If their communities are consistently making decisions with which they disagree, they can vote with their feet by moving to communities that provide a basket of public goods closer to their preferred market basket.

Metropolitan areas composed of many independent local governments are often criticized for not taking advantage of the economies of scale by integrating their police, fire, education, and sewerage services. They are also criticized for neglecting the external effects that decisions in one local governmental unit can have on the residents of other governmental units. These criticisms of competitive governments existing in a metropolitan area may be valid, but they overlook one substantial advantage. In a metropolitan area composed of many local governments, such as St. Louis County, the costs of moving from one government to another are fairly low, and individuals can be expected to move from one suburb to another that provides the political market basket they prefer. Economists generally approve of "voting with one's feet" because it offers options to individuals and provides signals to the community that it is doing something wrong. We have seen that voting mechanisms are beset with many imperfections and that an individual has virtually no control over the policies enacted. One way to avoid these difficulties is to let people sort themselves out into communities of similar tastes. An individual who doesn't like the mix of public goods provided in one community can move to a neighboring community where the market basket of goods, or quality of life, is more in accord with his preferences.

EXIT BEHAVIOR AND THE FEDERAL SYSTEM OF GOVERNMENT

Exit behavior is encouraged by the federal system of government and by the existence of metropolitan areas composed of many local governments. This decentralization of political power not only provides another layer of political checks and balances, but it enables more citizens to realize their preferences, thus increasing total welfare in the country.

Suppose that there is a country with a total of 100 citizens and that 60 citizens prefer Policy A and 40 citizens prefer Policy B. In a unitary political system with majority rule, the 60 citizens preferring Policy A would be able to get Policy A enacted, while the other 40 citizens would have to remain in the minority and suffer from the imposition of Policy A.

Now assume that a system of decentralized political power is introduced and the 100 citizens disburse themselves into two communities, X and Y, with a distribution of preferences as shown in Table 8-4. The 40 citizens in Community X who prefer Policy A are able to outvote those who prefer Policy B. The 30 citizens who prefer Policy B in Community X are able to outvote those who prefer Policy A. Thus, 70 citizens in the decentralized system, rather than only 60 citizens, can have their preferences satisfied. The example could be made even stronger. If all those who preferred Policy A moved to Community X and all those who preferred Policy B moved to community Y, 100 percent of the citizens could realize their preferences. This ability of citizens to move to communities in which there are many individuals with similar preferences is a strong argument in favor of a decentralized political system.

Recent research suggests that the responsiveness and efficiency of the country's 80,000 local governments are due primarily to people's opportunity to select their government by moving rather than their opportunity to participate in local politics. The extended commuting range provided by expressways and an efficient metropolitan housing market are probably the strongest contributors to the responsiveness and efficiency of local governments. Even if each of the municipalities were governed by a political clique, the ability of citizens to migrate to neighboring municipal dictatorships would have the effect of forcing the clique to operate somewhat efficiently and to provide combinations of public goods and services preferred by at least a substantial number of citizens. Larger political units such as states or countries are likely to be less efficient and responsive because it is more costly for individuals to move out of them when undesirable policies are enacted.

FURTHER ADVANTAGES AND DISADVANTAGES OF EXIT BEHAVIOR

Disadvantages of exit behavior include the high costs of mobility for many citizens, externalities produced by migration, spillover effects among

---

TABLE 8-4

Community X 50 Citizens	Community Y 50 Citizens
40 prefer Policy A	20 prefer Policy A
10 prefer Policy B	30 prefer Policy B
Policy A wins	Policy B wins

communities, geographical constraints on income-earning abilities, and a large variety of public goods that could be demanded by citizens.[8] Another limitation is that some individuals may not be able to find a community that provides the optimal combination of public goods for them, because the number of communities required to provide all possible combinations of public good alternatives increases geometrically as the number of public goods increases arithmetically. If the number of public goods is very large, the requisite number of communities may equal the entire population. However, some choice is always preferable to no choice, and the advantages of migration should not be discarded because it cannot fully satisfy all preferences. Yet another criticism of "voting by one's feet" is that migrants may impose external costs or benefits on members of the communities they leave or to which they move. The economies and diseconomies of scale applied to firms in chapter 3 can also be applied to governments. When economies of scale exist in the provision of public goods, the addition of one more person to the community decreases the cost of the public good for each citizen and the loss of one individual increases the cost. If there are diseconomies of scale, such as overcrowding or traffic congestion, the addition of another person increases the cost for everyone else. Pareto optimality is not obtained in either case. One possible solution is to use taxes and subsidies to "correct" for these externalities. If externalities are positive for in-migration, a community can offer a subsidy to newcomers and levy an identical tax on out-migration. Individuals are then forced to consider the effects of their external costs imposed on the communities. However, citizens may be reluctant to give such powers to their local governments because, in an imperfect political market, the power can easily be abused by politicians and bureaucrats.

Some effects of citizen mobility on local governments or public enterprises may not be immediately evident. When consumers exit from the consumption of one private good and begin consuming a competing product, the usual result is that all affected firms begin investigating the reasons for their revenue or market share loss, and they make improvements in their goods and services. Similarly, competition from other political units or private enterprises in metropolitan areas should stimulate local governments to make quality improvements or to adjust their market

---

[8] For further information on voting by moving see Albert Hirschman, *Exit, Voice and Loyalty* (Cambridge: Harvard University Press, 1970); C. M. Tiebout, "A Pure Theory of Local Expenditures," *Journal of Political Expenditures* 64 (October 1956): 416–24; J. M. Buchanan and C. J. Goetz, "Effeciency Limits of Fiscal Mobility: An Assessment of the Tiebout Model," *Journal of Public Economics* 1 (April 1972): 25–43; and W. E. Oates, *Fiscal Federalism* (London: Harcourt Brace, 1972).

baskets of public goods to retain or attract citizens. We would expect local politicians and voters who have higher costs of migration from these political units (their homes and businesses are located there) to react to an out-migration from their communities by making them more desirable places to live.

Some political scientists argue that out-migration might produce undesirable consequences for municipalities by permitting dissatisfied citizens an "easy way out." Political units may be more responsive to voice behavior than to exit behavior, and when citizens exit there may be less voice pressure for correcting deficiencies. Albert Hirschman offered an interesting example of exit availability lessening the pressures of voice activity.[9] The public Nigerian railways had a long-term record of poor performance in long-haul competition (in which railroads are supposed to be most efficient), despite the fact that they faced long-haul competition from trucks. The reason was that the presence of comparatively efficient truck competition reduced voice pressures for tough reforms in the administration and management of the national railroad. Those who would otherwise have complained about poor railroad service simply took their business to the trucks, and the subsidized public railroads—which were not particularly concerned about their loss of traffic revenues— continued their inefficient operations. Had the railroad not had competition from trucks, transportation users would have demanded better service from the railroad and, perhaps, reformed it. However, rather than attempt to reform an inefficient bureaucracy through a clumsy and uncertain political process, shippers simply took advantage of the alternative offered in the private market and switched to trucks.

The availability of low-cost alternatives to publicly provided goods has led to a muting of voice behavior in this country as well. In communities where the quality of public education is poor, it is easier for parents who have a high preference for quality education to place their children in private schools instead of engaging in voice efforts to change the policies and administration of the public education system. Citizens did not criticize the U.S. Postal Service for its late development of overnight mail service because it was provided by Federal Express a decade earlier. Where subdivisions or shopping malls can employ private police, voice behavior criticizing police inefficiencies becomes less vociferous.[10] Hence, unlike

---

[9] Albert Hirschman, *Development Projects Observed* (Washington: Brookings Institution, 1967), 146–47.

[10] When the police chief in the author's home town of Baton Rouge stated that a "crime is a crime" and that the apprehension of speeders and drivers without automotive inspection stickers was as important as catching robbers, burglars, and muggers, there was surprising little public criticism. Subdivision associations simply hired more private police to patrol their streets.

the private market, exit behavior in the political market may simply lead to less voice behavior, which otherwise might stimulate reform and improvements in the political unit. Therefore, if the costs of self-provision, private substitutes for public services, individual adjustments, and inter-governmental mobility are lower than the costs of exercising voice behavior in the form of lobbies, pressure groups, and social movements, we would expect to see more of the former and less of the latter. Traditional political scientists believe that voice behavior leads to more reforms in local political units, whereas economists believe that exit behavior is more powerful, because for most citizens it is easier to move than to attempt to change the government bureaucracy or the values of fellow citizens. Though overlooked by Hirschman, his Nigerian railroad example provides an excellent insight into the underlying reason for exit behavior not improv-ing the operations of the railroad. One reason for the Nigerian railroad not responding to the loss of its customers to the trucking industry was the subsidy provided to the railroad by the central government. If the railroad had had to obtain all its revenues from its own operations, it most probably would have reacted more positively to the exit behavior. If local governments are not subsidized by federal government grants designed to "maintain the central cities," exit behavior can normally be expected to result in improved operations and policies.

Exiting can be a very effective means for expressing displeasure and instigating reforms, but it might be destabilizing to the firms, parties, or governments involved. If consumers of private or public goods have a high elasticity for quality (or low-cost alternatives) for the good in question, a relatively small deterioration in quality (or increase in tax-price) can stimulate massive exit movement by consumers or citizens before the firms or governments have time to react and make improvements. If this occurs in the private market, the affected firms or divisions of firms exit from the industry and resources become employed in other industries. When citizens exit from a political unit, it seldom disappears because the resources are generally much less mobile. Many individuals whose costs of relocating are relatively high or who have a strong preference for the basket of public goods provided in that jurisdiction will remain, and depending upon the slope of the cost curves (economies or diseconomies of scale) these individuals could suffer long-term negative externalities from the out-migration of others. Unlike the assets of most bankrupt firms, the assets of a city cannot be easily sold and moved into other industries. The physical effects of exiting from communities seldom disappear, and the scars—empty buildings, lower tax bases, lower real estate prices—of elastic exit behavior remain visible for many years. The deterioration of central cities can be partially explained by the high elasticity of the exit behavior of previous residents and the lack of voice behavior that often accompanies exit behavior as well as by federal and state subsidies to them.

Nevertheless, the existence of alternative political units not only provides valuable competitive stimuli to governments and enables individuals to locate in communities that offer preferred market baskets of public goods, it also provides the bases for individual freedom. Migration has stimulated progress, economic advancement, and political rights among American municipalities and states as well as among many countries in Europe and Asia.

CLUBS AS PROVIDERS OF QUASI PUBLIC GOODS

Governments must exist to provide public goods, but due to the inefficiencies in political market decision making it is desirable to examine other institutions that can provide certain types of quasi public goods. One alternative is the private market as suggested above; another is the private club. Some quasi-public goods generally provided by local governments can also be provided by private clubs. These joint supply goods, such as swimming pools and athletic facilities, are generally characterized by economies of scale, that is, the addition of new members lowers the average cost of these goods to all other members. If average costs fall indefinitely, the optimal club size is the entire population and traditional public sector problems exist. If costs eventually rise, either because scale economies are exhausted or from the additional costs imposed by overcrowding, an optimal club size smaller than the population in the political unit might exist.

Assume that a few citizens in a community are thinking of forming a swimming club. Most of the costs of the pool are fixed, so the cost per member decreases as more members are added. However, at some point the marginal costs of overcrowding will begin rising, and the optimal size of the club will be determined where the marginal crowding costs of an additional member just equal the reduction in the other members' dues from spreading the fixed costs over one more club member. For a pure private good such as eating an apple, crowding takes place when the first additional person tries to take a bite. For a pure public good, an additional member does not detract from the enjoyment of the benefits of club membership to the other members. If optimal club sizes are small relative to the population, each individual can select a club or initiate a new one, and government does not have to provide that good. However, where the optimal club size is a large fraction of the population, only one such club can exist and no stable distribution of club size exists.

The voluntary formation of clubs to allocate public goods is socially attractive when the optimal club size is small and the goods have a limited degree of publicness. The voluntary formation of clubs may enable governments to let certain types of goods be financed by neighborhood clubs, which is less disruptive than people moving to other communities that provide the good or to those communities that don't provide it but have lower taxes.

QUESTIONS AND ANSWERS

THE QUESTIONS

1. Do you believe that the low-cost availability of referenda in Switzerland may help explain the low turnout of Swiss voters on election days when their political representatives are selected?

2. Some critics argue that referenda are not desirable because they give too much power to the media, which can sway voters' opinion for or against the subject of the referendum. Do you agree? Why?

3. Can you list five pieces of legislation that Congress enacted during the past few years that would have been defeated by citizens voting in a national referendum.

4. **a.** If you were an unborn spirit, would you rather be born into a country that had a well-developed system of referenda or one that had a strong representative government without referenda?

b. What are some of the factors you would have to consider in making your decision?

5. Candidate X says that all Nevada citizens should vote against the incumbent running for reelection in Nevada because he voted for deepening the Mississippi River channel to the port of New Orleans. "Why," she asks, "should Nevada residents pay taxes for a project that will yield few, if any, benefits to the citizens of Nevada?" Would this argument convince you to vote against the incumbent if you were a Nevada resident? Why?

6. **a.** Can you explain why so much legislation has been passed within the last few years granting benefits to blacks, when they constitute only 11 percent of the population and less than 9 percent of the voters?

b. Why wasn't such legislation passed years earlier?

7. No matter where you live in the country the odds are high that the political, social, industrial, educational, and commercial leaders in your community have stated repeatedly that the economic development of the community depends upon the strengthening of the public school system: "We cannot attract industry, entrepreneurs, and competent technicians and professionals unless we improve our public education system." If your community is similar to those in which this author has lived, most of these very same leaders are sending their children to private schools. If Hirschman is correct about exit behavior silencing voice behavior, it certainly does not seem to apply to many community leaders. Why?

8. Your boss comes to you one day and says that you have a choice of being transferred to a metropolitan area that has a large and strong consolidated county government with weak municipal governments or no municipalities permitted within the county, or to a metropolitan area that has a weak county government and numerous strong municipal governments.

    a. Which would you prefer? Why?

    b. Which metropolitan area do you think has more numerous, serious, and "colorful" political conflicts. Why?

    c. Which metropolitan area do you think has the most serious problem with a deteriorating central city area. Why?

    d. Which metropolitan area do you think has the best-developed peripheral area? Why?

THE ANSWERS

1. Swiss voters may believe they have less reason to concern themselves with the selection of their politicians because the legislature always has to shape legislation so as to be acceptable to most blocs or face the threat of a referendum. The brokerage and intermediary functions of politicians and representatives are reduced when referenda are widely used.

2. The question is not so much whether the media can influence voter opinion on referenda but whether such influence is more or less extensive and desirable than the influence of the media on the selection of legislative representatives and on the legislation they produce. There are many arguments on both sides and no a priori conclusion can be reached.

3. You are on your own. Most of us have our favorite pieces of legislation that we believe Congress placed on the heads of unwilling citizens.

4.   **a.** Can't help with your answer to (a) but consideration of (b) may help you form your own answers.

    b. *Advantages or benefits of referenda:*

        —they eliminate all the slippages and imperfections in democracy that are caused by the intermediation of politicians, power brokers, lobbyists, influence peddlers, and special interests groups.

        —they probably produce a mildly heightened interest in public issues by the average citizen.

—they place strong pressure on the legislature to enact laws that citizens want.

—they reduce special-privilege legislation for certain groups and industries.

Disadvantages or costs of referenda:

—they increase the costs of decision making for the average citizen. Rather than obtaining information on the values and general philosophy of competing politicians, the citizen wanting to make informed decisions would have to invest much time and effort about each of the subjects of the referenda. Because of the free rider problem, most citizens would not undertake much search activity, and many individuals would vote differently than if they had become more fully informed.

—they eliminate the possibility of logrolling, so general expenditure programs would have to be very thorough, complete, and detailed. Citizens would not approve an expenditure that would provide benefits to other groups or regions unless it provided benefits to them as well. This would result in very complex proposals being submitted to the voters. Consider the details that would have to be included in a simple road-building referendum.

5.   This argument shouldn't convince you to vote against the incumbent, because he might have been voting for the Mississippi River project as part of a logrolling agreement in which the Louisiana delegation agreed to vote for a project in your state in return.

6.   **a.**   Blacks have let their black and white representatives in Congress know that their votes depend almost exclusively upon how their representatives vote on such race-related issues. While a majority of whites *may not* approve such legislation, their votes are determined by a number of other issues on which they have greater intensities of preference. Thus, legislators in districts that have a sizable number of blacks engage in logrolling activity with legislators in other districts to secure votes to pass such legislation.

b.   Blacks didn't vote in significant numbers because of various restrictions.

7.   "Dunno," says the author while scratching his head, but public figures seem to be an exception to the Hirschman thesis that exit choices diminish voice behavior. One possible explanation is that public leaders believe that most citizens expect them to promote "public" institutions in the city. They might fear that if they said that "low taxes and good private schools would stimulate economic development as much, if not more, than high property taxes and good public schools" they would diminish their powerful public images. Obviously, when "public" figures make personal decisions to exit from public provision, they continue to engage in voice behavior.

Hirschman and others have not discussed such exceptions to the exit-voice interrelationships. Perhaps you have some other explanations to offer.

8. **a.** You first might want to compare the tax rates and services to see if there are economies of scale in the provision of public goods in the strong county government. (Economists would tell you that, contrary to a widely held opinion, economies of scale do not exist for most local public goods.) One factor that might determine your answer is that the metropolitan area composed of numerous competing municipalities would offer you many "market baskets" of public goods and taxes from which to choose. If the community you initially selected imposed a market basket not to your preferences, you could move to another location at a relatively low cost.

b. Individuals who live in the central city area in the weak county government can easily "escape" an undesirable market basket of public goods by moving a few blocks or miles to another municipality. Those who live in a strong county government area find it more costly to move (commuting distances are too far), so we could expect individuals with a wider range of views on public goods and taxes to live within its jurisdiction. Consequently, we would expect voice behavior, political action, and protest to be more prevalent in the area that has a strong county government.

c. Since exit is less costly, you would expect more exit activity and a greater decline in the central city area in the weak county, strong municipal government.

d. The weak county government area, because the majority of voters who live in the central area would oppose taxes to support development, such as roads, on the periphery. [*Note:* This author lives in East Baton Rouge Parish of Louisiana, which was one of the first city-county (parish) consolidated governments in the country. With the exception of two small municipalities that were grandfathered in at the start of consolidated government, independent municipalities, school districts, etc. are not permitted in this expansive parish of 460 square miles and 400,000 people. There are few roads (about a half-dozen) to the periphery of the parish, and they emanate from the center of the city outward to the fringes like the spokes in a wheel. There are *no* roads that traverse from the southern part of the parish to the northern part of the parish, and there is no road, or beltline, encircling the parish. Commercial and residential developments on the fringes have been seriously retarded by the refusal of the voters and parish council to vote funds for road development in this area. Residents of East Baton Rouge Parish who strongly prefer a different market basket of public goods have to leave the parish and commute considerable distances to their work locations in the parish.]

CHAPTER NINE

POLITICAL PARTIES

What businessmen do not understand is
that exactly as they are dealing in oil
so I am dealing in votes.
—ATTRIBUTED BY J. A. SCHUMPETER
(*CAPITALISM, SOCIALISM AND DEMOCRACY*)
TO FRANKLIN ROOSEVELT.

POLITICAL PARTIES ARE THE FIRMS OF THE POLITICAL MARKET AND POLITICIANS ITS ENTREPRENEURS

Firms organize resources and produce goods in the private market in order to gain profits; political parties organize resources and produce party platforms in the political market in order to gain political power. Political parties are coalitions of individuals seeking to control the government by winning elections. Parties perform the essential task of simplifying choices for voters, who cannot possibly be familiar with all candidates for every office and their positions on all public issues. Even though party labels in the United States cover wide segments of the political spectrum, they reduce the costs of gathering information about candidates because voters are able to make some rough first approximations about the political philosophy of candidates based on their party affiliation. Where candidates do not run under the labels of specific parties, voters have less information about the candidates and often do not vote as a result. For example, nonpartisan elections in municipal contests, where candidates do not have party labels, have much lower voter turnout.[1] Communities that

---

[1] See, for example, Robert R. Alford and Eugene C. Lee, "Voting Turnout in American Cities," *American Political Science Review* 62 (1968): 796–813.

prohibit straight party voting require voters to wade through lengthy and complicated ballots, which increases the costs and uncertainty of voting.

Ideally, competition among political parties should educate the public about major public issues, stimulate new ideas about solving public problems, and educate and train young people to seek public office. Politicians, who are the entrepreneurs in the political market, have an important role to play in the country's division of labor. They are intermediaries who specialize in the discovery and representation of the preferences of voters and the presentation of their party's positions to citizens. Information and knowledge are passed both ways: (1) from the citizens to their representatives, and thus to the government and parties, and (2) from the parties and government to the citizens. Political parties and their candidates are nearly as essential in the political market as firms and their managers are in the private market.

Political parties are much less pivotal in the American political system than in the parliamentary systems that characterize most democracies. Unlike the United States, in which the legislative and executive branches are separated, most other countries select the top administrators of government from members of the party or the coalition of parties that has a majority in parliament. Thus, representatives in parliamentary systems must follow the official party line in order to support their party and to keep it in power. For example, if the conservative party had 201 members in parliament and the liberal party had 199 members, the deflection of only two members from the conservative party's position on a major issue would result in the fall of the government. Unlike members of a parliament, U.S. representatives and senators need not vote the party line in order to keep their executive leaders in office. Consequently, they have considerable freedom to represent their constituents' interests when they conflict with party interests, and most election campaigns in the United States are centered around the candidate rather than around the party.

Although it is convenient to discuss political parties as decision-making units in much the same way that firms are discussed as decision-making units, political parties, of course, do not make decisions. The individual members of political parties make the decisions for reasons best known to them. The reader who recalls the free rider analysis in chapter 4 might wonder why individuals join political parties at all. Why would individuals provide money or time to the Republican or Democratic party? The analytical answer is *not* that they want to ensure the election of the party that espouses their political philosophy; they know that the Republicans or Democrats will win or lose the election regardless of what they, as individuals, do. Hence, they have an incentive to do nothing. The answer to this free rider dilemma is the same for political parties as it is for firms, governments, and other large organizations. There are several selective incentives motivating individuals to join political parties just as there are selective incentives motivating individuals to join firms. Working in political parties enables individuals to make contacts and to gain experience valuable to their careers, to obtain business contracts from governments captured by the party, and to participate in a wide variety of patronage, which yields economic, educational, professional, and social benefits.[2] Party members are motivated not by a desire to enact certain policies but to procure some of the benefits of office for themselves or to develop contacts with those who do hold office. Just as private "greed" motivates the butcher, baker, and candlestick maker, it also motivates the politician and party volunteer.

This is not a criticism of party members, because there is absolutely nothing wrong with selective interests motivating individuals to take their role in the country's division of labor. Just as a prosperous nation has to have specialists in science, construction, journalism, and medicine, it also needs to have specialists in discovering, organizing, and reflecting public opinion and in making decisions on public goods. Politicians and members of political parties are necessary components in the division of labor, and it is not being unduly critical or cynical to recognize that selective private interests motivate them just as they do owners, managers, and laborers in the private sector. Party members, therefore, formulate policies in order to reap the benefits obtained from winning elections. They manipulate their policies and platforms in order to maximize their votes without violating the Constitution. The private market analyst postulates that the pursuit of profit is the immediate stimulus shaping the behavior of market suppliers; the public choice analyst postulates that pursuit of votes is the primary stimulus shaping the behavior of politicians. Just as profits are the lifeblood of the profit market entrepreneur, votes are the lifeblood of the political market entrepreneur. Regardless of ultimate motivations, political competition forces politicians to pay attention to the effects their actions will have on their electoral prospects. If politicians refuse to support popular policies, they run a good risk of being replaced by competitors who pay closer attention to voters' preferences.

Let's continue to assume that information and voting are costless, that is, all citizens have the requisite amount of knowledge and that they do

---

[2] Federal patronage is still alive and well despite civil service. The president has more than 2,400 positions to fill in the federal bureaucracy. Many "workers" in political parties become part of the salaried executive staff. Congress is a major source of patronage. *Excluding* the General Accounting Office, the Library of Congress, and the Congressional Budget Office, Congress employs 20,000 workers.

exercise their franchise. Let's also initially assume that individuals vote directly for one of two political parties, Party X and Party Y. The rational voter will vote for the party that will provide the greatest flow of benefits or utility to him. He will compare the utility gained by him if Party X wins (U^X) with the utility obtained if Party Y wins (U^Y). The difference between the two is called the party differential: if $U^X > U^Y$, the individual will vote for Party X; if $U^Y > U^X$, the individual will vote for Party Y.

A party formulating a platform for a forthcoming election must consider the utility payoffs of each plank to the voters. Assume there is a constitutional provision that requires government expenditures to be financed out of current taxes. The party knows that it would increase its party differential by increasing expenditures but decrease its party differential by raising taxes. Hence, the vote-maximizing party[3] must weigh the additional votes it would receive by increasing expenditures against the marginal votes it would lose by imposing higher taxes. If the party expected to gain 10,000 votes by spending an additional billion dollars on defense but lose 60,000 votes by increasing taxes, it would quickly drop the proposal. The positions taken by a party on a number of such issues reflects the party's ideology.

PARTY IDEOLOGY AND DOWNSIAN ANALYSIS

More than 30 years ago Anthony Downs illustrated the rational behavior of political parties by representing political ideology on a linear scale. His methodology is still one of the most useful analytical devices for understanding political parties and the effects voter preferences have on the number and stability of political parties.[4] Political ideology, according to Downs, is a verbal or written image of the good society and the means for constructing such a society. It is a public statement about a party's

---

[3] We are assuming that the party would attempt to maximize votes. Some political economists have assumed that parties limit their supporters to the minimum necessary to win elections. After all, these critics argue, a candidate does not win more by receiving 65 percent of the vote rather than 55 percent. However, the larger the plurality, the freer the winner becomes from individual supporters who make claims for benefits. Secondly, large victories make a candidate more likely to be considered as a contender for higher office in the future than do small victories.

[4] Spatial competition shown on a linear scale was first used by economists to analyze the location of retail stores. The seminal articles were Harold Hotelling, "Stability in Competition," *The Economic Journal* (1929): 41–57 and Arthur Smithies, "Optimum Location in Spatial Competition," *The Journal of Political Economy* (1941): 423–39. It was first systematically applied to political parties by Anthony Downs in *An Economic Theory of Democracy* (New York: Harper & Row, 1957).

general proposals for action if elected. Ideologies describe a party's general position on a wide number of issues, and they reduce information costs because the voters, knowing the party's ideology, do not have to investigate the party's position on every issue. Individuals can vote for a party that has an ideology similar to their own, knowing that the party's position on most issues will be close to theirs.

Party ideologies can be represented on a linear scale running from 0 to 100; the extreme left-wing would be represented by 0, and the extreme right-wing would be represented by 100. An ideology, of course, represents a collection of positions on many issues, but for ease of presentation assume there is only one issue in the forthcoming election, which is the relative size of the defense budget. The horizontal axis in Figure 9-1 represents the percentage of the country's budget that will be allocated to defense. Individual A is a moderate pacifist who prefers that 25 percent of the nation's budget be allocated to defense, whereas Individual B is a moderate militant who prefers that 75 percent of the budget be allocated to defense. Their relative positions on the linear scale represent their first preferences, and it is assumed that their preference rankings are single peaked (that is, they would prefer alternative budget sizes closer to their first preferences to those that are more distant). Individual A would prefer a political party that would advocate 25 percent of the budget to defense, but she would vote for the party that came closest to that percentage. If Party X, for example, advocated 40 percent and Party Y advocated 50 percent, she would vote for Party X.

NORMAL DISTRIBUTION OF VOTERS

Linear analysis is most useful when it is applied to all voters in a political unit. Assume that there are one million voters whose distribution of first preferences is shown in Figure 9-2. Further assume that each voter would vote for the party that came closest to espousing his or her preferences.

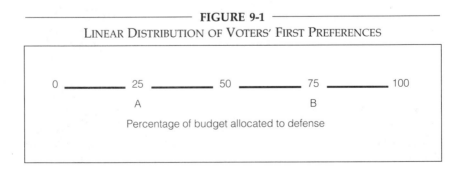

FIGURE 9-1

LINEAR DISTRIBUTION OF VOTERS' FIRST PREFERENCES

0 ——— 25 ——— 50 ——— 75 ——— 100

A   B

Percentage of budget allocated to defense

———————————— **FIGURE 9-2** ————————————
NORMAL DISTRIBUTION OF VOTERS' FIRST PREFERENCES
INITIAL POSITIONS OF PARTIES X AND Y

FIGURE 9-2
NORMAL DISTRIBUTION OF VOTERS' FIRST PREFERENCES
INITIAL POSITIONS OF PARTIES X AND Y

Percentage of budget allocated to defense

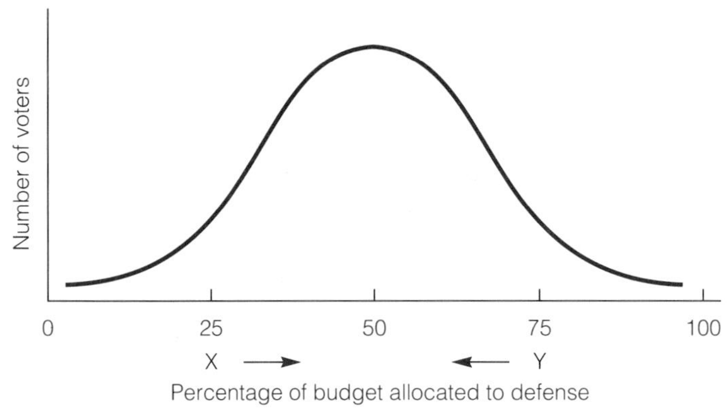

Although a few voters do have first preferences at the extremes, the overwhelming majority of them have preferences that are grouped around the middle of the ideological spectrum. This is a normal statistical distribution with a mean of 50. Though simplistic, the underlying political conditions reflected in this graph have much significance for political stability in a country.

Assume that Party X initially took the position that 25 percent of the government's budget should be allocated to defense while Party Y wanted 75 percent. Obviously, both parties would see that they could obtain more votes by moving toward 50 percent, which is the first preference of the largest number of voters. If the two parties adjusted simultaneously, parties X and Y would end up supporting approximately 50 percent of the budget allocated to defense. If Party X supported 40 percent, then Party Y would quickly move further to the left, say to 41 percent, because it would capture all voters to the right of 41 percent whereas Party X would receive only the votes of those to the left of 40 percent. Party X, of course, would never let itself be put in such an inferior position, so it would strive to position itself in the center of the spectrum, which is occupied by the majority of voters at 50 percent. Hence, both political parties would occupy the centrist position with not a "dime's worth of difference between them." They would have no incentive to change their positions as long as voters clung to the preferences represented in Figure 9-2.

Figure 9-3 represents the important median voter theorem, which states that the median voter holds the dominant position in the political market. According to the theorem, voters on the left can move further to the left or right, and voters on the right can move further to the right or left, but this will have no impact on government policy or on the policy positions taken by political parties. Political parties will still maximize their votes by staking out a position held by the median voter. If the median voter moves to the left or right, the political parties will follow. The median voter theorem states that it is the median voter who determines policy in a democracy; shifts of positions among voters other than the median voter simply don't matter. The median voter theorem operates well when the distribution of voters is normal, when voters don't abstain in protest, and when new parties cannot enter the political market easily. These limiting cases will be discussed below.

If one of the two political parties, say Y, ignored the position of the median voter and staked out a position to the right of the median voter, say at 75 on the ideological scale, Party X could simply stay in the middle and get the votes of all voters to the left of 50 percent, which it would have gotten previously, *plus* the large number of voters located between 50 and 62 percent. By being the first party to abandon its median position, Party Y would certainly lose the election because Party X could get even more votes by moving to the right and positioning itself at 74;

FIGURE 9-3

NORMAL DISTRIBUTION OF VOTER'S FIRST PREFERENCES
POSITIONS OF PARTIES AFTER ADJUSTMENT

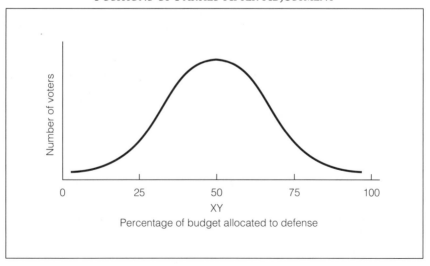

Party Y would get only a few votes of those who held ideologies to the right of 74.

Occasionally, candidates or parties misread the distribution curve and the position of the median voter, and they stake out a position to the left or right of the median voter. They suffer the consequences of their error. Barry Goldwater evidently thought the median voter had moved far to the right in 1964. He staked out a well-defined position to the right of the median voter and refused to move toward the center even after it became apparent to most observers that he had misread the distribution curve. He lost the election by a landslide. George McGovern championed leftist causes in 1972 and refused to move toward the center and lost the election by a landslide. Ronald Reagan correctly saw that the median voter had moved somewhat toward the right during the latter seventies, and he moved right along with the median voter and won the 1980 election. George Bush, who was able to isolate Michael Dukakis as advocating an ideology far to the left of the median voter, won the election in 1988.[5]

Critics of the American political system with its bell-shaped curve charge that the Democratic and Republican parties are as similar as Tweedledee and Tweedledum and that the ability to choose between them is essentially meaningless. The nearly identical positions of the two political parties can be compared to a cartel market and a competitive market that produce identical or nearly identical prices on contract bids. One analyst might argue that the closeness of the price bids indicates that a few firms colluded to rig the bid; another observer examining the same data might conclude that the nearly identical prices indicate a competitive market, because in a competitive market the prices charged by all firms will be the same. A similar analysis could be applied to political parties: the closeness of political party positions may indicate that the system does not work from one perspective or that it works very well from another perspective. The convergence of the two political parties toward the center is not unlike the convergent pressures that induce soap manufacturers to produce nearly identical products while trying to persuade consumers that their brand of soap is much superior to all other brands. Political parties take nearly identical positions while trying to convince voters—especially the voters grouped around the median—that their policies are different.

---

[5] This analysis assumes that voters can be set along an ideological spectrum. Data from the National Election Study (1980) showed that citizens with various levels of political sophistication could be placed along a liberal-to-conservative spectrum based on answers given to 11 policy issues. The normal bell-shaped curve was obtained with one exception and most respondents tended to be moderates. The exception was those with a high degree of political sophistication who tended to be extreme liberals or extreme conservatives. W. Russell Neuman, *The Paradox of Mass Politics* (Cambridge: Harvard University Press, 1986), 78.

The warm and cozy conclusion derived from the above analysis, based on a distribution of preferences around the center of the spectrum, is that a normal distribution of voters around the median and a single vote ballot is likely to generate only two parties and that no matter which party wins the election, there will be relatively few voters who are greatly disappointed.[6]

MULTIMODAL DISTRIBUTION OF VOTERS

If the distribution of voters is multimodal, the conclusions are much less satisfying than those above. Assume that the distribution of voters' preferences is bimodal, as shown in Figure 9-4. Voters' preferences are now widely separated and concentrated at both ends of the ideological spectrum. The two vote-maximizing parties would continue staking out positions in the middle, and the preferences of the median voter would dominate so long as new parties could not enter the race and all individuals voted for the party with the closest ideology. Assume now that voters

---
FIGURE 9-4
BIMODAL DISTRIBUTION OF VOTERS' FIRST PREFERENCES

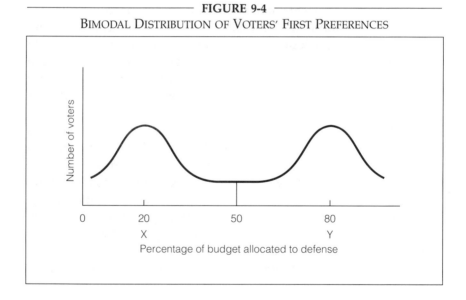

---

[6] Political scientists sometimes refer to the proposition that the simple majority single ballot system produces a two-party system as Duverger's law. He first mentioned the "law" in 1951 (Maurice Duverger, "Les partis politiques," *La Vie Intellectuelle* 20th ser., 70: 62–73), but he was not the first to discover the relationship between a simple majority system and a two-party system, nor did he discuss the effects of multimodal preference distribution on the law.

would abstain if their closest party moved too far away from their preferred position. With both parties taking a centrist position, it is likely that large numbers of voters would abstain to protest their party being located too far from their preferred position. Abstention by rightists and leftists poses no great threat in the single-modal distribution of Figure 9-3 because there are very few voters on either extremity. But if the distribution of voters were similar to that depicted in Figure 9-4, the abstention of a small percentage of the large number of voters located on the extremes could cause a party to lose the election. This would induce both parties to move toward their respective extremities, and the median voter's preference would no longer dominate. Parties would abandon the median voter to avoid losing the votes of the large number of individuals located on the extremities.

Two parties in a political market with such widely divergent preferences as those depicted in Figure 9-4 would have more to worry about than abstaining voters. If both parties stuck to their middle-of-the-road ideologies, there would be a strong incentive for new parties to emerge and to position themselves at points 20 and 80. Hence, to discourage voter abstention or new parties from entering on their flanks, Party X would move to the left and position itself at 20 and Party Y would position itself at 80. Both parties would place themselves in the ideological center of their supporters, but they would distance themselves from each other and from the median voter. There would be much more than a "thin dime" separating the positions of the two parties, and democracy would likely be unstable, chaotic, and highly prone to coups and revolutions. A large percentage of voters would be violently opposed to the policies of whichever party won the election. Unfortunately, it would be unlikely for any centrist party to emerge and remain a viable party. If a third party, Z, took a position at 50, it would draw only a few votes from the small number of voters in the center and it would have to move toward the left or right in order to attract voters. Thus, Party Z could win the election only by positioning itself immediately to the right of Party X or immediately to the left of Party Y. One of the parties would be squeezed out, and the two remaining parties would continue to have widely different platforms.

The fault lies not in the parties or in the political mechanism but in the widely divergent preferences of the electorate. Just as the private market will produce boomboxes, deafeningly loud music, and unwashed musicians if people's preferences run in these directions, so will the political market produce instability and chaos if people's preferences support it. The "solution" to such chaos is the same in both markets: the distribution of people's preferences has to change.

If voters' preferences are distributed as shown in Figure 9-5, then many parties are likely to exist. Each of the parties would stake out a position that appealed to its node of voters, and no party would have an incentive to move along the spectrum. For example, if Party X were to move toward the center—that is, toward Y—it would lose as many votes to W as it took away from Y. Hence, if voters' preferences were distributed as shown in Figure 9-5, each party would maintain its distinct ideological purity and identification and it would attempt to convince voters that it was different from the other parties. Voters in a multipeaked political market are much more likely to be influenced by ideologies and policies and to identify more closely with "their" party than are voters in a single-peaked, two-party system. Once again political instability would be likely to result because the supporters of parties at either extreme (Parties W and Z) would be quite upset if the party at the other extreme won.

The number of major parties existing within a democracy is affected by the distribution of voters' preferences. A single-peaked, normal distribution tends to produce two centrist parties; a multimodal distribution tends to produce many parties. New parties are most likely to emerge when new classes of voters are enfranchised, when major events shift preferences, when older parties drift from their positions, or when voters' preferences drift along the spectrum while the parties do not change their ideologies.

The origin of the British Labour party in the early twentieth century is the best example of newly enfranchised voters producing a new party.[7]

FIGURE 9-5

MULTIMODAL DISTRIBUTION OF VOTERS' FIRST PREFERENCES

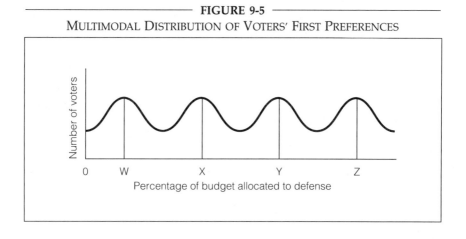

---

[7] There were independent Labour candidates for Parliament during the latter nineteenth century, but the Labour party was organized in 1900 by trade unions and socialist organizations. The party did not have individual members until 1918.

Males in the British working class were enfranchised in the latter nineteenth century, and they found that the Liberal party, which was the slightly left-of-center party, had an ideology that was too far to the right of theirs. Hence, the small Labour party positioned itself far to the left of the Liberal party. The single peak of the distribution was shifted to the left by the enfranchisement of working-class citizens. This eventually prompted both the Liberal and Conservative parties to shift to the left as well. As a result, the Liberal party—squeezed between the new Labour party and the Conservative party moving to the left—became a minor party. The Democratic party in the United States, followed somewhat haphazardly by the Republican party, moved to the left during the 1930s as the electorate's political ideology moved to the left. That preempted the emergence of a strong third party on the left. No new party in the United States has attained national standing since 1856, when the Republican party was organized.

MORE THAN ONE POLICY ISSUE

The Downsian analysis presented above dealt with a single ideology and ignored the complications that arise when there are many issues to be decided. Just as the consumer in the private market has certain brand, color, and size preferences for particular goods in the private market, so does the voter have certain preferences on a number of issues in the political market. In the private market, the individual can realize these preferences by purchasing a market basket of goods that suits her preferences. She can purchase a blue Toyota, a pink shirt, sugar-coated cereals, cowboy boots, and a book on gourmet cooking. The purchase of one good is not tied to the purchase of other goods.[8] Unfortunately, the individual is unable to similarly adjust her consumption of public goods for two reasons. First, the nature of public goods and collective decision making means that she must consume the market basket that is provided by the collective decision-making process. Second, the individual cannot find a party that reflects her preferences on *all* issues. Because there are far fewer parties than the number of policy combinations, the voter has to accept a party that advocates some policies with which she disagrees.

---

[8] Some firms have attempted to engage in a practice of full-line marketing, in which consumers are constrained to purchase a firm's high-profit lines in order to get a low-profit product. Generally, such practices have been declared to be anticompetitive by Congress and the courts, and—where they have not been protected by patents—competition in the marketplace has generally eliminated them.

Each party offers a basket of policy positions, and the individual must select the one that comes closest to reflecting the combination of her own preferences. Parties realize this, and they are able to include some unpopular policies in their electoral packages on the ground that voters will still support them on the other issues. When putting their platforms together they have to weigh the relative intensities of voters on the various issues.[9]

One of the most important lessons a vote-maximizing party or politician has to learn is that the majority of voters are seldom in the majority on *every* issue, that is, the composition of the majority varies from issue to issue. Assume that there are three voters, A, B, and C. If A and B agreed on every issue and C disagreed with them on every issue, then Party X would take A and B's position and C would lose on every issue. For example, if A and B had the same preferences for the defense budget to be increased by 20 percent (prodefense) and tariffs to be reduced by 10 percent (protrade), Party X's platform would be prodefense and protrade, no matter how intensely the three voters felt about each issue.

However, it is highly unlikely that the majority of voters would have identical views on all issues. More likely there would be majority coalitions composed of different voters on different issues. For example, assume that A, B, and C have the following preferences:

A	B	C
Prodefense	Prodefense	Antidefense
Antitrade	Protrade	Protrade

A majority of voters hold prodefense (A and B) and protrade (B and C) positions, but the composition of the majority changes on each issue. A and B constitute the prodefense majority, whereas B and C make up the protrade majority. When the composition of the majority varies among issues, the relative intensity of voter preferences becomes important to parties seeking to put together a winning campaign platform.

Assume that A just slightly prefers the prodefense position but that he is strongly opposed to free trade. Individual C, on the other hand, is strongly antidefense while slightly preferring protrade laws.

A	B	C
Slightly Prodefense	Prodefense	Strongly Antidefense
Strongly Antitrade	Protrade	Slightly Protrade

---

[9] Why would parties take positions with which a large number of voters would disagree? One possibility, which will be discussed below, is that parties appeal to the intense preferences of a small minority while hoping that the large majority has a slight intensity for the issue. Another possibility is that parties take positions that are favored by those who hold chokepoint positions in the dissemination of information.

Assume that Party Y ignored the intensity of voter preferences but listened to its polling experts who told the party that the majority of voters were prodefense and protrade. Party Y would adopt the majority positions of prodefense and protrade as its platform. Assume that Party X, on the other hand, was advised by political economists that it could win the election by appealing to the strongly held preferences of A and C by putting together the two planks of antitrade and antidefense. How would the two parties fare in the election? Individual A prefers the prodefense position of Party Y to the antidefense policy of Party X but he feels most strongly about the antitrade position, so he votes for Party X. Individual C prefers the protrade position of Party Y, but because he is a strong pacifist he votes for Party X. Only Individual B votes for Party Y. Hence, the party (Y) espousing each of the positions preferred by the majority of the voters loses the election to a party (X) espousing the *strongly held* positions of the minority. A party wishing to maximize its chances of winning an election must determine not only the preferences of the electorate but the *intensities* of these preferences.

Note that the vote-maximizing party does not compare relative passions from one voter to another; rather it compares them within each voter. Given the one-person-one-vote rule, it doesn't matter whether Individual A views a prodefense policy to be worth $10,000 to him or Individual C views a pacifist policy to be worth only $100 to him. What is important is that Individual A prefers an antitrade to a protrade policy more than he prefers a prodefense to a pacifist policy and that Individual C prefers a pacifist to a prodefense policy more than he prefers a protrade to an antitrade policy. Individual A has relatively intense preferences for an antitrade policy while Individual C has a relatively intense preference for an antidefense policy.

One of the serious failures in the political market is that voters cannot express the intensity of their preferences through any voting system. However, there are two institutions though which such preferences can be partially realized. One is logrolling, which was discussed in chapter 8, and the second is through parties attempting to build platforms composed of the most intensely held preferences of voters. The ability of the voters' intensities to be reflected in legislation, however, is still severely limited; logrolling—that is, trading votes—is limited to only a few issues. As for the second institution, hundreds of thousands of political parties would be necessary to reflect the relative intensities of voter preferences among all feasible issues, yet virtually all democracies have less than a dozen parties.

Parties have used surveys, polls, grass-root canvassing, consultations, trial balloons, and many other devices to gather information about the preferences of voters, but they have not yet become very sophisticated about determining the intensities of voter preferences. This lack of a general methodology for determining preference intensities has increased the power of lobbyists for single-issue organizations who simply assert that members of their organizations and "millions" of other voters feel most intensely about their favored issue. Lobbyists are constantly trying to convince congressional representatives that members of their supporting organizations are deeply concerned only about one issue and will vote accordingly. If politicians are truly convinced that members of an organization or pressure group will actually base their political decisions on a single issue, they will vote favorably on the issue, even if the overwhelming majority of voters has opposing views. Individuals with intense preferences who do not belong to lobbying organizations lose out to individuals who do. This is most evident in the so-called race and sex quota legislation in which women and members of minorities have set up effective organizations to lobby Congress whereas those who suffer from such laws have no comparable organizations to express their own intensities.

KNOWLEDGE OF A POLITICIAN'S PERSONAL VALUES PROVIDES LOW-COST INFORMATION

Social scientists and editorial writers are very much concerned about the professional, social, and religious background of politicians, but they seldom are interested in the backgrounds of businessmen. One frequently cited reason for this asymmetrical treatment of politicians and businessmen is that businessmen's decisions are guided by the narrow confines of profit maximization while politicians have no such objective guide and they must rely upon their own social values when making legislative decisions.

At the theoretical level this view is incorrect. The politician is guided as much by vote maximization as the entrepreneur is by profit maximization. It should not matter whether the politician is an attorney, a minister, a butcher, or a scientist. All politicians attempt to construct political platforms that appeal to the median voter, and, given a certain electorate, their political platforms should be very similar. However, the reader should now be aware that many impediments exist in the political market such as costly information searches, barriers to entry, choke points in the dissemination of information, unequal distribution of political power, inefficient voting systems, and others. Because of these impediments, a politician can pursue a "hidden agenda" that does not reflect the median voter's preferences, or he may not know the preferences of his constituents and it is too costly for him to determine them. Hence, he can use his lowest-cost sources of information for his decision making, which are his own experiences, education, and advice obtained from professional colleagues and friends. To the extent that such impediments enable the politician to stray from the actual preferences of the median voter, the occupation and social background of the politician are important to voters because they may be good proxies for the politician's values.

It has become intellectually fashionable to state that voters and the media should be concerned only about a candidate's ideas and policies and not about a candidate's personal values. There is *no* analytical basis for such statements. The editorial writer who proclaims that a candidate's personal life-style and values should be disregarded in a political campaign is ignoring the simple fact that it is too costly for voters to obtain information about the politician's views on all potential issues. A rational voter has no incentive to invest time and resources in making his own decisions on the hundreds of complicated issues confronting the country and then investigating the candidate's views on all of these issues. Furthermore, the voter doesn't know whether he can trust the politician to actually vote according to his platform. The voter wants the politician to make the same decisions that he—the voter—would make if he had the same information. One of the most reliable indicators about the likelihood a candidate will vote the way a voter would want him to vote is the candidate's personal set of values. Rather than search out information about the numerous issues and the politician's stand on them, it is far less costly for the voter to ask himself which of the candidates has values that most closely approximate his own values. If the voter shares many values with the candidate, he can expect that candidate to vote the way he would on most issues.

The voter can minimize the costs of obtaining information about the candidate and the issues by examining the candidate's life-style and set of values. Politicians, of course, will try to develop external indicators of values they may not actually hold if they believe a large number of voters prefer a certain set of moral or social values. The media has as important a role to play in ferreting out a candidate's real values as it does in reporting a candidate's campaign pledges. Both can be reliable sources of information to voters.

SOME CHARACTERISTICS OF POLITICIANS AND PARTIES IN THE UNITED STATES

One of the variables determining a politician's values and views on legislation is his or her prior and current occupation. Politicians come from many, but certainly not all, occupations; many occupations are not represented at all in Congress. A disproportionate percentage of congressional legislators are attorneys, which, at least at the margin, has to affect legislation. Attorneys constituted only six-tenths of 1 percent of the 1987 civilian labor force but about 60 percent of the 100 senators and at least 20 percent of the 435 members of the House (see Table 9-1). When those House members, whose occupations could not be determined, are subtracted from the total, attorneys account for more than 25 percent.

The United States Congress has a much larger percentage of lawyers than any other legislative body in the world. Only about 12 percent of the British Parliament in 1980 were lawyers. This predominance of attorneys in Congress, and in the state legislatures, is caused by a number of factors: lawyers who are trained in the law and the legislative process have a comparative advantage in some areas of politics; their occupations provide them with a flexible schedule; political campaigns provide publicity, which can be valuable in their professions; and participation in the political market provides numerous selective incentives for lawyers. Lawyers become involved in the political process to obtain clients, make

TABLE 9-1

OCCUPATIONS AND PROFESSIONS OF MEMBERS
OF CONGRESS 1987–88

	Senate	House
Attorneys	60	87
Politicians/Public Administrators	0	35
Communications Personnel	8	22
Bankers/Financiers	4	25
Businesspeople	10	88
Educators	3	26
Engineers/Scientists	2	5
Military Personnel	2	1
Physicians	1	4
Farmers	3	13
Pilots	1	1
Professionals	3	17
Social Workers	1	4
Clergy	1	3
Others	1	13
Not Determined	0	91
Total	100	435

SOURCE: *Congressional Yellow Book,* Washington: Washington Monitor, Inc., Spring 1988.

valuable contacts, acquire knowledge, obtain appointments to offices and judgeships, and influence legislation. A successful political career almost always assists a legal career; more than any other occupation, a legal career benefits from the externalities generated from political activism. While the interests of other occupations may not be proportionately reflected in the political market, there is little doubt that the interests of the legal profession are amply represented.

The dominance of the American political market by attorneys is not confined to the legislature. The third branch of government, the judicial system, is composed entirely of lawyers; this is not true of some other countries, which set aside some judicial seats for average citizens. This exclusive role of attorneys is especially important because the American judicial system possesses more power than that of any other country.

Another characteristic of American politics is that incumbents seldom lose elections. In recent decades more than 90 percent of the members of the House of Representatives have sought reelection, and all but 1 or 2 percent have survived the occasional challenges for nomination. Rarely do as many as 10 percent of those seeking reelection get defeated. Even in a year of stunning upsets of incumbents, such as 1980, only a small percent (7 percent for 1980) of the incumbent members of the House were defeated. The power of incumbency is due to barriers to entry in the political market, restraints on campaign contributions and financing, information choke points (which tend to favor incumbents), the single-mode distribution of American voters, free advertising by incumbents, and the ability of incumbents to reward supporters.

The Republican and Democratic parties have overwhelmingly dominated American politics for nearly 150 years. There have been marginal shifts in the allegiances of Americans between the two parties, but there have been only three major political realignments in American history. The first was the emergence of the Republican Party at the time of the Civil War and the alienation of southerners from that party. The second occurred during the 1890s, when the Republicans became identified with the gold standard and conservative economic policies. Republicans increased their dominance in the Northeast while the South and West tended to identify more with the Democrats. The third was the depression of the thirties and the formation of the Roosevelt coalition, which included white southerners, blacks, northern urban labor union members, and first- and second-generation immigrants and intellectuals. The Republicans gained back some ground in the latter forties and early fifties, but since 1952 Democrats have consistently outnumbered Republicans by an average ratio of 1.7 to 1.

During the 1970s and 1980s there have been three gradual shifts taking place that might constitute a fourth major realignment. The first is the geographical party realignment among voters, with those in the Northeast becoming much less Republican and those in the South becoming much less solidly Democratic. The second is that many blue-collar workers have shifted from the Democratic to the Republican Party. The third is that there has been a significant increase in the percentage of voters who identify themselves as conservative, especially on social issues.[10]

Another characteristic of American politics has been the decline in the influence of both political parties. National political parties in the United States have never possessed the power held by parties in other countries. American national parties are loose alliances formed for electoral purposes, but the real party managers operate at state and local levels. In Britain, on the other hand, the national political parties possess significant power. Local party organizations have little real power except over the nomination of local candidates. As discussed in the appendix to this chapter, political parties played a major role in the United States during the early part of this century. They selected candidates, they financed the candidates' campaigns, they controlled patronage, and they articulated issues. The rise of special interest groups, such as Common Cause, the Sierra Club, and the Hoover Institute, has decreased the issue-articulation role of parties. Voters identify less strongly with either the Republican or Democratic parties than they did a few decades ago.[11] Polls have shown that party affiliations of candidates are not as important as during the forties and fifties and that the perceived abilities and personalities of the candidates are more important. The net result of these trends is that there has been a rise in the proportion of independents in the electorate, a decline in the number of strong partisan voters, and an increase in split-ticket voting. The percentage of the electorate identifying themselves as Independents remained very stable at about 20 percent between 1940 and 1964. After 1964 it began increasing to a high of 38 percent in 1978 and has fallen slightly to 34 percent in 1984.[12] Between 1920 and 1944 only about 10 percent of the 435 congressional districts elected a representative from a party different from the one that received a majority of the presidential votes. In other words, most districts that elected a Democratic congressman were also likely to cast a majority of votes for the Democratic candidate

---

[10] In 1984, 43 percent of the respondents in a national poll stated that they were conservative, versus only 26 percent liberal.

[11] See Jerrold G. Rusk and Helmut Norpoth, "Partisan Dealignment in the American Electorate: Itemizing the Deductions since 1964," *American Political Science Review* 76 (1982): 522–37 and Martin P. Wattenberg, *The Decline of American Political Parties, 1952–1980* (Cambridge: Harvard University Press, 1984).

[12] Survey Research Center/Center for Political Studies National Election Studies.

for president. In the 20-year period between 1944 and 1964 split-party election results rose to 30 percent, and it was almost 50 percent in 1980.

One of the most frequently cited reasons for the recent decline in the significance of political parties is the diminishing role played by party officials in selecting candidates. Throughout most of the nineteenth and the early part of the twentieth century, party officials selected candidates with little, if any, input from ordinary members. Caucuses of party members serving in Congress were used to select presidential and vice presidential candidates until 1832, when the first Democratic national convention, under the prodding of Andrew Jackson, was held in Baltimore. The national conventions held in the nineteenth century had little appeal to the public and were dominated by local and state party bosses. After World War I, the proportion of primary-elected delegates at national conventions rose slowly, but it greatly accelerated during the sixties and seventies. Between 1960 and 1980 the proportion of delegates elected or bound by direct primaries rose from 30 to 78 percent for the Democrats and from 29 to 77 percent for the Republicans. The new convention rules for selecting delegates effectively destroyed the control previously exercised by national and state party leaders.

The United States is the only country in which all major party candidates for the legislature are chosen by the votes of ordinary party "members" in direct primaries. Although many American institutions were adopted by other countries, not one country has adopted the American direct primary, and most foreigners have difficulty understanding that ordinary voters, loosely defined as "party members," actually select party candidates. Most European parties use committees or conventions of active party members to nominate their candidates. National party leaders in Austria, Belgium, Columbia, Ireland, and Turkey can nominate local candidates even if opposed by local party organizations. Most national parties have the power to veto the selection of a candidate by a local party, and in most countries there are no government regulations or limitations on the party's nomination of candidates. The constitutions or regulations of the parties themselves determine the candidate-selection procedure.

Unlike most other countries, the candidate-selection procedure in the United States is prescribed by law and not by the parties. Each state has its own laws for nominating and selecting winners for state offices. Furthermore, each state has laws that determine how delegates are selected for the national presidential conventions. These procedures are a continuing mystery to foreigners who are accustomed to the political parties making such rules and to government-legislated details being uniform throughout the county. The variety of presidential primaries are even confusing to American citizens. The major types of presidential primaries follow:

1. Voters elect slates of delegates pledged to specific candidates, and the slate that secures the plurality of votes takes all of the delegates in the district. New York, Texas, and Alabama use this form of primary.

2. Individuals cast their votes for their favorite candidate, but their votes are merely preference indicators and are not binding. Delegates are elected in a separate election. New Hampshire, Illinois, Nebraska, New Jersey, Pennsylvania, Vermont, and West Virginia use this form.

3. Individuals vote for their preferred candidate whose name appears on the ballot, and then delegates are awarded to the candidates according to a formula based on the popular vote totals. The Republicans use the winner-take-all principle, in which the candidate who wins the plurality takes all of the delegates. One of the reasons Democrats have abandoned winner-take-all primaries is that George McGovern got 65 percent of all of the primary states' delegates in 1972 with only 25 percent of the vote.

4. Twenty states use the caucus-convention method, in which voters hold meetings on the precinct level to elect delegates to the county or congressional district conventions. The county conventions, in turn, select delegates to the state convention, and the state convention selects delegates to the national convention. Iowa is the best-known caucus state.

The nominating primary and caucus were adopted to reduce the power of party bosses and to enable individual citizens to express their preferences among the candidates. But they have produced many undesirable effects, because the important public choice theorems of rational abstention and rational ignorance were unknown or unheeded. The fundamental problem with all varieties of primaries is that relatively few voters turn out to cast their ballots, because most individuals face few social pressures or other selective incentives to vote. This enables a small activist minority to select the nominees. The nominating caucus is especially susceptible to control by a few activists. The average caucus attracts only the highly active, highly motivated ideologues and extremists as well as those peddling their own influence for future political favors; fewer than 5 percent of registered party members attend state caucuses or conventions. Those citizens who do vote have little incentive to obtain information about the candidates, which also increases the influence of an activist minority. Decisions made in the primaries and caucuses reflect not the preferences of the median citizen but the preferences of a minority who have selective incentives to go to the polls.

This self-selection distortion is exacerbated by the use of the plurality voting system to select the nominees. As discussed above, the plurality system, which expresses only the first preference of the voters and suppresses the rankings of all other preferences, is the most inefficient voting system. The low voter turnout at primaries and caucuses and the lack of knowledge about candidates coupled with the use of the inefficient plurality system constitute a very serious threat for American democracy. It is quite possible for the nominating process in one or both parties to return a candidate who is the first preference of a very small activist minority but the least desired candidate of the overwhelming majority of citizens.

Previously, when party officials selected the candidates, they had an incentive to select individuals who appealed to the median voter. They might not have liked the candidate, but if they wanted to continue or to expand their own political power, they had to select a candidate who was likely to win the election. The power of selecting candidates also imposed some cohesion, discipline, and authority in parties and made parties more responsible for their campaign promises. Today, national and state conventions no longer have much significance and authority. National conventions used to be places where party leaders investigated and discussed the candidates and traded political support for various concessions. Now they are meetings where the delegates can have a good time, meet old friends, and ratify the decisions made in the primaries. Even the widely reported party platform, over which bitter battles have been fought during conventions in the last 30 years, binds no one, says little of substance, is largely ignored by the candidates during the election campaign, and is virtually abandoned once the candidates are in office.

The primacy of primaries has produced other changes in the political market. Primary elections inhibit the formation of new parties because they encourage dissident groups and individuals to contend for office in the primary of an established party rather than forming an opposition party. The primary has elevated the importance of the media and those who occupy information choke points. They often select the "early leader in the horse race" who gets the initial publicity necessary to win the primary election. Primaries have changed the personal attributes that are required by a successful candidate. Administrative abilities, analytical logic, and reflective thinking are less important then a smiling face and the ability to read the television prompter. The most important characteristic of candidates is that they look and speak well on television.

Remedies are available to correct some of the worst distortions caused by the popular nomination process. The first is to eliminate the nominating caucus. The time required to attend caucuses increases the cost of participation and discourages attendance by all except a few activists with strong personal incentives. Attendees are not representative of party membership, and the candidates nominated are unlikely to be the candidates who, on average, rank highest on the preference orderings of all party members or citizens. The second remedy is to abandon the plurality voting system and to adopt the weighted ranking method or some other voting system that reflects the entire preference rankings of every voter. The third remedy is to make the costs of voting as low as possible. If banking by telephone is possible, certainly voting by telephone is possible. It would be an excellent way of lowering the cost of voting to the individual.

FINANCING PARTIES AND ELECTIONS

One obvious characteristic of American elections is that they are very costly. The media and academicians make unfavorable comparisons with the costs of financing campaigns in other countries, and editorial writers ask why election campaigns in the United States have to be so expensive.[13] One reason for expensive campaigns is the expansiveness and diversity of the United States. A candidate for a Senate seat in Texas, the second largest state, has to travel 870 miles, east to west, from one state line to the other. This is equivalent to traveling from London to Venice, passing through parts of Belgium, France, Luxembourg, West Germany, and Switzerland.

Another reason for high campaign expenditures in the United States is the length of election campaigns, on which many other countries place limits. The United Kingdom has a minimum campaign period of 17 days after the dissolution of the House of Commons, not counting Sundays, bank holidays, or the Easter or Christmas breaks. This means that British politicians have about three to four weeks in which to campaign. They cannot buy time on radio or television. Campaign expenditures are controlled at the local level, where each candidate has to appoint an election agent who approves all campaign expenditures, which cannot total more than £5,000 (about $8,000). Campaigns for the French National Assembly begin about three weeks before the first election and one week before the second. Canada has an election campaign lasting about two

---

[13] The 1984 presidential primary elections cost more than $100 million: Mondale and Reagan each spent $40 million of federal funds; $17.5 million of independent contributions were made to the presidential candidates; and millions more probably slipped through the reporting cracks. The congressional races of 1985–86 involved campaign expenditures of at least $240 million, or about $3.70 for every vote cast in the final election.

months. Candidates in Germany are selected in June and then sit on their hands until six weeks prior to the October election. By contrast, the United States has no fixed time period for campaigning. The campaigns of House representatives are virtually continuous but are most feverish after the nomination of candidates, which varies in each state. Presidential campaigns officially begin during the summer when the conventions are held, but they really start months earlier, before the Iowa and New Hampshire primary contests.

American parties rely more heavily upon the contributions of individuals, corporations, and labor unions than do parties in most other countries. Many political parties, especially in Israel and continental Europe, are actively engaged in quasi-commercial enterprises. British Conservatives run bingo games and lotteries and sell advertising yearbooks. German Christian Democrats own printing plants and publish economic bulletins. Israeli parties publish daily newspapers and own publishing firms, sports teams, banks, housing projects, wholesale and retail cooperatives, hospitals, and kibbutzim. The Italian Communist party owns retail chain stores, garment manufacturing firms, travel agencies, and import-export agencies, which handle a large part of the country's trade with Eastern Europe. The French Communist party runs banks, real estate companies, publishing and public relation firms, and it owns a large urban firm, which sells services to municipalities controlled by the Communist party.

American political parties have never been so enterprising. They and their candidates have to rely more heavily upon contributions, which many critics argue has added yet a third meaning to the phrase "Want to have a party?" American candidates and parties depend much more heavily upon expensive political advertisements, especially on television. Only a few major countries permit paid political advertisements on television and radio (Australia, Canada, Japan, and the United States), and virtually all countries (with the exception of Norway, Sri Lanka, and the United States) provide free television time to political parties. Although television networks and stations are not required to provide free time to candidates and parties in the United States, television coverage *is* the electoral campaign. Since the election campaign of John Kennedy in 1960, television has become the dominant ingredient of every political campaign at the district, state, and national level.

Television, radio, and other media require enormous amounts of money, which, in turn, requires candidates and parties to solicit contributions. Between 1925 and 1971 the Federal Corrupt Practices Act was the principal law regulating political finances. Covering only general elections, the law limited candidates to maximum expenditures of $25,000 and $5,000 for Senate and House races, respectively. As amended in 1940, it prohibited federal contractors from contributing to federal candidates, extended the coverage to primary elections, established an individual contribution ceiling of $5,000 for any federal campaign, and established a $3 million limit on expenditures by a multistate political committee. These limitations were widely ignored or had wide loopholes.

The Federal Election Campaign Act of 1971 (amended in 1974 and 1976) attempted to remedy the deficiencies of previous laws by placing many limits on campaign contributions. No individual could contribute more than $1,000 to any one candidate, and no organization could contribute over $5,000. A companion law, the Revenue Act of 1971, provided for tax credits or deductions for contributions to electoral campaigns. This act also established the checkoff fund that has financed presidential campaigns since 1976. A presidential candidate who could raise at least $5,000 in small individual contributions was eligible for matching federal assistance up to a limit of $5 million, but the candidate could not then spend more than $10 million. A duly nominated candidate could not spend over $20 million in the general election if federal funds were accepted. However, the limitations did not cover local and state party spending or the numerous independent groups campaigning for the candidates.

Because individuals could not contribute more than $1,000 on a candidate, there was an incentive to establish Political Action Committees (PACs) to send unsolicited money to candidates. PACs are private organizations established to support candidates for public office. Although labor unions are now among the most vocal opponents of PACs, they were the original PAC organizers during the 1940s. Corporations were barred from organizing PACs until the passage of the Federal Election Campaign Act of 1971 (FECA). By lifting prohibitions against corporate contributions to PACs, FECA legitimized a new and much larger role for trade associations and corporations in politics. After a PAC is registered with the Federal Elections Commission, it can collect up to $5,000 per member and can contribute up to $5,000 per candidate per election with no overall limitations. The FECA spawned a dramatic change in the way political money is raised and fostered an enormous growth in the numbers of PACs involved in active politics. There is no upper limit on either the number of candidates a PAC can support or the number of PACs that can support one candidate. In 1974 about 600 PACs contributed $12.5 million to congressional candidates; by 1983, 4,000 PACs distributed more than $100 million (see Table 9-2).

The rapid growth of PACs, most of which represent specific interest groups, has also contributed to the decline of parties. Congressional candidates during the eighties received more than one-third of their campaign funds from PACs and less than 10 percent from the parties. PAC

TABLE 9-2
CONTRIBUTIONS TO CONGRESSIONAL CAMPAIGNS BY PACS
PERCENTAGE DISTRIBUTIONS

	1979–80	1981–82	1983–84	1985–86
Contributions (in millions)	$55.2	$83.7	$105.4	$132.2
From: Corporations	34.6%	33.1%	33.6%	34.7%
Trade Associations	28.6	26.0	25.3	24.8
Labor Unions	23.9	24.3	23.5	22.7
Other	12.9	16.6	17.6	17.8
Given to: Democrats	52.4%	54.2%	57.2%	56.4%
Republicans	47.5	45.6	42.6	43.5
Incumbents	60.7	65.8	71.3	67.6
Challengers	26.3	19.2	16.7	14.5
Open Seats	13.0	14.9	12.0	17.9

SOURCE: Statistical Abstract of the United States, 1988.

contributions come from a variety of sources, with corporate PACs contributing about one-third of the total and trade associations and labor unions about one-half.

EVALUATION OF FUNDING LIMITATIONS

There are frequent calls for limiting the amount of political contributions, although the reasons for doing so are not always clear. Presumably, a financial contribution could place a "donee" in an indebted relationship to the "donor," and the elected candidate might vote for legislation benefitting the donor or put pressure on executive departments on the donor's behalf. More likely, the donor might make a contribution with the expectation that he would have greater access to the politician and his aides. But such access is not granted only to financial contributors; members of the politician's family, professional colleagues, friends, and those who contribute shoe leather and brains to the campaign have at least as much access.

Furthermore, limitations on financial contributions are not necessarily desirable. The first problem is that reductions in campaign expenditures would hurt challengers more than incumbents. Incumbents are already well known to voters in their districts; they have staffs to assist in organizing campaigns; they are frequent guests on television news and public interest programs; they can mail letters to constituents with the postage paid by the taxpayer. Hence, it is far more important for the challenger than the incumbent to be able to advertise. The only way the challenger can hope to compete with the inherent advantages possessed by the incumbent is to present his name, face, positions, and arguments in advertisements. The political challenger is in a position similar to a small firm that has developed a new motor oil. If the firm cannot advertise extensively, it has little chance of competing against Mobil and Quaker State. Incumbent politicians, like established brands, have an incentive to limit advertising expenditures in order to keep the new kid on the block from establishing a foothold in the market. Mobil and Quaker State have not been able to convince Congress to limit advertising expenditures in the private market, but incumbent politicians have been able to limit advertisements in the political market.

The second problem with limitations on campaign contributions is that such limitations have been directed solely at monetary contributions and not at contributions of time or talent. The National Association of Manufacturers has a comparative advantage in raising funds to support candidates, the American Federation of Labor has a comparative advantage in organizing workers to devote time, and the National Education Association has a comparative advantage in writing position papers for candidates.[14] If monetary contributions were limited, but not contributions of time or talent, the political process would be distorted. Those who had high incomes but little time would be discriminated against, while those who had much spare time but low incomes would be benefitted. The political favors and access accorded to those who contribute time or control groups of volunteer labor can be as dangerous to the political process as the favors given to financial contributors. There is a countervailing power at work in the political market. Some candidates get relatively more financial contributions while others get relatively greater contributions of time and effort. The appointment to ambassadorships and other positions of power in government of those who have made campaign contributions is well known and discussed in the media. Less publicized, but at least as important, are the appointments of those who have contributed time and professional skills to the candidates' campaign. Limits placed on one source of contributions (money) without placing limits on the other (time) would upset this countervailing balance. There is no simple solution to the "obscene" campaign contributions of money, time, or skills—and the influence that accompanies all such contributions—as long as the political

---

[14] In 1976 labor unions estimated the value of their support to the Carter campaign to be worth an equivalent of $11 million. Teacher organizations, which have become very active during the past two decades, have considerable influence in the legislatures of many states.

market is able to provide special benefits to some groups or individuals and not to others and so long as government is not constitutionally restricted to more limited powers.

THOSE SPECIAL INTEREST GROUPS

Special interest legislation provides substantial benefits to a small number of constituents while imposing a small cost on a large number of individuals. Special interests can be economic, social, religious, racial, ideological, and military, among many others. They clearly are not confined to economic issues. Since special interest legislation directly affects a small number of voters, members of special interest groups have an incentive to gather information about the presumed benefits of various legislation and to lobby their representatives to vote accordingly. They provide their representatives with financial and time contributions and inform them that members' votes will be determined by the representatives' positions on specific issues. The majority of voters who will have to pay taxes for special interest legislation have few incentives to gather information on the issues or to talk to their representatives about them. It is simply not worth the effort because the tax will exert little impact on each of them.

There are three types of pressure groups: those that represent producers, those that represent consumers, and those that represent do-gooders (altruists, the socially concerned). The theory of special interest producer groups has not received the scholarly attention that the amount of public discussion about them would imply; there have been few explanations of their very existence. A special interest producer group can be compared to several firms attempting to form a cartel in the private market. All firms have a common interest in procuring higher prices for their industry's output, but it is in the interest of each firm to let the other firms reduce their quantity in order to achieve that price. Hence, economists have long argued, competitive firms are not able to sustain boycotts or artificially reduced supply. Similarly, all firms have a common interest in the establishment of government price supports, tariffs, and limited entry into the industry. It requires considerable time and money to finance a professional lobbying association with a staff of public relations, marketing, organizational, and legal experts. Why do individual firms finance such associations? If it is irrational for a competitive firm to reduce its output in order to get a higher price, it's just as irrational for it to contribute to a lobbying association. Even if each firm were convinced that the lobbying association would bring benefits to the industry and to the firm, there would be no incentive to contribute to such an association. The benefits would be common to all firms in the industry, and they would or would not be provided whether the individual firm contributed or not. The free rider problem once again! How is the free rider problem avoided and special interest associations financed? One answer is found in the market structure of the industry. If the industry is characterized by a few large firms, the free rider problem is not serious because each firm knows that its own efforts will make a significant difference to the organization and financing of the interest group and the other firms in the industry will be able to identify and ostracize the free rider.

Not all special interest producer groups are in industries with a few firms. In fact, the most influential ones, such as the Farm Bureau and the American Medical Association, represent industries composed of many small firms or individual participants. Effective special interest groups exist in industries characterized by a large number of firms and individuals because they have found ways to minimize the impact of the free rider problem by providing selective benefits to contributing members as well as providing public benefits to the industry through their lobbying efforts. These selective benefits include meetings and technical seminars, publications, awards, recognition banquets, personal contacts, and research advisories. They offer a "tied sale" of a collective and a noncollective good. The major economic lobbies—labor unions, farm organizations, and professional organizations—obtain support because they provide many selective benefits to members in addition to their lobbying activities: malpractice insurance, pensions, and technical publications. Trade associations distribute trade statistics and provide technical research, advisory services, and education and training to workers and managers. The Farm Bureau offers low-cost insurance and farm cooperative activities to its members. Some organizations obtain members through coercive powers. Unions are often able to coerce workers to join unions; doctors, dentists, lawyers, and other professionals must belong to their state association by law or professional pressure. State governments have given some guild-like producer-professional associations authority to govern themselves and to discipline members of the profession who do not maintain ethical standards such as lawyers, barbers, undertakers, plumbers, and beauticians.

Special interest producer groups tend to be more powerful than consumer groups because the special legislation benefits to them are large and visible, whereas the benefits of consumer legislation are spread among a large number of individuals. For example, auto firms and auto unions— unions are the most effective special interest producer groups—can effectively lobby Congress to place limits on auto imports because such limits will have a significant impact on the income of each member. The total loss to consumers from import limitations may far exceed the gains of the producers, but the losses are spread over millions of consumers, and each consumer believes that his own loss does not justify the expenditures and effort it would take to fight such legislation. This explains why certain industries, unions, and other who benefit from such legislation have been so successful. A few consumer groups have been able to organize special interest groups by offering selective, excludable benefits, such as magazines, product analyses, and bumper stickers to induce members to join. Environmental groups have utilized similar techniques. Members of the American Automobile Association receive insurance, bail money, maps, towing, and other services. Contrary to common opinion, the National Rifle Association gets most of its money and power from ordinary members who are the consumers of guns and ammunition and not from gun producers. The NRA is successful because it provides selective incentives such as monthly magazines, targets, hats, and stickers to obtain members.

Special interest groups perform social benefits in the political market. They are valuable sources of information for representatives who otherwise would have to rely upon the government bureaucracy. They lower the costs of seeking information for members, and they can organize and effectively represent members scattered throughout many states. The social problem of special interest groups is that they can "tilt" the legislation on their behalf, and not all individuals belong to the same number of equally effective lobbying organizations; accordingly, some individuals have more representation than others.

All forms of political and special interest activity require time or money or both. This is true for political parties, special interest groups, volunteer organizations, and religious organizations. The relative amount of time or money an individual possesses will determine the form of contribution he or she will make. Voters with high incomes and relatively little time tend to participate by donating money to favored causes, parties, and special interest groups, whereas those with little wealth and much time tend to donate their time. This explains why wealthy individuals generally contribute money and why college students, whose time opportunity costs are lower, tend to participate in demonstrations and political meetings.

QUESTIONS AND ANSWERS

THE QUESTIONS

1. It has been suggested that the United States eliminate elections, say, for the House of Representatives and that it select representatives by lottery. What are some of the advantages and disadvantages of this suggestion?

2. Assume that you and your friends, who are unknown on a large campus, are organizing a party to "capture" student government.

a. Would you support a proposal made by the university administration that all advertisements for candidates seeking student offices be banned from campus? Why?

b. Would you support a limit on the length of the campaign?

c. A supporter with a major in business comes to you with $1,000 in contributions he has collected from some friends to finance your campaign. Another friend, a philosophy major, comes to you with a dozen friends he has talked into helping you do some personal campaigning. If you won the election, which one would you appoint to a prestigious university committee?

d. Assume that there are two major issues on campus. The administration is trying to decide whether to improve the football team or the library; the other issue is whether beer should be allowed on campus. Assume that you ask a friend in statistics to survey the students to see how they stand on the issues. A few days later he returns and tells you that he and his girlfriend in psychology have devised a survey instrument that not only measures preference rankings but also intensities. He says that there are three groups on campus, each with 5,000 members with the following preferences and intensities. The entries show their preferred positions and associated intensity differentials, measured in utils.

	Group A	**Group B**	**Group C**
Football/Library	Library	Library	Football
Intensity Differential	100,000	3,000	10,000
Beer/No Beer	No Beer	Beer	No Beer
Intensity Differential	40,000	5,000	6,000

Example: Group A prefers the library to football by 100,000 utils and No Beer to Beer by 40,000 utils.

(1) What policies are preferred by the majority of the students?

(2) What would happen if your party advocated the majority positions?

(3) How could you win the election?

(4) Which set of positions would maximize the welfare of students?

(5) If vote buying were allowed, what would be the outcome?

(6) What would happen if you decided that the morally correct position to take at a university was to promote the library and to ban beer?

3. Would the Republicans or the Democrats benefit more if campaign contributions to representatives were limited?

4. Two individuals are running for mayor in your home town. You know nothing about either individual except that Candidate A is a "politician who bends to all political winds" while the Candidate B is a "rock of moral integrity who pursues his concept of right regardless of the political consequences." Which one would you support for mayor? Why? Which one would you support for director of new product development if you owned a corporation? Which one would you want as a friend?

5. You are playing cards with some friends and one of them tells you that the mayor was "playing politics" with some recent appointments. What do you think your friend meant? Do you think he approved of the appointments? Is "playing politics" socially desirable?

6. You are a left-wing radical. Your friend is a right-wing radical who is trying to move the Republican party further to the right. Should you help your friend? Why?

7. a. Can you think of a selective incentive motivating certain owners of newspapers and television stations to oppose campaign financing reform? How might your answer be affected if the media firm were large and prosperous versus small and marginally profitable?

b. Can you think of a selective incentive motivating certain members of the working media (reporters, editorial writers, news analysts) to criticize special interest groups and to support campaign financing reform?

THE ANSWERS

1. One definite advantage of random selection is producing a House membership that would more clearly represent the values and occupations of the populace. One problem of having professional politicians is that, as in any other field or occupation, the process of self-selection tends to attract individuals with certain qualities, ambitions, and values that are not representative of the entire nation. The major disadvantage is merely the reciprocal of this primary advantage. Civilization has benefited from the specialization and division of labor in many fields, including politics. Would you select your dentist, doctor, or economics teacher by lottery? Why, then, would you want to select your representative by lottery? One answer you might give to this last question is that dentists, doctors, and teachers deal with technical matters, whereas politicians deal with values. This is not the place to discuss this further. Talk it over with your friends, teachers, and parents.

2. a. You have an incentive to oppose it because advertising is the most effective way of obtaining recognition in the campaign. If your opponent were the captain of the football team, you certainly would oppose it. Those who are known and recognized always have an incentive to oppose advertisements, while the unknowns have an incentive to support them.

b. No, for the same reasons as mentioned in 2. a. The longer the campaign, the longer the time you have to obtain name recognition. Of course, if you thought you were more recognized on campus than your opponent, you would support limiting the length of the campaign. By the way, how would you define the activity (campaigning) you are trying to limit?

c. If you said that it would depend upon the relative quantities of workers and money you had and that it would depend upon the marginal value of $1,000 versus the marginal value of twelve additional campaigners, you understand the point of the question.

d. **(1)** The majority positions are to fund the library and to ban beer on campus. Groups A and B prefer the library to the football team and Groups A and C prefer no beer to beer.

(2) Your party would lose the election. You would get only the votes of the 5,000 students in Group A. Group B would vote against you because its members have a greater relative intensity for having beer on campus than having the library. Group C's members would vote against you because your party took the wrong position on its more intense preference.

(3) Take a position on supporting football and permitting beer on campus. Group C would support you because football is their more intense preference. Group B would vote for you because beer is their more intense preference.

(4) Because of the large number of utils (intense preferences) of the Group A students, welfare would be maximized by having the library improved and beer banned on campus.

(5) The welfare-maximizing outcome would be produced. Group A students, who have strong preferences, would be able to bribe Group B voters to vote for the library and against beer.

(6) You would lose the election.

3. If you accept the stereotyped view that Republicans have a comparative advantage in collecting money and the Democrats have a comparative advantage in collecting volunteers' time, then the answer is the Democrats. Do you think that the stereotyped view is an accurate generalization?

4. You would, of course, want Candidate B (the "rock of moral integrity") if you knew that his morals were your morals, but we are assuming that you *don't* know the content of his morals. The function of a politician is to represent the views of citizens in his constituency and, like Candidate A, "bend to all political winds." If he puts aside his own personal views and strives to maximize votes, he will not only be a successful politician but he will play an important social role in transferring the preferences of individuals into social policy. The politician should be praised and not criticized for performing this very important function. Hitler and Stalin knew what was "right" for the German and Soviet people and they pursued their concept of right regardless of the political consequences. Consider the private market. You would not want, nor expect, a director of new product development to pursue only those products he personally liked. You would expect him to take market surveys and to develop a market basket of goods preferred by consumers. You would also want a politician to take market surveys and to develop a market basket of positions (a platform) that would appeal to the majority of voters. You realize, of course, that there will be some products in the private market that you will dislike and there will be some positions taken by your representatives that you will dislike, but consider the alternatives in both markets. You might want the "rock of moral integrity" to be a friend.

5.   Unfortunately, "playing politics" has taken on a pejorative meaning, and your friend was most likely being critical of the mayor's appointments. The phrase "playing politics" has many shades of meaning. One interpretation of "playing politics" is developing policies and making appointments that appeal to the median voter. In this sense, "playing politics" is socially desirable. If the mayor is secretly making deals or appointing people clearly opposed by the median voter, then it might be undesirable. A popular interpretation of "playing politics" is that the mayor is appointing his supporters—often thought unqualified—to positions in the administration. While this practice might not be socially desirable, it is widely practiced at all levels of politics, and the possibilities of such appointments motivate many individuals to participate in politics. It is, after all, the source of our administrative assistants, cabinet officers, judges, commissioners, and, occasionally, university presidents.

6.   Careful! Your strategy might backfire. Assuming you neglect the message of the free rider analysis and you believe that your efforts will have some perceptible effects on the outcome, you want the Republican party to move to the right so that it will lose the election to the Democrats. So far your strategy is good. However, what is going to happen to the radical left influence in the Democratic party? You certainly hope to have some influence in moving the Democratic party to the left. Depending upon the primary voting system, your radical colleagues might even capture the Democratic party (see the analysis of primaries in chapter 6). The problem is that if the Republican party moves to the right, the rational policy for the Democratic party is to follow it to the right, and your group of radicals might well lose influence in the Democratic party. You might even be an "embarrassment" to Democratic leaders who will be attempting to position the party "in the mainstream," that is, appealing to the median voters. Of course, you could always threaten to form a third party, but after reading the previous chapters and the appendix that follows you will know that your chances of success are very small.

7.   **a.**   Ambition and greed . . . for profits. Political advertisements are major sources of revenue for the media, and they often charge higher rates for advertisements appearing prior to an election (supply and demand again). The owners of large and profitable media firms might

be willing to sacrifice some profits for the additional influence and power the elimination of special interest groups and advertisements would give them (see the answer to 7. b.), but the owners of the small, marginally profitable media could be expected to place a higher marginal value on the additional profits generated by the advertisements financed by campaign contributions and special interest groups. The owner of the small-town newspaper or television station, for example, would have a greater incentive to oppose campaign financing reform than the owners of the Washington Post media empire.

b. Ambition and greed . . . for power, control, and influence. Citizens obtain information and guidance on public issues from special interest groups and advertisements, which compete with the information they get from public media sources. The elimination of competing special interest groups and advertisements would increase the importance and power of those who occupy information choke points in the public media.

APPENDIX C: HISTORY OF AMERICAN POLITICAL PARTIES

INTRODUCTION

The United States is a two-party country that comes very close to replicating Downs's single mode distribution. Even though minor parties occasionally field a candidate or two, the simple truth is that for more than a century virtually all elections have been won either by a Democrat or by a Republican. The American Constitution does not mention political parties, and few American citizens are aware of the history of the country's two major political parties. The first significant party was the Federalist party formed by Alexander Hamilton to promote federal power and economic growth. The opposing party, to which both the Democratic and Republican parties claim ancestral rights, was the Democratic-Republican party, also known as the Jeffersonians because it was founded by Thomas Jefferson. The Democratic-Republican party supported the interests of farmers, veterans, and urban immigrants and was in favor of minimum government, individual liberty, and easy credit and money policies. Between 1800 and 1820 the Democratic-Republicans were able to elect Thomas Jefferson, James Madison, and James Monroe—the "Virginia dynasty"—to the presidency for two full terms, and federalist strength declined throughout the country except in New England.

THE DEMOCRATIC PARTY

Small feeder roots of the Democratic party can be traced back to the Democratic-Republican party of Thomas Jefferson, but its tap roots were sunk when Andrew Jackson "lost" the presidential election in 1824. Jackson, the populist hero of the Battle of New Orleans in the War of 1812, received a plurality of popular votes in a four-man contest for president, but he was unable to secure the required majority of electoral votes. When the House of Representatives selected John Q. Adams, Jackson vowed to restructure the Democratic-Republican party, and he finished the task after solidly defeating Adams in the 1828 elections. The restructured party was called the Democratic party, and it supported suffrage for white male citizens, thereby bringing urban workers into the electoral process and the party.

The first national party convention was held by the Democrats in Baltimore in 1832. It not only renominated Jackson but, at his urging, it adopted the requirements of a two-thirds vote for presidential nominations. This two-thirds nomination requirement, which lasted for more than 100 years, was to give future southern Democrats a disproportionate degree of power in the Democratic party, because no nomination could be made without their approval. The new Democratic party was successful. It controlled the House and Senate for most of the next 25 years, and it elected four of the next six presidents. During the 1850s, however, questions of tariffs, slavery, and states' rights began dividing the Democratic party, which had supporters in both the South and North. The internal crisis came to a climax in 1860, when the party split and separate conventions were held by southern Democrats, who nominated John C. Breckinridge, and northern Democrats, who nominated Stephen A. Douglas. This division resulted in the election (with only 40 percent of the vote) of the nominee of the newly created Republican party, Abraham Lincoln.

Democrats had little success at the national level between the end of the Civil War and the beginning of the twentieth century. They were only able to elect Grover Cleveland to the presidency, while all the other presidents were Republicans. Democrats controlled the Senate for only 4 of the 34 years, but they had more success in the House of Representatives, which they controlled for 18 years. They had much more success at local and regional levels. After Reconstruction, southern Democrats, who had suffered during and after the Civil War under Republican administrations, wanted nothing to do with Republicans. The "solid South" married and lived with the Democratic party for the next century. The Democratic party also thrived in northern urban areas, where Democratic political machines were sharpening their tools of political influence, service, and corruption. Most democratic urban political machines obtained their power from the services provided to the millions of immigrants streaming into the country between the Civil War and the Depression of the thirties. Immigrants were met at the dock and enrolled in the party by representatives of the Democratic machines who "took care" of the immigrants for decades. Ward or precinct "bosses" helped immigrants find employment, they ran interference with judges, landlords, and police, went to funerals, weddings, and baptisms, and settled overdue rent and electricity bills. The Democratic machines were powerful because they were able to provide essential social services to the immigrants in return for their votes. The machines also controlled most of the jobs in city government, and they readily used patronage to maintain discipline and to reward dedicated workers. Machine politics continued in many northern cities until the 1930s, when civil service reforms and social welfare were legislated by a Democratic-controlled Congress.

A number of populist causes such as free trade, control of railroads, and big business began emerging after the Civil War, but the most potent political and economic issue revolved around money supply, prices, and the gold standard. The last three decades of the Civil War were characterized by deflation. Although it might be difficult for the current generation of Americans to conceptualize, prices decreased more than

25 percent between 1866 and 1900. It was commonly believed that the gold standard was responsible for the deflation, tight credit, and frequent financial panics, which occurred in the latter nineteenth century. Those hurt most by the deflation were farmers, small businessmen, and western silver interests, and they began to agitate for the abandonment or modification of the gold standard. Grover Cleveland, the only Democratic president during the period, supported some reforms, such as lower tariffs, but he strongly supported the gold standard. Democratic party leaders in the South and West, however, strongly supported liberal coinage of silver currency, the issuance of silver certificates, and any other means to increase the money supply. This issue of "free silver" made William Jennings Bryan the party's nominee for president in the 1896 convention, where he delivered his famous "cross of gold" speech.[1] Bryan aligned the party with workers and farmers by supporting decreases in tariffs and various social and economic reforms. Although he lost the election to William McKinley, Bryan was nominated again in 1900 and 1908, but he lost to Republican candidates both times.

Woodrow Wilson, reform governor of New Jersey and former president of Princeton University, became only the second Democrat to win the presidency (1912) since James Buchanan won in 1856. He and the Democratic Congress had to deal with millions of immigrants from southern and eastern Europe, corrupt machine politics rampant in many cities, a revival of the Ku Klux Klan, the revolution in Mexico, World War I, a more active labor movement, and the suffrage and prohibition movements. Despite his academic interest in political parties, Wilson neglected the Democratic party organization, and he left the party split between city bosses and white southerners, wets versus drys, and conservatives versus progressives. The Democrats lost control of both houses of Congress in 1918 and the presidency in the elections of 1920 and 1924. The Democrats thought they had a good chance of winning the presidency when the urban political machines and progressives joined in 1928 to nominate Governor Alfred E. Smith of New York, the first Roman Catholic

---

[1] After verbosely elevating the status of the struggling masses of workers and farmers and deflating the egos of the "idle holders of idle capital," Bryan uttered the most quotable phrase ever made in a political convention: "Having behind us the producing masses of this nation and the world, supported by the commercial interests, the laboring interests, and the toilers everywhere, we answer their demand for a gold standard by saying to them: You shall not press down upon the brow of labor this crown of thorns; you shall not crucify mankind upon a cross of gold." Bryan was later appointed secretary of state in the Wilson administration but resigned to protest Wilson's anti-German policies. He then traveled around the country giving speeches, and he drew large crowds to real estate seminars in Florida. His last public appearance was in the Scopes trial in Tennessee, where he defended a literal interpretation of the Bible and opposed Clarence Darrow, the attorney for the defendant.

to receive a presidential nomination. Although Smith attracted votes from millions of recent immigrants, workers, and advocates of repealing prohibition, he lost the solid South and the election to Herbert Hoover.

The Depression rescued the Democratic party when the Democrats captured the House of Representatives in 1930 after more than a decade of control by the Republicans. The 1932 election was a landmark year for the Democrats and the country. Their presidential nominee, Franklin D. Roosevelt, was able to join plowmen and professors, blacks and southerners into a coalition that made the Democrats the nation's majority party for nearly the next half century. The Democrats won huge majorities in both houses of Congress, and Roosevelt was able to get most of his New Deal legislation passed without most congressmen even bothering to read the bills. Although the New Deal was unable to eliminate the Depression, it spurned a massive increase in the size of the federal government, which mobilized hope and relief for the starving, work for the unemployed, credit and agricultural price supports for the farmers, reform for the nation's financial institutions, and Social Security for the elderly, and it increased power to labor unions, which spurred a phenomenal growth in unionization. The New Deal era also brought many structural changes to the Democratic party. Most ironic was the damage done to the urban Democratic party machines by the New Deal's provision of welfare benefits and services, which had been the political base of the machines. The growth of the New Deal's welfare state robbed both parties of opportunities to use welfare and charity as political weapons. The replacement of the patronage system with the civil service merit system further reduced the parties' opportunities to reward workers. As the federal government provided new social services to the poor and immigrants, the resources and power of Democratic machines in the cities diminished. Political bosses in many cities were swept away by insurgents and reformers and replaced by labor unions.

The 1936 Democratic convention repealed the two-thirds nominating rule, and the influence of the southern wing of the Democratic party began its long and gradual decline. Roosevelt and congressional Democrats continued to dominate the political market through most of World War II. Roosevelt died soon after being elected to an unprecedented fourth term[2] in 1944 and was succeeded by Vice President Harry S. Truman, who strongly supported organized labor and civil rights programs for blacks. Truman lashed out at the "do-nothing Congress," which the Republicans

---

[2] No president had ever served more than two terms until Roosevelt was elected to his third term in 1940.

had captured in the 1946 elections. The 1948 Democratic convention was the first of many stormy ones for Democrats. Southern Democratic leaders registered their disapproval of Truman by supporting the States' Rights (Dixiecrat) ticket headed by maverick Democrat Strom Thurmond. The Democrats recaptured control of both Houses in 1948, but Truman barely won the presidency with slightly less than 50 percent of the vote. He declined to run for reelection in 1952, and the party nominated Adlai E. Stevenson, former governor of Illinois and grandson of Adlai Ewing Stevenson, Grover Cleveland's vice president. Stevenson's candidacy attracted intellectuals and liberals to the party, but his Republican opponent, Dwight D. Eisenhower, a popular World War II general, won easily. Eisenhower received a substantial number of votes in the South, which was one early indicator that the Democrats were losing influence in that region. The Democrats lost control of both houses in 1952 but won them back again in 1954, and they did not lose control of the Senate until 1980. Since 1954, they have never lost control of the House.

Democrats won the White House in 1960, when John Fitzgerald Kennedy became the youngest man and the first Roman Catholic to be elected president. Kennedy accelerated the trend of intellectuals to the Democratic party while driving southerners away from it. His liberal New Frontier program and active, though belated, support of civil rights led to significant new legislation, most of which was passed, however, under his successor. Kennedy's assassination in Dallas on November 22, 1963, brought Vice President Lyndon B. Johnson, former Senate majority leader, to the presidency. Although his personal style and stand in Vietnam alienated intellectuals and liberals, Johnson's Great Society programs of educational, welfare, and civil rights legislation transformed the nation and made government a large source of patronage once again. His refusal to abandon the Vietnam War divided the Democratic party and the nation. After his narrow victory over Senator Eugene McCarthy in the New Hampshire primary election, which the media claimed was a "victory" for McCarthy, Johnson announced that he would not be a candidate in 1968, and Vice President Hubert H. Humphrey won the nomination at the tumultuous convention in Chicago. Governor George Wallace of Alabama, hoping to capitalize on racial tensions in northern cities and the South and the "privileged treatment of blacks" by Great Society legislation, entered the race on a third-party ticket.

The 1968 Democratic convention, the most chaotic and violent one in the nation's history, contributed to Humphrey's defeat by Richard M. Nixon. But the most serious blow to the Democratic party was the massive defection of blue-collar and southern voters, who thought their old "bread and butter" party had abandoned them. The party was in considerable disarray for the next two decades. At the 1972 convention, antiwar, black, young, and women delegates were pitted against labor representatives and party regulars. Humphrey, who had championed traditional liberal causes for decades, was defeated for the nomination by Senator George McGovern, who stressed radical party reform and an end to the Vietnam War. McGovern hastened the dissolution of the Roosevelt coalition with his policies. Most white southerners and many blue-collar workers and Catholic ethnics once again abandoned the Democratic ticket and voted for Nixon. McGovern carried only Massachusetts and the District of Columbia.

Democratic fortunes were improved considerably by Nixon's Watergate scandal in 1974. Democrats dominated the congressional and state elections in 1974, and they produced a new party charter in their first midterm national conference. Jimmy Carter, former governor of Georgia, began to campaign early for the Democratic presidential nomination in 1976. His lack of experience in Washington and born-again Christianity helped him win enough primary election victories to ensure the nomination. Aided by an unusually high turnout of black voters, Carter won a close race against President Gerald R. Ford, and some thought that the Democratic coalition forged by Roosevelt in the thirties was still alive. The Carter presidency, however, marked a precipitous decline in the fortunes of the Democratic party. Carter's most serious problems were with Congress, which was less susceptible to party discipline and presidential direction than in the years before the Vietnam War and Watergate. Many of Carter's initiatives were ignored or defeated, and his administration was plagued by a reputation for inefficiency and weakness. Although Carter created new departments of education and energy, signed the second Strategic Arms Limitation Treaty (SALT II) with the Soviet Union, and played a key role in negotiating a peace treaty between Israel and Egypt, his energy initiatives were ridiculed (Moral Equivalent of War = MEOW), stalled, and watered down. Inflation was rampant and unemployment high. U.S. citizens were captured and held hostage in Iran, and the Soviet Union occupied Afghanistan. Carter faced serious opposition within his own party, especially after he began stressing military preparedness at the expense of social programs. Senator Edward Kennedy challenged Carter for the 1980 Democratic presidential nomination, but Carter won enough primary victories to ensure his nomination.

Republican Ronald Reagan, who combined criticism of Carter's domestic, military, and foreign policies with a conservative philosophy and an excellent ability to communicate to voters, easily defeated President Carter in 1980. The Democrats kept their majority in the House of Representatives, but the Republicans won their first Senate majority since

1954. The 1984 Democratic convention was comparatively quiet, and Vice President Walter F. Mondale was easily nominated. He broke with tradition by selecting a woman, New York Representative Geraldine A. Ferraro, as the vice presidential candidate. But President Reagan, one of the most popular presidents in history, easily defeated the Democratic candidate by obtaining 59 percent of the popular vote. The Democrats retained their majority in the House and had 34 governorships, but they were unable to win a majority in the Senate until 1986.

The Democratic party was strongest in the years following its creation in 1832 and during the Roosevelt years of the thirties and early forties. Since 1952, it has been very successful in congressional races, but it has been able to elect only three presidents to office. Its coalition of southern whites, workers, intellectuals, and blacks has been disintegrating. Its strongest national support is now found among Jews and blacks. Although conservative Democrats still do well in the South, the party is gradually losing the votes of white southerners, while many workers in the north have not supported the leftward drift of the party. The key to future Democratic successes is for the party to return to the middle of the ideological spectrum on defense and social issues and to stress the economic populist issues of income distribution and corporate responsibility.

THE REPUBLICAN PARTY

The Republican party was born amidst disputes over the expansion of slavery into the new western territories during the middle of the nineteenth century. After the passage of the Kansas-Nebraska Act (1854), which repealed earlier compromises that had excluded slavery from the territories, two meetings of slavery opponents were held in Ripon, Wisconsin, in 1854. The attendees decided to form a new party and call it the Republican party because they professed to be political descendants of Thomas Jefferson's Democratic-Republican party. The first Republican national convention, held in Philadelphia in 1856, nominated Senator John C. Fremont for the presidency, but he was defeated by Democrat James Buchanan. Republicans won control of the House of Representatives in 1858, but one Republican, Abraham Lincoln, was defeated in his bid for a U.S. Senate seat by Stephen A. Douglas.

The second Republican national convention, in 1860, nominated Abraham Lincoln. Running on a platform that included a promise not to extend slavery to new territories or states, the free-homestead legislation, the establishment of an overland mail service and a transcontinental railroad, and the support of the protective tariff, Lincoln was elected with only 40 percent of the popular vote in a field of four candidates. Party leaders attempted to broaden the base of the party in 1864 by nominating Andrew Johnson, a prowar Democrat, as Lincoln's running mate. Recent military victories contributed to Lincoln's reelection, and he helped build the new party by appointing many of its members to government offices. After Lincoln's assassination in 1865 the Radical Republicans fought President Johnson's moderate reconstruction policies. Johnson was impeached by the House but was acquitted by a single vote in the Senate.

The defeat of the South left the Democratic party—closely allied with the Confederacy—in shambles, and the Republicans dominated Congress and the presidency for more than seven decades. Republicans occupied the White House for 56 of the 72 years between 1860 and 1932. They controlled the House of Representatives for 48 of the 72 years and the Senate for 60 years. They had many troubles in the White House during this period. Ulysses Grant's two terms were riddled with scandal and corruption, probably the worst in the nation's history. The scandals and the financial panic of 1873 caused the Republicans to lose control of the Congress in 1874, but they obtained a new party symbol, the elephant, after it appeared in a magazine cartoon by Thomas Nast.

The Republicans nominated Rutherford B. Hayes in 1876, but the Democratic candidate, Samuel J. Tilden, received the greatest number of popular votes. Widespread reports of voting fraud led to the appointment of a congressional electoral commission to review the results and decide who should receive disputed votes in four states. The commission, controlled by Republicans, granted all disputed electoral votes to Hayes, which enabled him to win an electoral margin of 185 to 184. Hayes did not seek a second term in 1880, and James A. Garfield was nominated as the Republican candidate. After winning a close election, Garfield was assassinated and Vice President Chester A. Arthur became president. Arthur became the only president not to be renominated by his party's convention when James G. Blaine received the nomination instead. Democrat Grover Cleveland defeated Blaine in 1884 by a narrow margin, but in 1888 Benjamin Harrison became the second person to win in the electoral college (233 to 168) despite losing the popular vote. Republicans also captured both houses of Congress in the elections of 1888, and they passed the Sherman Antitrust Act and the highly protective McKinley Tariff Act. President Harrison was renominated in 1892, but in the worst defeat suffered by a Republican candidate since the founding of the party, he lost the election to Cleveland.

The election of 1896 was the most important election since 1860. It pitted a "socially concerned" candidate who wanted to revamp the monetary standard and make several reforms against a candidate who represented conservatism, business, and the market system. In effect, the campaign and the election set the future directions of the Republican and Democratic parties. William McKinley, who wanted to maintain the gold standard and to proceed slowly in social and economic reform, defeated William Jennings Bryan, who championed a bimetallic monetary standard, by a substantial margin. McKinley's first term was dominated by the brief Spanish-American War (1898) and the resulting acquisition of Guam, Puerto Rico, and the Philippines and the annexation of Hawaii, which thrust the United States into world politics.

Governor Theodore Roosevelt of New York was selected as the vice presidential candidate on the Republican ticket headed by McKinley in 1900. McKinley again defeated Bryan but was assassinated after six months in office. Roosevelt, who succeeded McKinley, was not only the most colorful president in history but also one of the most active reform presidents. Conservation, antitrust, and economic and social reform laws were passed during his 7½ years in office. He spoke softly, but often, in international affairs, and he carried a big stick tipped by naval power. He refused to run again in 1908 and recommended William Taft, who easily defeated Bryan, who was running for the third and last time. Taft's personal style, conservatism, and opposition to many reforms alienated liberal Republicans led by Robert M. La Follette of Wisconsin, who organized the National Progressive Republican League to wrestle party control from Republican conservatives in 1911. At the Chicago convention in 1912, Roosevelt challenged Taft for the nomination but failed to receive it. He bolted the party and ran as the Progressive party candidate. The split in the Republican party enabled Woodrow Wilson to win the presidency with less than 42 percent of the vote.

The decade of the twenties was another Republican decade. The party captured control of both the House and the Senate in 1918 and did not relinquish control until the elections of 1930. Republicans were able to thwart Wilson's plan to have the United States join the League of Nations by refusing to ratify the Treaty of Versailles. Republicans gained control of the White House again in 1920, when the ticket of Warren G. Harding and Calvin Coolidge won by a landslide. Harding's administration was plagued by the Teapot Dome scandal, but after his death in 1923, Coolidge controlled the political damage to the party by appointing a bipartisan team of special prosecutors to deal with the scandal. Harding died in office, and Coolidge was reelected by a large margin in 1924 and led the country through the roaring twenties. In 1928 Silent Cal shocked the nation by declaring "I do not choose to run," and the Republicans nominated Herbert Hoover, whose administrative work during and after World War I brought him public attention as the Great Humanitarian. President Harding appointed Hoover to be secretary of commerce in 1921, and he held that post until he began his own presidential campaign in 1928. Hoover easily defeated Alfred E. Smith, a Catholic and strong critic of Prohibition, with 58 percent of the vote. The worldwide economic depression brought a quick end to this post–World War I Republican resurgence. Although the Hoover administration took many steps to reverse the economy, including sharp increases in government spending, Hoover was unable to shake the blame citizens placed upon him. Hoover, renominated in 1932 during the worst crisis the country faced since the Civil War, was defeated by Franklin D. Roosevelt in one of the greatest landslides in American history.

The Republican party remained a minority party until 1946, when it became the majority party in the House and the Senate for the first time in 16 years. Thomas Dewey lost a close election to President Truman in 1948, and Republicans also lost control of the Senate and House after only 2 years of being the majority party. But the Republicans made a more durable comeback in 1952. The Republican convention in 1952 was split between war hero Dwight D. Eisenhower and "Mr. Conservative," Senator Robert A. Taft of Ohio. The convention selected Ike as the presidential nominee and Richard M. Nixon as his running mate. Despite a controversy over Nixon's campaign funds, the two won decisively in 1952 (55 percent) and then again in 1956 (58 percent). Ike skillfully ended the war in Korea, supported civil rights, created the Interstate Highway System, and pursued a moderate, though firm, foreign policy. However, the Republicans lost control of both houses in 1954, and they never again regained control of the House and did not achieve a majority in the Senate until 1981, which they lost again in 1987. Vice President Nixon easily won the nomination of his party in 1960 but lost the election to John F. Kennedy of Massachusetts by the smallest popular margin in the twentieth century, a difference of only about 115,000 votes out of more than 68 million cast.

The Republican party had been dominated by eastern moderates since World War I, while an increasing number of Republicans were conservatives from the Midwest, South, and West. Senator Barry M. Goldwater and fellow conservatives were able to wrestle control of the Republican party from the moderates in the 1964 convention. Goldwater stuck to his principles and refused to move to the left after his nomination, while the Democrats made it appear that he was a "right-wing nut." His unprecedented landslide defeat left the party organization in disarray.

After Nixon lost the governor's race in California, he traveled around the country giving speeches to Republican groups and supporting Republican candidates. Consequently, he had solid support among Republicans in 1968 and, after receiving the party's nomination, he selected Maryland Governor Spiro T. Agnew as his running mate. Nixon won the election over Democrat Hubert H. Humphrey, who headed a Democratic party deeply divided by the Vietnam War and many social issues. President Nixon's first term was marked by many accomplishments, including improved relations with China, a more cooperative relationship with the Soviet Union, significant reduction of U.S. involvement in Vietnam, and an improved economy. Under the banner of "A New Federalism," Nixon shifted important elements of governmental power and responsibility back to state and local governments. He cut back federal welfare services, proposed antibusing legislation, and used wage-and-price controls to fight inflation. In 1972 Nixon defeated George S. McGovern, a liberal, antiwar senator from South Dakota, with more than 60 percent of the popular vote. He won every state except Massachusetts and the District of Columbia, but the Democrats continued to control both houses of Congress by considerable margins.

Shortly after his victory in 1972 disaster fell upon the Nixon White House. Vice President Agnew was forced to resign in 1973 after being convicted of income tax evasion, and Gerald R. Ford, a representative from Michigan, was appointed vice president. A burglary of the Democratic National Committee headquarters in the Watergate office complex during the 1972 campaign led to revelations of widespread civil and criminal misconduct within the campaign organization and the administration. Impeachment proceedings were underway when Nixon resigned in 1974. Ford, who succeeded Nixon, faced serious economic problems of high unemployment, inflation, and interest rates and worsening budget deficits. His Whip Inflation Now (WIN) program was ridiculed, and he was strongly criticized by conservatives for granting amnesty to Vietnam-era draft evaders and for appointing Nelson Rockefeller to the vice presidency. Ford barely won the Republican nomination after a bitter fight against Ronald Reagan, but he lost the election to Jimmy Carter by a narrow popular and electoral margin.

Reagan and conservatives in the Republican party perceived that Carter's inability to solve economic, military, and foreign policy problems as well as an ideological shift to the right among the electorate would give them a good chance to win in 1980. Reagan, the oldest man (69) and the first movie actor to move into the White House, easily won the party's presidential nomination and went on to a landslide victory over Carter with 51 percent of the popular vote in a three-man race. Reagan received 489 electoral votes against Carter's 49. At the same time, the Republicans won 12 additional seats in the U.S. Senate and took control of that body for the first time in 25 years.

The swing toward Republican candidates was aided by the aggressive campaigning of the Moral Majority and other groups affiliated with Christian religions. These religious groups represented individuals, concerned about social and moral issues, who had been ignored by the media and by previous politicians. Reagan and conservative Republicans courted them as well as ethnics and working classes in a successful attempt to destroy the coalition forged by Roosevelt and to form a new majority for the Republicans. This new Republican coalition helped Reagan defeat Walter Mondale in the 1984 elections with 59 percent of the popular vote, which was the fourth largest landslide in history (Harding's win, Roosevelt's first election, and Nixon's landslide against McGovern were the others). Reagan received a record-breaking 525 electoral votes, while Mondale garnered only 13. The Republicans lost 2 Senate seats in 1984 but retained a majority while the Democrats continued to control the House. The Democrats won solid control of the Senate in 1986 by 55 seats to 45.

Reagan pushed his conservative programs through Congress in 1981—a major tax cut, $43 billion in budget cuts in domestic programs, and cutbacks in environmental and business regulation. At first Reaganomics seemed to worsen the economy, but by 1983 the economic picture had brightened with a resurgent stock market, low inflation rates, falling interest rates, and an unemployment rate inching downward. The economic recovery, although menaced by enormous budget and trade deficits, continued until Reagan left office in 1989. Reagan built up military defenses and showed that he was not afraid to use the armed might of the United States in various parts of the world. He took a tough stand against the "evil empire" of the Soviet Union but made more progress toward ending the cold war than any other President, with the possible exception of Nixon. George Bush, Reagan's vice president, easily defeated Michael Dukakis in 1988 and continued the post–World War II Republican dominance of the White House.

Between 1860 and 1988 the Republicans held the White House for 80 years and the Democrats for 48 years. The Republicans controlled the House of Representatives for 50 years and the Senate for 56 years, while the Democrats controlled the House for 78 years and the Senate for 92 years. The Democratic party has been considered by virtually all analysts to be the potpourri of American politics, but the Republicans also have many ingredients in their stew. During this century the Republicans have been composed of fairly wealthy individuals and representatives of business corporations, farmers, members of "Norman Rockwell's America," and individuals from all segments of the country who believe in the competitive private market system. Many of those from the business community would like to see their party put tariffs on imports and proceed slowly on business regulation and antitrust enforcement. Most other Republican supporters oppose these policies. More recently, the

Republican party has reached out further to capture the votes of ethnics and working classes by stressing social issues. In effect, the Republicans have said to these groups, "forget your traditional economic populism, which has led you to support the Democrats, and come to the Republican party, which will join you in your more serious concerns about social issues, such as abortion, crime, racial quotas, family life, and religion." These latter groups are now the marginal voters who will determine the future success of the Republican and Democratic parties. If their preference intensities for social issues are greater than their preference intensities for economic issues, then the Republicans may be able to form a working majority. If not, then the Democrats will continue to dominate Congress and win more presidencies during the next couple of decades.

CHAPTER TEN

THE BUREAUCRACY

Government offices are as acceptable here as elsewhere, and whenever a man has cast a longing eye on them, a rottenness begins in his conduct.
—THOMAS JEFFERSON, 1799

Of the various executive abilities, no one excited more anxious concern than that of placing the interests of our fellow-citizens in the hands of honest men, with understanding sufficient for their stations.
—THOMAS JEFFERSON, 1801

The king reigns but does not govern.
—JAN SAMOYSKE, 1605

INTRODUCTION

Bureaucrats are damned and demeaned from Pretropavlovsk to Peoria and from Rosario to Regina. Many Americans believe that the typical bureaucrat's workday begins when he stumbles sleepily into the office about 10 A.M., pours a cup from the ubiquitous—but illegal—coffeepot, and then works the crossword puzzle in the *New York Times*. A few telephone calls are made to fellow bureaucrats to catch up on agency news and intrigue, to maintain those valuable personal contacts, and to enter the office pool for the next football game. At a luncheon meeting the hard-working bureaucrat delicately tries to obtain information about the other bureaucrat's bureaucracy amidst congenial questions about family, old friends, and the necessary discussion about the prowess of the Redskins. The luncheon is cut short because the bureaucrat must attend a meeting with other bureaucrats in which they will either discuss their agency's image until an appropriate percentage of the participants are yawning or they will energetically hatch schemes to expand their agency's size and to increase its appropriations. The meeting must end, however, before the evening rush hour, and the bureaucrat leaves with a briefcase, stuffed with memos written by fellow bureaucrats, which is set in the entrance hallway of his suburban home, where it will be waiting for him when he leaves the next morning as the workday grind begins once again.

This is a slightly exaggerated but common view of bureaucrats held by those who are convinced the bureaucracy is staffed by individuals who couldn't "make it" in the real world of the competitive private market and have settled into the warm and cozy labyrinths of the bureaucracy until they have put in the required number of years (too few, at that!) for their generous retirement. Some economists and political scientists too readily dismiss this average citizen's view of bureaucrats by stressing that bureaucrats have the same weaknesses, strengths, abilities, and values as workers in private industry. However, there is no reason to think that priests and ministers, scientists and academicians, politicians and newscasters, computer programmers and accountants are randomly selected from the population. Similarly, there is no reason to expect individuals attracted to bureaucratic careers to be a microcosm of the working population. Organizations and occupations differentially reward varying talents and abilities, and workers tend to sort themselves out by their perceptions of alternative rewards and their own skills and interests. It would be a mistake to assume that bureaucrats do not have differentiating characteristics, although the differences do not mean superior or inferior . . . just different. The major sources of bureaucratic problems, however, are not to be found in the personal attributes of those who staff the bureaucracies. Although they are not a microcosm of the population, they are very much like the rest of us, and we would be very much like them if we held the same positions. The source of bureaucratic problems lies not in the bureaucrats but in the nature of public goods and the incentives, controls, and institutions existing in the bureaucracy. Hence, any solution to bureaucratic problems must involve the discovery and alteration of these institutions and incentives so that the decisions of bureaucrats will more clearly serve the public interest.

In the following analysis it is important to remember that while government bureaucrats might not be a microcosm of the population, bureaucracy is alive and well in all of us. One of life's more amusing moments is to listen to a professor decry the imperialistic and rent-seeking activities of government bureaucrats after leaving a university meeting in which she joined her colleagues in requesting funds to hire two or three additional professors, to lower teaching loads to one class per year, to provide funds to travel to the national convention in San Francisco and the new "policy" convention in Hawaii, and to offset the deplorable unavailability of competent graduate assistants by increasing their stipends.

WEBER VERSUS PARKINSON

Scholars' views of bureaucratic behavior and incentives are divided into at least two widely divergent camps. One view, initially associated with Confucius and Plato, was brought to the attention of the modern world by Max Weber (1864–1920),[1] who stressed the idealized operation of a bureaucracy in a democracy. Weber's views, which have been widely adopted by public administration professors, maintained that the bureaucratization of the political and economic spheres of society was the most significant development in the modernization of Western civilization. Weber assumed that voters are knowledgeable and public-spirited individuals who make meaningful decisions on policies by electing politicians to office. These political representatives pass legislation that is clear and unambiguous, and then bureaucrats objectively administer the laws. Bureaucrats are assumed to be knowledgeable, talented, and interested only in the administration of policies without implementing their own policies or pursuing their own objectives.

The opposite view is most often associated with C. Northcote Parkinson's tongue-in-cheek "observation" that bureaucrats are bungling and inefficient and that they serve only their own interests.[2] Parkinson's insights— especially his view that the number of bureaucrats tends to grow at a constant rate over time—were given academic respectability when economists began focusing their analytical eyes on the utility-maximizing behavior of bureaucrats and concluded that bureaucrats, as other individuals, pursue their selfish interests and not solely those of the public or their political or bureaucratic bosses.[3] While the Weberian view remains strong in public administration, it is fading in political science and nonexistent in public choice or political economy.

Bureaucracies are easier to criticize than they are to identify or define. There are many acceptable definitions of bureaucracies, but a barebone definition is that they are organizations that share *at least* two characteristics: (1) they produce an output that is not evaluated by the price

---

[1] Max Weber, *The Theory of Social and Economic Organization,* trans. A. M. Henderson and Talcott Parsons (Glencoe, Illinois: Free Press, 1947). Weber, one of the founders of modern sociology, achieved a reputation for his studies in the sociology of religion and his influential book *The Protestant Ethic and the Spirit of Capitalism.* His political sociology built the foundation for much modern analyses of politics, social stratification, and bureaucracy.

[2] Parkinson's law states that work expands to fill the time available for its completion. C. Northcote Parkinson, *Parkinson's Law: or, The Pursuit of Progress* (London: J. Murray, 1957) is a satire that ridicules industrial and government bureaucracies.

[3] Ludwig Von Mises was one of the first economists to write about bureaucracy [*Bureaucracy* (New Haven: Yale University Press, 1944)], but his book was more philosophical and normative than analytical. Gordon Tullock examined bureaucratic behavior directed at personal advancement in the bureaucracy [*The Politics of Bureaucracy* (Washington, DC: Public Affairs Press, 1967)]. Anthony Downs examined management processes within bureaus [*Inside Bureaucracy* (Boston: Little Brown & Co., 1967)]. Much of the analysis of bureaucratic behavior is based on Niskanen's major work, *Bureaucracy and Representative Government* (Chicago: Aldine-Athortan, 1971). Also see A. Breton and R. Wintrobe, *The Logic of Bureaucratic Conduct* (New York: Cambridge University Press, 1982).

mechanism, and (2) they obtain at least part of their revenue from sources other than the sale of their output. Other characteristics can be added. Many bureaucracies are large, and the income of most bureaucratic managers is not affected by the revenues or costs of the organization. However, some organizations exhibit the two primary characteristics of a bureaucracy except that they are small (for example, Office of Pet Control or Mosquito Eradication in medium-size communities). Another bureaucratic characteristic is that it is not necessary that the income of a bureaucrat be separated from the revenues and costs of the bureau; it is only necessary that the bureaucrat not be able to significantly affect the bureau's revenues or costs. This definition includes all government agencies, nonprofit organizations, and those divisions of private corporations that are not obvious profit centers.[4] Virtually all staff departments of corporations— including the legal, accounting, public relations, research, and advertising departments—would fall within this definition. Since this book is about the political market, the emphasis will be on government bureaucracies, but much of the following analysis could be applied to such nongovernmental entities as corporations, the Red Cross, hospitals, universities, United Funds, arts and humanities councils, and the March of Dimes.

CAUSES OF BUREAUCRATIC INEFFICIENCIES
ADMINISTRATIVE CONTROL LOSS

Bureaucratic problems have many origins. The first is the division between those who consume the outputs of bureaucracies and those who provide them. The social goal of government bureaucracies is to provide public goods and services to citizens, but bureaucrats report not to their consumers/citizens but to elected officials in the executive office and the legislature. Hence, unlike private firms, which are subject to the daily review and evaluation of consumers who purchase their goods and finance their development and production, the government bureaucracy is subject to control and review from the legislature from which it also obtains part or all of its operating funds. This produces a level of decision makers—the legislature—that is separate from the mass of citizens who consume the output of bureaucrats. This intermediary level introduces the possibility of serious distortions arising in the decision-making process. Theoretically, legislators represent the preferences of citizens, but this

---

[4] Profit centers in corporations are administrative units that have revenues and costs assigned to them even though they may not independently sell goods and/or buy resources.

assumes a frictionless political market. The reader should now recognize that the political market is characterized by such market failures as rational abstention, rational ignorance, inefficient voting systems, choice among only two parties, bundling of political issues into a single market basket, special interests, donations of time, labor, and money to political campaigns, and disproportionate influence of communicators and professionals. These and other political market failures produce distortions between the preference patterns of citizens and the voting patterns of legislators.

The Weberian view that representatives of the people are supposed to make laws and establish policy and that bureaucrats are supposed to carry them out is increasingly difficult to apply to large modern governments in which legislators seldom have the time necessary to consider important details or even, in many cases, to read the bills. Legislators delegate much work and—as anyone who has worked on Capitol Hill knows—decision making to their staff members, who are also overworked. The busy schedules of legislators and their staffs, plus the innate complexity of legislation in a country of 250 million people, result in broad and ambiguous legislation that leaves immense discretionary authority to bureaucrats. During the tenure of the Ninety-ninth Congress (1985–86) nearly 10,000 measures (bills and joint resolutions) were introduced and 483 were passed. This was not an isolated one-year event. In fact, the output of the Ninty-ninth Congress suffered from legislative depression when compared with the previous ten congresses (1965–84), in which the average number of bills introduced *each* session was 17,500 with more than 800 measures enacted.

Congressional representatives, of course, have many duties other than reading, researching, and voting on legislation. Most representatives serve on at least a dozen committees or subcommittees, and they have to respond to numerous requests from their constituents. One cost of a large government and a busy legislature is that policy making does not end when Congress approves a bill and the president signs it. The loose language embedded in virtually every piece of legislation and the lack of attention to details make it inevitable that bureaucrats will form important policy decisions as they administer the law. This is why it appears to many citizens that most public decisions are made not by their representatives but by unelected officials including administrators, bureaucrats, and judges. In the view of many citizens, bureaucrats constitute the permanent government, while presidents and congressional representatives come and go.

Because legislatures have numerous agencies to oversee, they assign committees to review the activities and determine the budgets of government bureaus. These committees, in turn, cannot handle the assigned tasks, so subcommittees are created. Except in very unusual circumstances, legislators attracted to particular oversight committees are those individuals who have an incentive to expand the bureaucracy that the committee reviews. Members often represent local interests that benefit from expansions in the bureau's activities. Representatives from districts with military camps and defense firms sit on armed forces committees; representatives from farm states serve on agricultural committees; members from urban areas sit on urban transit committees; and members from racial minority districts serve on civil rights committees. Even members from "neutral districts" can easily develop an expansionist mentality for the bureaucracy they oversee. Committees and their members that oversee small and insignificant bureaucracies that have few employees, purchase few materials from contractors, and are not publicly visible are ignored by the press, contributors, and fellow legislators. Such committees do not provide platforms from which legislators can spring to higher political office. Thus, even "neutral" legislators have strong incentives to expand the size and influence of the agencies they oversee. At the least, as noted by William Niskanen, the legislative committee is a "passive sponsor of the agency it oversees."

Even if "objective" legislators sat on oversight subcommittees, the information they would receive from the bureaucracies could be misleading or slanted. Although other sources of information (not necessarily unbiased) have become available to the Congress and to some state legislatures during the past decades, most detailed information on a bureau's activities, performance, and costs comes from the bureaucracy itself. High-level bureaucrats have an incentive to give only the most favorable information to the legislature, and very often the information received by the top-level bureaucrats has been diluted, slanted, or biased by lower-level bureaucrats through a process called *control loss*. Control loss arises in many ways. Analysts can select data or methodologies that will produce results known to be favored by the department head. Studies that give the "wrong" answers are ignored, while those that give the "right" results are "sent forward." Control loss can occur when bureaucrats summarize voluminous studies into a few pages of "executive summaries" that become smaller as the report makes it way up the bureaucratic ladder. The most damaging data, comments, and qualifying phrases can be ignored, while the positive comments are emphasized. Control loss also occurs when selective information is leaked to the media. One of the most serious sources of control loss is the difficulty of imparting detailed instructions to bureaucrats. Bureaucracies exist because it is difficult to define their services sufficiently well so that they could be contracted out to private firms. This, of course, means that it is also difficult to give precise instructions to administrators in the bureaucracies. Bureaucrats are able to give their own interpretations to the general instructions they receive and, thus, gain valuable flexibility.

Even when the legislature is able to obtain accurate information, it is unable to evaluate it properly because there is no acceptable yardstick to measure the value of most bureaucratic output. Public goods and services are not priced in the marketplace, and one bureau's performance cannot be compared with the performances of other bureaus because it is the only one supplying the good or service. This lack of an acceptable yardstick to measure the value of a bureau's output produces uncertainty and gives bureaucrats and legislators considerable flexibility in determining "social needs." At the theoretical level the political market does have a measure of overall performance, which is equivalent to profits in the private sector. This measure is votes. Unfortunately, profits and votes are not useful guides or incentives for the individual worker in a large corporation or government, because the individual's contribution to profits or votes is seldom measurable.

Just as the separation of ownership and control between stockholders and managers—first evaluated by Berle and Means[5] in the thirties—creates incentive and monitoring problems in private corporations, so the separation of control between voters and government managers creates incentive and monitoring problems in government. Academic research on the role of modern corporate managers and the role of public managers has developed very similar themes. Where stockholdings are widely dispersed, corporation managers tend to neglect the owners' interests in favor of their own. Corporate managers, like public bureaucrats, become motivated to expand their departments and to acquire the nonpecuniary forms of consumption and the quiet life (sometimes called organizational slack). The corporation is able to narrow the area of measurement problems by evaluating upper management on profit performance and lower management, where possible, on profit center results. Government managers cannot be evaluated by profits or profit centers, and the measurement problem is much more serious in government bureaucracies than in corporations.

BIG IS BEST

Although bureaucrats seldom benefit in a direct monetary way from their agency's monopoly position, they can benefit in many indirect ways.

---

[5] A. A. Berle, Jr., and G. C. Means, *The Modern Corporation and Private Property* (New York: Macmillan, 1934).

Among a minor list of benefits are small dining rooms for cabinet secretaries and special restaurants for senior or flag officers, redecorated offices for incoming bureaucrats, chauffeured limousines, travel allowances, and costly recreational facilities. The media tend to highlight such fringe benefits, but the most serious inefficiencies of bureaucracies are to be found not in the trappings of office but the waste of resources resulting from bureaucratic incentives to enlarge agencies beyond their optimal size. Bureaucrats are motivated by promotions, power, prestige, perks, influence, reputation, and an easy life. All but the last are related to the size of the bureau a bureaucrat manages.

But the most important reasons motivating a bureaucrat to enlarge the bureaucracy are more subtle and are generated by the bureau's lower-level employees. To workers everywhere, power-hungry bureaucrats are the unprincipled directors of *other* departments or agencies, while the ideal director for *their* agency is an aggressive and active leader who is able to convince others of the important mission of their agency and who is able to procure resources and enlarge their department. Agency employees want their director to aggressively promote and to expand the agency because expansion will increase their own chances of advancement, provide new desks and equipment, enlarge travel budgets, and generally make life more pleasant. It is extremely difficult for any director to resist such pressures from employees with whom he must associate on a daily basis and whose respect he must have if he is to be a successful administrator. Furthermore, civil service rules makes it difficult to discipline workers and virtually impossible to fire anyone, so the only way a senior bureaucrat can motivate subordinates is to offer them promotions generated by an expanding bureaucracy. Also, review committees, the media, and often the general public build monuments and heap praise on those bureaucrats most successful in expanding their agencies. Seldom does one read about the agency head who downsized an agency; even less often does one hear about a university president who increased educational efficiency by decreasing the number of faculty and cutting peripheral and nonessential activities in the university. The unwritten but most important mission of the senior bureaucrat is to expand the agency.

The universal practice of appointing as the head of a bureau an individual who is a champion of the bureau's mission exaggerates the normal expansionary incentives in a bureaucracy. Seldom is the secretary of defense a dove, the secretary of health and welfare an opponent of welfare, the secretary of education a foe of the education establishment, or the chief of the civil rights division a critic of "equal opportunity." Furthermore, many executives in every bureaucracy are likely to be selected from among the industries or occupations that will benefit from an expansion of the bureau's activity. Employees are often attracted to a bureau because of the opportunities they will have to promote their professional careers. The typical example highlighted by the media is the appointment of an executive of a corporation that sells goods or services to the bureau. Far more numerous are the government appointees who are former employees of associations, nonprofit organizations, research institutions, and professional firms that benefit from the agency's activities. They, too, have self-interests and personal constituencies to serve. The explosion of expertise in ever-narrowing fields has generated an exclusive sense of dedication among those who specialize in them, and they take this dedication and the concerns of their fellow experts into government with them. The university bureaucrat who has spent her life with colleagues who view government financing of education as the sine qua non of enlightened public policy cannot be expected to be objective when she is appointed to the Department of Education. The head of a metropolitan museum appointed to the Foundation of Arts and Humanities is not likely to argue that fewer funds should be given to the arts. The scientist who has studied the mating patterns of shrimp in coastal wetlands cannot be expected to decrease shrimp research if appointed to the National Marine Fisheries Service. The Washington lawyer, on leave with the State Department, who is appointed to head a delegation negotiating a complicated international treaty cannot be expected to take an objective view of the proposed treaty.[6]

Every bureau has a strong incentive to satisfy its clients because they are important sources of political influence, and most bureaus and their employees become lobbyists for the interests they serve. Bureaucrats form implicit lobbying partnerships with those who provide materials and supplies to the agency and those who have a high demand for the services of the agency. Labor unions and the Department of Labor, farmers and the Department of Agriculture, defense industries and the Department of Defense, universities and the National Science Foundation conduct campaigns to expand budgets of the relevant agencies. Bureaucrats argue that their clients have "special needs" that only their bureau can satisfy, and, of course, the client groups reinforce this with their own campaigns advertising their "special needs" and the irreparable harm that will be done if these "needs" are not satisfied.

Sometimes their joint efforts to "serve the public interest" are humorous as well as costly. Edward Banfield, author of *The Unheavenly City,*

---

[6] If the treaty is successful, he becomes celebrated as the "Father of Treaty X"; if it fails, he is unknown. If he leaves government service after negotiating a successful treaty, he possesses a strong comparative advantage in procuring clients who have to deal with the treaty's provisions.

held a public relations position for one of the lesser agencies in the Department of Interior.[7] One of his duties was to draft a letter to the secretary of interior to be formally signed by the president of a citizens' group requesting that the agency be financed at higher levels. The letter was sent to the secretary and it was referred to Banfield to draft a reply for the secretary's signature. He was, in effect, carrying on a correspondence with himself.

There are many other methods that can be used by bureaucrats to expand their bureaus. They can inflate estimates of benefits and underemphasize costs in benefit-cost studies; they can adopt low discount rates that make large projects look more attractive;[8] they can support the introduction of complicated and elaborate machinery to deal with personnel issues; they can systematically redefine the objectives of a program to ensure that it remains "up to date"; they can support the introduction of new legislation to correct the bad effects of some previous policy instead of recommending the abolition of the old policy; they can support programs that require specific expenditures rather than transfers in money, since the former requires a larger bureaucracy; and they can make "radical innovations" to correct problems that the agency has not been able to solve in previous years. A major motivation for broadening the service line of a bureau is to hedge against the possibility that its mainline service may be terminated by the legislature. Virtually all major federal departments supply some service that does not seem to fit in with the major services provided. The United States Army builds and maintains inland waterways. The Department of Agriculture advises urban housewives on family budget planning. The Department of Transportation oversees the Coast Guard.

Bureaucrats have little incentive to allocate the bureau's resources efficiently over time. Unlike a private firm owner, a bureaucrat does not own property rights to future increases in the value of the agency or to its reputation after he leaves it. The benefits of any investment decision made by him are likely to accrue to his successors and not to him. Thus, the bureaucrat has an incentive to make decisions that enlarge the agency's size and output only during his tenure at the agency. However, a bureaucrat faced with a decision, say, between a large capital expenditure made today that will reduce future labor staffing and a small capital expenditure made today that will require a large labor staffing in the future

---

[7] Edward Banfield, *The Unheavenly City,* (Boston: Little,Brown, 1970).

[8] See chapter 11 for a discussion of discount rates. Basically, low discount rates tend to exaggerate the benefits of government projects and, thus, make them more likely to be funded.

has an incentive to select the large capital expenditure today and a smaller staff in the future. The bureaucrat will be able to expand the influence of the department today by designing and administering the capital project and awarding the construction grants while leaving future agency heads a smaller staff.

Budget-maximization behavior by bureaucrats is not necessarily bad for society. If marginal benefits of the agency's services are greater than marginal costs, bureaucrats who are working diligently to expand the agency's services are performing a valuable public benefit for society. Bureau chiefs may also provide a public service when they propose new programs to the legislature. As technology, population, and the tastes of the public change, government needs to provide some new services. If bureaucrats didn't act as entrepreneurs by providing information on changing conditions and potential new programs, legislators would have to do so. Since legislators lack the information and expertise necessary to make detailed proposals, it would be more expensive for them to initiate new programs. In fact, the legislature, which is accustomed to receiving information and new proposals from departments, might be rudderless if these proposals were to cease suddenly. Congress, for example, did not like Secretary of Defense McNamara proposing a stable defense budget for a number of years and then defending it against increases as well as decreases.

The bureaucratic problem is that, for the many reasons mentioned above, bureaucrats will continue to push for larger budgets even when marginal costs are greater than marginal benefits. Legislative control over bureaucracies is complicated, because inefficient performance does not lead to the termination of bureau activity and it often leads to requests for additional funds and an expansion in the bureau: poor performance by students leads to larger education budgets; cost overruns in the Department of Defense lead to supplemental appropriations; and increased crime rates and fewer apprehensions lead to larger police forces.

BUREAUCRATIC MONOPOLIES: SINGLE PROVIDERS OF PUBLIC GOODS

Many bureaus are the sole providers of public goods and services and the sole purchasers of certain resources. Many economists believe that the monopoly nature of most bureaus frees bureaucrats from competitive pressures to be efficient, innovative, and customer oriented and encourages them to pursue nonpecuniary gains. This view is correct, but the monopoly/monopsony emphasis may be misdirected. The costs of pursuing nonpecuniary gains such as leisure, large offices, and generous travel budgets are fairly much the same to a monopolist as they are to a perfect competitor: in each case there is a sacrifice of profits. Monopoly per se does not lead to the pursuit of the quiet life; the inability to profit from "correct" decisions does. Bureaucrats have less incentive to be efficient—or more incentive to pursue nonpecuniary rewards—not because they are monopolists but because they cannot take home the profits or benefits of great efficiency. Bureaucratic decision making reflects the ancient adage that "no one spends someone else's money as carefully as he spends his own." This adage is reflected in a variety of bureaucracies. University bureaucrats want the best faculty and largest and fastest computer; hospital administrators want the latest and best brain scanner; police chiefs want fast and large cars; and fire chiefs want the shiniest and most advanced fire engine. Bureaucrats strive to obtain nonmonetary income because they have little incentive to be efficient, their salaries are fixed and unrelated to efficiency, and they seldom worry about losing market share or becoming subjected to government regulations.[9]

THE SITUATION IS SERIOUS: SEND MORE MONEY

There is an unconfirmed apocryphal anecdote that has floated around the economics profession for decades. Supposedly, a number of Swiss cantons experienced problems with rats in the middle of the nineteenth century. All but one of the cantons let current government bureaus and private citizens eliminate the rats. However, one canton established an independent rat eradication agency, and the only canton that had rats into the middle of the twentieth century was that canton. Perhaps this story is nothing more than the product of a professor's fertile imagination attempting to provide an interesting illustration in class. However, it does illuminate a potential danger of creating a bureaucracy to eradicate a public bad. Bureaucrats always have an incentive to convince the legislature that the "bad" they were hired to eliminate is still present. Obviously, the Department of Defense has an incentive to emphasize the external dangers to the United States so that it will receive larger budget allocations. However, the incentive is just as strong in other agencies. After decades of poor educational attainment, no education budget is too large, no

---

[9] This incentive is not confined solely to bureaucrats. To the extent that performance is not objectively measurable and efficiency is not rewarded, corporate managers have a tendency to pursue personal rather than corporate objectives. A casual glance at the typical offices of senior management in public agencies compared with those in private corporations—the quality of the carpets, the drapes, the chairs, the desk, and the secretary, as well as travel and expense budgets—suggests that it is the corporate rather than the public sector that offers greater possibilities for at least these kinds of nonpecuniary consumption.

pupil-teacher ratio is too small, no new experiment—except the voucher system—is too costly, and no education research project is too bizarre. The fire marshall will always find hundreds of dangerous construction practices; a metropolitan mass transit agency will always find too much traffic congestion generated by automobile travel and find subsidies for mass transit too low; OSHA will always find dangerous shop practices and equipment; the EPA will always find dangerous levels of pollution; and the FBI will always have too many "armed and dangerous criminals" to track down.

There is a problem in establishing an agency or authority to look out after a particular activity because it will ignore the possibilities that consumers can substitute other goods for the ones they are responsible for. For example, a metropolitan transit authority for a medium-size city can solve the "problems of the poor getting around the city" by running large buses—with fewer than 20 percent of the seats occupied—while totally ignoring alternative methods of transit: for example, the rich could pay their maids to travel to work (which generates much of the travel in medium-sized cities) or the city could subsidize taxicabs or small vans to provide the same service at much less cost. The Delaware Basin Commission mounted a massive attack on pollution in the estuary, spending hundreds of millions of dollars to make the river only slightly more fishable and smellable. People could easily do their swimming and fishing in the Poconos or at the Jersey shore rather than in the highly industrialized Delaware Valley. This is typical bureaucratic behavior. Instead of considering whether consumers had other and better locations for swimming, boating, or fishing, the commission confined itself to the estuary for which it was responsible. By narrowing the range of recreational alternatives available to residents of the estuary area, the study considerably overestimated recreational benefits.

One budgetary practice used in virtually all bureaucracies is designed to produce blatant inefficiencies. This is the fiscal-year accounting system, in which all budgetary allocations have to be spent or committed by the end of the fiscal year or the money has to be surrendered to the budget office or to the legislature. Anyone who has served in the military is familiar with the feverish activity that occurs during the last month of the fiscal year: millions of bullets and shells are expended; millions of gallons of aviation fuel are used on "training and refresher missions"; and warehouses are stuffed with pencils, papers, typewriter ribbons, rifles, clothing, and tires. Anyone who has worked in a university is familiar with the urgent request for faculty to list their requirements for new desks, computers, and other equipment at the end of the year. Lawns are trimmed and trees are planted on the university grounds. The bureaucratic anthem that "we have to spend it or return it" echoes in every government building from Bangor to Bakersfield, and those innocent neophytes in the agency who ask "Why not return it?" are given that cold bureaucratic stare and told that the accountants would not know how to handle such returns. Another reason, of course, is that senior bureaucrats are afraid that subsequent budgets will be reduced unless they spend all of their allocations before the end of the fiscal year.

The lack of competitive pressures and monetary incentives in public agencies is reflected in many little but cumulatively important ways. The following are a few questions relating to everyday services provided by the private and political markets. The answers represent not random events but many of the theories that were presented in the previous pages.

1. Why do private retail stores stay open evenings and on Saturdays and Sundays while government offices close at 4:30 on weekdays and are never open on Saturdays or Sundays?

2. Why do retail stores and most utilities have branches located throughout metropolitan areas but government agencies require their customers to travel to the central part of the city?

3. Why do private malls provide free parking to their customers and require employees to park at the far edges of the parking lot whereas governments provide no parking for their customers but assign reserved places (often empty) for politicians, agency executives, and many other government employees?

4. Private utilities and other private companies send a bill to their customers with two parts: one is sent back to the company with a check and the other provides detailed information for the customer's records. Why does the local tax assessor send out the property tax bill on only one piece of paper that has to be returned with the check?

5. Why are a department store's telephone lines seldom busy and the government lines always busy?

6. Why do you always have to wait in line to get a driver's license but never to buy a car?

7. Why do faulty telephone or electricity lines get repaired within hours and potholed streets get repaired within months or years?[10]

---

[10] The answer to this question is not immediately obvious because the utilities, though private, are regulated monopolies. One plausible reason is that they are regulated by political agencies that provide external checks on their performance. Government agencies, on the other hand, seldom face external checks on their performance by the private sector. Government agencies that do face checks from the private sector perform much more efficiently. One of the most efficient *public* agencies is the U.S. Postal Service, which faces competitive pressures from United Parcel Service (one of the most efficient *private* firms in the world), Federal Express, telephones, fax, and computer communications.

8. Why did Federal Express, and not the U.S. Postal Service, inaugurate overnight delivery?
9. Why do private detectives hired by bail bonding firms have a better record of retrieving bail jumpers than the police?

POSSIBLE REMEDIES

What can be done to correct the problems inherent in today's bureaucracies? Various solutions can be offered, but they often produce their own problems, difficulties, and costs, and each proposed remedy needs to be carefully evaluated in its specific departmental and institutional environment. However, a few general solutions that may yield benefits in some bureaucracies are set forth below.

One of the most simple improvements in bureaucratic behavior would be anathema to government accountants, but bureaucrats should not be tyrannized by the traditional, "generally accepted" principles of accounting, which are often inefficient when evaluated by any other criterion. Millions of dollars, and the resources that such dollars represent, could be saved by the simple expedient of encouraging agencies to return unused budget allocations to the general fund. Those agencies that return such unspent allocations should be allowed to keep some percent, say 40 percent, to spend on whatever activities or capital goods, within broad guidelines, they wish to. One department may want to spend the unallocated funds on a new car, more desktop computers, building maintenance, or more secretaries. These funds should be completely fungible, that is, the accounting and budgetary practices should not be constrained by those artificial categories—personnel, operating, and capital funds—that budget officers require because it simplifies their jobs. If an agency's operating funds are not spent during the fiscal year, the portion that is not returned should be spendable on equipment, personnel, or operations, or, if it so desires, the agency should be able to accumulate these funds over the years and earn interest on them. Auditors should not be allowed to dominate decision making in the agency by requiring that these funds be spent on "approved" activities. General guidelines would have to be established to avoid spending money on parties and personal benefits, but the widest latitude should be given. It is the incentive provided by the flexibility in the use of these saved funds that would induce government managers to make socially correct decisions.

The current perception of the legislature, the media, and the public of a "successful administrator" as one who expands the budget, size, output, activities, construction, reputation, or number of employees in an agency, university, or hospital must change. The most successful administrator may be one who refuses to be pressured by employees or by the inherent expansionist incentives of all bureaucracies and reduces rather than expands the agency's size, output, budget, and number of employees. Such an administrator is likely to have an employee rebellion, so he needs to have the flexibility of increasing the monetary income of employees so that productive workers will be willing to work for the agency even if their own department is not expanding, their travel budgets are limited, their offices are small, and they do not have the latest technological gadgets. It is always less expensive and more socially efficient to retain employees by increasing their salaries than by providing nonincome perks. All workers would like to have large offices, desks, and the latest technological devices if they didn't have to pay for them. However, an increase of $10,000, or possibly even $1,000, in annual income would be much more appreciated than an increase of $10,000 in additional perks.

Every major department should have some bureaucrats who are not committed to the mission of the department. The Department of Defense should have doves; the civil rights division should have people not committed to civil rights; universities and the boards that govern them should have some officials not committed to formal education. These employees should have the right to present minority positions and papers to review committees, to the legislature, and to the media. Legislative oversight committees should not be dominated by members who are sympathetic to the agency or its missions. In fact, members should be assigned randomly and rotated from committee to committee so they do not develop vested interests in the success of a particular agency.[11] Professional review and evaluation committees should be developed in the executive branch and the legislative branch. Auditors should investigate whether proper administrative and accounting procedures are followed by the departments and whether the funds and resources of the agency are used for proper purposes. Auditors should detect fraud, embezzlement, and dishonesty. Evaluation committees should investigate the efficiency and effectiveness of the programs and their administration. While a minority of these committee members should be allowed to specialize in certain large and complicated programs, the majority of members should be rotated among evaluation committees.

The source of much bureaucratic inefficiency is the monopoly power possessed by many agencies. One way to decrease this monopoly power is to privatize, or contract out, the supply of public goods to competing

---

[11] Gordon Tullock pointed out in a private communiqué that until recently the French legislature assigned committee members randomly.

private firms. Most government buildings in the United States are constructed by private firms; most military weapons, highways, space research equipment, and government telephone, electric, and computing services are developed and produced by private firms, and the food services and concession stands in most government buildings and military bases are supplied by private firms. There is no reason the current list of privatized activities could not be expanded. Governments could use competing private companies to repair roads and administer Social Security and government retirement programs. Private firms could bid to manage the postal services, fire protection services, air traffic control system, and routine paper processing of various types. There would be many advantages realized from such privatization. It would introduce competition in the provision of public goods; it would increase responsiveness to consumers; it would reduce bureaucratic empires; it would reduce the monopoly power of public sector unions; and it would provide a yardstick for evaluating the public sector provision of these goods. In the 1930s a major argument for the creation of the TVA was to provide a public sector benchmark that could be used to evaluate the efficiency of private electric utility monopolies. The use of the private supply of some public services would provide a yardstick to evaluate the performance of budget-maximizing monopoly bureaus.

Many municipal and state governments have begun the privatization of public services. During the nineteenth century, cities, states, and territories paid bounty hunters to capture lawbreakers, and private companies still track down bail jumpers. Scottsdale, Arizona, discovered that contracting out fire prevention services cut nearly 50 percent of fire service costs;[12] cities contract out the collection of garbage to private firms that are able to provide the service at two-thirds of the cost of municipal government production.[13] The voucher system, in which school boards give vouchers to parents for use as tuition payments in any school, would be an excellent way of introducing competition into education. Local governments could also contract out municipal services to other governmental units. Scotland Yard contracts out its detective services to local governments throughout Britain, and many municipalities purchase snow removal, fire department, and sewerage treatment services from other municipalities.

---

[12] Roger Ahlbrandt, "Efficiency in the Provision of Fire Services," *Public Choice* 16 (1973): 1–15.

[13] E. S. Savas, *Privatizing the Public Sector: How to Shrink Government* (Chatham, NJ: Chatham House Publishers, 1982); Robert Bish, "Improving Productivity in the Government Sector," in *Response to Economic Change*, ed. David Laidler (Toronto: University of Toronto Press, 1986), 203–37.

Another way to induce competitive pressures into the political market is to permit numerous bureaucracies to provide the same good. Economists tend to emphasize the advantages of competition in public goods provision, but the traditional public administration view is that monopoly bureaus are absolutely necessary to eliminate duplication and overlap among agencies. Many public administration reforms actually group bureaus supplying similar services into larger specialized monopoly bureaus because competing agencies are thought to be wasteful. A monopoly bureau has several potential advantages: there may be economies of scale in the production of the public good; fewer resources may be devoted to competitive advertising; consumers and the legislature may have lower information-seeking costs; and single producers keep down monitoring and evaluation costs for the review committees.

Traditional public administrators are obviously correct when they say that the provision of public goods by competing agencies would produce duplication. However, General Motors, Ford, Chrysler, Toyota, Volkswagen, and Honda duplicate each other's services. So do IBM, Apple, Commodore, Toshiba, and dozens of other computer companies. Similar competition may be good for the public sector. Monopoly agencies do not always benefit from economies of scale. Several studies of the economies of scale in the provision of local government services conclude that the unit cost of these services increases with the absolute size of the local government. Several other studies of teaching, police, and fire services have concluded that quality is higher in smaller districts.[14] Competition and efficiency may be increased by permitting independent local governments in metropolitan areas to compete with each other. At the national level more than one bureau could be allowed to compete in the provision of services already provided by other bureaus. The legislature would obtain more information about costs, and citizens would be able to enforce some consumer sovereignty by changing from one public provider to another. The little competition among bureaus that has existed has already produced some benefits. The Navy and Army competed to develop missiles and planes and to put the United States into space.[15] The Coast Guard played a valuable role in Vietnam because the Navy had produced very few small boats that could traverse the narrow and shallow streams in the delta. The Army Corps of Engineers and the TVA build dams.

Legislators, the press, and political scientists appear to be more interested in how honestly public activities are conducted rather than how well

---

[14] See William A. Niskanen, "Bureaucrats and Politicians," *Journal of Law and Economics*, 18, 3 (December 1975): 617–43.

[15] The first United States satellite was launched by the Navy.

they are conducted. Many public administration reforms are primarily designed to insulate bureaucrats from opportunities for personal gain. Corruption in government makes good news copy, but the waste in bad programs administered by honest men and women is hardly mentioned. This may be attributable to the dominant role in the American political system of lawyers who have a comparative advantage in writing laws and identifying illegal behavior but who have no special background in deciding what constitutes good law. Citizens and legislators must emphasize efficiency as well as honesty in the administration of government programs.

Even if the above measures could be applied to most bureaucratic activity, they would lessen but not eliminate bureaucratic inefficiencies. In fact, if the analysis presented in this and previous chapters is correct, even these measures will not be adopted. There simply are few, if any, reliable external yardsticks to evaluate the performance of most public agencies, and there are no simple answers to the malaise. Most improvements would not be in the interests of the legislators or the bureaucrats, so we could hardly expect them to be enthusiastic about reforms. Citizens are too concerned about their daily activities to demand efficient governments. The best method of controlling bureaucratic inefficiency is to control the size of government, which is going to be difficult in an age of increasing interdependencies and externalities. Some new government programs will be needed and others should be expanded, but every time an expenditure bill is passed citizens must consider that the expenditure will not only involve higher taxes—and the additional inefficiencies that such taxes produce in the private market—it will also expand a current bureaucracy or create a new one.

QUESTIONS AND ANSWERS

THE QUESTIONS

1.   One of the quotes at the beginning of this chapter states that "the king reigns but does not govern." Why did the author use this quote to start a chapter on bureaucracy in a democracy?

2.   One of the potential market failures discussed in chapter 3 was the collusion by firms to divide markets and raise prices. Such collusive behavior is determined to be so undesirable that there are civil and criminal sanctions for those corporations and executives engaged in such activity. When public bureaucracies and bureaucrats get together to divide markets and raise taxes, such behavior is praised as consolidation. Why is there such inconsisent treatment of what appears to be similar actions in the two markets?

3. The following questions relate to positions that various bureaucrats and politicians may take on a number of issues. Based on the material presented in this chapter, what possible positions would bureaucrats take in the following situations?

   a. If you were a general in the U.S. Army, would you agree with the following statement: "The country needs to declare war on drugs"?

   b. If you were a bureaucrat in an underdeveloped country, which of the following plans would you prefer?

   (1) A U.S. foreign aid plan in which the United States sent checks directly to poor people in the developing country.

   (2) A U.S. foreign aid plan in which the United States specified the projects in the developing country.

   (3) A U.S. foreign aid plan in which the United States sent money to the government, which, in turn, approved or channeled funds to various projects.

   c. If you were a member of the Municipal Housing Authority, would you publicly support a rent subsidy plan in which the poor found their own apartments and then received a subsidy directly from the government equal to some percentage of the rent paid by the poor family?

   d. If you were the director of the local Red Cross blood bank, which obtained blood from volunteers, would you support a bill prohibiting monetary payments for blood?

   e. West Germany has a much smaller percentage of its high school graduates go to a traditional university than the United States. Many high school students begin interning in an industrial or craft position and then further their education at technical schools, which are independent of the traditional universities. Would you expect the chancellor of your university to propose such a program—as well as administrative independence—for your state or country?

4. **a.** If your boss offered to redecorate your office at a cost of $10,000 would you take him up on the offer?

   b. If your boss offered you the choice of a $9,000 cash bonus or a redecorated office costing $10,000 which would you choose?

   c. What is the relevance of this example to bureaucracies?

5. Assume that a state legislator proposed that the state should no longer continue to subsidize state universities and instead should send a higher education voucher to parents of college-age youth. Parents could use the voucher to pay, say, $5,000 of tuition at any university in the country.

   a. Do you believe that the chancellor of the state university would approve of the plan? What about the chancellor of the largest private university in the state?

b.   Assume you are attending a private university and you ask five of your professors if they approve of the plan. Do you think you would get a different response if you asked five professors at a state university? Why?

c.   What changes do you think would occur in the state universities if such a proposal were adopted in your state? What changes do you think would occur in the state universities if such a proposal were adopted in all states? Why?

6.   **a.**   How would you rank the following groups at your university in terms of parking privileges? That is, which of the following are most assured of parking close to their offices or classrooms: administrators, faculty, employees, students?

b.   How would you rank the following groups in terms of parking privileges at the largest shopping center in your city: administrators, employees, customers?

7.   You wake up tomorrow and your telephone and refrigerator are broken and the public sidewalk in front of your home has caved in. You call the telephone company, the refrigerator repair company, and the city's department of public works to come and make repairs.

a.   About how long would you wait for each of the repair crews to fix your respective problems?

b.   What are some explanations for the differences?

8.   A deep pothole emerged in a major thoroughfare about three miles from the author's subdivision. The Department of Public Works put in a quick asphalt patch repair, which was soon eroded. The DPW was called again, and it once again put in a temporary repair. The pothole re-emerged within a few days. Dozens of citizens called the bureaucracy to complain that the pothole was a serious safety problem and that it was causing expensive damage to cars hitting it. Nothing was done for more than a year. One Sunday afternoon the mayor talked to a meeting of the subdivision's homeowners' association and he was told about the pothole. He said he would take care of it. The *next* morning at 7 A.M. a city work crew was repaving the road.

a.   Would you give the mayor high marks for his administrative efficiency?

b.   Does this episode illustrate one of the problems of bureaucracy discussed in the chapter? Which one?

THE ANSWERS

1.   A modern interpretation: "Voters reign but do not govern." Voters are considered to be sovereign in a democracy, but it is the bureaucracy that appears to govern. The bureaucracy has enormous power because of the various impediments in the political market.

2. For unknown reasons many people believe that competition is desirable in the private market but not in the political market. General Motors should compete with Ford, Chrysler, and Honda, and K-Mart should compete with Target and Wal Mart; but when the FBI competes with the CIA or suburbs compete with the central city, it is called wasteful duplication.

3. **a.** Sure, and no government agency knows more about fighting wars than the U.S. Army.

b. Answer (3), because this would give the bureaucracy additional power. However, you would want to know whether you were actually in one of the bureaucratic agencies that would benefit. Read the history of foreign aid programs, especially the Alliance for Progress.

c. Unlikely. You would derive your income and power from an agency that administered housing and housing services for the poor. If the rent subsidy program were a success, your agency would shrink in power and political visibility.

d. Yes. Bureaucractic imperatives exist in nonprofit as well as in government bureaucracies. Red Cross bureaucrats correctly believed that their agency had a comparative advantage in obtaining "volunteer" blood. During the early 1970s the Red Cross bureaucracy led the campaign to eliminate commercial blood banks. A few years later it led the campaign against "blood credits" (used primarily by the members of the American Association of Blood Banks).

e. Unlikely. There is no public record of a univeristy chancellor proposing such a program.

4. **a.** Certainly, you're no fool. Even if you placed a personal value of $2,000 on the redecorated office, you would want the office decorated if your opportunity cost were zero.

b. Unless you have a very strong preference for a redecorated office (greater than $9,000), you would prefer the $9,000 in cash because you could spend it on goods that yielded $9,000 in marginal benefits to you.

c. Legislatures often place unrealistically low ceilings on salaries for certain positions in governments. Bureaucracies then compete for personnel by offering large travel budgets, generous retirement benefits, and large offices and staffs. The local, state, and federal governments could save money (society's resources) by paying higher salaries and providing fewer fringe benefits.

5. **a.** The chancellor of the state university would most likely denounce the plan as destroying higher education in the state. The chancellor of the largest private univeristy would say that it offered competition and would inject renewed vigor into the state's system of higher education.

b. What do you think? Play it safe, though, and ask five professors not in the economics department.

c. The adoption of this proposal would probably result in more emphasis on teaching, closer interaction with students and student organizations, smaller classes, and less emphasis on research. However, the university would likely lose faculty to state universities in other states where research was emphasized. If other states enacted a similar program, there would be fewer attractive alternatives for faculty and they would be less likely to move. Each university would place a greater emphasis on teaching and student-related activities.

6. **a.** At the author's university the ranking of parking privileges is clearly:

> (1) Administrators
> (2) Faculty and employees
> (3) Students

b. The largest shopping center in the author's home town has the following pecking order for parking privileges:

> (1) Customers, including students
> (2) Administrators and employees

7. **a.** Your experiences are probably not much different from the author's:

> Telephone repairs—one to three hours.
> Refrigerator—one-half to one day.
> Caved-in sidewalk—Don't know. Sidewalk caved in about 18 months ago, and despite repeated calls to the bureaucracy, the city repair truck has not shown up yet.

b. The refrigerator company, which has competition in the repair industry, has an incentive to provide optimal repair service to its customers. The repair company has to balance the additional costs of having "excess" repair capacity that can respond quickly with the revenue lost from having smaller repair capacity and a slower response. Thus, the refrigerator repair company does not respond immediately, but it is able to respond within a reasonable time period.

The department of public works has no competition, and it does not derive its revenue directly from the customers it serves. It faces no market pressure to respond quickly, and it has no benchmark for evaluating response time. See the answer to the next question for advice on getting a quick response in the political market.

The amazingly quick response of the telephone repair crew is more difficult to analyze. Quick response to calls for telephone repairs are not universal. Responses in many countries where the governments run the telephone systems can take weeks or months. Certainly part of the reason for the quick response time in the United States is to be found in the strong tradition of service developed by the American

Telephone and Telegraph Company when it was competing for service areas against hundreds of other phone companies during the 1920s. As a regulated local monopoly, the phone company can allocate an "excessive" quantity of resources to repair services and raise prices accordingly.

8. **a.** Once informed, he moved very quickly, but the previous persistence of the problem illustrated that he was unable to organize the bureaucracy to respond to citizens' complaints.

b. Yes, the bureaucracy reports not to the citizens who pay the taxes but to the politicians who determine the budget of the bureaucracy. "The people are sovereign but they do not govern." Thus, hundreds of desperate calls to the bureaucracy do not have the impact that a single request from a mayor or council member has. Most politicians want to perpetuate this indirect accountability because it increases their power and ability to get votes. The mayor won many votes from the members of the subdivision when the street was repaired so quickly after he was asked to intervene.

CHAPTER ELEVEN

INTERTEMPORAL RESOURCE ALLOCATION

Time discovers truth.
—SENECA, A.D. 40

Remember that time is money.
—BENJAMIN FRANKLIN, 1748

WHALES AND TURTLES, BUT NOT HEREFORDS AND HOGS, ARE BECOMING EXTINCT

One of the more serious problems confronting mankind is the appropriate utilization of the earth's resources over time. Unfortunately, much of the public debate on conservation and resource utilization reflects an ignorance of the social role performed by private capital markets, interest rates, and prices. There is more misunderstanding and ignorance of intertemporal allocation decision making in the private and political markets than there is about temporal resource allocation. While intertemporal resource allocation is often covered in other economic theory courses, it's real-world significance for public choice requires that a chapter be devoted to it.

The most frequently heard complaint about the private market is that individual consumers and producers have no concern about the impacts of their economic decisions on the availability or condition of resources in the future. According to critics, this shortsightedness endemic in private market decision making results in an overuse of resources today, which leaves too few resources and too much pollution for future generations. Too much oil and gas are produced, too many animals are killed, too many fish are caught, and too many trees are cut. Hence, the critics argue, we should rely upon the political market to correct this overconsumption and overpollution produced in the private market. This argument has immediate appeal to many citizens who concentrate upon the constraints of Spaceship Earth and who are not familiar with political economy.

Before issuing a blanket condemnation of private market decision making and an uncritical acceptance of political market decision making, however, the conservation incentives in both markets need to be analyzed and compared. First, the private market should not be blamed for failures where it is not involved. Rapid depletion and extinction of many kinds of resources are blamed on the private market when the proper blame should be placed on the courts or the legislatures for not properly defining private property rights in the depleted asset. Where property rights are simply not feasible to define or to defend, the private market cannot work, and the conservation of such resources becomes the natural concern of the political market.

Certain species of fish, eagles, wolves, and whales are in danger of becoming extinct because no one owns them and the only way to acquire property rights to them is to kill them.[1] Common property resources such as these are the ones that are most quickly depleted, and they have nothing to do with private market failure and everything to do with political market failure. Buffalo, which previously roamed freely on the Western plains, are a frequently cited example of a resource that was not owned by individuals. As the buffalo began disappearing, each hunter probably knew that he and all other hunters would be better off if fewer buffalo were killed each year. But in the absence of private property rights in buffalo, each hunter also knew that the buffalo he did not shoot today would be shot by someone else tomorrow. The only way property rights in buffalo could be obtained was to kill them. It didn't pay anyone to take a long-term perspective on buffalo, and as a result they nearly became extinct. The buffalo were not initially protected by political market action; the buffalo that did survive were those in private herds enclosed on private lands. The same is true of many species of fish, seals, and whales, as well as streams, rivers, and lakes.

The key to the private conservation of resources is private ownership, if it is feasible. If private goods are not owned by individuals, private market forces cannot work because no one can reap direct benefits from conservation. If resources are privately owned, there are strong forces working toward the efficient intertemporal utilization of resources. Unfortunately, there are many resources that are not subject to private market ownership. It is too costly to assign and defend private property ownership rights to such resources as highly migratory species of fish in the ocean, so their use needs to be restricted through political market decision making which might involve auctioning off fishing rights.

---

[1] Most states that permit the hunting of animals such as moose and deer prohibit the capture of such animals. An individual can obtain private property ownership only by killing these animals.

INTERTEMPORAL DECISION MAKING

The three most important factors determining the intertemporal allocation of resources in the private market are interest rates, current prices,
and expected future prices. Interest rates arise not from the exploitation
of the poor by the rich but from the fact that people prefer early availability
to delayed availability and that decreased consumption today makes capital
production and greater future consumption possible.

Assume an individual is deciding between a gallon of gas available
today and a gallon of gas available a year from now. The rational individual
will not be indifferent between these two choices. If she selects a gallon
of gas available a year from now, she has to consider that the gallon of
gas will not be available for her consumption during the year. She also
has to consider the possibility that she will not be alive a year from now
to enjoy the gallon of gasoline. On the other hand, if she selects the gas
available today, she has to consider that she can sell the gas and use the
income to invest in capital goods that may yield a higher income in the
future. The individual recognizes the advantages of earlier availability
(assured consumption and the ability to use the earlier availability to
increase total income) and compares them with the advantage of future
availability: "I value one gallon of gas more highly today than one gallon
in the future. Hence, if I am going to give up one gallon today, I must
receive in return more than one gallon in the future. Based on my
preferences between current consumption and future consumption"—
called the time preferences of consumers—"I am willing to give up one
gallon today if I am able to get 1.10 gallons one year from now." The
individual, in effect, is stating that her *time preference ratio*, or her trade-
off between present and future consumption, is: 1.1 gallon of gas to be
received one year from today to 1 gallon of gas today. We could also state
that the *present value* of 1.1 gallons received a year from now is 1.0 gallons,
or we could state that the interest rate is $(1.1 - 1.0) / 1.0 = 10\%$. Thus, the
interest rate reflects the higher value of earlier availability expressed as
a percent of the present value of a good.

Interest rates are normally expressed in monetary terms; for example,
a lender will receive $110 a year from now if he foregoes the current
consumption of $100. An interest rate of 10 percent [($110 – $100) / $100]
applied to the loan of $100 should not disguise the fact that the lender
is giving up a certain amount of current consumption in order to consume more in the future. For example, if shirts cost $10 each, the lender
would be giving up current consumption of 10 shirts in return for the
future consumption of 11 shirts. The person borrowing the $100 is gain-
ing purchasing power of 10 shirts today in return for giving up the

consumption of 11 shirts in the future. The borrower's real cost of consuming 10 shirts today is the 11 shirts he will have to forego in the future. Earlier consumption is going to cost him an additional shirt.

Because the interest rate is stated in monetary terms in the financial world, the real costs to society, which the interest rate represents, are often ignored. For example, assume a private developer is considering the construction of an office complex costing $100 million. One of the costs to the developer *and* to society is the interest rate, which expresses the cost of delaying consumption and the productivity of alternative investments. If the interest rate is 10 percent, one of the real costs of constructing the office building is the $10 million of interest. This cost is the same regardless of the amount the builder actually borrows. If he only borrows $60 million, the interest cost (opportunity cost once again) is not $6 million but $10 million. Those who lend $60 million to the builder are foregoing current consumption and other alternative investment projects; those who provide the builder with the $40 million, presumably the stockholders, are also foregoing consumption and alternative investments. The interest rate and profit return are their incentive to forego current consumption and alternative investments.

The same logic is applied to government projects. If a local, state, or federal government plans to build a new $100-million office building, society's costs include an interest cost of $10 million. Even if the government does not include the interest costs in its calculations, someone in society will have to forego current consumption for future consumption, and the country will lose the use of capital in other projects. The capital could have been used to build a public school or a private office building. These are real costs that should not be ignored. The reader should be alert for the frequent error committed by those who want to ignore interest costs and concentrate on the "real costs" of some project. The opportunity costs to society represented by interest payments are as real as the opportunity costs represented by payments for labor and materials.

A short but very valuable lesson will be provided on the meaning and calculations of interest rates and present values. Today's present value (PV) will grow over one year to a larger future value (FV) depending upon the interest rate (r):

$$(1)\ FV = PV(1 + r)$$

Using the previous example:

$$(2)\ \$100(1 + .1) = \$110$$

Or we can rearrange and solve for the interest rate:

$$(3)\ r = (FV - PV) / PV$$
$$.10 = (\$110 - \$100) / \$100$$

Or we can rearrange and solve for the present value:

$$(4)\ PV = FV(1 + r)$$
$$\$100 = \$110 / (1 + .1)$$

Equation (4) gives the present value when the interest rate and future value are known. It tells us that the present value of $110 to be received one year from now is $100 today. Another way of saying the same thing is that $100 invested at 10 percent will grow to $110 a year from now.

Present Value Decreases as "Time Goes By"

The longer consumption must be delayed or the revenue received, the lower the present value is today. If the interest rate is 10 percent, $100 received one year from today is worth $90.91 today:

$$(5)\ \$90.91 = \$100 / (1 + .1)$$

If the $100 is to be received two years from today, the present value is:

$$(6)\ \$82.64 = \$100 / (1 + .1)^2$$

The present value of $100 to be received three years from today is:

$$(7)\ \$75.13 = \$100 / (1 + .1)^3$$

The present value of any amount to be received n years from today is:

$$(8)\ PV = FV / (1 + r)^n$$

If the present value is invested today at r interest rate compounded annually, the amount will equal FV at the end of n years. The present value of some amount to be received many years from today will be quite small. For example, the present value of $100 to be received 50 years from now, at an annual interest rate of 10 percent, is only 85 cents.

$$(9)\ \$0.85 = \$100 / (1.1)^{50}$$

The further in the future that some amount will be received, the lower the present value of that amount.

THE LOWER THE INTEREST RATE, THE HIGHER THE PRESENT VALUE

The calculation of present value is straightforward; the selection of the interest rate to use is not. There are many rates of interest, and the selection of the appropriate one depends upon the methodology used in the study, the purpose of the study, and the questions being asked. This is not the place to discuss all relevant factors that must be considered in determining the appropriate interest, or discount, rate to be used in present value calculations. However, the reader should understand some fundamentals about the importance of selecting the proper discount rate because such knowledge is useful in analyzing debates about current and future resource usage and the economic feasibility of government projects.

Consider the following differences in present value produced by using alternative interest rates:

At r = 5 percent, the present value of $100 to be received
in three years is: $86.38 = $100 / (1 + .05)^3$

At r = 10 percent, the present value of $100 to be received
in three years is: $75.13 = $100 / (1 + .1)^3$

At r = 20 percent, the present value of $100 to be received
in three years is: $57.87 = $100 / (1 + .2)^3$

The higher the interest rate, the smaller the amount that must be "invested" today in order to have $100 three years from now. Thus, a low discount, or interest, rate yields a relatively high present value, and a high discount rate yields a relatively low present value.

Because the selection of the proper discount rate often determines the feasibility of a capital project, individuals with vested interests often argue for the adoption of discount rates that will support their arguments. Assume that you are trying to convince your boss to buy a new computer. The computer costs $5,000, so you must convince him that the new computer will save at least $5,000 during its expected life, which is assumed to be three years. You are able to gather data showing that the new computer will save your agency $2,000 per year for the next three years, or a total of $6,000. Since your boss recognizes the significance of the time value of money, you know that you cannot simply state that total benefits are $6,000. After all, the present value of the $2,000 to be received two years and three years from now is less than $2,000. You tell your boss that you will determine the present value of the benefits and report back. You scurry back to your office and calculate the present value of $2,000 each year for the next three years at the alternative discount rates of 13 percent, 10 percent, and 7 percent:

(10) $4,722 = $2,000 / 1.13 + $2,000 / (1.13)^2 + $2,000 / (1.13)^3$
$$\$1,770 \quad + \quad \$1,566 \quad + \quad \$1,386$$

(11) $4,973 = $2,000 / 1.1 + $2,000 / (1.10)^2 + $2,000 / (1.1)^3$
$$\$1,818 \quad + \quad \$1,653 \quad + \quad \$1,502$$

(12) $5,249 = $2,000 / 1.07 + $2,000 / (1.07)^2 + $2,000 / (1.07)^3$
$$\$1,869 \quad + \quad \$1,747 \quad + \quad \$1,633$$

Since you have a personal interest in procuring the new computer, you would not want to use the present values generated by the 13- or 10-percent discount rates because they would produce present values of the benefit stream that are less than the cost of the computer. Your boss surely would not want to spend $5,000 for a computer that generated only $4,722 in benefits, so you would not use the 13-percent discount rate.[2] You would want to use a discount rate of 7 percent because it would generate a present value of $5,249, which is greater than the $5,000 cost of the computer. By selecting the appropriate discount rate (a low rate from your point of view), you would "tilt" the data in your favor and hope that you had convinced your boss to buy the new computer. If your boss had been exposed to some finance or economic courses, he might not be so easily fooled. He might tell you the discount rate the company uses in calculating present values.

When the discount rate is not clearly specified or if the instructions are ambiguous, those who have a selective incentive to report a high present value of future benefits of some project will utilize a low discount rate; those who have an incentive to report a low present value will utilize a high discount rate. A conservationist who wishes to emphasize the future benefits of conservation policies today could use a low discount rate in calculating the present value of the benefits of a program. In fact, one who places a high value on preserving resources for the future is often described as a person who has a low discount rate. One who places a low value on preserving resources for the future is often described as a person who has a high discount rate.

The reader should not be surprised by the fact that there has been considerable debate about the appropriate rate to use in discounting the stream of future benefits and costs on government projects. This debate is especially important for government projects, such as highways or dams,

---

[2] Your boss would correctly point out that he could obtain greater benefits by simply investing the $5,000 at 13 percent.

in which most of the costs are incurred at the time of construction but the benefits are strung out over many decades. A low discount rate will apply its powerful effect most on the benefits, which are long term, and thus produce an artificial and incorrect high benefit-cost ratio for such projects. About 30 years ago, when Treasury bonds were yielding about 6 percent, the Corps of Engineers was using a discount rate of 2 percent. The corps was widely criticized for using a "ridiculously low" discount rate in order to obtain high benefit-cost ratios that would maximize the number of construction projects. The 2-percent rate might have been a bit low, but the criticism—most of it coming from economists—was based on an ignorance of the methodology used by the corps in evaluating benefits and costs.

Future costs and benefits can be estimated by using either constant, or fixed, prices or current prices. If fixed prices and costs are used, then one needs to exclude the inflation rate from the discount rate. If current or nominal prices and costs are used, the inflation rate should be included in the discount rate. The best way to understand this important and often neglected principle is through an example.

Let's return to the computer example. Assume that you know that the computer will reduce one month of secretarial time per year and that one month of secretarial time, at current wages and benefits, is valued at $2,000. Hence, annual benefits of $2,000 for three years produced by the new computer represent one month of a secretary's time each year for three years *at today's wages and prices*. Because you are using today's prices and wages and holding them constant in future years, you are said to be using the *constant wage and price method* for estimating benefits. You are taking one month of saved labor and valuing it at today's wage rates and saying that this wage rate is assumed to be held constant in future years. You are making *no* adjustment for the effect of inflation on prices and wages. Let's assume that your boss tells you to use as a discount rate the market rate of interest on AAA corporate securities, which is 10 percent. You calculate the present value as:

$$(13)\ \$4{,}973 = \$2{,}000\,/\,1.1 + \$2{,}000\,/\,(1.1)^2 + \$2{,}000\,/\,(1.1)^3$$
$$\$1{,}818 \quad + \quad \$1{,}653 \quad + \quad \$1{,}502$$

The $2,000 in annual benefits represents a saving of one month's labor at $2,000 per month, which is the current wage rate. The present value of saving one month's secretarial salary in each of three years is $4,973.

There is another acceptable method of calculating present values. You can calculate the benefits by using *current wages and prices* expected to exist in each of the future years. Assuming you expect an inflation rate of 7 percent per year, you apply the 7-percent inflation to the saved wages.

One month's labor-saving benefits from the computer will be $2,140 ($2,000 × 1.07) at the end of the first year, $2,290 ($2,140 × 1.07) at the end of the second year, and $2,450 (2,290 × 1.07) at the end of the third year. Utilizing these *current, or inflation-adjusted, price-wage estimates* and the 10-percent interest rate, you calculate the present value of benefits to be:

$$(14)\ \$5,678\ =\ \$2,140\,/\,1.1\ +\ \$2,290\,/\,(1.1)^2\ +\ \$2,450\,/\,(1.1)^3$$
$$\$1,945\quad+\quad\$1,893\quad+\quad\$1,840$$

The present value obtained by using current dollar prices (14) is considerably greater than the present value you obtained when the money wages were assumed to be constant (13). Since the two methods yield widely different answers, the reader may wonder which method is right and which is wrong. The answer is that both methods are correct but the *same* discount rate cannot be used in both methods!

Benefits can be calculated using either constant or current prices, but the appropriate discount rate will differ depending upon which method is used. If the constant dollar method is used, the effect of inflation is *not* included in the estimates of future costs and benefits. Hence, the discount rate should *not* include the inflation rate either. Since the market interest rate will always reflect the expected inflation rate, the inflation rate needs to be subtracted out of the market interest rate. If the market interest rate is 10 percent and the expected inflation rate is 7 percent, the discount rate to use in the constant price method is 3 percent. Economists use the terms *nominal, or market, rate* to mean the rate that actually exists in the market and the term *real rate* to indicate the rate of interest with the inflation rate—sometimes called the *inflation premium*—subtracted from the market rate of interest. If the market rate of interest is 10 percent and the expected rate of inflation is 7 percent, the nominal rate is 10 percent and the real rate is 3 percent. If the market rate of interest is 15 percent and the expected inflation rate is 10 percent, the real rate of interest is 5 percent. Therefore, the appropriate rate to use with the constant dollar method is the real rate of interest, or the market rate of interest less the inflation rate.

When using the constant dollar method of estimating future benefits and costs, use the following discount rate:

(15) Market (nominal) rate of interest   10%
Less inflation rate (premium)   − 7%
Equals real discount rate   3%

When using the current dollar method of estimating future benefits and costs use the following discount rate:

(16) Market (nominal) rate of interest: 10%

If constant dollar prices and wages are used to estimate future benefits and costs, then a real rate of interest (3 percent) must be used as a discount rate. If nominal, or current dollar, prices and wages are used to estimate future benefits and costs, then the market or nominal rate of interest (10 percent) should be used as the discount rate. The use of constant dollar estimates *and* the real rate of interest will yield the same present value as the use of current dollar estimates *and* the nominal interest rate.

Constant dollar estimates used for future benefits and real rate of interest used as discount rate:

(17) $5,657 = \$2,000 / 1.03 + \$2,000 / (1.03)^2 + \$2,000 / (1.03)^3$
$\qquad\qquad\quad \$1,942 \quad + \quad \$1,885 \quad + \quad \$1,830$

Current dollar estimates used for future benefits and nominal, or market, rate of interest used as discount rate:[3]

(18) $5,657 = \$2,140 / 1.1021 + \$2,290 / (1.1021)^2 + \$2,450 / (1.1021)^3$
$\qquad\qquad\quad \$1,942 \quad + \quad \$1,885 \quad + \quad \$1,830$

The present values are the same because we are comparing "apples with apples and oranges with oranges." In the constant dollar method [equation (17)] the inflation premium is not included in the estimates of benefits in the numerator, and the inflation premium is not included in the discount rate. In the current dollar method the inflation premium is included in the numerator and in the denominator. As expected, the two present values are equal.

One reason we worked through the above exercise was to illustrate that the criticism of the Corps of Engineers or any other agency using a real rate of interest is unwarranted. Some economists heard about the 2-percent rate used by the corps back in the fifties and sixties and observed the 6-percent rate on bonds and immediately criticized the corps for using such a drastically low discount rate. They did not inquire into the methodology used by the corps for estimating benefits and costs. Since the corps used the constant dollar method for estimating future costs and benefits, the 2-percent discount rate was not far off the mark. At the time

---

[3] Note that the denominator in the calculation is 1.1021 instead of 1.1. The discount rate *is* 10 percent, but there is a statistical anomaly that exists when combining two growth rates into one and applying them to the same time period. The 3-percent discount rate is also being applied to the 7-percent increase in prices during this period. Thus, to correct for this anomaly, the correct discount factor is $(1 + r + xy)$ where x and y are the independent growth factors. In this example it is $[1 + .1 + (.03)(.07)] = 1.1021$.

the inflation rate was about 3.5 percent, so the real rate was approximately 2.5.[4] A 6-percent rate of discount coupled with constant dollar price estimates would clearly have been excessive.

INTEREST RATES AND THE MARGINAL PRODUCTIVITY OF CAPITAL

If capital markets are allowed to function freely and if there are no controls on interest rates, no taxes on interest earnings, no international flows of capital, and if bond debt finances all capital investment, the interest rate should reflect the marginal productivity of capital in the economy as well as the time preference of individuals. A profit-maximizing firm wishing to build a new plant or assembly line would equate the interest rate it had to pay on borrowed funds with the marginal productivity of capital. Most companies have a list of potential investments they would like to undertake. They estimate the labor and other costs as well as the revenue associated with each project. They then estimate the rates of return on the capital investment for each of the projects. Assume a firm can undertake the capital projects shown in Table 11-1.

TABLE 11-1

Capital Project	Marginal Return on Investment	Captial Project	Marginal Return on Investment
A	45%	F	15%
B	38	G	13
C	24	H	10
D	22	I	8
E	18	J	5

[4] The corps was using a slightly lower rate than was warranted by conditions at the time. Its discount rate was 2 percent when it should have been closer to 2.5. The reader may think that this ½ percent is insignificant. However, if you pay $100 for a pair of shoes today, a 2-percent annual increase will result in the shoes costing $269 in 50 years; a 2.5-percent annual increase will result in the shoes costing $345. If prices continue to increase at the recent inflation rate of 4.5 percent, those same shoes will cost more than $900 in 50 years.

We have not presented all of the analysis or information pertinent to selecting the appropriate discount rate. We have assumed that all capital funds were obtained by selling bonds, but in the real world capital funds are also obtained from equity capital, which has a higher rate of return because the rate of returns are more risky.

The most important limiting factor on the firm's investment plans is the availability of financial capital at a cost that would make a project feasible. Assuming that all capital projects were financed by bonds, the firm would compare the interest rate it would have to pay to borrow funds for each project with the marginal return on capital. If the market interest rate were 15 percent,[5] the firm would undertake all capital projects from A through F because the return earned from the projects would be greater than the interest rate paid for the use of funds. The firm would continue to earn money so long as the capital project yielded a return greater than the interest rate. In other words, the firm would invest in capital projects until the marginal return on capital obtained from the last, or marginal, project were equal to the interest rate. With an interest rate of 15 percent, the marginal project would be Project F; the firm would not undertake any more projects because it would cost more to borrow the funds than the expected return earned on the project. For example, Project G would yield a return on capital of 13 percent, but it would cost the firm 15 percent to borrow the money, so the firm would not invest in Project G. It would not undertake fewer projects because each of the Projects A through E would have a rate of return greater than the cost of borrowing the funds. Project E, for example, would yield a return on investment of 18 percent, so the firm would find it profitable to borrow funds at 15 percent and to finance the project. If the interest rate should increase to 25 percent, the firm would borrow funds only to finance Projects A and B; if the interest rate should drop to 5 percent, the firm would borrow to finance all ten projects.

Hence, if the interest rate were 10 percent, we could expect all firms to adjust their planned capital investments so that, at the margin, the return on capital investments would be equal to the 10-percent interest rate. Assuming that all financing were obtained from the sales of bonds, a market interest rate of 10 percent would mean that all marginal capital projects being built in the country would be yielding benefits at least at the rate of 10 percent. That is, the marginal (revenue) productivity of capital would be 10 percent.

Interest rates also reflect the time preferences of consumers. If individuals have a strong preference to consume goods and services today rather than in the future, they will save little and provide few funds to the bond market, which will force interest rates up; if individuals have a strong preference for future consumption, they will have a high savings rate and provide funds to the market, which will drive interest rates down.

---

[5] The firm could use the constant or current price methods of estimating future costs and revenues associated with the project. We are assuming that the firm used the current price method of estimating benefits, so it uses the market interest rate for comparison.

Given their preferences for present and future consumption, they will adjust their quantity of savings to the interest rate. Hence, if there were no taxes on interest earnings, the interest rate would reflect the marginal preference or trade-off between present and future consumption. If the interest rate were 10 percent, individuals would be willing to forego $100 of marginal consumption today in order to obtain $110 of consumption a year from today.

An interest rate of 10 percent means that the marginal rate of return on capital in the country is equal to the marginal time preference of individuals. A 10-percent interest rate means that consumers are willing to sacrifice $100 of current consumption for $110 of consumption next year and that a $100 invested in capital will yield a $110 of increased production. Pareto optimality is obtained in the intertemporal allocation of goods, because no further allocation of goods over time could improve resource allocation. Some imperfections that drive "wedges" between the time preferences of individuals and the marginal returns of capital are taxes on interest and on capital returns. Despite these imperfections, however, interest rates do provide valuable information about the relative marginal returns on capital.

There are many different types of interest rates in the marketplace. One explanation for this variation is the difference in the time to maturity of the securities, that is, maturity dates can be one week, one year, or one decade away.[6] Another explanation is that some bonds are more risky than others because it is possible that the interest or maturity value of the bond will not be paid. Generally, United States government bonds have the lowest interest rates because the government has the taxing and money-creating ability to ensure that the interest and maturity value will always be paid. The bonds of private firms, which must convince consumers to buy their products in order to get the revenue to pay interest and principal, are more risky, and their interest rates reflect a risk premium. Some bonds are so risky that the annual interest rates, including the risk premium, are more than 50 percent. Interest rates also vary because they are subject to different treatment by tax laws. Interest earned on bonds issued by state and local governments are not subject to federal income taxes, so their market interest rates are lower as a result.

---

[6] Generally, long-term bonds pay higher interest rates than short-term bonds because the prices of long-term bonds are much more sensitive to changes in the interest rate. If the interest rate doubles, the market value of a 40-year bond will decrease by nearly 50 percent. Thus, even "risk-free" federal government bonds are subject to market risk because even though there is no risk of the holder receiving interest and the maturity value, there is the market risk that interest rates will rise and bond prices will fall. If the bond holder has to sell the bond before maturity he will suffer a capital loss.

Interest rates, as prices, perform a communicative and inducement function in a free market. They communicate information about the relative scarcity of capital to entrepreneurs who are making investment decisions, they communicate information about the rate at which consumers are willing to trade off current consumption for future consumption (time preferences), and they communicate information about the marginal productivity of capital to consumers and investors. The interest rate not only allocates funds to their most productive capital uses in society today, but it also provides valuable information to those who are thinking of conserving resources for the future. If the future price of a resource is expected to be higher than the current price because of future "shortages," investors can make a potential profit by holding resources for future consumption. However, investors must consider the opportunity cost of holding those resources for the future. If the resource were sold today, the funds could be invested in bonds and an interest rate earned. Thus, the profits that an investor can obtain by holding some resource must be compared with the interest rate, which represents the value of that capital in other industries.[7] If the expected annual percentage increase in future prices is greater than the interest rate, then consumption will be postponed for an even greater consumption in the future. From a social welfare viewpoint, society does not want resource conservation to occur if it yields less than the interest rate. If the interest rate is greater than the annual growth rate in the price of the resource, this indicates that future citizens will benefit more from having other goods produced or resources conserved than the one in question.

Let's take a real-world example concerning the "excessive" harvesting of trees, which presumably will denude the forests and leave few trees to future generations. An individual investor who expects a future shortage of trees will also expect that the price of trees will increase relative to other goods. The rational investor will compare the expected rate of return from an investment in a tree farm with alternative investments. If the future tree shortage is estimated to be especially severe, future prices of trees will increase and the rate of return from the tree farm can be expected to be greater than the rate of interest. This means that, based

---

[7] If future prices include the effects of inflation, then the investor will compare the annual percentage gain in prices with the nominal market interest rate. If inflationary premiums are factored out of future prices, then the percentage gain in prices has to be compared with the real interest rate, that is, the market interest rate with inflationary effects extracted.

Since future events are much less certain than present events—that is, they are more risky—an allowance for risk must be included in income calculations. There are many ways of doing this and many assumptions that can be made about the willingness of the investor to assume risks. These are too complicated to explore here.

on the expectations and preferences of members in the current generation, future members of society will benefit more from a tree farm than from other investments whose rates of return do not equal the rate of interest. An interest rate that is higher than the growth in prices of forestry products indicates that other investments, perhaps in coal mines, will yield more benefits to future consumers. If the return on trees is higher than the interest rate, an investor will plant trees today, even though they may not be harvested for 20 or even 50 years. As the trees grow, the value of the tree farm will increase each year, so that even if the investor does not expect to live long enough to see the trees harvested, he can sell stock in the tree farm or sell the forest land for an increasingly higher price. Thus, the private wealth of a tree farm is transferred from one generation of owners to successive generations of owners, with each generation profiting from its decision to let the trees grow. When individuals have private property rights in resources, prices and interest rates tie the future with the present and provide owners both the information and the incentive to allocate resources efficiently over time.

Private farmers also have an incentive to conserve and to protect their resources. If a tree farmer is having trouble with bug infestation he can decide to invest in an eradication program or he can ignore the bugs and let the value of the tree farm decrease. If he ignores the bugs, his current income will be greater and his future income will be lower because the loss of trees will reduce the future value of the land. The farmer cannot escape the future consequences of his private actions today. If the discounted benefits of protecting the farm are greater than the costs, resources will be conserved and protected. The social function of capital markets is to finance investments that provide future benefits to society. Since capital is scarce, we want only those projects that will generate the most highly valued benefits in the future to be undertaken today. The role of capital markets is to bring together those who have excess funds and those who need funds to enlarge the capital base or to conserve resources. The person who provides the funds may not have a direct knowledge of the investment being financed; the savings of a plumber may be financing an office building or a tree farm in another part of the country. The role of the saver is to reduce consumption in order to free resources that can be utilized to conserve resources or to build new capital projects. The concomitant funds are channeled through the capital markets to those investors who are willing to pay the highest rates for the funds. The investors who are able to compete successfully for these funds will be those who have projects with the highest expected rate of return, that is, those who will utilize the resources to produce the most valuable goods in the future.

The private market allocates resources over many time periods by rewarding those who save and conserve today in order to invest in capital projects that will yield returns in the future. The reason the market works well is that individual owners possess exclusive and transferable ownership rights to property so that they or their heirs will bear the costs or benefits of their present stewardship. Thus, there is a tendency for scarce resources to be conserved for future use. There is no similar mechanism connecting future benefits or costs with present benefits or costs in the political market. Unlike private individuals and firms, politicians and political parties are almost exclusively concerned about the votes they will receive in the next election; they cannot trade present votes for future votes the way an entrepreneur can trade present income for future income. Furthermore, voters have little incentive to gather information about future events because there is no payoff in doing so. Instead, they tend to evaluate incumbents by conditions prior to election day. Thus, politicians have an incentive to make conditions look good prior to election, even if the result is a worsening of the budget or the economy at some time in the future. This does not make politicians bad or antisocial individuals. The political market just does not generate the appropriate incentives. Unlike the tree farmer and other entrepreneurs in the private market, politicians are unable to capture the benefits from making decisions that are costly today but yield many benefits in the future. There are many examples. Quantitative limitations on foreign oil imports stimulate the domestic oil industry today but result in a "Drain America First" policy that sets the stage for future oil crises. Budgetary deficits to finance short-term programs directed at special interest groups result in higher interest rates, lower capital investment, and higher taxes in the future.

Frank Knight, an eminent economist at the University of Chicago during the middle of this century, used to say that he could never determine whether critics of the market system disliked it because it didn't work or because it worked too well. He was referring to the market's tendency to provide goods preferred by many individuals but disliked by the critics. But his concern could also be directed at those who criticize the intertemporal allocation of resources. Perhaps consumers want to consume "too much" during current time periods and leave "too little" for future consumers. This does not mean that the market system is not working; it is reflecting the values of those consumers who prefer current consumption to future consumption for themselves or their heirs. Private market critics disagree with the preferences of these consumers and believe that *fewer resources should be consumed* in the present and *more should be saved* for the future. They believe that the role of government is to regulate or to displace the collective judgment of millions of individuals who comprise the market. It is not clear, however, why the critics think that in the private market—where there are incentives to make correct decisions—citizens will make wrong decisions and that in the political market—where there are no selective incentives to conserve resources—they will make socially correct decisions. They forget that the individual who is overfishing, "overusing" gas and electricity, and throwing away bottles and cans is the same individual who will be voting on government conservation policies.

The private market does not work perfectly. Private market supporters stress market incentives to conserve resources but often neglect the frictions and imperfections that exist in the marketplace. Interest rates are affected by monetary and fiscal policies and by flows of foreign funds, so they reflect more than individual preferences for present and future consumption. Corporate executives are moved from job to job so frequently that they seldom have personal incentives to "take the long-run view" and they seldom benefit from making decisions that will benefit the corporation in the future.[8]

Individuals may have short-term horizons because they ignore the longer-term effects of their private decisions; it stands to reason that these same individuals have short-term horizons in their political decision making. Some individuals not satisfied with the intertemporal allocation of goods in the private market may want to make corrective decisions in the political market. Their efforts, however, are likely to produce political market burden shifting, similar to those discussed in chapters 5 and 6. Some individuals may not voluntarily restrict their present consumption in order to conserve certain resources for future generations, nor may they be willing to save to make such investments possible. However, since they do place some positive value on conserving future resources, they can vote to conserve resources while placing the current costs on others.

Assume that a conservationist places a marginal value on preserving wild wolves in Montana and is not a consumer of sheep or sheep products. Ranchers, on the other hand, are assumed to place no value on conserving wolves. No one owns the wolves to protect and conserve them, so if the wolves are killing privately owned sheep, ranchers have an

---

[8] Some large corporations have instituted stock options, which give at least the senior officers who receive them an incentive to consider future benefits when making their decisions. A senior corporate officer could maintain or sell her option rights in the firm, independent of her decision to maintain or to change her managerial position. Thus, if the corporate officer made a decision to allocate resources, say to the research department, that would produce hefty profits in the future, the price of the corporation's stock would reflect this future profit potential. Upon her retirement, or even at a later date, the officer could sell her options and be rewarded for making the correct decision.

incentive to kill the wolves. Conservationists may react by criticizing the farmers and lobbying the legislature to pass laws prohibiting the killing of wolves. Conservationists will want to have the wolf herd protected until the value of the marginal wolf to them is zero. This is a classic example of some group seeking to obtain benefits for themselves but placing the costs on others, in this case on farmers and consumers of sheep products. Compared with the Pareto optimal quantity of wolves, the legislation desired by the conservationists will result in too many wolves living in the future and too few sheep and sheep products.[9]

One policy decision the government can make to assist intertemporal allocation of resources is to define and enforce property rights, where feasible, in those resources that are becoming extinct. Where such assignments are too costly to define or maintain, such as the saltwater fisheries, the government might place restrictions on access to the resource and auction off these limited rights to the highest bidder. If an auction were deemed to be undesirable for some reason, the resources might be given away to certain groups or individuals who would then have a stake in their wise conservation. The Homestead Act of the last century is one example. Zimbabwe and Botswana have given rights to kill a certain number of elephants each year to local villages. These villages, in turn, sell these rights to individual hunters for as much as $25,000. Part of the proceeds of ivory and hides from elephants are returned to the local villages. Thus, the villages have a stake in protecting the herd so they can continue to earn these fees. As a result, the elephant herd has nearly doubled in these two countries during the past decade, while it has plummeted from 65,000 to less than 20,000 in Kenya, where local villages and farmers receive no personal benefits from protecting and conserving the elephants.[10] Prohibition of trade in ivory and elephant hides has not produced the desired results in central Africa, but making the elephants valuable to rural villages in southern Africa seems to have worked.

---

[9] We must also recognize that farmers do not consider the positive externalities generated by live wolves. Thus, they will kill wolves until their marginal cost of killing them equals the expected gains in fewer dead sheep. There will now be more wolves killed than is Pareto optimal. If the conservationists have their way, there will be too many sheep and too few wolves. Optimality could be obtained by having the conservationists bribe the farmers to quit killing some wolves and to suffer some sheep losses. The optimal quantity would be where the marginal dollar loss from the damage on sheep wrought by the marginal wolf equaled the value placed on the marginal wolf by the conservationists. However, the protection of wolves would be a public good for individuals with such conservationist preferences, and the free rider problem would become operable. Conservationists would have no incentive to reveal their preferences and to be taxed accordingly.

[10] See Randy T. Simmons and Hurs P. Kreuter, Fall (1989) issue of *Policy Review* for more information on the comparative practices of conserving elephants in central and southern Africa.

A last resort of government should be to tax, subsidize, or regulate resource usage or extraction, but there are cases, such as highly migratory species or air pollution, where such action may be necessary. But, as stressed throughout this book, the political market is composed of individual politicians, bureaucrats, and voters. There is no reason to assume that individuals who apparently prefer present consumption to future consumption in the private market will necessarily prefer future consumption to present consumption when making decisions in the political market. They are the same individuals.

Questions and Answers

THE QUESTIONS

1. If Bank A says that it will pay an interest rate of 8 percent on your $1,000 deposit and Bank B says it will pay 6 percent, what is the nominal difference in the income you would earn after three years? Assume the banks compound annually.

2. If you borrowed $1,000 today at an interest rate of 8 percent, what amount would you have to pay the bank in three years?

3. If the bank paid an interest rate of 6 percent to you when you deposited your money and then charged 8 percent to borrowers, what would be the gross profit of the bank out of which it had to pay for bookkeeping, overhead, etc.?

4. Assume that you want to borrow $1,000 for three years and every bank in town charges an interest rate of 8 percent. Your rich uncle visits town and tells you that he will lend money to you at a 6-percent interest rate. What is the net value of his loan to you? If he offered to give you $60 today or the low-interest loan, which would you take?

5. Assume that the federal government offers a student a low-interest loan (4 percent) to finance a college education. The maximum amount of the loan is $10,000, and the market interest rate is 9 percent. Assume that the student can borrow the full amount of the loan on the first day of school and that the principal plus interest must be paid back six years later. Also assume that the interest rate the student has to pay on non-government loans and the interest she receives on deposits is the same 9 percent.

    a. Should the student borrow the money? Why?

    b. If the proceeds of the loan can be applied only to tuition and fees, can one conclude that the federal loan program increases educational opportunities?

    c. What is the present value of the government "gift" to the student or her parents?

d. If you were that student would you rather have the government give you an outright gift of $1,500 or the low-interest loan?

6. Assume you and your friends have grown tired of eating beans and hot dogs every night and you decide to start a business putting designs on T-shirts. You visit a firm that sells the machines that make the T-shirts, and after considering the data shown by the salesman you agree that the machine would generate about $1,000 in profits to you each year for the next 20 years. The machine costs $10,000.

a. The salesman says that at a 5-percent interest (or discount) rate the present value of the future profits produced by the machine is _____ (you provide the amount), so the machine is a bargain.

b. One of your friends, a conservative accounting student, points out that the market rate of interest is closer to 10 percent and that the present value of the future earnings for 20 years is only _____ (you provide the amount), so the machine is not a bargain.

c. Why do think the salesman used a low rate of interest in calculating the present value of the benefits provided by the machine?

d. What are some questions you would like to have answered before making your decision on any *profit-seeking* seller's proposal about future benefits?

e. Do you think most buyers have an incentive to ask those questions? Why?

7. Assume that you read in the newspaper that Bluepeace, a *nonprofit* environmental organization, has just completed a study that shows that $10,000 invested in preserving the wetlands today will yield a total of $12,462 of benefits over the next 20 years.

a. What discount rate did Bluepeace use in its study?

b. Why do you think it used that rate?

c. What are some questions you would like to have answered before making your decision on the Bluepeace proposal? Why?

d. Do you think most voters/contributors would ask those questions and attempt to find the answers? Why?

8. Assume that you read in the newspaper that the Pleasant Valley River District (PVRD), a *government agency,* has just completed a study that shows that $10,000 invested in a dam today will yield a total of $12,462 of flood-control benefits over the next 20 years.

a. What discount rate did PVRD use in its study?

b. Why do you think it used that rate?

c. What are some questions you would like to have answered before making your decision on PVRD's proposal? Why?

d. Do you think most voters would ask those questions and attempt to find the answers? Why?

9. Separate the two crucial issues and analyses implied in the following statement: Current generations are cutting too many trees today and not enough will be available for future generations.

THE ANSWERS

1. Bank A: $1,000 × 1.08³ = $1,260
Bank B: $1,000 × 1.06³ = $1,191
Net Difference $ 69

2. $1,260

3. $69

4. Did you say the value of your uncle's loan was $69. Tsk! Tsk! Did you say you would rather have the low-interest loan than the $60? Tsk! Tsk! Tsk! You were comparing the value of $69 saved over three years with the $60 gift received today. You were comparing apples ($69 received in the future) and oranges ($60 received today). You can make the proper comparison through either one of the following methods:

a. Your uncle's low-interest loan would save you $20 each year for three years. Assuming you could earn 6 percent on your money, the present value of this "income" stream to you today would be:

$$\$53.46 = (\$20 / 1.06) + [\$20 / (1.06)^2] + [\$20 / (1.06)^3]$$

This means that your uncle's low-interest loan would be worth $53.46 to you *today*, which would be less than the value of the cash gift of $60 *today*. Another way of saying this is that the present value of the low-interest loan would be less than the present value of the cash gift.

b. If your uncle gave you a $60 gift today, you could earn 6-percent interest on it each year for three years, or:

$$\$71.46 = \$60(1.06)^3$$

This means that at the end of three years your uncle's low-interest loan would have saved you a nominal $69, but his cash gift of $60 would be worth a nominal $71.46 at the end of the three years. Another way of saying this is that the future value of the low-interest loan would be worth less than the future value of the cash gift.

5. **a.** Certainly! The government is giving the student, or her parents, a very valuable gift, and she should borrow the money even if she does not "need" it. She can take the money and reduce her other debts, she can lend out the money and earn a net 5 percent on it, or she can spend the money on clothes or computer games if current consumption is more valuable to her than future consumption. If she put the money in a certificate of deposit earning 9 percent, she would earn $500 per year on the interest rate differential.

b. Only a few students receiving loans would not attend college if the low-rate loans were not available. The low-interest loan will affect the college decisions of only those who would not attend college if they had to borrow $10,000 at 9 percent but would attend if they could borrow $10,000 at 4 percent. The educational opportunities of these students would be increased. But other students who would attend college without the subsidized interest rates can also borrow the money. In effect, they receive a "gift" from the government (the value of which is calculated in the answer to 5. c.) that does not affect their educational decisions or opportunities.

c. The student can earn a net $500 [$10,000(.09 − .04)] on the loan each year. Over five years she can earn $2,500, but the reader should recognize that the real value of this income is the present value of $500 each year for the next five years. This is equal to $2,165 ($500 $\{[1 − (1.05)^{-5}] / .05\}$).[11] Thus, the government is providing the student with a gift worth $2,165.

d. Of course, you would rather have that loan, with a present value of $2,165, than $1,500.

6. a. If the machine earns $1,000 a year for 20 years and the discount rate is 5 percent, the present value of its future earnings is:

$$\$12,462 = \$1,000\{[1 − (1.05)^{-20}] / .05\}$$

b. If the machine earns $1,000 a year for 20 years and the discount rate is 10 percent, the present value of its future earnings is:

$$\$8,514 = \$1,000\{[1 − (1.1)^{-20}] / .1\}$$

c. He wanted to show that the present value of the revenue stream produced by the machine was high. He wanted to sell the machine to you and earn a commission and/or to impress his boss.

d. What rate of discount did he use in determining the present value of a stream of future revenue? What methodology did he use in calculating future costs and benefits?

e. Yes, if they didn't ask the appropriate questions, they could lose money. They have a profit-maximizing selective incentive in asking the questions.

7. a. 5 percent.

b. To convince citizens of the value of the project, to maximize their affirmative votes and possibly to enlarge the Bluepeace bureaucracy.

---

[11] This present value formula is the same as ($500 / 1.05) + [$500 / (1.05)^2] + [$500 / (1.05)^3] + [$500 / (1.05)^4] + [$500 / (1.05)^5].

    c.   What rate of discount did Bluepeace use in determining the present value of a stream of future revenue? What methodology did it use in calculating future costs and benefits?

    d.   The questions might fly through their minds, but they would have no selective incentive in asking the questions because of the free rider and rational ignorance problems discussed in chapter 5.

8.   You should have the gist of the this series of questions now.

9.   Trees apparently produce both private and public goods. They produce lumber and wood products, which can be sold to current and future generations through the private market price mechanism. If private market ownership and the price mechanism are utilized, there is a incentive to cut the correct quantity of trees today. Future "shortages" of trees will mean high prices for wood products and high prices for future trees. Hence, new trees will be planted and certain hardwood trees, which require decades to mature, will have greater value to current generations if they are *not* cut.

    However, trees apparently produce such public goods as generating oxygen, cleaning the air, and regulating global temperatures. To the extent these statements reflect reality about public good impacts, the private market cannot provide for the socially efficient allocation of trees among the generations, and some government subsidies, taxes, or regulations may be more efficient.

CHAPTER TWELVE

RENT SEEKING

A reg'lar pollytician can't give away an alley without blushin', but a businessman who is in pollytics jus' to see that th' civil sarvice law gets thurly enfoorced, will give Lincoln Park an' th' public libr'y to th' beef thrust, charge an admission price to th' lakefront an' make it a felony f'r annywan to buy stove polish outside iv his store, an' have it all put down to public improvemints with a pitcher iv him in the cornerstore.
—MR. DOOLEY (FINLEY PETER DUNNE), 1902

DEFINITIONS OF RENT

To most people the term "rent" means the exorbitant payments made to owners of apartment or office complexes. However, economists, who seemingly excel in obfuscating the obvious, have used the term "rent" in many different ways since the middle of the nineteenth century. Traditionally, economists have used the term *economic rent* to indicate the amount paid for the use of land or other nonreproducible resources that are in fixed supply. Unlike wages, interest, and profits, payments for land perform no incentive function because the supply of land does not respond to changes in price. A high demand for raw land will result in a high price —called rent—while a low demand will result in a low price, or rent. High prices for land increase the welfare of landsellers while decreasing the welfare of land buyers, but they do not bring forth an increased supply of land. During the latter part of the nineteenth century the single tax movement, spurred by Henry George's *Progress and Poverty* (1879), proposed that economic rent earned on land sales could be taxed completely without impairing the available supply of land or the productive potential of the economy.[1]

At the beginning of this century the concept of rent was extended much beyond land rent and was applied to nonreproducible assets such

---

[1] Market prices for land have no affect on the supply of raw land. However, land prices do have an allocative function by distributing land to those who can put it to its most productive uses.

as natural resources, unique skills, paintings by dead artists, and even to resources or goods (strawberries is a favorite example) that were fixed in supply during the short run. Since the supply of the resource was fixed, the price received by the resource owner was determined by the demand for the resource. When OPEC drove the price of oil from $3 per barrel to $10 per barrel to $40 per barrel between 1973 and 1983, those who owned land that had easily accessible crude oil found that the price of their land was driven up, and they earned considerable amounts of economic rent. Similarly, Rudolf Nureyev, Madonna, Paul McCartney, Jascha Heifetz, and Terry Bradshaw have earned economic rent because of their nonreproducible skills.

Around the middle of this century economists began referring to monopoly profits as "monopoly rents" because they served no productive purpose; they represented wealth transfers from consumers to monopolists, and they could be taxed without impairing the efficiency of the economy. These definitions of rent, however, are not the subject of this section. Economists have now further extended the general concept of rent to rent-seeking activities. Economic rent now refers to a higher return, income, or receipt that cannot be reduced or eliminated by the normal competitive factors in the economy. Short-run rents can readily exist in any industry, because it takes time for other firms to enter an industry and adapt to a new market or productive process. However, economists are particularly concerned about economic rent earned in the long run because of barriers to entry in an industry. The most persistent and pervasive entry barriers are those created by government that exclude or reduce competition. Thus, government is a major source of economic rent, and those who attempt to use government to obtain such rents are called rent seekers.

SOCIALLY GOOD AND SOCIALLY BAD RENT SEEKING

During the seventies, public choice economists began analyzing the ability of some individuals, whom they called *rent seekers*, to use government legislation and regulations to transfer wealth (rent) to themselves. Before discussing the economic misallocations caused by certain types of rent seekers, it is necessary to understand that all individuals are potential rent seekers and that all rent seeking is not inefficient and socially undesirable.

All entrepreneurs are rent seekers, and they move their resources into those industries where rents appear to be highest. An entrepreneur who produces a new service or commodity or builds a better tool or machine hopes to earn some economic rent before other firms offering a similar product enter the market and compete with his product. The prospect of earning economic rent motivates such entrepreneurial activity and is responsible for much of the wealth-creating activity in a private economy. But such rents are short lived. As long as an industry is competitive, producers are unable to earn rent in the long run because new firms and resources enter the industry and drive prices down. Consumers benefit from this rent-seeking activity because they have a variety of new products at competitive prices. Although rents cannot exist in a long-run competitive environment, the possibilities of earning rent in the short run motivates entrepreneurs to produce new products that provide many social benefits. Such wealth-creating rent seeking activity is socially desirable.

When economists talk about rent seeking, they are not referring to the socially good rent-seeking activity that occurs in a competitive environment. Rather, they are referring to the socially bad rent seeking that occurs when government restricts competition, erects entry barriers, or grants special privileges to certain segments of society and not to others. Suppose that an entrepreneur lobbies to enact legislation that makes his firm the sole provider of some good. This rent-seeking action by the entrepreneur adds no wealth to society but instead produces a government-sanctioned monopoly, which means that fewer units are produced at higher prices. The benefits of competitively low prices are diverted to the profits of the government-created monopolist. The social "bad" of this rent-seeking activity, however, is not the higher price of the monopoly good, because this is a transfer (which is the rent) from some members of society (consumers) to other members of society (producers). Nor does the bad rent seeking create the lower monopoly output, because such resource misallocation is a characteristic of all monopolies and is represented by what economists call "deadweight welfare loss." Rather, the social waste produced by this bad type of rent seeking is the use of resources to obtain, promote, and retain this monopoly position. The social bad of rent seeking is not the rent, which once again is merely a transfer from consumers to the monopolist; it is the resources utilized in "chasing" or trying to obtain the rent. The rent-seeking monopolist has to utilize resources such as lobbyists, lawyers, accountants, press agents, and maybe even an economist or two to convince government to grant the monopoly to him. The monopolist pays these individuals because, if successful, they produce a valuable right for him. The nation's resources are withdrawn from productive activity and put to rent-seeking activity by the monopolist because he is willing to pay a higher price. The monopolist gains a monopoly right, but citizens lose because the resources, which could have been producing real goods and services, are used to chase rents. In this case rent-seeking activity produces not wealth creation but wealth destruction.

A useful analogy that illustrates the impact of bad rent seeking on society is theft. Why is theft a social evil? It merely involves a transfer of wealth from the victim to the thief, and the total welfare of society, which includes the thief as well as the victim, remains the same. Does this mean that stealing involves no social waste? The answer is no, because an increase in theft induces individuals to install more burglar alarms, locks, and window bars, to purchase firearms, and to employ private and public police forces to prevent theft. This is a waste of resources that, in the absence of stealing, could be used to produce other goods and services. Successful stealing also induces other individuals to enter this "profession" rather than socially productive occupations. The opportunity costs of the resources used in committing and preventing theft constitute the social costs of theft. Similarly, the opportunity costs of most resources used to procure special benefit legislation from government constitute the social costs of rent seeking. Both rent seeking and theft lead to a social waste of resources.

Rent Seeking Adds a Third Dimension to Monopoly Analysis

Rent seeking adds a third dimension to the analysis of monopoly power presented in chapter 3. Monopolies produce higher product prices, which transfers wealth from customers to monopolists; they distort resources by producing less than the social optimal of the monopolized good; and they use resources in their rent-seeking endeavors to obtain and maintain their monopoly position. But the most serious resource waste is probably not generated by the firm that obtains the monopoly right but by those who don't.

Assume that the government decided to grant monopoly rights to only one among ten competing sellers and that the firm that received the monopoly right would obtain $10 million in monopoly profits. At the very extreme, the maximum amount each firm would want to spend to get the monopoly right would be $10 million. However, each firm would have to possess certain knowledge that if it spent that much money on procuring the monopoly it would, indeed, get the monopoly right. No firm could reach such a conclusion, because it would have to consider the real probability that one of the other firms might be selected. Hence, each firm would have to make some subjective probability estimate of obtaining the monopoly right. If each firm reasoned that it had the same chance of obtaining the monopoly right as each of the other nine firms, then each firm's expected value from the monopoly right would be $10,000,000 × $\frac{1}{10}$, or $1 million. Hence, each firm competing for this right would spend up to $1 million in lobbying and public relations efforts, technical studies, and legal arguments to procure the monopoly right. A total of $10 million would be spent on rent-seeking activities by all firms. Of course, the amount could be greater than or less than $10 million if the firms thought their chances of getting the monopoly right were different than one in ten. Since business executives are generally optimistic, each firm might believe that it had a one-in-five chance of obtaining the monopoly right, in which case each firm would be willing to spend $2 million in rent-seeking activities. The firm that got the right would reap a net $8 million monopoly profit, consumers would pay an additional $10 million because of the monopoly pricing, there would be a consumer loss resulting from the reduced output of the monopoly product, *and* there would be a rent-seeking waste of resources equal to $20 million. The rent-seeking loss to society could be greater than the monopoly profits or the deadweight loss resulting from the monopoly output. Until the advent of rent-seeking analysis, economists were underestimating the social costs of government-created monopolies because they ignored the social waste of rent-seeking efforts by all firms competing for the monopoly power.

Whether the natural propensity of individuals to seek rents is socially useful or socially wasteful depends upon the moral, legal, and social constraints in society. When the power of government is constrained by the constitution, custom, or morality, the benefits from socially bad rent seeking are limited. When individuals know that they are unable to lobby government to obtain special benefits for themselves or their industry, they waste fewer resources in attempts to do so. Similarly, there is no need to have counterlobbying groups that oppose those seeking special benefits for themselves. However, when government is not so constrained—and it normally provides benefits to some firms, local governments, universities, industries, or individuals but not to others—a significant proportion of the country's resources are allocated to rent seeking. Resources that would otherwise be used to produce goods and services are channeled into nonproductive rent-seeking and rent-protecting activities. Lobbyists, lawyers, accountants, economists, public relations experts, reporters, political scientists, sociologists, and others involved in political persuasion expand in number and influence, while engineers, physical scientists, craftsmen, assembly line workers, mechanics, machine operators, and others involved in the production of goods and services decline. If government's role in the economy is restricted to protecting individual rights, enforcing contracts, and providing a minimum of public goods, rent-seeking activity is not entirely absent but it is insignificant.[2] As government grows in size and as it increases its interferences in the private market, rent-seeking activity continues to grow at least as rapidly. Many firms now find it more profitable to switch from pursuing wealth-creating activities to pursuing rent-seeking activities. Resources that are used to capture these rents yield a valuable return to those seeking the rent but reflect a social waste for all other citizens.

The analysis has been framed in terms of the government granting monopoly rights, and the reader may wonder whether this analysis has real-world relevance. After all, doesn't the United States government enforce antitrust laws to prevent monopolies. Yes, it does with various degrees of enthusiasm and success. But both the federal and state governments create various degrees of monopoly power through legislation, which, of course, is never called "monopoly creating." Examples of government activities that stimulate rent-seeking behavior are licenses, permits, regulations, tariffs and other import restrictions, and race and sex quotas. Regardless of whether or not these government activities are socially justified by other criteria, they generate rent-seeking activities and a waste of resources. This rent-seeking activity is one important reason, though certainly not the only one, for the much discussed rise in the service sector and the decline in domestic manufacturing. Legal, lobbying, public relations, accounting, and economic professionals have populated service firms and organizations seeking rents in Washington (the beltway bandits) and state capitols, leaving fewer individuals producing real goods and services.

Rent Seeking Caused by the FCC

One illustrative example of the type of rent-seeking activity that can be generated when government creates monopoly power is the granting of licenses in cellular telephone markets. Cellular technology was available for many years, but the Federal Communications Commission did not know how to allocate the rights to cellular markets among the many possible competitors. When it did announce during the latter 1970s that

---

[2] Rent-seeking behavior exists in any society in which governments provide public goods or in which a bureaucracy exists to manage government programs. However, the smaller the extent of government activities, the smaller the relative role of rent-seeking activities. Be sure to read the questions at the end of this chapter for some further examples.

it was taking applications for cellular licenses in the top metropolitan markets, it also announced that for various reasons only two operators were to be allowed to provide cellular services in each metropolitan area: one telephone company and one nontelephone company. Since it was widely believed that cellular service would be quite profitable with such limited entry, the FCC was confronted with the problem of selecting cellular providers from among many applicants. Initially, the FCC said that it would make a selection among the competitors upon the basis of an evaluation—using several public interest criteria—of each applicant's proposal. Based on the theory of rent seeking just discussed and knowing nothing else about the cellular market, we would expect firms to hire attorneys to counsel them on the proper form of their proposals and to represent them before the FCC, to hire marketing experts to take surveys, to hire financial, economic, and accounting experts to juggle the numbers, to hire graphic experts to render attractive graphs and drawings, and to hire journalists to write the appropriate bureaucratese.

This is exactly what happened. Applicants sought out every technical, legal, marketing, and financial advantage imaginable, and they made promises in their applications to the FCC that were impossible to fulfill or to enforce after the licenses were granted. The result was that the FCC was literally inundated with *rooms* full of applications. Several applications were submitted for a single market that were more than 4-feet thick. After putting up a good bureaucratic front and using such phrases as a "socially beneficial cellular coverage plan" in making its first awards, the FCC had to confess that it was unable to make rational selections from among the many applicants and that it would use a lottery system to select those who would be awarded franchises. During the approximately two years that the FCC was using its "socially desirable" criteria an entire new industry of rent-seeking cellular consultants and attorneys emerged. These resources, costing many millions of dollars, were engaged in valuable work for their clients, but they were essentially unproductive from a social viewpoint.[3]

---

[3] The author was one of those engaged in such work for several clients. One benefit of economics training is the quick realization that, although one might believe such laws are harmful to the economy, the free rider analysis (see chapter 5) teaches us that our own refusal to work within the environment produced by such laws is not going to change them. What does remain a mystery is why economists, who often benefit personally from such legislation, continue to attack the legislation in their lectures and writings. One seldom hears attorneys calling for fewer and less complicated laws or accountants criticizing more time-consuming audits. Perhaps the answer is to be found in the fact that the economics profession is largely driven by academic economists who remain untainted by such real-world experiences.

OTHER EXAMPLES OF RENT SEEKING

There are numerous examples of rent-seeking activities. Trunk line airlines devoted considerable resources to maintain government control and limited entry in the airline industry for 40 years; major interstate trucking companies fought to get the same benefits for themselves. The maritime industry probably has more lobbyists, public relations experts, and attorneys working in Washington than it has sailors on the high seas. These rent-protecting resources work hard to maintain the Jones Act requirement that domestic coastal shipping and all shipments of North Slope oil be made on high-priced American-flag vessels and that the federal government continue its subsidies for the operation, maintenance, and construction of American-flag vessels. Various agricultural interests have extensive rent-seeking outposts in all state capitols and especially in Washington to protect agricultural subsidies and acreage restrictions. American sugar producers, whose costs of production are about three times higher than in many Caribbean countries, have a coterie of lobbyists attempting to sweeten the subsidies and import restrictions on sugar.[4] Various occupational groups, ranging from medical doctors to chiropractors to pharmacists, teachers, mechanics, barbers, and beauticians, have agents representing their interests in protecting Americans from low-priced "quacks" and prohibiting or discouraging their entry into the industry.

Most states require that "any person who shaves and trims the beard; cuts, trims, shampoos dresses, tints, bleaches, colors, relaxes, arranges, or styles the hair . . . " be licensed by the Board of Barber Examiners and be a practicing barber.[5] Applicants for a barber license must have completed high school, completed an accredited barber school, and passed a daylong written and practical examination. All applicants must have successfully completed 1,500 hours of instruction in a licensed barber college during nine consecutive months of full-time instruction.[6] No part of a barber shop can be connected to a residence. Cosmetologists and

---

[4] The nation's 10,000 sugar farms received an average of about $140,000 per farm in 1987, but most of this was absorbed in higher operating costs.

[5] This and the following examples are required by law or regulations in the state of Louisiana, but they are typical of most state regulations.

[6] Those who sit on the various regulatory commissions claim that regulations requiring barbers or members of other occupations to obtain training and education are designed to protect the public welfare from uneducated and inexperienced practitioners. Economists who have done empirical research have generally found no difference between the quality of services of those who met the regulations and those who did not. However, to the extent that such restrictions do improve the quality of services, part of their resource costs would have to be subtracted from the rent-seeking losses.

beauticians have similar requirements. Hearing aid dealers, horticulturists, plumbers, shorthand reporters, securities agents and brokers, landscape architects, music, art, and dance therapists, race horse trainers, radio and television repair persons, social workers, and nursing home administrators must successfully pass an exam administered by a commission or board controlled by current practitioners in these occupations. A pest control operator must pass a four-part examination and have four years of experience or a degree in entomology. A tree surgeon must have a college degree and pass an examination administered by the Horticulture Commission.

Bankers have representatives working feverishly to enact legislation that would protect their industry from the unprincipled intrusions of nonbanks onto their turf while enabling them to invade the securities and investment industries. All major universities have gaggles of employees in Washington to (1) enlarge the education and research trough and (2) ensure that their employers are first in line at feeding time. Local and state governments hire lobbyists and engage in extensive "planning" to obtain funds from the federal government. Given the opportunity, we would all be rent seekers. Where or when such opportunity exists, we should not be surprised that the economy allocates its scarce resources accordingly.

CONCLUSIONS

Traditional tax analyses focus on the extent to which a tax induces individuals to change their behavior with respect to the good taxed. An excise tax on electric pencil sharpeners would induce individuals to change the quantity of electric pencil sharpeners purchased. This would result in a loss of welfare, because the excise tax would produce a wedge between the marginal cost and price, thus artificially restricting the quantity provided. However, an additional social loss caused by rent seeking would occur as individuals, firms, and industries allocated resources to avoid taxation of their goods by government. They would hire lobbyists, lawyers, economists, and accountants to convince government that taxation would produce social bads and result in a loss of votes.[7]

Most rent-seeking activity has been associated with government, but it can and does exist within a corporate bureaucracy as well. Corporate executives whose departments are shielded from competitive rigors have incentives to develop procedures that magnify their own power and

---

[7] For those students with a bit more economic education: the more price inelastic—or unresponsive to price—the supply of the good being taxed, the greater the incentive to allocate rent-seeking resources to avoid this taxation.

increase rent-seeking activities both inside and outside the corporation. Purchasing agents, for example, may be influenced by lavish gifts, dinners, and trips; corporate lawyers or accountants may design internal controls that serve their own goals rather than the stockholders'. But the most serious rent seeking is caused by government, because only government has the power to create and enforce monopoly powers and to create and finance a system of special privileges without the possibility of competition eroding the values of these monopoly powers or special privileges.

Some of the economic literature implies that rent-seeking waste could be eliminated simply by restricting the size of government and its interferences in the economy. Undoubtedly, government's influence could be reduced from current levels, but a larger population, more pollution and other externalities, increased mobility, and national and international interdependencies mean that the federal government will remain a significant factor in the economy. Hence, it is very important that we recognize this fact and develop rules and institutions that will minimize rent-seeking activity. For example, if there are valid technical reasons for government to grant monopoly rights, then it should first consider auctioning off these valuable rights to the highest qualified bidders. Taxpayers would recoup some or all of the monopoly rents, and rent-seeking social wastes would be avoided. The FCC, for example, could have auctioned off the rights to the cellular markets, but this alternative was not seriously considered. Another, but less desirable, method of allocating monopoly rights is to use a lottery, which the FCC used in allocating cellular licenses. The disadvantage of the lottery is that it does not allocate the right to those who can make the most efficient use of it. Both the auction and the lottery would be resisted by bureaucrats because their adoption would decrease the power and the size of the bureaucracy.

QUESTIONS AND ANSWERS

THE QUESTIONS

1. Firms waste the nation's resources by engaging in rent-seeking activities in order to procure favorable treatment from government. Do you believe that it would be more efficient to have government bureaucrats simply allocate monopoly rights to those firms that pay the highest bribe to bureaucrats instead of wasting perfectly good resources to produce bureaucratic mumbo-jumbo? Why?

2. If you wanted to maximize the standard of living in your country, which of the following would you institute if you were dictator? Your answers should relate to the rent-seeking discussion above.

a. A strong centralized government or a strong decentralized federal government? Why?

b. A large centralized government that exercised detailed control over the economy or a centralized government that left most economic decisions to the private market? Why?

c. Trial by judge or trial by jury for determining innocence or guilt of those accused of violating monopoly rights granted by the government?

3. Why did the Industrial Revolution come first to Great Britain, and why did the United States economy perform so well between 1900 and 1929?

4. If you owned a set of apartments on or near the California coast, would you have an incentive to expend rent-seeking resources to establish a Coastal Commission that would restrict the "unbridled development" of the California coastlands? Why?

5. During the latter seventies and early eighties several cable companies competed for cable franchises in major cities. Many city councils awarded the franchises on the basis of the number of public service broadcasts the company would make. Were rent-seeking activities encouraged by such activities?

6. "All lawyers are rent seekers." Comment!

7. Assume that your professor gives difficult questions on the exams, asks "impossible" questions of students during class, and assigns 50-page term papers.

a. Is this professor encouraging rent-seeking activity among students?

b. Is the professor encouraging rent-seeking activities if she says that only the top 10 percent of the students will receive A's?

c. Is the professor encouraging wasteful rent-seeking activities if she says that only those students who help with her yard work at home will receive A's?

d. When this author was an undergraduate student, a certain management professor was widely known to assign grades based on the thickness of reports submitted by students. Whether he actually graded on this basis or not, it certainly appeared as though he did, and students stuffed their reports with pages of pictures and magazine clippings they had not even read. If the professor did use thickness as his criterion in determining grades, was he encouraging wasteful rent-seeking activity?

e. You go to see your professor during his office hours and he is not there. You come back the next day and he is not there. You ask him after class when he is going to be in his office. He answers that he is working on a particularly difficult mathematical model describing the reaction of a common housefly to a reduction in its real wealth in a perfectly competitive environment. He states that he cannot be bothered by students asking elementary questions while he is engaged in such important research. You scratch your head and ask the professor why the work is so important; who will read the results of the study? The professor answers that other professors engaged in similar research will read his paper and that his reputation and salary from the university will be enhanced if he publishes the paper. Is this professor engaged in wasteful rent-seeking activity?

THE ANSWERS

1. A bribe is only a transfer from the "briber" to the "bribee" and involves no waste of the nation's resources. Hence, it may appear logical to have firms bribe government decision makers rather than waste real resources. However, if government bureaucrats could become rich by capturing the monopoly rents for themselves, then individuals would very quickly utilize resources to become qualified bureaucrats. This happened among the mandarins of ancient China and is happening among the bureaucrats of many third world countries today. If the number of firms or licenses in the marketplace have to be restricted by governments for technical (such as cellular licenses) or conservational (such as commercial fishing licenses) reasons, the government could auction off the rights to those willing and able to pay the highest price with the proceeds going to the Treasury.

2. **a.** A strong centralized government could award rights or special privileges to national monopolies. Hence, there would be strong incentives to allocate rent-seeking resources to obtain such attractive monopoly rights. A decentralized system of government would have many competing local and state governments, which would make it more difficult to establish monopolies. Thus, rent-seeking activities would be less.

b. The more decisions made by government, the greater the incentives for firms and individuals to use rent-seeking resources to obtain favorable decisions. A limited government and the existence of competitive firms is the best way to minimize the granting of monopoly privileges and the rent-seeking activities they generate.

c. Many, if not most, monopoly rights granted by government produce higher consumer prices, so a jury would be unlikely to convict those who violated monopoly rights. For example, before the modern era of deregulation, which began in the early 1970s, the Civil Aviation Board tightly regulated the airline industry and did not license a new major trunk line airline for more than 20 years. One result was that airline passengers had to pay high prices. If an airline meeting the FAA's safety standards operated without a CAB license and charged lower fares than licensed airlines, it is unlikely that a jury would have convicted the airline for violating such anticompetitive laws. Similarly, a jury would unlikely find an independent trucker guilty of charging illegal low rates and breaking into the Interstate Commerce Commission–sanctioned trucking monopolies. In fact, most such anticompetitive laws are not enforced by prosecuting the violators, because the defendants can always request a jury trial. Generally, the prosecutor's office requests a judge to issue an injunction, which orders the "offender" to obey the law and cease the illegal activity in the controlled industry. If the offender does not obey the order, he must appear before the judge who issued the injunction. Though not the only reason for injunctions, the federal and state agencies that enforce such laws know that it is difficult to get a guilty verdict from a jury, so they seek judicial orders.

3. There are many possible reasons for the Industrial Revolution, most of which have nothing to do with rent seeking. On the other hand, the absence of rent-seeking incentives in Britain at the time may provide one plausible explanation for industrial and economic growth. A nation that devotes a considerable part of its resources to chasing rents is unlikely to stimulate the thoughts and efforts of creative individuals and risk-taking entrepreneurs. Rather than creating new manufacturing processes and products, these talented and hard-working individuals directed their energies towards obtaining the privileges dispensed by the king, government, or aristocracy. The British governments of the seventeenth and eighteenth centuries encouraged rent-seeking activities for *government* posts, most of which could be purchased from government officials or Parliament, but governments interfered relatively little with the private sector. Also, during the seventeenth and eighteenth centuries trial by jury limited the abilities of government monopolies to operate without competition from interlopers. Because rent-seeking opportunities were not available for most nonaristocrats, they directed their energies and skills to innovation, invention, and entrepreneurship.

The United States benefitted from the wisdom of Adam Smith, jury trials, enterprising immigrants, and the Victorian ethic, which also limited government activities and rent-seeking attempts. With the exception of the railroads, most nineteenth- and early twentieth-century Americans never even thought of Washington or their state capitols as sources of personal wealth, benefits, or sinecures. Unable to obtain position or wealth from governments, individuals turned their attention to taming the frontier and nature and tinkering with new ideas and gadgets. It was their own hard work and creativeness that secured success for themselves and, thus, their country.

4. Rent seeking is not confined to governments and large corporations. Given the proper set of incentives, all of us could be rent seekers. Individuals owning homes or apartments in the coastal area would like to see restrictions on development because it would increase their quality of life and their property values. The movie star who owns a home on the Malibu coast and is supporting such "socially worthwhile" causes as protecting our valuable land for future generations is a rent chaser.

5. Yes. The winning cable companies were those that offered to broadcast the greatest number of "public service" and community broadcasts that they otherwise would not have shown. Those community broadcasts of city council and school board meetings are terribly expensive to produce, and very few people watch them. They are a waste of society's resources, and the community would be served better if the cable franchises were awarded to the highest bidder or to those offering the lowest prices for specified cable services.

6. No. Society benefits from having some individuals specialize in defending and prosecuting criminals, advising clients and corporations, and even drawing up lawsuits. These are not socially wasteful activities. However, when lawyers are employed in rent-seeking activities, such as special government treatment of their clients, their time is lost to society and no useful goods or services are produced. Since the rent-seeking activities of lawyers are valuable to the clients that employ them, many receive high salaries or fees, but their real social marginal product is very low, if not zero. This is not the fault of the lawyers who are engaged in these activities but the rules of society in which the lawyers operate and, we might add, the rules many lawyers and the American Bar Association help write.

7. **a.** Students are using more time, paper, computers, and other resources to obtain a passing grade, but their efforts are producing human capital, which is useful to society. No rent-seeking waste here.

b. No, for the same reason as answer a. She is merely encouraging competition in acquiring knowledge and learning how to think.

c. Shame on her! She is a poor professor; she is wasting the resources of the university and should be dismissed. However, the yard work done by the students is beneficial for society. No significant rent-seeking activity here.

d. Students were wasting resources attempting to secure a valuable "right"—a good grade—from the professor. No useful service was being performed by such activities. He was encouraging wasteful rent-seeking activities. He, too, should have been dismissed.

e. Hmmmm . . . ask your professor during posted office hours, if you can find him.

CHAPTER THIRTEEN

CONSTITUTIONAL ECONOMICS

Free government is founded out of jealousy and not in confidence.
—THOMAS JEFFERSON

TWO LEVELS OF DECISION MAKING

Constitutional economics, a fairly recent development in political economy, is the application of economic analysis to the selection of efficient rules and decision-making institutions. Constitutional analysis begins with the recognition of the difference between operational and constitutional levels of decision making. The *operational* level consists of decisions made within a given set of already-existing rules. Operational-level decision making has been the traditional field of concern among most political scientists and economists specializing in public choice. According to this traditional approach, which was presented in previous chapters, individuals make decisions through some voting mechanisms, and if these mechanisms work reasonably well, the preferences of the median voter will determine the outcome. Decisions made at the operational level, for example, could be the size of the defense budget, the size of the education budget, the level of tax rates, or the number of parks. Traditional public choice and economic analyses have been concerned with individuals choosing among alternatives within a given set of rules, and they have emphasized the limitations imposed by the scarcity of resources—limited land, oil, trees, minerals, time, and labor.

Constitutional decision making is at a higher level, where the "rules of the game" are established. These constitutional decisions determine the rules in which future operational decisions about the procurement and allocation of resources will be made. Perhaps the easiest way to understand the reasons for constitutional decision making is to consider the confusion that would exist in a card game if the rules were decided after the cards had been dealt. Card players are able to agree on the rules before the cards are dealt because they are impartial at this stage. At this constitutional level of decision making the players can discuss the rules that would make the game interesting, efficient, and equitable without worrying about how each rule would affect them personally. They don't know what cards they will get to play. There are two quite distinct stages or levels of choice involved in card playing. First, there is the choice of the rules themselves, the constitutional choice, and then there are the choices made within these rules, the operational choices. Examples of the operational choices would include holding or folding, drawing to an inside straight, bluffing, or deciding the size of the bet to make on two pairs.

BENEFITS OF CONSTITUTIONAL DECISION MAKING

Constitutional choices introduce impartiality into an otherwise highly partial world. Just as card players would find it difficult to determine the rules after the cards had been dealt, so individuals would find it difficult to determine institutional rules after they had an established position in life. Individuals have various stakes in their occupations, locations, age, and education, and they can be expected to use operational decision making in the political market to improve these known stakes and positions. If all rules were made through operational choices in normal elections, individuals would attempt to use the political mechanism to improve their own known positions. They could not be impartial about the rules for which they would vote. Constitutional rules, on the other hand, are determined in an atmosphere of conceptual impartiality, because decision making individuals do not know which particular individuals will eventually benefit from the rules. Thus, rules made at the constitutional level, where there is uncertainty about the specific future interests of individuals, yield a fair amount of impartiality and fairness to the system. After the constitution, or set of rules for the game, has been decided, individuals can make operational, or postconstitutional, choices.

In addition to instructing individuals how they should play the game and providing impartiality to the decision-making process, another advantage of rules is that they inform each individual how other individuals will behave. This is a valuable social benefit, because individuals planning their own behavior and commitments need to estimate how others will behave. If individuals don't have some bases upon which to predict the behavior of others, the resulting uncertainty makes it very costly for them to make decisions, commitments, or investments. A simple example can illustrate these benefits. An individual driving an automobile from Mankato to Morris, Minnesota, will rely upon some elementary rules of the road: drive on the right side of the road, stop at stop signs, yield to cars on the right in intersections. Without such rules it would be very costly for the individual to attempt this trip because he wouldn't know how *other* individuals would behave. If other individuals could travel on the left, right, or center of the road, the individual might simply expect the roads to be too dangerous and decide to remain in Mankato. In this case, as in many others, the content of the rules is not important. It is only important that the rules exist. The rules could specify that individuals drive on the left-hand side as they do in Britain, but all drivers would need to adhere to one set of rules.

These constitutional rules of the road do not prohibit individuals from making certain operational choices in the future or pursuing their own ends. The purpose of rules is not to proscribe a certain social outcome or to restrict the freedom of individuals but to enable them to pursue their own objectives. Rules need not be uniform throughout a country, but individuals do need to know the location where the rules change. The costs of switching from one set of rules to another set should be acceptably low. For example, individuals are required to drive on the right-hand side of the road in all states because the costs of changing the rules at each of the 50 state lines would be prohibitively costly. All major railroads in the United States also observe the right-hand rule on double tracks, with one exception. The Chicago and Northwestern Railroad had a left-hand running rule, which it initially adopted because of the location of a passenger depot and station parking lot at a high-traffic suburban Chicago station. The left-hand rule worked well for the C&NW because its rail limits were clearly marked and known to all engineers, and traffic from other lines seldom traveled on C&NW tracks.

Rules need not be written; they may simply be conventions such as a gentleman allowing ladies to enter an elevator first or individuals queuing up at a bus stop. The important requirement for efficient rules is that they be known by those who use the facilities or resources and that they be stable over time. If rules were changed constantly, the transition costs from one set of rules to another set would be high and the new rules would be difficult and costly to learn. Frequent changes would also increase the uncertainty about the behavior of others: Did all individuals get "the word" about the changes? Will they habitually observe the new rules? Hence, there is an efficiency advantage in conservatism. Rules should not be changed unless the benefits of the changes clearly outweigh the costs.[1] The philosophical French say, "unless it is necessary to change, it is necessary not to change," and the practical Americans say, "if it ain't broke, don't fix it."

---

[1] Constitutional economists stress that they are "rule conservatives" and not "outcome conservatives"; they want the rules to be changed infrequently, but they are not necessarily opposed to radical changes in outcomes.

Despite considerable international pressures for the British to adopt a right-hand driving rule, they have remained with the left-hand rule because a change would be too costly. Despite the women's liberation movement, gentlemen still step aside to let women enter an elevator first, and they quickly file into the elevators with the knowledge and expectation that males will permit them priority entry. The efficiency of this convention is clearly shown when many men, whose social status or pecking order are unknown, attempt to enter elevators. Each dances around in an attempt to defer first-class status upon the others. The lack of social rules defining which men have priority of entrance results in excessive boarding time. Many economists illustrate the importance of rules by quipping, "If you agree with me that we need a rule, I'll let you determine the rule."

Conceptually, individuals can reach agreement on rules at the constitutional level of decision making, even when an individual recognizes in advance that he may well be damaged in the future by these rules. For example, assume that an individual who does not know his future life path must make a constitutional decision about rules for protecting private property. The individual must consider that there is some probability that he might become a thief, but he also recognizes that even if he became a thief he would want to have laws protecting his property. He would support laws against theft, even if he might be subjected to punishment by these laws. An individual would assent to a law prohibiting murder even if he knew he might want to murder someone in the future. Without such a prohibition, he would be in much greater danger of being murdered himself. Thus, constitutional economists can go through civil and criminal laws as well as tax and expenditure laws to see if they pass the constitutional test.

Constitutional rules provide benefits other than an institutional framework within which efficient operational decisions may be made. Rules, for example, often are the only way to evaluate the morality or acceptability of an outcome. For example, the acceptability of the outcome of a card game is determined by whether all participants played according to the rules. The winner is allowed to keep his loot if he played fairly, that is, according to the rules that were established and known prior to the game. The outcome of a political election cannot be evaluated by any moral or efficiency criterion, but the winner is allowed to take office if the campaign rules were followed. A wealthy person may have procured wealth by stealing it or by earning it in a competitive environment. We let him keep his wealth if he obtained his wealth fairly, that is, by following the rules. But if his wealth was accumulated unfairly, by breaking the rules through stealing or stock manipulation, we condemn him and take away his wealth.

Part of the literature in constitutional economics stresses the importance of having constitutional rules to govern operational decision making without discussing the relative merits of alternative constitutional rules. Another part of the literature stresses that it is not only important to have constitutional rules, but it is necessary that these rules be efficient so that individuals can effectively interact with each other. Specifically, these latter constitutionalists believe that improvements in welfare are constrained not only by limited resources but also by limited institutional arrangements. In a society consisting of a few individuals the scarcity of physical resources is virtually the only factor limiting improvements in the standard of living. In a modern, complex society with millions of individuals, interdependencies, and externalities, improvements in the standard of living become increasingly dependent upon an efficient set of institutions that provide the correct signals, information, and incentives to other members of society. These institutions, which are the rules within which operational choices are made, are very important for an orderly, prosperous, and peaceful society. Constitutional economics focuses on these institutional alternatives. Very casual empiricism—reading the front pages of newspapers is enough—suggests that millions of individuals live in poverty not because of a lack of physical resources within their country but because of a lack of an efficient set of institutional rules in which these resources can be mobilized, utilized, and allocated.

LEVIATHAN GOVERNMENT

Much recent work in constitutional economics has centered on analyzing rules limiting the power of governments, which the constitutionalists argue is *the* source of much uncertainty about the future application of rules and *the* source of inefficient rules in both the private and political markets. In order to analyze constraints that might be placed on government, they have posited the existence of a Leviathan government[2] that is beyond the control of individuals. The concept of a Leviathan government that exists apart from the collection of individuals constituting society seems to violate the first postulate of political economy. However, there is an analytical foundation for Leviathan government that makes the contradiction more apparent than real. The individual knows his influence over the operational decisions of government is very limited and that government is

---

[2] The English philosopher Thomas Hobbes titled his famous political treatise *Leviathan* (1651) after the whale, or leviathan. The state, said Hobbes, was like a whale. It required a single controlling intelligence with absolute power to direct its motion.

going to make decisions regardless of his own views. That is, even *if* the political market's decision-making mechanisms effectively reflect majority preferences and even *if* there are no impediments in the political market, the individual will confront the prospect of having little individual control over government decisions. When the likely impediments in the political market—bureaucracies, imperfect competition, fixed market baskets, pressure groups, unequal distribution of political power, information costs, and imperfect voting mechanisms—are considered, the individual has even more reason to treat the government as a Leviathan beyond his control. In such circumstances the individual will want to control the degree of harm the government can do to him. Hence, many constitutionalists argue that the Leviathan government attempts to maximize government revenue and expenditures, subject only to the limitations imposed on it by the constitution. Citizens cannot rely upon majority rule or the median voter model to constrain governments, so they attempt to limit the power of governments through constitutions.

Assume that individuals were making constitutional decisions today. They would want a government to provide public goods and services that could not be provided by the private market. At this constitutional stage of decision making they would realize that they could not know the specific quantities of goods and services they would want provided in the future, so they would be willing to let such decisions be made at the operational level by majority decision making in the future. They would also realize, however, that once government were established it would be very difficult, if not impossible, to control. They would want to protect themselves against exploitation by the Leviathan-like government institutions that might be virtually uncontrollable once established. The rational individual would want to limit the ability of government to raise revenue in the future by placing in the constitution a clearly defined and narrow tax base that could not be expanded. Similarly, an individual might want to limit government to a balanced budget because otherwise it would have virtually no limits on its expenditures.

This type of constitutional reasoning has led many economists to advocate certain constitutional amendments that would limit government's budgets, limit the growth of money supply, limit economic activities that could be taxed by the federal government, and tie growth in government expenditures to the growth rate in the GNP. They believe that these amendments would limit perceived dangers in government caused by the existence of impediments in the political market. Not unexpectedly, the constitutionalists' fundamental assumption that these political market imperfections would create a Leviathan government has been sharply criticized as being too cynical and pessimistic.

The constitutionalists have replied that the search for an appropriate social contract should be approached like the search for an efficient contract with a building contractor.[3] Individuals planning on building a home search for a conscientious builder whom they trust and with whom they can work amicably. They do not expect to have difficulties with the contractor, but when they sit down to draw up the contract, they implicitly assume that the contractor is a shyster without any principles. They make this assumption not because they believe that their contractor is actually this kind of person but because they are making the contract to cover the worst eventuality. The constitutionalists argue that when setting out rules for future government action this same kind of cynical behavior is necessary. They know that even the best governments are beset with impediments that require some limits, but they do not necessarily assume that their government will actually be the Leviathan they assumed in their analysis. However, the purpose of a political constitution is similar to a building contract, and one has to write into a contract a number of provisions limiting the damages that can be done under the worst case scenario.

WEAKNESSES IN CONSTITUTIONAL ANALYSES

There are many weaknesses in constitutional economics. Perhaps the most salient is the practical inability of individuals to make decisions completely devoid of any knowledge about their future lives. If the United States Constitution were to be amended, it would have to be done by real flesh-and-blood individuals whose interests in life had already been established. Also, the remaking of the Constitution would probably be dominated by the same special interests that have disproportional influence in Congress and the bureaucracy as well as by those—lawyers, judges, and professors—who have developed human capital in administering and interpreting the present Constitution. Constitutionalists have various defenses for this criticism. One solution would be to have individuals making constitutional decisions at a stage in their lives where they still possessed much uncertainty about the future course of their lives. For example, young men and women, whose career paths, income, and social status were not yet clearly determined could vote on constitutional rules. However, even young adults already have knowledge about their family wealth, skills, temperaments, intelligence, and future occupations. Furthermore, constitutionalists have

---

[3] Geoffrey Brennan and James M. Buchanan, *The Power to Tax* (Cambridge: Cambridge University Press, 1980).

offered no feasible suggestions as to how such constitutional decision making can actually occur. Would a new constitution be required every two or three years? Would the older generation be bound by the contract they made or by the new constitution made by the younger generation? Would there be many constitutions for different generations?

Some constitutionalists argue that they are not suggesting that frequent constitutional decisions actually be made. They use constitutional decision making as an analytical tool to evaluate the efficiency of alternative decision-making rules under varying sets of assumptions. The reference individual in these analytical models is assumed to be an unborn spirit, acting behind a "veil of ignorance" about his future state in life,[4] who is about to embark on life's journey with no knowledge about his specific endowments or experiences. Within this analytical framework the political economist can examine the decision-making processes of a rational spirit who has to weigh the pros and cons of alternative institutional rules. Some scholars use this theoretical mechanism to examine the efficiency properties of alternative rules. They focus on the ability of rules to enable individuals to pursue their objectives at the lowest cost. A conceptual voluntary acceptance of certain rules is merely one way of stating that the rules are efficient.

Constitutionalists have written little on how constitutional amendments can be enacted, implemented, and interpreted. They have examined the impediments in voting, the bureaucracy, and the legislature, but, surprisingly, they have paid little attention to the judicial bureaucracy. The general and loose language necessary in any amendment that would receive voter approval would require interpretations by the judiciary, over which present and future voters exercise less control than they exercise over the legislature. Individuals attempting to limit an uncontrollable legislature and executive bureaucracy might merely be substituting an even less controllable bureaucracy than is found in the judicial system.

The distinction between constitutional and operational decision making is not totally clear. At the conceptual level the distinction is useful, but its application to any area—taxes, expenditures, money supply, individual rights—is fraught with difficulties. The criteria that can be used to separate those rules that should be placed in the constitution and those that should be left to future majority votes have not been clearly delineated.

---

[4] This approach, as well as the terminology "behind the veil of ignorance," was used by John Rawls in his important book *A Theory of Justice* (Cambridge: Harvard University Press, 1971). Rawl's book, which has much in common with constitutional economics, was based on a rational and selfish individual who was about to enter the game of life and was able to select the rules of the game.

Constitutionalists have ignored the practical difficulties inherent in the rules themselves. Seemingly simple tasks such as defining government revenues, expenditures, and money supply are extremely difficult in the real world. For example, some constitutionalists have argued that a constitutional rule should require the Federal Reserve to abandon discretionary monetary policy and, instead, keep the money supply growing at some fixed percent per year. The problem is that there are many definitions of money supply, and innovative financial managers are constantly devising new liquidity substitutes. Which money supply definition should be subjected to the constitutionally determined growth rate? What should happen when new forms of money are devised and old forms are discarded? Constitutions can protect individuals only if the rules are clearly delineated in the constitutions, but they cannot be specified if the subjects of the specifications are constantly being revised, altered, or abandoned.

Constitutionalists have said little about the processes of amending the Constitution. Decision-making costs involved in altering the present Constitution, which could be quite high, have not been examined.[5] Other questions remain. What are the most efficient procedures to amend the Constitution? How can the amendments be worded so that judges will have fewer opportunities to interpret them as they wish? Is there a more efficient and accountable way to interpret the Constitution than through the Supreme Court? Why would individuals devote resources to obtain information on a proposed constitutional amendment? Why would they even take part in the decision-making process? Could the media distort the revelation of preferences in constitutional decision making?

It takes much thought and knowledge to write an effective constitution, including knowledge about the role that the private market and price mechanism can play in integrating the diverse preferences and abilities of individuals. Since individuals have an incentive to remain rationally ignorant about public issues, they would also remain rationally ignorant about the issues involved in constitutional decision making. The net result is that they might well make constitutional decisions that would give more, rather than less, discretionary power to government. This would be particularly likely to occur because of the past uneven development of analytical thought on the two markets that was mentioned in chapter 1. Although the problem is less serious today, many people still believe that

---

[5] Some difficulties were discussed by William Craig Stubblebine, "Practical Problems of Constitutional Reform," in *Constitutional Economics*, ed. Richard B. McKenzie (Lexington, MA: Lexington Books, 1984).

the government can easily correct failures in the private market without introducing additional failures in the political market.

Lastly, constitutions are virtually worthless unless they are maintained and respected over time, and the strongest constitutions are those, such as the British and American constitutions, that have been in existence, with few major alterations, for centuries. People respect and obey the constitutions because of their longevity and unwillingness to alter rules that have served both countries fairly well for so long. Both the British and American people take pride in the longevity of their constitutions, whereas people in countries that have new constitutions seldom have developed the respect and reverence for their constitutions, which are frequently repealed or ignored. Drastic changes in the American Constitution might jeopardize this reverence and respect and there might not be a lengthy period of stability during which a new constitution could gain the requisite support.

Despite these problems and oversights, constitutional economists have raised some meaningful issues. Social and economic institutions and rules are becoming increasingly important as Victorian morality and small-town ethics are becoming faint memories of a less interdependent era. Governments as well as individuals are less constrained by tradition, convention, and morality than, presumably, they once were. The almost religious fervor to which most people clung to the concept of a limited government providing general benefits for all citizens rather than expenditures to benefit a few and to the "Golden Rule" of a balanced budget disappeared more than 50 years ago.

As the necessity for limits and rules guiding individuals to cooperate with each other increases, larger populations and less efficient political mechanisms leave the individual with little power to control government. Social science scholars scoff at the rube's colloquial quips that the generalized and unspecified *they* are "out to get us." These scholars admonish their students that "they" do not exist in a democracy, because it is "we" who make the decisions. One of the inescapable, though embarrassing, implications of the material presented in this book is that the rube is correct. From the viewpoint of the representative individual, there is a "they" over which he has no meaningful control. The "they" in the legislature, the "they" in government bureaucracy, the "they" in the corporate and special interest bureaucracies are making decisions that affect him but that he, as an individual, can neither alter nor avoid. He can lessen the interferences "they" impose on him and obtain at least some control over his welfare by escaping to the competitive choices offered by the private market and, perhaps, by participation in local clubs and associations. But in other important aspects of his life, he is at the virtual mercy of "them." Since he is no longer protected by traditions or moral imperatives, he has to depend upon a set of respected rational rules and institutions to protect him from "them." He can seek protection in a constitutional set of rules with which "they" cannot tinker.

This, in the view of this author, is the focus of the constitutionalists. As pointed out by Brennan and Buchanan, Anglo-American legal scholarship has emphasized the rules of reason; but it has neglected the reason of rules.[6] Constitutionalists want to reignite the interest in the reason for rules that were emphasized by James Madison, Benjamin Franklin, and Thomas Jefferson. Constitutionalists are attempting to analyze, construct, and recommend a set of rules that would constrain the amount of harm that "they" can impose on the reference individual but that would still provide the essential ability of individuals to collectively solve the problems generated by externalities and interdependencies. It is an important but difficult quest.

QUESTIONS AND ANSWERS

THE QUESTIONS

1. Did your professor tell you the rules for the course—the class constitution—on the first day of class? Did such information help you organize your notes and your methods of studying for the tests?

2. During the past 30 years the Supreme Court has been accused of "rewriting" the Constitution. List and analyze some arguments supporting and criticizing such judicial changes. Do not discuss specific cases or topics.

3. Do the Ten Commandments represent a set of constitutional rules?

4. List some common and widely accepted social conventions that are generally recognized by individuals as having the status of an unwritten constitution or set of rules.

5. Do you think there is some connection between the relaxation of the Victorian "Golden Rule"—that federal and state budgets should be balanced except in wartime—and the large deficits of the past decade?

6. Article 1, Section 8 of the United States Constitution states: "The Congress shall have power to lay and collect taxes, duties, imposts and excises, to pay the debts and provide for the common defense and general

---

[6] Geoffrey Brennan and James Buchanan, *The Reason of Rules,* (Cambridge: Cambridge University Press, 1985).

welfare of the United States; but all duties, imposts and excises shall be uniform throughout the United States."

    a.   What potential problems in the future do you think this constitutional rule was designed to avoid?

    b.   Looking over the past 200 years, do you believe it accomplished its purpose? Why?

7.   The Constitution of the United States is more than 200 years old, which has led us to believe that the making of political constitutions is a part of history. For most countries of the world, however, constitution making is a relatively recent experience. There are about 160 written national constitutions in the world, more than one-half of which have been written since 1975. A few countries have even written more than three constitutions since 1950. Egypt had constitutions written in 1956, 1964, and 1971. The latest constitution was significantly amended in 1980. Article 23 of the 1971 Egyptian Constitution stated: "The national economy shall be organized in accordance with a comprehensive development plan that ensures raising the national income, fairly distributing it, raising the standard of living, solving the problem of unemployment, increasing work opportunities, connecting wages with production, and fixing minimum and maximum limits for wages guaranteeing smaller disparities in income."

    a.   Do you think that the "longevity" of the Egyptian constitutions have something to do with their amount of detail?

    b.   What "rules" are embodied in this article of the Egyptian Constitution?

THE ANSWERS

1.   The rules announced at the beginning of class form the class constitution. They should have been helpful to you in this class.

2.   You are on your own here. One of your major arguments against judicial changes in the Constitution should be that they are changing the "rules of the game" after people have made their plans based on the old rules. A major argument supporting such changes should be that since people's preferences and technology have changed, the Constitution should reflect such changes.

3.   Yes. Though often violated, they are recognized and respected rules by which millions of people have lived.

4.   "Women and children first" on sinking boats. The aged and handicapped get first priority on seats in public transportation. Raise your hand in class when you have a question. The bride's family pays for the wedding. You stand in line at grocery checkout counters. You eat with a fork, knife, and spoon.

5. The relationship is difficult to prove, but some political economists believe that prior to the Depression, Victorian morality made it impossible for politicians to vote for a deficit except during wartime. Individuals would have viewed votes for budget deficits as immoral and quickly voted the politicians out of office. The result was that governments did not run deficits and countries did not experience the undesirable consequences of deficits such as inflation.

6. **a.** One potential problem the constitutional framers obviously wanted to avoid was a majority of voters living in one region of the country enacting taxes on the minority living in another section of the country. The requirement that taxes had to be "uniform throughout the land" was meant to constrain Congress from such discrimination. Another was to constrain Congress from voting specific benefits for certain localities, groups, or individuals. The tax revenues were to be expended "for the common defense and general welfare."

b. The uniformity clause did keep Congress from passing seriously discriminatory tax laws but the "common defense and general welfare" clause has not kept Congress from granting benefits to specific groups, industries, or localities. The Supreme Court has so broadly interpreted that clause that it has lost its original meaning.

7. **a.** It is certainly plausible.

b. Very few. This constitutional clause certainly does not imply that there will be constraining limits on the national government in economic matters. The clause suggests possibilities of serious intervention in the Egyptian economy by the Egyptian government without specifying details or defining terms. What do the following terms mean: "connecting wages with production," "fairly distributing [income]," and "smaller disparities in income"? This clause is both too specific and not specific enough. It gives the government various general powers in the economy but then does not define or limit the terms of such government intervention.

CHAPTER FOURTEEN

MARKET COMPARISONS

*There are four classes of Idols which beset men's minds. To these
I have assigned names—calling the first class, Idols of the Tribe;
the second, Idols of the Cave; the third, Idols of the Marketplace;
the fourth, Idols of the Theatre.*
—FRANCIS BACON, 1605

COMPETING MARKETS

Nearly four centuries ago Bacon discussed four idols of human beings that
we would now term government (Tribe), the home or family (Cave), the
private market (Marketplace), and the media (Theatre). We have examined
two of these idols—more neutrally called market mechanisms—through
which individuals can express their preferences and pursue their goals. One
is the private market, characterized by profit-seeking firms and commodity-
seeking individuals who exchange millions of goods and services without
chaos and with a maximum of individual freedom. But the private market
is not a universal social solvent. Even if the private market operated with
perfect efficiency and equity, it could not provide public goods. For this,
political market—which organizes the collective preferences of individuals
for public goods and arranges their financing—is necessary.

Although many functions of the two markets are complementary to
each other, they have become, at least at the broad margins, substitutes
for each other even in such free market countries as the United States.
From the beginning of the century until at least 1980 the political market
made ever-greater intrusions in the private market. Initially, laws were
passed to limit monopolies and regulate the working conditions of children
and women and the safety of workers. As the century progressed,
additional government legislation intruded on the private sector. The
following are a few examples of the political market intrusion in the private
market during this century: income taxation, labor legislation, Social
Security, minimum wages, licenses and occupational requirements,
securities regulations, price and wage controls, limits on land usage,

corrective taxes and subsidies, protection of animal species, historic structures, public lands, and the environment, sex and race quotas, maximum hours of work, local "blue laws," a second round of health and safety legislation, pension regulations, and a relative increase in the general expenditures of government. During the past few years there has been an intrusion of the private market and the price mechanism into some areas of the political market. Privatization, the establishment of semi-autonomous units such as the United States Postal Service, and user fees are some examples. There is little doubt that the political market's intrusion in the private market through economic regulation is now viewed much less favorably than it was in mid-century, but social, conservation, and environmental legislation is still viewed as being unquestionably beneficial by many. Though washed by the ebb and flow of changes in deep-rooted philosophies and intellectual clichés, the battle between the markets will continue.

Factors Affecting Future Competition between the Markets

NEGATIVE EXTERNALITIES

The outcome of the worldwide battle between the two markets is uncertain. Future attitudes and trends about the relative roles to be played by the two markets are going to be shaped by at least three major trends. One is the increasing importance of negative externalities caused by expanding populations, urbanization, and technology. Unless some major technical breakthroughs are made, it appears that national, and even international, political markets are going to have to deal with such externalities as acid rain, air and water pollution, and ozone destruction. While the private market may be able to internalize some of these externalities through private contracts and the establishment of retail and industrial centers, the role of government in solving these real problems will likely increase.

A NEW INTELLECTUAL MILIEU

The second major trend shaping the outcome of the battle between the markets is the rejection of the absolute power of government in Western countries and even in the economies of Eastern Europe. The world is currently witnessing significant shifts in attitudes and policies in communist countries away from the supremacy of command economies and toward increasing decentralization, and toward the recognition of the important roles played by prices, monetary incentives, interest rates, and private investment. It is too early to evaluate the long-run effects of these trends on the future of the private market or on the democratization of the political markets in these countries, but the fact that they are occurring with such depth, support, and speed is phenomenal. Even if these current tendencies should diminish, they are generating impacts that will last well into the next century.

One obvious cause of these shifts is the practical realization by the citizens and even the leaders of these countries that political market decision making may be able to focus development efforts on a few "visible" segments of the economy, but it has failed miserably in stimulating general economic progress for the average citizen. The progress, energy, and vitality of market economies in the West have been so sharply contrasted with the failure, lethargy, and inflexibility of economies in the communist countries that even the most dedicated ideologue has run out of excuses.

Perhaps the most significant cause of the shift in attitudes and policy in Eastern Europe is more subtle and obtuse but very instructive about the role ideas—or the acceptability of ideas—play in the modern world. Keynes was right about academic scribblers:

> The ideas of economists and political philosophers, both when they are right and when they are wrong, are more powerful than is commonly understood. Indeed the world is ruled by little else. Practical men, who believe themselves to be quite exempt from any intellectual influences, are usually the slaves of some defunct economist. Madmen in authority, who hear voices in the air, are distilling their frenzy from some academic scribbler of a few years back.[1]

Ideas are important, but they have power to change the world only after they have become intellectually and socially fashionable. This occurs when such ideas are accepted by some critical percentage of those to whom others look for intellectual leadership. Socialism, communism, welfare-statism, and government management of the economy reached their academic zenith in the period between 1930 and 1970, because it was intellectually acceptable if not de rigueur for those aspiring to intellectual pretensions to espouse such views. In student unions and faculty clubs on campuses throughout the Western world during those decades one's intellectual sophistication was evaluated by adherence to a socialist ideology. It was widely accepted in academia that only those professors who prostituted themselves by taking grants from the Liberty Foundation

---

[1] John Maynard Keynes, *The General Theory of Employment, Interest and Money* (New York: Harcourt, Brace & World, 1936), 383.

or were afflicted by mental dry rot defended the free market or classical economics. Modern socialist economics was new, exciting, and intellectually chic, and many of those who questioned socialism or welfarism sulked into dark allies wondering if they indeed were the intellectual rednecks the majority of their colleagues thought them to be.

Socialist economics was a rising tide that carried most professors and students with it. Soon these students became professors, consultants, advisors, and political leaders who applied the exciting views and theories of their youth to the problems of the real world. They supported each other and their novitiate with grants, projects, promotions, and, most importantly, the imprimatur of progressive intellectualism. There was more than the critical mass of "true believers" among opinion leaders to make socialism and welfare statism a powerful force in changing the world. The chain that connected the academic scribbler to the "madmen in authority" was the creation of this "correct" intellectual milieu. Without this milieu the ideas would have been lost on dusty library bookshelves.

An intellectual milieu loses its power only when it is replaced by another milieu. The milieu of classical economics was replaced by that of socialism, communism, and Keynesianism in the thirties. This milieu, in turn, was replaced by that of neoclassicism in the seventies. It is this modern milieu that eventually elected Thatcher, Reagan, and Bush and that set the fingers of the Invisible Hand moving once again in Eastern Europe. This promarket milieu was started by a few academic scribblers who were initially ignored by government foundations, most private foundations, and virtually all major universities. Frank Knight, Friedrich Hayek, Ludwig Von Mises, Milton Friedman, James Buchanan, Gordon Tulloch, Warren Nutter, Ronald Coase, and W. H. Hutt were a few of the "defunct economists" who began building the long road of intellectual respectability for free market economics.

At first their collective writings—criticizing socialism, communism, Keynesianism, the Soviet economy, and government decision making; praising the inherent orderliness of the private market; and analyzing the relationships between political freedom and economic freedom—caused them to be ridiculed as right-wing apologetics. Their few students who went on job interviews were subjected to severe inquisitions by members of the then-current liberal milieu. There were simply not enough supporters of free market economics to make their views respectable. But like the young socialists and Keynesians of the thirties and forties, they were bright, enthused, well trained, and very creative. Although they would not like the analogy, they were the Jesuit missionaries in the midst of a tribe of heathens. They wrote extensively, expanded neoclassical economics to new fields, and made economics, which had become stale, exciting once again.[2] They began making converts, and, most importantly, they showed a few young students of the sixties that free market economics was intellectually respectable and that they did not have to be ashamed of their research or policy conclusions. They no longer had to sulk in the back alleys of intellectual respectability. Their ideas were fresh, logical, and increasingly proven by empirical research.

Not surprising to them was that some of their first, and most enthusiastic, converts were young economists in Eastern Europe who could personally relate to these "radical" free market views. By the 1970s these economists were beginning to displace the old intellectual milieu of socialism, communism, and welfare-statism with their own milieu, which began percolating over into the world of policy. The practical result of the work of those few academic scribblers in the fifties and sixties was Thatcher, Reagan, Bush, and the developments in Eastern Europe during the eighties. Keynes's economics might have been wrong, but his insights about the delayed significance of defunct economists were shown by the displacement of his own ideas and the intellectual milieu they created by a new generation of academic scribblers with their now well-established milieu.

PUBLIC CHOICE

The third remaining trend affecting the future roles of the private and political markets is the impact of the research currently being done in public choice, rent seeking, and constitutional economics. Though related to the free market economics milieu, it is a separate branch. Its central objective is not to examine the operations of the private market but to lay bare the mechanisms of the political market. Although the agenda of public choice researchers is often unclear, it appears that they are striving to utilize the tools of private market economics to develop a consistent and comparable theory of the political market. Adam Smith's *Wealth of Nations* has yet to be written for the political market, but, hopefully, this book (and especially the summary that follows), will show that a few chapters have been completed.

Much of the public choice research has yielded conclusions critical of the political market simply because it is not very efficient in reflecting individual preferences or enabling individuals to realize their preferences. Despite these inefficiencies, however, one can interpret public choice

---

[2] It is not surprising that the most exciting decades for economics students were the thirties and the sixties. The debates of ideas, policies, and relevance and a sense of mission were similar in the two decades, even though their views were radically different.

research as attempting to improve government decision making and to limit unnecessary bureaucracy so that government will be able to deal with those very important issues, such as pervasive externalities, that cannot be solved by the private market and that require enlightened and energetic government action.

SUMMARY

A frequent mistake made by novices in political economy is to believe that the private market serves only private interests and that the political market serves only public interests. Both markets serve the public interest by enabling individuals to pursue their private interests. Providing individuals with food, clothing, housing, automobiles, and entertainment serves the public welfare at least as well as providing citizens with a national defense, courts, and fire and police protection. The private market, as well as the political market, provides goods that increase the welfare of citizens in the country.

Another mistake made by political economy novices is to assume that individuals are motivated by personal, selfish interests in the private market and by altruistic social interests in the political market. There is no analytical or empirical reason to believe that motivations differ in the two markets. While some decisions in both markets are obviously motivated by genuine altruism, the majority of decisions in the two markets are made for selfish reasons. However, independent individual decision making generated by selfish desires does not mean that chaos exists.

Provided certain conditions are met, the competitive pursuits of profits and income through the private market mechanism will procure and allocate private goods efficiently. The political market is characterized by individuals pursuing their own self-interests, but total chaos does not exist. Parties and politicians, seeking to maximize political power and votes, formulate platforms designed to appeal to the median voter. Unfortunately, there is no set of conditions, similar to those posited in the private market, that enable one to conclude, even at the theoretical level, that resources are allocated efficiently. The nature of public goods, collective consumption, and collective decision making makes it impossible for efficiency to be achieved even under the best of conditions.

The fact that a comparison of the two markets at a highly abstract level produces a favorable comparison for the private market does not enable one to conclude that the private market should always be the preferred mechanism. At the theoretical level the political market is less efficient than the private market, but the only meaningful evaluation of the two markets is at the level of the real world, where both markets are characterized by imperfections and impediments. A brief comparison of a few of the theoretical and practical characteristics of the two markets follows.

COMPARISONS BETWEEN THE PRIVATE AND POLITICAL MARKETS

The Private Market

1. Private goods are provided, which nonpayers/noncontributors can be excluded from consuming.

2. Individuals can adjust the quantity of goods they consume.

3. Individuals can express the intensities of their preferences as well as their rankings.

4. Transactions, which are voluntarily undertaken in the private market, represent increases in the welfare of all parties to the transactions. No individual would engage in a voluntary transaction that would decrease his or her welfare.

5. Private market entrepreneurs are motivated by profit maximization, and they produce according to consumer demands.

The Political Market

1. Public goods are provided from which individuals cannot be excluded from consuming. The political market is necessary because of the existence of public goods and services, externalities, and the free rider problem.

2. Individuals cannot independently adjust to the quantity of public goods. Each person must consume the quantity decided upon by the collectivity over which he or she has virtually no influence.

3. Individuals can express the ranking of their preferences if efficient voting systems are used, but—except for logrolling and the parties' formulation of platforms—the intensity of individual preferences are not reflected in the political market.

4. Transactions undertaken in the political market will not represent an improvement in the welfare of all citizens unless Wicksellian unanimity is used. If (second-best) efficient voting systems (such as the weighted ranking method) are used and if there are no other failures in the political market, the welfare of the majority will be improved, but the welfare of the minority could be decreased. If inefficient voting systems (such as the single vote plurality) and/or other impediments exist in the political market, the welfare of a minority could be improved and that of the majority decreased by any expenditure and/or tax bill.

5. Political market entrepreneurs are motivated by vote maximization, and they formulate policies preferred by the median voters.

continued

Comparisons between the Private and Political Markets *(continued)*

The Private Market	The Political Market

The Private Market

6. Individuals can pick and choose the goods they want to purchase. Consumers can buy cars made by Ford or GM, computers made by IBM or Apple, colas by Pepsi or Coke, toothpastes made by Pepsodent or Colgate, and any combination from among millions of goods and services. Consumers can pick and choose among competing goods and suppliers, putting together a bundle of goods that best suits their preferences.

7. Individuals in the private market have incentives to reveal their preferences for private goods but not for public goods.

8. Individuals have selective incentives to obtain information about the prices and qualities of private goods. Information on the prices of goods in the private market is easy to obtain. Information about the qualities of various goods is more difficult to obtain (that is, more costly), but the individual knows that he or she will be rewarded for searching out such information because he or she alone will make the decision.

9. Individual demand curves are added horizontally, reflecting the fact that units of a private good consumed by one individual cannot also be consumed by another individual. Efficiency conditions for private goods can be stated as $P = MC$. Welfare is maximized when the value consumers place on an additional unit is equal to the opportunity cost of producing it.

The Political Market

6. Voters cannot engage in the collective choice analogy of choosing one supplier for one good and another supplier for another good; they cannot select one candidate's proposal on welfare, a second candidate's proposal on foreign policy, and a third candidate's views on national defense. Rather, voters must choose among the bundles of issues that the different candidates represent. Individuals cannot pick and choose their preferred positions on all policies. They must accept the basket of positions offered by the limited number of political parties and candidates.

7. Individuals have no incentive to reveal their preferences for public goods, that is, they have no incentives to vote unless they are taxed for not voting or they have professional or social incentives that are unrelated to making effective public choices. They have an incentive to be rational abstainers.

8. Individuals have no incentive to gather information about the prices and quantities of public goods, unless motivated by professional or social reasons. They have an incentive to remain rationally ignorant. Furthermore, the individual tax-prices of all goods—private and public—provided through the political market are very difficult, if not impossible, to obtain.

9. Individual demand curves are added vertically, reflecting the fact that all individuals can "consume" the services of a public good. Efficiency conditions for public goods can be stated as $\Sigma ME = MC$ and $MTP^i = ME^i$. The total marginal evaluation for the public good should equal the marginal cost of producing the public good, and each individual should be charged a tax-price equal to his or her marginal evaluation.

continued

COMPARISONS BETWEEN THE PRIVATE AND POLITICAL MARKETS (*continued*)

The Private Market

10. If there are no impediments in the market, competitive firms and those firms that face unlimited entry tend to produce an optimal quantity of goods, where $P = MC$.

11. Private market monopolies that can limit entry will restrict production and price above marginal cost. Private market monopolies are seldom able to restrict entry unless aided by government.

12. Corporations can suffer from a separation of ownership from control. Corporate executives can pursue empire building, various perks, or a quiet life rather than profit maximization. However, corporate executives are limited by the preferences of consumers, who can easily switch their allegiance to other producers.

The Political Market

10. Optimality cannot be obtained even in the pure theory of the political market because the median voter will vote for a quantity of public goods that equates his own ME with his MTP. He ignores the marginal evaluations of all other voters, which means that the *sum* of the marginal evaluations will most likely be greater than or less than the marginal cost of producing the public good.

11. (a) Agency monopolies result in a lack of competition, innovation, and meaningful data for oversight committees.

(b) The existence of only two major parties restricts the alternatives available to voters. Parties restrict entry of new parties by adopting voting systems and prohibiting proportional representation, and they vote to restrict advertising by limiting campaign contributions. Some competition is introduced in the political market by the federal system of government, in which small governmental units can compete for residents and taxpayers by offering various combinations of public expenditures and taxes. Competition can also be stimulated by having private firms provide quasi public goods, although this is likely to reduce "voice" behavior on the part of citizens.

12. Government agencies can suffer from a separation of ownership and control. Citizens are the consumers of an agency's output, but agencies report not to their customers but to legislative committees. This additional layer of decision making probably permits bureaucrats a greater degree of latitude than possessed by corporate executives to pursue their own social goals, to build empires, to expand their perks, and to ignore the preferences of their consumers.

continued

COMPARISONS BETWEEN THE PRIVATE AND POLITICAL MARKETS (*continued*)

The Private Market

13. According to certain equity norms, economic power can be poorly distributed. Some individuals inherit economic wealth, which gives them too much influence in the allocation of resources. Children of Donald Trump and Sam Walton might have an "undeserved" influence in the private market.

14. Most advertisements provide a social good by identifying a company with a particular product and permitting new firms a chance to break into the market, but misleading and uninformative advertisements do exist in the private market. The ad showing a beautiful girl sitting on the hood of a used car and the dealer with a bright red tie saying "Trust me, I've got a deal for you" provides little information on private goods, and it might be another example of a socially wasteful advertisement.

15. Some individuals, such as movie, fashion, and automotive reviewers, are able to influence preferences, but such influence is constrained because consumers have selective incentives to gather information about private goods from many different sources.

16. Externalities are a serious problem in the private market. As the world becomes more populated and urbanized, externalities—especially pollution and waste products—will become more important. Some externalities can be internalized in the private market, but others require the actions of government, or at least a set of enforceable laws and incentives.

The Political Market

13. According to certain equity norms, political power can be poorly distributed. Some individuals inherit political wealth, which gives them too much influence in the allocation of resources. The children of Ted Kennedy and Hubert Humphrey might have an "undeserved" influence in the political market.

14. Advertisements provide a social good by enabling new entrants to break into the political market, but misleading and uninformative advertisements exist. The ad that shows a politician with a hard hat standing next to a factory gate saying "Vote for me and I'll work for you" provides little information, and it might be an example of a socially wasteful advertisement.

15. Because individuals have few incentives to gather information about public goods or policies, those who occupy choke points in the distribution of low-cost information have some degree of monopoly power in political market decision making.

16. Though less publicized, externalities are also a problem in the political market. Municipal, county, and state sewage and garbage disposal units dump sewage in streams and pollutants in the air. Military planes create sonic booms, nuclear tests have polluted the atmosphere, political signs and billboards create visual pollution. Licensing and the creation of rent-seeking opportunities generate extensive externalities. Halfway houses for convicts are located in residential neighborhoods.

continued

COMPARISONS BETWEEN THE PRIVATE AND POLITICAL MARKETS *(continued)*

The Private Market	The Political Market
17. Individuals have an incentive to conserve an optimal quantity of resources for the future. They will conserve all resources that have an expected risk-adjusted rate of return greater than the interest rate. Thus, decreased consumption or abstinence today will be rewarded by increases in future income. Those resources that are not subject to private property rights can be expected to be consumed or destroyed quickly.	17. There is no inherent tendency in the political market to conserve resources for the future. Abstinence today cannot be converted into political wealth in the future. Politicians, unlike private entrepreneurs, do not have a market in which they can capitalize future benefits into present political "wealth" or power.
18. Private entrepreneurs are rent seekers, but their short-run rent-seeking activities produce socially beneficial goods and services at efficient prices, unless entry into their industry is difficult or prohibited. Long-term economic rent can be earned by owners of nonreproducible factors of production and by those who are given special privileges by government. Such rents might not be considered equitable, but the resources dedicated to obtaining the rents represent a social waste.	18. Some rent seeking in the political market is socially beneficial because it provides some information to legislators, but much of it is socially wasteful. The greater the ability of government to provide special privileges to some citizens, firms, or industries, the greater the quantity of resources wasted in rent seeking. Rent seeking also occurs for political power, and such political rents might not be considered to be equitable.
19. Concentrated economic power possessed by firms, families, or individuals can produce distortions in the private market and pose a threat of increasing the concentration of power in the political market.	19. Concentrated political power possessed by parties, families, or individuals can produce distortions in the political market and pose a threat of increasing the concentration of economic power.
20. Private market firms, such as United Parcel Service or private garbage collectors, can serve as "yardsticks" or examples for the political market.	20. Political market bureaucracies, such as the TVA and NASA, can serve as "yardsticks" or examples for private firms.

QUESTIONS AND ANSWERS

THE QUESTIONS

There is a large plot of land on the edge of the city that is owned by the city. The city council has to decide what to do with the land, and many individuals, companies, organizations, and government agencies are competing for the land. We will concentrate on just three of these individuals. Individual B is a bureaucrat who is the director of the city's environmental enrichment board, which is attempting to obtain the land so that it can be managed for future generations as a walk-through sanctuary for trees, plants, and animals. Individual E is an entrepreneur who owns a retail development firm and is attempting to buy the land on which she would build a shopping center. Individual P is a politician who was elected to the county's recreation board, which is attempting to obtain the land in order to develop a public park. Each of these three individuals, as well as others, are attempting to obtain the land from the city.

1. Assume that the three individuals are going to appear before the city council and argue their respective cases. You are assigned to write a few key ideas or "talking points" for each of the three. Note that you are not to be objective here. Your assignment is to put yourself in their place and to write what you think they would say to convince the council to award the land to them.

2. Based on the material presented in this book, what motivations might you initially ascribe to each of these three individuals?

3. Which of the proposals serves the public interest?

4. Are the motivations of the sponsors valid reasons for accepting or rejecting the proposals?

5. Each of the three individuals is making estimates about future benefits and costs. Which one would lose the most if the benefits proved to be overestimated and the costs underestimated?

6. Go through the talking points of each of the sponsors and pick out the emotive terms and phrases.

7. Independent research studies often produce the results desired by their sponsors. This does not necessarily mean that the research organizations are dishonest. There are many assumptions that have to be made in any study, and the researchers can be expected to select at least some of the assumptions that produce favorable results. With such information, the sponsors in our example might report only the favorable results and keep other data or conclusions hidden. Based upon what you learned in this class, what would be one of the first questions about the research studies you would ask each of the sponsors? Why?

8. Assume that you are employed to do an *objective* analysis of the three proposals. How would you go about doing your job?

9. Which of the three proposals would provide primarily private goods?

10. Which of the three proposals would generate externalities?

11. Can you think of a simple way for the council to make its decision and still provide benefits to the taxpayers?

THE ANSWERS

1. For Individual B, stress that the current citizens of the city and especially their children *need* (note the use of this emotive term to convince others) to have this nature sanctuary. Solicit the support of the conservation and environmental groups. Talk about the shortage of air-purifying, beautiful trees, the benefits to those living close to the preserve, and the need to have a bit of nature in the midst of the noise and confusion of the city. Mention the benefits to the poor who would be able to stroll through the preserve, observe the animals and trees, and obtain some of the benefits that the rich enjoy when they take costly trips to the mountains. Criticize the proposals of your competitors with points: "The city certainly doesn't *need* the crass commercialization of another shopping center"; "Put the *needs* of humanity (or your children) before the interests of profits"; "The handicapped cannot use a sports field"; "We already have far too many recreational parks"; "We *need* to conserve." Ask some independent research firm to do a benefit-cost study of alternative uses of the land and then show the favorable results to the council.

For Individual E, stress that the citizens of the city *need* another shopping center because the nearest comparable shopping center is located 10 miles away. Solicit the support of the construction unions and the chamber of commerce to show the employment benefits to labor and the present and future economic benefits to the city today. Be sure to mention the benefits of increased competition and lower prices for the poor as well as the advantages that would accrue to the children in the city as the higher tax base resulting from the shopping center would provide more revenues for education. Stress "jobs for our workers," "revenue for our children," and "convenience for the housewife." Oops!! Strike that as sexist. Make it "convenience for shoppers." Subtly mention that Mr. P and Mr. B are "playing politics" with the future of the city and future employment opportunities and that they are not very realistic about the hard realities of life.

For Individual P, stress that the citizens of the city *need* another recreation park because the nearest comparable park is located 10 miles away. Solicit the support of the recreation and sports associations. Mention that children of poor families would have a healthy outlet for their energies and they would have an opportunity to learn different sports. Argue that the shopping center developers are interested only in profits for themselves and are not concerned about the city. The preserve proposal is antiprogress and ignores the *needs* of the citizens.

2. B wants a larger bureaucracy and greater power for himself and his employees on the board. E wants to make additional profits from the land development. P wants to obtain additional votes and to increase the bureaucracy over which he exercises some control.

3. All three.

4. No, as Adam Smith pointed out more than 200 years ago, the public interest is often served best when individuals are pursuing their private interests. We may or may not agree with the motivations of the sponsors. We need to examine the costs and benefits of their proposals.

5. Individual E, the shopping center developer.

6. Most of the statements of all three are emotive. Examples are the use of the words "need," and "crass commercialization," the appeal for benefits for our children, and the criticism of the motivations of the opposing sponsors.

7. You would want to ask what discount rate was used in the studies. All three projects would involve most of the costs being incurred at the beginning of the project with the benefits strung out over many years. Hence, a low discount rate would produce a high present value of benefits. You would also want to ask about the methodologies used in estimating benefits and costs.

8. All three proposals would provide benefits to the citizens of the city. The question is which one would provide the most benefits per dollar expended. Hence, a benefit-cost study should include all relevant benefits and costs, including positive and negative externalities. The principle of marginalism should be used: what is the benefit of having *one* more shopping center, park, or preserve. What are the marginal costs associated with each project? Benefit-cost studies are very difficult to do well, and further details will have to be left to another course.

9. All three. Individuals not paying to enter or not paying for the goods could be excluded.

10. All three.

11. Auction off the land to the highest bidder. However, some of the externalities might not be internalized by the price mechanism.

INDEX